GERMAN KRIEGSMARINE
IN
WWII

ORDER OF BATTLE
GERMAN KRIEGSMARINE IN WWII

CHRIS McNAB

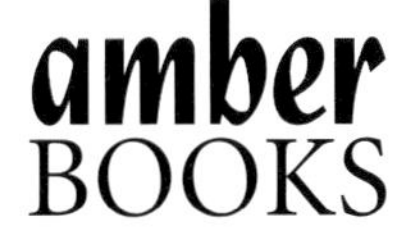
amber BOOKS

First published in 2009 by
Amber Books Ltd
Bradley's Close
74–77 White Lion Street
London N1 9PF
United Kingdom
www.amberbooks.co.uk

ISBN: 978-1-906626-19-8

Project Editor: Michael Spilling
Design: Hawes Design
Picture Research: Terry Forshaw

Printed in Thailand

Picture Credits
Art-Tech/Aerospace: 13, 42
Art-Tech/MARS: 100
Cody Images: 6, 18, 50, 68, 77, 160, 170
Public domain: 66, 102, 124, 161, 176

All artworks: Art-Tech/Aerospace

Maps
Cartographica: 29, 80, 86, 93, 110, 117
Mark Franklin: 3 0, 49, 53, 54, 85, 90, 98, 122
All maps © Amber Books

CONTENTS

The Pre-War Kriegsmarine

Shattered by the experience of World War I, the German Navy had to build itself into a war-capable force in only 20 years, something it achieved, albeit with a collection of significant strategic mistakes.

U-boats in harbour during the 1930s. The U-boat proved to be the *Kriegsmarine*'s most successful weapon during World War II.

The *Kriegsmarine* holds a curious place in the history of Germany's armed exploits in World War II. On the one hand, it was a hugely influential arm of the services, principally through its ruthlessly effective submarine war in the Atlantic, which undoubtedly came close to strangling the United Kingdom's maritime lifeline between 1940 and 1943. It is now common knowledge that British Prime Minister Winston Churchill once declared that the German wolf packs were the only thing of which he was truly afraid during the course of the entire war.

Yet on the other side of the equation, the *Kriegsmarine* was in many ways a marginalized service. Although Hitler was undoubtedly enthused by the successes of the U-boats in the Battle of the Atlantic, the *Kriegsmarine* remained an under-resourced arm, the *Heer* (Army) and *Luftwaffe* (Air Force) attracting the overwhelming bulk of financial and technological investment. This disparity is partly understandable. Apart from its coast on the Baltic, Germany was a largely landlocked nation, and Hitler and most of his staff thought primarily in terms of offensive land grab, not war on the high seas. Furthermore, there was a recognition that countries such as the United Kingdom and France, both of which had far more powerful surface navies than did Germany, made comparable development an impossible prospect, given German limitations on natural resources and the need for rapid rearmament.

The converse of the argument against the limitations of naval development depends on the logistical realities of warfare during the late 1930s and 1940s. During this period, the Allied war in particular hung upon maritime logistics, the Allies having to fuel invasion armies in theatres separated by major expanses of water. Had the *Kriegsmarine* been able to sever any of these lifelines decisively, the balance of the war might have tipped in Germany's favour.

Such an argument, however, is easily made in the light of hindsight. As we first focus our attention on the pre-war *Kriegsmarine*, we see a service struggling to break free from the severe limitations of Allied-imposed treaties after World War I, and working out its future strategic role in a world of rapidly transforming military technology.

As we shall see, there were several options on the table, ranging from the *Kriegsmarine* as simply a Baltic goalkeeper through to the service as a truly oceanic instrument of war, capable of taking on the Royal Navy on its own terms. As with so many aspects of the German military during its rearmament period, the final path chosen was a compromise that arguably satisfied none of the strategic concepts. Yet while its ultimate role in the forthcoming conflict may not have been as strategically epic as that of the German Army, the battles fought by the *Kriegmarine* would constitute some of the most distinctive campaigns in military history.

Low point

At the end of World War I, the *Kriegsmarine* was a humiliated and battered service, forcibly armed with obsolete ships in limited numbers. Breaking free from its position would be an intense technological and diplomatic challenge.

The lowest point in the fortunes of the interwar German Navy came on 21 June 1919. The *Kaiserliche Marine* (Imperial Navy) had been broken by the epic battles of four years of conflict, and following the Battle of Jutland on 31 May 1916, most of the *Hochseeflotte* (High Seas Fleet) remained confined to its home ports. With the armistice in November 1918, however, the Allies were determined to hobble German naval power once and for all. The German fleet was ordered to sail under escort to the Royal Navy base at Scapa Flow in the Orkney Islands. The fleet consisted of nine battleships, five battlecruisers, seven light cruisers and 49 destroyers

BATTLESHIPS, BATTLECRUISERS AND CRUISERS INTERNED AT SCAPA FLOW			
Name	**Sunk/beached**	**Time**	**Fate**
BATTLESHIP			
Kaiser	Sunk	1315 GMT	Salvaged March 1929
Prinzregent Luitpold	Sunk	1315 GMT	Salvaged March 1929
Kaiserin	Sunk	1400 GMT	Salvaged May 1936
König Albert	Sunk	1254 GMT	Salvaged July 1935
Friedrich der Grosse	Sunk	1216 GMT	Salvaged 1937
König	Sunk	1400 GMT	Unsalvaged
Grosser Kurfürst	Sunk	1330 GMT	Salvaged April 1933
Kronprinz Wilhelm	Sunk	1315 GMT	Unsalvaged
Markgraf	Sunk	1645 GMT	Unsalvaged
Baden	Beached		To Britain, sunk as target 1921
Bayern	Sunk	1430 GMT	Salvaged September 1933
BATTLECRUISER			
Seydlitz	Sunk	1350 GMT	Salvaged November 1929
Moltke	Sunk	1310 GMT	Salvaged June1927
Von der Tann	Sunk	1415 GMT	Salvaged December 1930
Derfflinger	Sunk	1445 GMT	Salvaged August 1939
Hindenburg	Sunk	1700 GMT	Salvaged July1930
CRUISER			
Bremse	Sunk	1430 GMT	Salvaged November 1929
Brummer	Sunk	1305 GMT	Unsalvaged
Dresden	Sunk	1350 GMT	Unsalvaged
Köln	Sunk	1350 GMT	Unsalvaged
Karlsruhe	Sunk	1550 GMT	Unsalvaged
Nürnberg	Beached		To Britain, sunk as target 1922
Emden	Beached		To France, scrapped 1926
Frankfurt	Beached		To USA, sunk as target 1921

– a truly formidable armada humbled. The fleet sat at anchor for several months while its fate was being decided at the Versailles conference.

Then, on 21 June, the deadline for deciding the future of the *Hochseeflotte*, the German crews scuttled their vessels in a massively violent act of defiance. The British were almost powerless to stop the destruction, and only a handful of vessels, amongst them the battleship *Baden*, were saved.

Future options

The destruction at Scapa Flow pretty well wiped out the German naval force in one stroke, and a week later the limitations of the Versailles Treaty came into force. Details of the treaty are explored in the next chapter, but it is worth assessing what was left after the scuttling of the *Hochseeflotte*. In total the remaining German military surface fleet consisted of eight battleships, eight light cruisers, and 32 destroyers and torpedo boats, plus

DESTROYERS INTERNED AT SCAPA FLOW		
Name	Sunk/beached	Fate
DESTROYER		
S32	Sunk	Salvaged June 1925
S36	Sunk	Salvaged April 1925
G38	Sunk	Salvaged September 1924
G39	Sunk	Salvaged July 1925
G40	Sunk	Salvaged July 1925
V43		To USA, sunk as target 1921
V44		To Britain, scrapped 1922
V45	Sunk	Salvaged 1922
V46		To France, scrapped 1924
S49	Sunk	Salvaged December 1924
S50	Sunk	Salvaged October 1924
S51		To Britain, scrapped 1922
S52	Sunk	Salvaged October1924
S53	Sunk	Salvaged August 1924
S54	Sunk	Salvaged September 1921
S55	Sunk	Salvaged August 1924
S56	Sunk	Salvaged June 1925
S60		To Japan, scrapped 1922
S65	Sunk	Salvaged May 1922
V70	Sunk	Salvaged August 1924
V73		To Britain, scrapped 1922
V78	Sunk	Salvaged September 1925
V80		To Japan, scrapped 1922
V81		Sank on way to breakers 1921

DESTROYERS INTERNED AT SCAPA FLOW		
Name	Sunk/beached	Fate
DESTROYER		
V82		To Britain, scrapped 1922
V83	Sunk	Salvaged 1923
G86	Sunk	Salvaged July 1925
G89	Sunk	Salvaged December1922
G91	Sunk	Salvaged September 1924
G92		To Britain, scrapped 1922
G101	Sunk	Salvaged April 1926
G102		To USA, sunk as target 1921
G103	Sunk	Salvaged September 1925
G104	Sunk	Salvaged April 1926
B109	Sunk	Salvaged March 1926
B110	Sunk	Salvaged December 1925
B111	Sunk	Salvaged March 1926
B112	Sunk	Salvaged February 1926
V125		To Britain, scrapped 1922
V126		To France, scrapped 1925
V127		To Japan, scrapped 1922
V128		To Britain, scrapped 1922
V129	Sunk	Salvaged August 1925
S131	Sunk	Salvaged August 1924
S132		To USA, sunk 1921
S136	Sunk	Salvaged April 1925
S137		To Britain, scrapped 1922
S138	Sunk	Salvaged May 1925
H145	Sunk	Salvaged March 1925
V100		To France, scrapped 1921

a motley assortment of minesweepers and auxiliary vessels. While these figures may sound respectable, the fact remained that almost all the types were obsolescent, particular the battleships, which had armour and performance that were utterly inadequate for the Dreadnought age. For example, the *Kaiser Wilhelm II*, a *Schlachtschiff* (battleship) commissioned in 1900, had no guns over 24cm (9.5in), deck armour of only 50mm (1.97in) and belt armour of no more than 225mm (8.86in). The armour situation alone was hopelessly deficient in an age of long-range plunging fire and torpedo attacks; consider that the *Bismarck* had deck armour of up to 120mm (4.72in) and maximum belt armour of 320mm (12.6in). Most of the surviving vessels were suited for little more than coastal defence duties. Many were siphoned off for use in the French and Italian navies.

There was also the problem of manpower. Even disregarding the restrictions of the Versailles Treaty, the personnel situation in the German Navy during the early 1920s was grossly unstable. Many former naval personnel had joined the paramilitary *Marinefreikorps* (Naval Free Corps), a violent anti-communist organization that eventually turned on the Weimar Republic itself. Their activities forced the German Government to oust the head of the navy, *Vizeadmiral* Adolf von Trotha, from his position and replace him with *Admiral* Paul Behnke. Behnke's key staff also included one *Konteradmiral* Erich Raeder, someone who would mark a new beginning for the *Kriegsmarine.*

Consolidation
One of the critical measures implemented by Behnke was the foundation of a *Bildungsinspektion* (Training Department) within the navy. The purpose of the department was to train up the next generation of German naval officers, albeit within the limited personnel mandates of the Versailles Treaty. The move was important because it introduced an element of structure and discipline within the *Reichsmarine* (*Reich* Navy), as the German Navy was known at the time, and provided a new generation of naval officers not enslaved to the doctrines of the past. It also gave a much-welcomed boost to naval morale. This department was Raeder's personal responsibility, and he was determined to build up a new professional navy from the skeleton of the old *Kaiserliche Marine.*

Beyond Versailles

Understanding the development of the post-World War I *Kriegsmarine* requires a fundamental appreciation of the treaties and limitations from which it had to escape and, over the course of the next 20 years, actively defy.

The fundamental restriction upon the post-World War I German Navy was the Versailles Treaty. Its naval clauses were particularly harsh, and included the following: 1) The total naval force was restricted to six battleships (Lothringen or Deutschland classes), six cruisers, 12 destroyers and 12 torpedo boats, plus a small collection of minesweepers. 2) Germany was not permitted to build or buy new warships except as replacements, and their displacements were limited to 10,000 tonnes (9842 UK tons) for battleships, 6000 tons (5905 UK tons) for cruisers, 800 tons (788 UK tons) for destroyers and 200 tons (187 UK tons) for torpedo boats. The conditions for replacement were that battleships and cruisers had to be at least 20 years old and destroyers and torpedo boats 15 years old. (Ships could also be replaced if lost at sea.) 3) Germany was not permitted to acquire or build submarines for any purposes. 4) The entire German naval establishment was limited to a maximum 15,000 personnel, including shore-based men, and only 1500 of those could be officers. 5) The Baltic became free waters to Allied vessels, and Germany was obliged to dismantle its coastal defences. Other elements of the Versailles Treaty sought to control everything from the factories that produced naval equipment to the content of military radio transmissions, and together they constituted one of the starkest humiliations to a once world-respected navy.

Below the radar
The economic, social and political chaos in Germany following the end of World War I meant that even building within the patrolled parameters of the Versailles Treaty was problematic. In a country suffering from war fatigue, what limited funding was available for military redevelopment was hotly contested between the army and the navy (and later the nascent German Air Force). Nevertheless, enough funds were acquired to enable the beginnings of a shipbuilding programme, aided by some clever circumventions of the treaty clauses. For example, a high percentage of civilian staff would be employed in shore-based and technical development roles, thus boosting the manpower but

FATE OF WWI BATTLESHIPS		
Name	**Commissioned**	**Fate**
BATTLESHIP		
Brandenburg	19 Nov 1893	scrapped 1920
Weissenburg	14 Oct 1894	sold to Turkey 1910, scrapped 1938
Wörth	31 Oct 1893	scrapped 1919
Kaiser Friedrich III	7 Oct 1898	scrapped 1920
Kaiser Wilhelm II	13 Feb 1900	scrapped 1922
Kaiser Wilhelm der Große	5 May 1901	scrapped 1920
Kaiser Karl der Große	4 Feb 1902	scrapped 1920
Kaiser Barbarossa	10 Jun 1901	scrapped 1919–20
Wettin	1 Oct 1902	scrapped 1921
Wittelsbach	15 Oct 1902	scrapped 1921
Zähringen	25 Oct 1902	sunk after bomb hits 26.03.1945, scrapped 1949–50
Schwaben	13 Apr 1904	scrapped 1921
Mecklenburg	25 Jun 1903	scrapped 1921
Braunschweig	15 Oct 1904	scrapped 1932
Elsass	29 Nov 1904	scrapped 1936
Hessen	19 May 1905	scrapped 1950s
Preussen	12 Jul 1905	scrapped 1931
Lothringen	18 May 1906	scrapped 1931
Deutschland	3 Aug 1906	scrapped 1920–22
Hannover	1 Oct 1907	scrapped 1944–46
Schleswig Holstein	6 Jul 1908	scuttled 25.06.1947
Schlesien	5 May 1908	blown up 04.05.1945
Nassau	1 Oct 1909	scrapped June 1920
Westfalen	16 Nov 1909	scrapped 1924
Rheinland	30 Apr 1910	scrapped 1920–21
Posen	31 May 1910	scrapped 1922
Helgoland	23 Aug 1911	scrapped 1924
Ostfriesland	1 Aug 1911	sunk as a target ship 21.07.1921

FATE OF WWI BATTLESHIPS		
Name	**Commissioned**	**Fate**
BATTLESHIP		
Thüringen	1 Jul 1911	scrapped 1923–33
Oldenburg	1 May 1912	scrapped 1921
Kaiser	1 Aug 1912	scuttled in Scapa Flow 21.06.1919
Friedrich der Große	15 Oct 1912	scuttled in Scapa Flow 21.06.1919, wreck raised 1936–37, scrapped
Kaiserin	14 May 1913	scuttled in Scapa Flow 21.06.1919, wreck raised May 1936, broken down
König Albert	31 Jul 1913	scuttled in Scapa Flow 21.06.1919, wreck raised 31.07.1935, broken down 1936
Prinzregent Luitpold	1 Aug 1912	scuttled in Scapa Flow 21.06.1919
König	9 Aug 1914	scuttled in Scapa Flow 21.06.1919, wreck sold 1962
Großer Kurfürst	30 Jul 1914	scuttled in Scapa Flow 21.06.1919, wreck raised 1936, broken down
Markgraf	1 Oct 1914	scuttled in Scapa Flow 21.06.1919, wreck sold 1962
Kronprinz Wilhlem	8 Nov 1914	scuttled in Scapa Flow on 21.06.1919, wreck sold 1962
Bayern	18 Mar 1916	scuttled in Scapa Flow 21.06.1919, wreck raised 1934, broken down 1935
Baden	19 Oct 1916	Sunk as a target ship 16.08.1921
Sachsen	–	construction stopped 9 monthes before completion, scrapped 1921
Württemberg	–	scrapped 1921

keeping the on-paper military personnel at the dictated levels. Budget allocations for certain areas would be excessive, allowing unspent resources to be filtered off unseen for unauthorized projects. As the *Luftwaffe* later did through civilian flying organizations and airlines, the navy also advanced its technology through ostensibly developing civilian craft – what appeared to be banana freighters and trawlers, for example, were actually test beds for future cruisers and minesweepers. Submarine design also continued through a Dutch company established in The Hague in 1922.

The year 1922 was also that of the Washington Naval Treaty, an attempt by the world powers to limit the naval arms race. Fleet size ratios were established, as were the tonnage and armament specifications of major fighting vessels. The principal signatories of the Washington Treaty were the United States, United Kingdom, Japan, France and Italy (China, Holland, Belgium and Portugal also joined later), but the treaty had an impact on Germany as well. First, it limited the power of the type of vessels that Germany might one day have to fight. Second, ship tonnage was to be measured in long tons of 1016kg (2235lb) instead of the metric tonne of 1000kg (2200lb), giving Germany a little more room to increase the displacements of its new ships.

New build begins

While furtive activities continued, the navy also began its new-build programme within the treaty limitations. The first vessel to emerge was the light cruiser *Emden*, laid down in 1921 and launched in 1925. From 1924, when Behnke was replaced by *Vizeadmiral* Hans Zenker, construction of 12 new torpedo boats began, divided equally between the Raubvogel (Bird of Prey) and Raubiter (Predator) classes. Completed by 1929, these vessels (classed as destroyers under the Versailles conditions) had a decent speed of 41km/h (22 knots) and were armed with six 53cm (21in) torpedo tubes and three 104mm (4.1in) guns.

In the late 1920s, German naval rebuilding took a new direction, and became much more controversial. Up to this point, the emphasis on light vessels reflected the belief that a future naval conflict would for Germany largely be conducted in the Baltic against French and Polish shipping, and speed and manoeuvrability were the most advantageous characteristics in those waters. In 1928, however, Zenker and his staff began to consider a new *Panzerkreuzer* (armoured cruiser) as the first battleship replacement became possible. This would be a large, fast, heavily armed ocean-going raider with

KRIEGSMARINE RANKS

Rank	Translation
SEEMÄNNER	**SEAMEN**
Matrose	Ordinary Seaman
Matrosen-Gefreiter	Able Seaman
Matrosen-Obergefreiter	Leading Seaman
Matrosen-Hauptgefreiter	Leading Seaman (4–5 years)
Matrosen-Stabsgefreiter	Senior Leading Seaman
Matrosen-Stabsobergefreiter	Senior Leading Seaman
UNTEROFFIZIERE OHNE PORTEPEE	**(JUNIOR) NCOS**
-maat (e.g. Funkmaat)	Petty Officer
Ober-maat	Chief Petty Officer
UNTEROFFIZIERE MIT PORTEPEE	**SENIOR NCOS**
Bootsmann	Boatswain
Stabsbootsmann	Senior Boatswain
Oberbootsmann	Chief Boatswain
Stabsoberbootsmann	Senior Chief Boatswain
OFFIZIERE	**COMMISSIONED OFFICERS**
Fähnrich zur See	Midshipman
Oberfähnrich zur See	Sub-Lieutenant
Leutnant zur See	Lieutenant (Junior)
Oberleutnant zur See	Lieutenant (Senior)
Kapitänleutnant	Lieutenant-Commander
Korvettenkapitän	Commander
Fregattenkapitän	Captain (Junior)
Kapitän zur See	Captain
Kommodore	Commodore
Konteradmiral	Rear-Admiral
Vizeadmiral	Vice-Admiral
Admiral	Admiral
Generaladmiral	no equivalent
Grossadmiral	Admiral of the Fleet

capabilities well beyond Baltic waters. Developing such a potent vessel not only pushed against and then beyond the limits of the Versailles Treaty, but also caused a political storm because of its extreme cost at a time of brutal austerity. The controversy led to Zenker being replaced as *Oberbefehlshaber der Reichsmarine* (Commander-in-Chief *Reich* Navy) by none other than Erich Raeder. Ironically, if anybody had expected that the appointment of Raeder would kill off the developments proposed by Zenker, they were mistaken.

Expansion, 1928–38

With Raeder at the helm of the *Reichsmarine*, the German Navy began a true period of expansion that switched its status from the subservient force of a defeated nation to a threatening new maritime power in the European continent.

From 1928, aided by the steady rise of the Nazi party and its stabilizing effect on German society and industry, German warship production began to accelerate. It was fuelled by important technological and conceptual developments. In terms of technology, Germany was moving away from the days of oil-fired vessels and investing more in diesel-powered warships. The development of operationally effective diesel engines by such companies as MAN of Ausburg had far-reaching benefits, primarily in major improvements in fuel economy, which made long-range operations into distant corners of the Atlantic and other oceans a practical possibility. Improvements in steel design from the industrial powerhouse of Krupp also meant that it became easier to armour ships while retaining their hydro-efficient properties.

Cutting-edge warships

Between 19 May 1931 and 30 June 1934, three new *Panzerschiff* (armoured ships – a redesignation of the former term *Panzerkreuzer*) were commissioned into the

ERICH RAEDER (1876–1960)

Erich Raeder joined the *Kaiserliche Marine* in 1894 and quickly demonstrated exceptional administrative discipline and tactical talent. During World War I, he was chief of staff to naval commander Franz von Hipper, gaining combat experience in engagements such as Dogger Bank (1915) and Jutland (1916).

- Promotions came rapidly in the interwar period, Raeder becoming a *Vizeadmiral* in 1925, then *Oberbefehlshaber der Reichsmarine* in 1928.

- Raeder entered World War II as *Großadmiral* (Grand Admiral) in command of the *Kriegsmarine*, and although he was a generally loyal officer his opposition to some of Hitler's tactical decisions, particularly the invasion of Russia, and some tactical failures in key engagements led to his resignation in May 1943.

MAJOR SURFACE VESSELS (1933–39)	
Name	**Commissioned**
BATTLESHIP/POCKET BATTLESHIP	
Gneisenau	21 May 1938
Scharnhorst	7 Jan 1939
Admiral Graf Spee	6 Jan 1936
Admiral Scheer	12 Nov 1934
Deutschland (renamed Lützow)	1 Apr 1933
HEAVY CRUISER	
Admiral Hipper	29 Apr 1939
Blücher	20 Sep 1939
LIGHT CRUISER	
Nürnberg	2 Nov 1935
DESTROYER	
Z1 Leberecht Maas	14 Jan 1937
Z2 Georg Thiele	27 Feb 1937
Z3 Max Schulz	8 Apr 1937
Z4 Richard Beitzen	13 May 1937
Z5 Paul Jakobi	29 Jun 1937
Z6 Theodor Riedel	2 Jul 1937
Z7 Hermann Schoemann	9 Sep 1937
Z8 Bruno Heinemann	8 Jan 1938
Z9 Wolfgang Zenker	2 Jul 1938
Z10 Hans Lody	13 Sep 1938
Z11 Bernd von Arnim	6 Dec 1938
Z12 Erich Giese	4 Mar 1939
Z13 Erich Koellner	28 Mar 1939
Z14 Friedrich Ihn	6 Apr 1938
Z15 Erich Steinbrinck	31 May 1938
Z16 Friedrich Eckoldt	28 Jul 1938
Z17 Diether von Roeder	29 Aug 1938
Z18 Hans Lüdemann	8 Oct 1938
Z19 Hermann Künne	12 Jan 1939
Z20 Karl Galster	21 Mar 1939
Z21 Wilhelm Heidkamp	10 Jun 1939
Z22 Anton Schmitt	24 Sep 1939

German Navy. These were the *Deutschland*, the *Admiral Scheer* and the *Admiral Graf Spee*, and they represented the latest in warship design thinking. They were fast, with top speeds of just under 56km/h (30 knots), and had operating radii of around 16,677km (9000nm). The first of the vessels commissioned, the *Deutschland*, had six 280mm (11in) guns, eight 150mm (6in) guns and twenty-four other guns, plus torpedo launchers. The new warships were designed purely as commerce raiders – ships designed to predate on Allied merchant shipping, utilizing their speed and gunnery to make hit-and-run attacks before escaping over the horizon.

In 1933, Adolf Hitler came to power as Chancellor of Germany. Hitler's thinking was very much oriented towards land warfare, but a good relationship with Raeder nonetheless ensured some continued, albeit limited, progression on naval development.

Renoucing the Versailles Treaty

Everything changed in 1935. Hitler publicly renounced the Versailles Treaty, and then signed the Anglo-German Naval Agreement on 18 May of that year. This agreement committed Germany to producing a naval fleet of up to 35 per cent of the tonnage of the Royal Navy surface vessels, and up to 45 per cent in submarines. The following year, the London Submarine Protocol was also agreed, which allowed Germany once again to develop its submarine technology, on condition that in time of war submarines only engaged those vessels carrying war supplies. Essentially, the *Kriegsmarine* (War Navy) – the name which was adopted for the German Navy in 1935 – could now develop into a complete warfighting machine.

The *Kriegsmarine* began to build for the possibility of Atlantic warfare, and to this end designed new classes of *Schlachtschiff* (battleship) and *Schwerer Kreuzer* (heavy cruiser). Five light battleships, regarded by some as battlecruisers, were planned, but only two were completed: the *Gneisenau* (commissioned 1938) and *Scharnhorst* (1939). They had long range, high speed and exceptional armament, including nine 280mm (11in) guns and 12 150mm (6in) guns. Combined with a projected five heavy cruisers – *Lützow, Seydlitz, Prinz Eugen, Blücher* and *Admiral Hipper*, of which only the latter three were eventually commissoned – the *Kriegsmarine* was approaching war-readiness.

Preparing for war

In the late 1930s, the *Kriegsmarine* went on to a full war footing. Although it was the period of the unrealistic Z-Plan programme, some of the world's finest warships and submarines entered German naval service.

Germany's increasingly muscular approach to naval planning became evident in 1936, when the foundations of two new and exceptionally powerful surface vessels were laid down. These were two of history's most famous fighting vessels – the *Bismarck* and *Tirpitz* – and were an extension of the 'pocket battleship' concept (heavy

KRIEGSMARINE COMMAND STRUCTURE (NOVEMBER 1939)

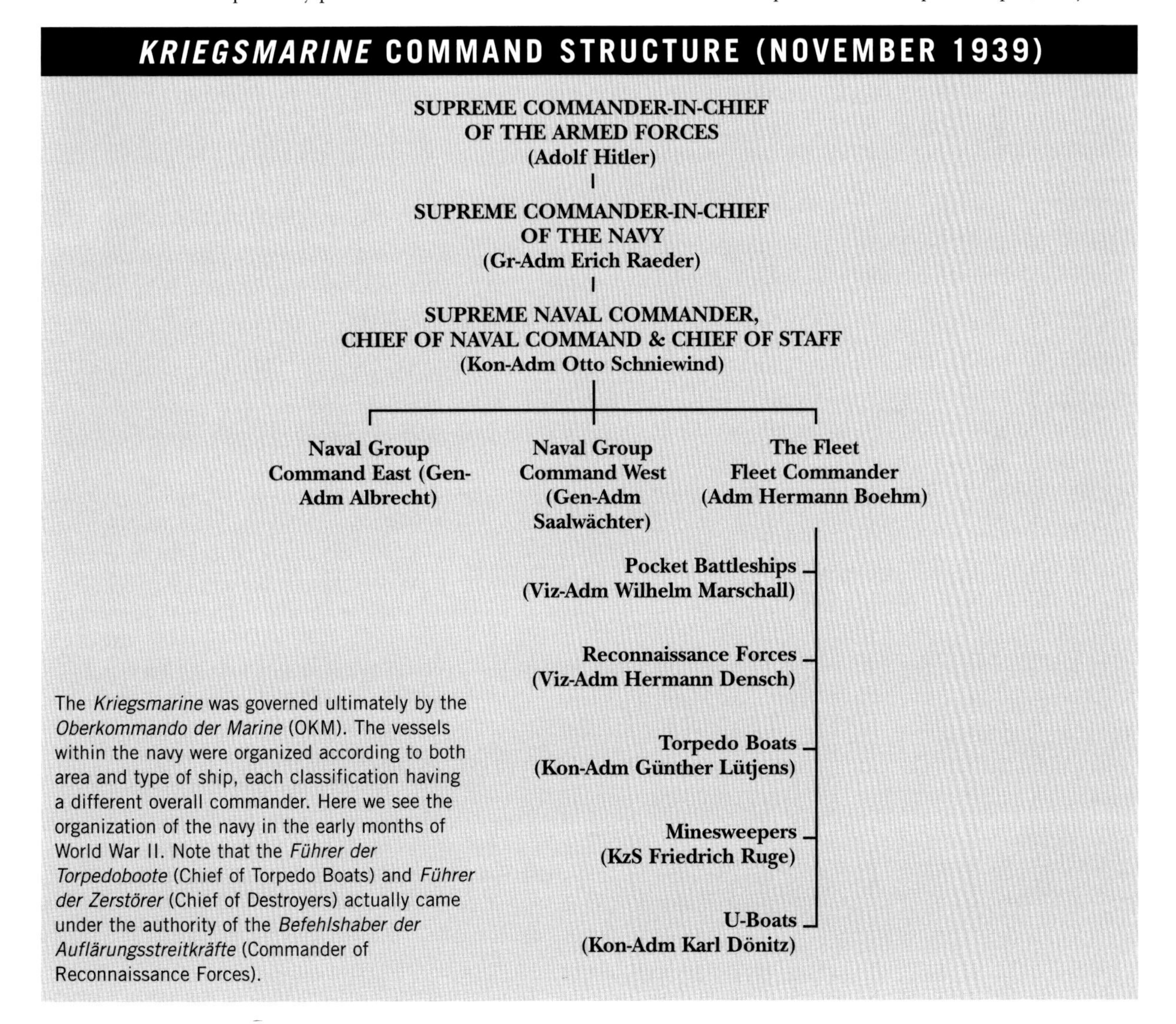

The *Kriegsmarine* was governed ultimately by the *Oberkommando der Marine* (OKM). The vessels within the navy were organized according to both area and type of ship, each classification having a different overall commander. Here we see the organization of the navy in the early months of World War II. Note that the *Führer der Torpedoboote* (Chief of Torpedo Boats) and *Führer der Zerstörer* (Chief of Destroyers) actually came under the authority of the *Befehlshaber der Auflärungsstreitkräfte* (Commander of Reconnaissance Forces).

armament in a comparatively small warship), which had been established by the Deutschland class *Panzerschiffe*. Once these battleships took to the seas, they provoked justifiable alarm amongst the Allied navies.

Not only did they have a top speed of 54km/h (29 knots), and an operational radius of 16,677km (9000nm), but they also each carried over 30 major guns, including an awesome battery of eight 380mm (15in) radar-controlled main guns. Each ship had a complement of 2400 officers and men, and it was merciful to the Allies that more such vessels did not mature beyond the planning stage.

In addition to the above-mentioned warships, the *Kriegsmarine* also acquired 22 new destroyers. Yet it was not only the German surface fleet that was expanding.

U-Boat production

Since 1922 German designers had been developing U-boat technology from foreign offices, ostensibly for overseas clients such as the Turkish and Finnish navies. In fact, Germany was laying the design framework for U-boat classes such as the Type IIA and Type VII. The head of the U-boat arm was Karl Dönitz, a passionate advocate of submarine warfare as the future of Germany's maritime strength. Following successful war games

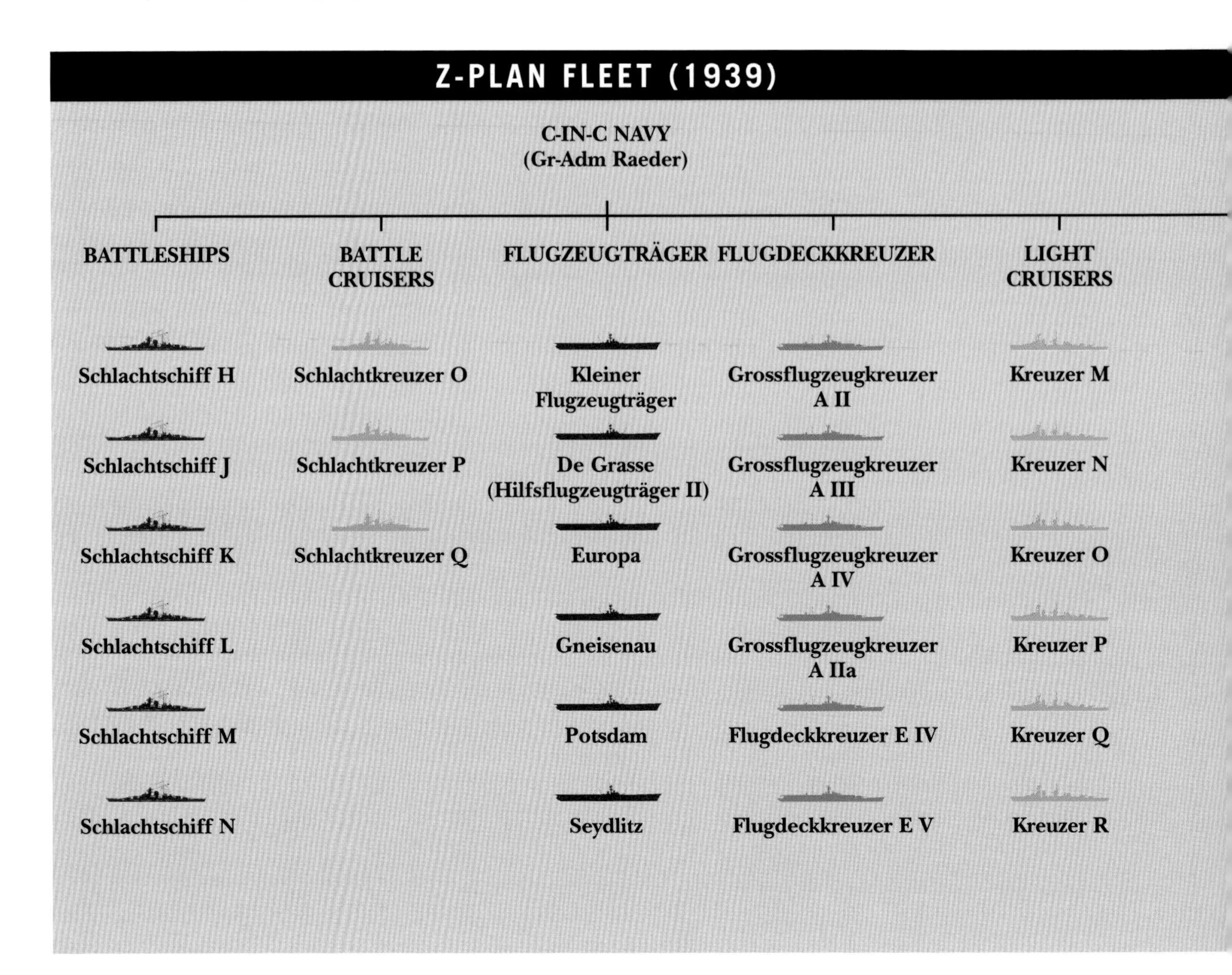

against test convoys in the Baltic, and with the evident approach of war, Dönitz pushed for a greater emphasis on U-boat production. He was to be disappointed.

The Z-Plan

Although diplomatically Germany had managed to set the conditions for much-accelerated submarine production, the massive competing demands of other German arms of service, particularly the *Luftwaffe,* meant that by August 1939 Dönitz had only 56 submarines on his establishment, of which less than half were capable of ocean-going operations. Dönitz was infuriated by what he saw as unrealistic strategic distractions, of which the most frustrating was the Z-Plan. The Z-Plan was an unusual point in the development of the *Kriegsmarine* just prior to the onset of World War II. Drawn up in 1938, the Z-Plan was the name of a shipbuilding programme intended to give the *Kriegsmarine* the capability of fighting the Royal Navy. After several drafts were presented to Hitler, the Nazi leader gave his authorization to the programme, which outlined the development of a large surface fleet, including aircraft carriers. Most of these vessels ultimately never saw life beyond those paper concepts, and the Z-Plan simply retarded the development of the critical submarine arm.

A picture of what might have been. Here we see the principal vessels envisaged in the German 'Z-Plan'. This was a serious attempt to provide Germany with a surface vessel fleet capable of taking on Allied navies. Note the emphasis on maritime aviation in the form of *Flugzeugträger* (aircraft carriers) and the aircraft-capable *Flugdeckkreuzer* (flight-deck-equipped cruisers). Most of the aircraft carriers actually commissioned ultimately served as passenger ships, and none of the *Flugdeckkreuzer* were built.

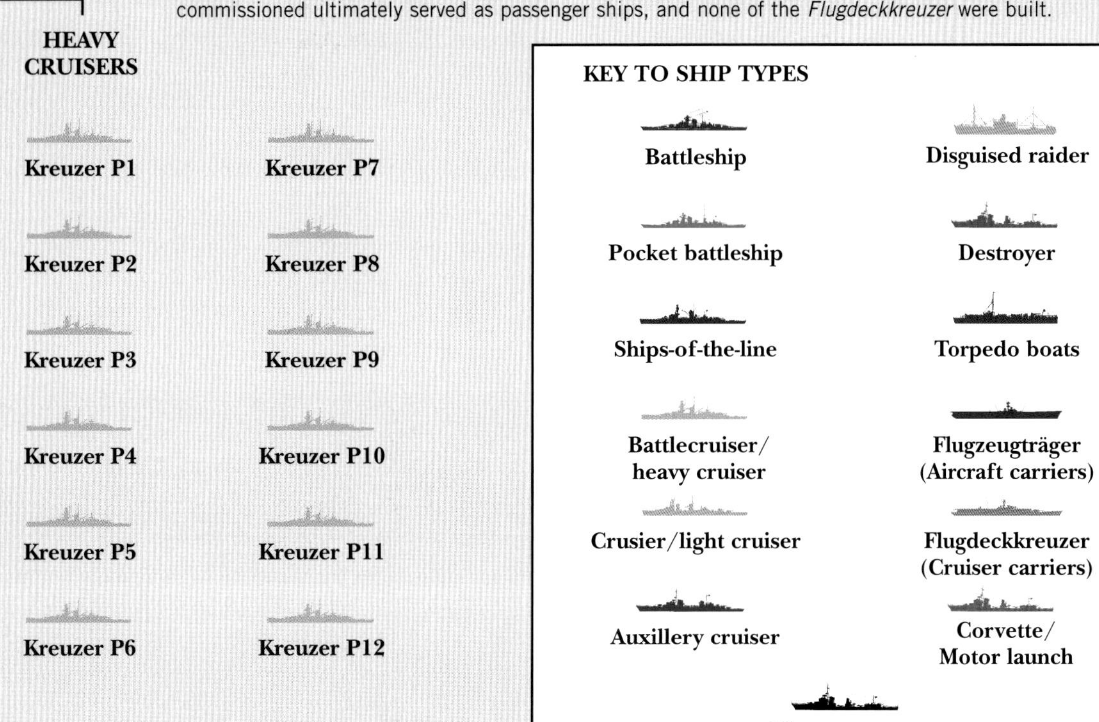

Early Operations: 1939–40

War broke out in 1939, but it was not until 1940 that the *Kriegsmarine*'s surface fleet would have the chance to express its combat potency in earnest. Its first major target was Norway, which would also be the place for one of its greatest defeats.

Otto Ciliax, commander of the *Scharnhorst* (until 23 September 1939), makes a crew inspection.

The German Navy that began combat operations in 1939 had undoubtedly managed to transform itself from the crippled service of 1919 to a professional, highly motivated and technologically advanced naval fighting force. At the outbreak of war, it was divided into two principal *Marinegruppen Befehlshaber* (Marine Group Commands) – these were essentially the *Kriegsmarine*'s operational commands, with Raeder presiding over both as supreme commander. The two commands were *Marinegruppenkommado Ost* (Marine Group Command East) and *Marinegruppenkommando West* (Marine Group Command West), the former overseeing operations around Poland, the latter for the North Sea and Scandinavian coastlines.

Strengths and weaknesses

At the beginning of the war, the *Kriegsmarine* went into battle carrying both major strengths and critical weaknesses. On the plus side, the quality of many of its larger vessels was quite simply superb, often beyond many of the equivalents possessed by the far larger Royal Navy. Its standards of training amongst both ratings and the officer class were very high, with an emphasis on technical excellence that gave initial advantages in areas such as long-range gunnery and submarine tactics.

Its weaknesses centred on the nature of its force composition. One element that the *Kriegsmarine* lacked at the beginning of the war, and would never correct, was maritime aviation. Hitler had never bought into the idea of aircraft carriers in a big way. Construction had started in December 1936 on the 23,200-tonne (22,833-ton) *Graf Zeppelin*, which was intended to carry an air group consisting of 28 Junkers Ju 97 dive-bombers and 12 Messerschmitt Bf 109 fighters. The vessel was never completed, and neither was a sister ship, *Flugzeugträger B* ('Aircraft Carrier B'), meaning that the *Kriegsmarine* had no carriers for the rest of the war, even as the type proved itself as the future of naval warfare.

Therefore, German naval aviation consisted of a few inadequate catapult-launched aircraft, plus, as the war developed, specific but limited maritime support from the *Luftwaffe*. The latter utilized a wide range of aircraft types, some capable of deep Atlantic reconnaissance (such as the 'Condor'), but as the war slowly turned against Germany its resources were frequently drawn away to other theatres and squandered in conventional ground-support roles. Add the lack of submarines mentioned previously, and the *Kriegsmarine* was actually ill-prepared to fight a long naval conflict once the British became involved in World War II.

KRIEGSMARINE BASES (SEPT 1939)

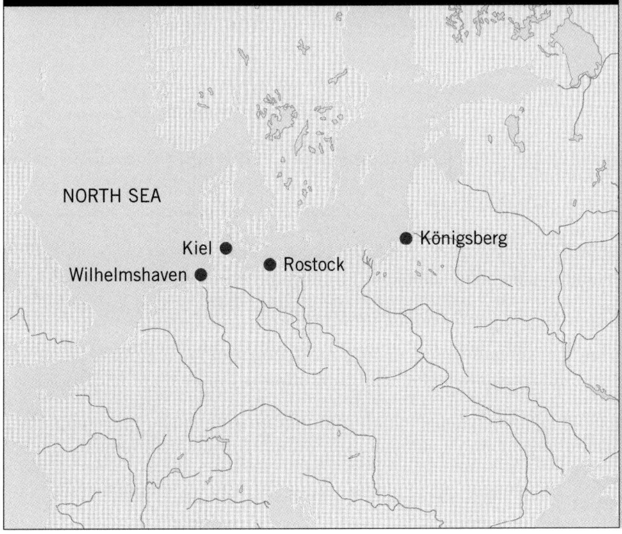

Operational bases

At the beginning of World War II in September 1939, the *Kriegsmarine*'s bases, for obvious geographical reasons, opened onto the Baltic and North Seas. The four principal ports were Kiel (original headquarters of *Marinegruppe Ost*) and Wilhelmshaven (HQ of *Marinegruppe West*), both major centres of German shipbuilding and facing outwards onto the North Sea, and Rostock and Königsberg on the Baltic. There were also shipbuilding production facilities at Bremen.

The limited dispersal of these bases illustrates why it was relatively easy for the Germans to prosecute the opening stages of the war against Poland and Scandinavia, but also shows how critical it was for future Atlantic operations to secure further bases along the western European coast. Without these, U-boat operations against the Allied transatlantic convoys would have been severely restricted.

Planning: September 1939

On 1 September 1939, German forces invaded Poland and so began what became World War II. Although the Polish campaign was overwhelmingly a land action, the *Kriegsmarine* had to prepare for the almost certain international response.

At the moment the war against Poland began, Raeder had to take immediate stock of his fighting resources and how they were deployed. In terms of fighting vessels, the *Kriegsmarine* had a respectable force at its disposal. It possessed a total of five capital ships, these consisting of the three Deutschland class vessels (*Deutschland*, *Admiral Scheer* and *Admiral Graf Spee*) and the two light battleships *Scharnhorst* and *Gneisenau* (*Bismarck* and *Tirpitz* were in production). Eight cruisers were also ready for action, including the two heavy cruisers *Admiral Hipper* and *Blücher*. Added to these heavy forces were a total of 34 destroyers and torpedo boats, plus the 56 submarines mentioned in the previous chapter.

Opposing forces

The German maritime forces undoubtedly dwarfed those of Hitler's victim, Poland, which at the beginning of the war had only four destroyers and five submarines at its disposal. The submarines and all but one of the destroyers quickly fled from Poland as the country's defeat became inevitable, and the campaign involved no significant maritime engagements. Poland was not really on Raeder's mind. His two primary concerns were France and the United Kingdom. In September 1939, France had a naval establishment of one aircraft carrier, seven battleships, 19 cruisers, 70 destroyers and 77 submarines. It was an impressive force, although its resources were quite widely scattered (numerous French vessels resided at North African ports) and its readiness for war was questionable.

An even greater concern for Germany was the Royal Navy, one of the most powerful surface navies in the world at that time (alongside the United States and Japan). The British naval establishment in 1939 was eight aircraft carriers, 12 battleships, 50 cruisers, 94 destroyers, 87 escort vessels and 38 submarines. It was apparent to the German high command that if one of these navies turned against it in force, the *Kriegsmarine* would be crushed in open battle. If both descended at once, there could be a true disaster in the making.

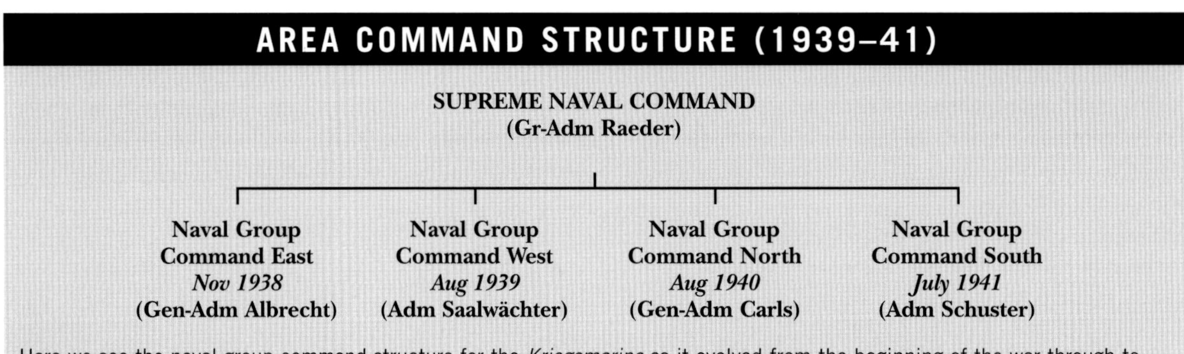

Here we see the naval group command structure for the *Kriegsmarine* as it evolved from the beginning of the war through to 1941, by which time four major area commands had been established (the dates are those on which the command was founded. *Marinegruppenkommando Nord* (Naval Group Command North) took over responsibility for the Baltic Sea Area, German Bay, Denmark and Norway, while *Marinegruppenkommando Süd* operated around the Balkans, Black Sea and Greece.

Battle plan

Of course, the naval war was just one part of the scenario playing itself out in western Europe, and ultimately the Germans knew that the land campaign would be the more significant and controllable element of their early offensives. Nevertheless, Raeder had to make plans for worst-case scenarios. First, it was predicted that the first British response would be to impose a blockade of German waters. It was important, therefore, that the German capital ships were deployed via the North Sea into the Atlantic beforehand to prevent being trapped against the German coast. *Admiral Graf Spee* and *Deutschland*, therefore, headed out into the Atlantic (the *Admiral Scheer* was undergoing refitting and would remain at Wilhelmshaven), while the shorter-range *Scharnhorst* and *Gneisenau* stayed closer to home waters, operating in distraction mode. It was hoped that the Deutschland class vessels would function in their commerce-raiding role in the Atlantic, made more viable by the two battleships pulling away Royal Navy warships from the Atlantic theatre. It was also intended that simply the threat of such powerful warships at large would increase the drain on and dispersal of both British and French maritime resources, as convoys of supply ships would require increased numbers of escort vessels and protective warships.

SCHARNHORST	
Name	*Scharnhorst*
Commissioned	7 January 1939
Crew	1840
Displacement	39,524 tonnes (38,900 tons)
Dimensions	Length: 239m (771ft); Beam: 30m (98ft)
Range	14,515km (9020 miles) at 28km/h (15 knots)
Armour	Belt: 330mm (13in); Decks: 50–100mm (2–4.25in); Turrets: 355mm (14in)
Armament	9 x 280mm (11in); 12 x 150mm (5.9in); 30 x AA guns; 6 x 533mm (21in) torpedo
Performance	59km/h (32 knots)

Submarine deployments

Although the *Kriegsmarine*'s U-boat arm would later become one of the most significant forces in the naval war against the Allies, in September 1939 its role was recognized even by Dönitz as being singularly limited. Dönitz himself commented: 'With 22 boats [ocean-going types] and a prospective increase of one to two boats a month, I am incapable of undertaking effective measures against England.' Dönitz issued a memorandum on the opening day of the war, stating that he required a total of 300 U-boats if he were to maintain 90 of them on station at any one time in the North Atlantic. Thankfully for Dönitz, the opening months of the war proved his point about the importance of the submarine, and the ambitions of the Z-Plan were promptly suspended.

Hopeful allies

It should be remembered that Hitler largely hoped to avoid conflict with the United Kingdom. Although Britain and France declared war on Germany only two days after the invasion of Poland, the *Kriegsmarine* was initially restrained in its actions, and its crews were instructed to be scrupulous in following the Prize Ordinance Regulations about avoiding surprise attacks on merchant ships and protecting the lives of their crews. Such niceties would quickly be forgotten over the coming year, however, as the war in the Atlantic became increasingly bitter.

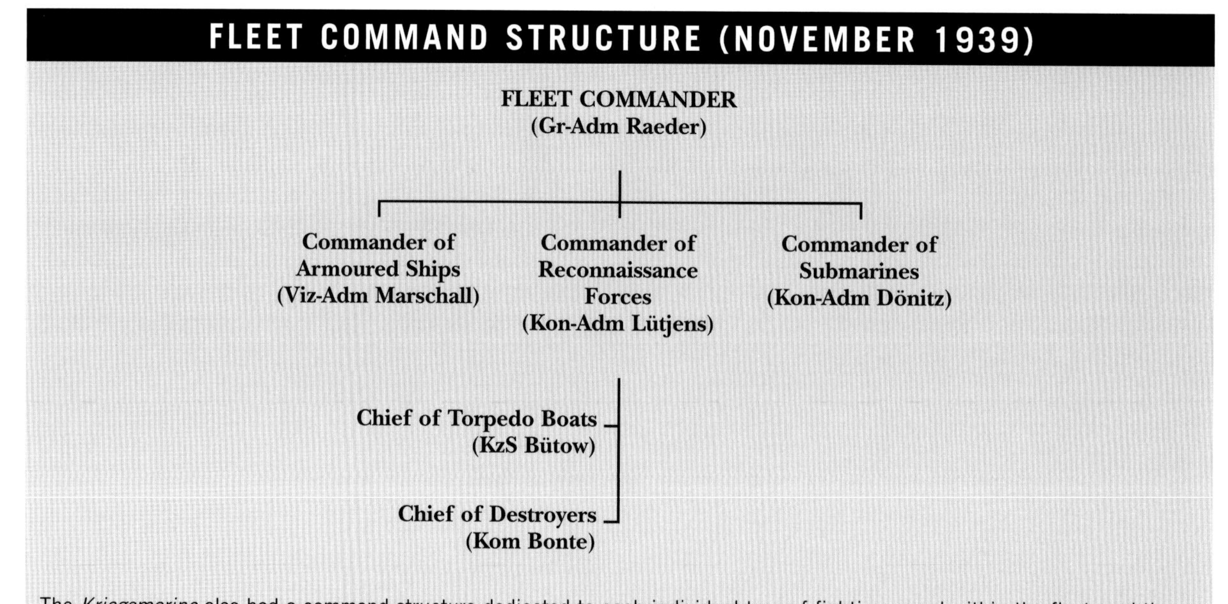

The *Kriegsmarine* also had a command structure dedicated to each individual type of fighting vessel within the fleet, and these are displayed here as the fleet was structured in November 1939, just two months after the beginning of World War II. Each of these individual commands had its own flag officer with responsibility for overseeing technical, tactical and administrative matters related to the vessel type. All these commanders came under the jurisdiction of the overall fleet commander.

Opening Actions

The early actions of the *Kriegsmarine* surface fleet in World War II were far from encouraging for Raeder or Hitler. By the end of the year, the German Navy had lost one of its capital ships and the remainder were back in German ports.

One of the first naval actions between the Royal Navy and the *Kriegsmarine* came in December 1939. Part of Raeder's initial plan for his navy involved laying an extremely dense minefield in the North Sea, to act as protection against British incursions into German waters. This operation, conducted by destroyers, ran from October 1939 to February 1940, and extended downwards as far as the waters off Norfolk, and it was here, off Cromer, that on 7 December two British destroyers, *Juno* and *Jersey*, happened upon two German equivalents, *Hans Lody* and *Erich Giese*, which had just laid their mines and were heading back home. The brief engagement, which lasted no more than four minutes (0310–0314), saw the German vessels launch a total of seven torpedoes, one of which struck and severely damaged the *Jersey*. It was a minor action, but one that encouraged both the two German crews and the German public at home.

Graf Spee

By the time of the Cromer engagement, the two German commerce raiders were already doing their damage. Between 30 September and 2 December, *Admiral Graf Spee* sank six merchant vessels at various points around the Atlantic, her operations sustained by the supply ship *Altmark*. The *Deutschland* added another three vessels to the mounting tally. In response, the British and French navies formed seven hunting groups of vessels designated Forces G, H, I, K, L, M and N, between them covering a massive territory from the North Atlantic to the Indian Ocean. Despite the Allied forces deployed, the German 'pocket battleships' had an immense oceanic space in which to hide. Nevertheless, further sinkings by the *Graf Spee* gave Force G – the cruisers *Exeter*, *Ajax* and *Achilles*, later reinforced by the *Cumberland* – a lead, and it eventually bore down on the German vessel around the River Plate estuary off the coast of Argentina and Uruguay. In this first big-gun engagement, the *Exeter* was heavily damaged by the *Graf Spee*'s 280mm (11in) guns, and *Ajax* had her forward turrets put out of commission. Yet the *Graf Spee* had also been hit, and its captain, Hans Langsdorff, took it into the neutral Uruguayan port at Montevideo. British propaganda claimed that its forces around or near Montevideo now included the aircraft carrier *Ark Royal* and battlecruiser *Renown*. This was a fabrication, but one that Langsdorff bought into. On 17 December, Langsdorff took his ship a short way out of harbour, and scuttled it. Langsdorff himself later committed suicide.

The destruction of the *Graf Spee* was a bitter loss to the *Kriegsmarine*, but the engagements with British ships at least proved the fighting power of a pocket battleship. For the British, it was a tremendous victory, one reinforced by the capture of the *Altmark* off Norway in February 1940, from whose hold 300 captured British merchant sailors were freed. Regarding the *Deutschland*, she had been called home on 5 November following a period of undetected raiding actions. She made it back to Gdynia (Gotenhafen), Poland, on 17 November, at which point she was renamed the *Lützow*.

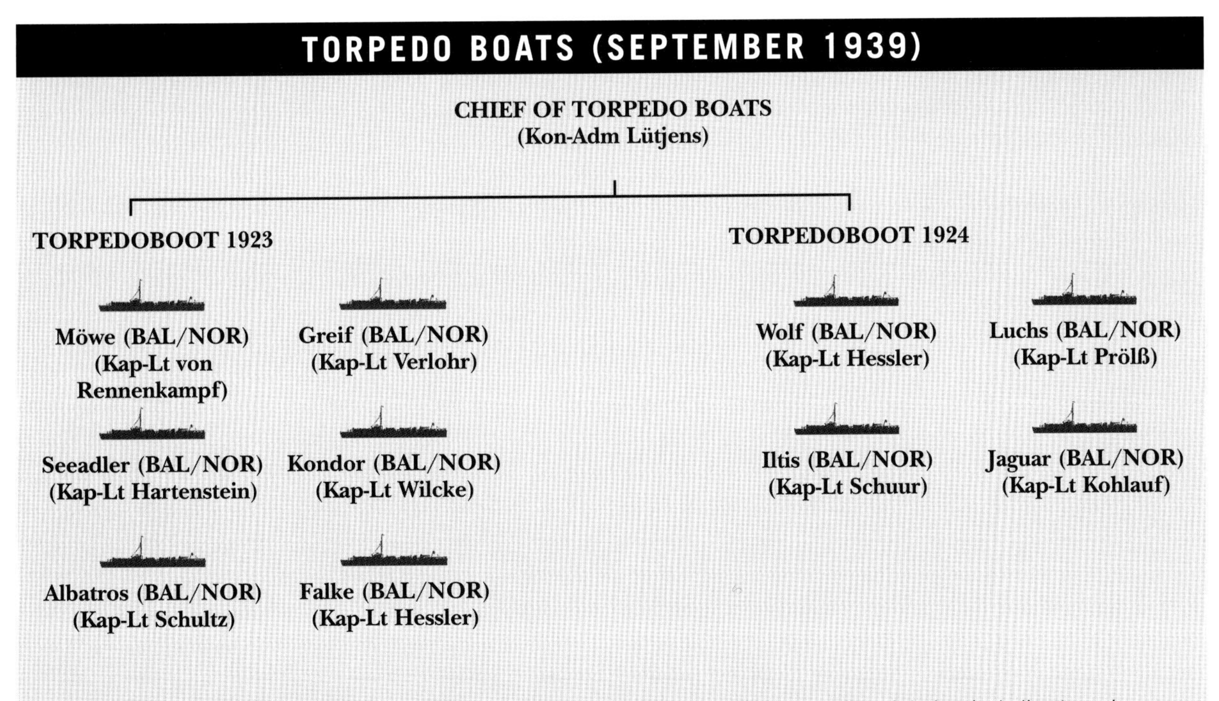

Torpedo boats in the *Kriegsmarine* were essentially small destroyers. They performed a range of duties, including torpedo attack, patrol and reconnaissance, minelaying and escort duty. Here we see the torpedo boat order of battle in September 1939, subdivided into specific vessel type. At this point in the war, the two main types in service were the *Torpedoboot* 1923 and *Torpedoboot* 1924. Updated Type 1935 vessels had been launched, but were not in commission until the end of the year.

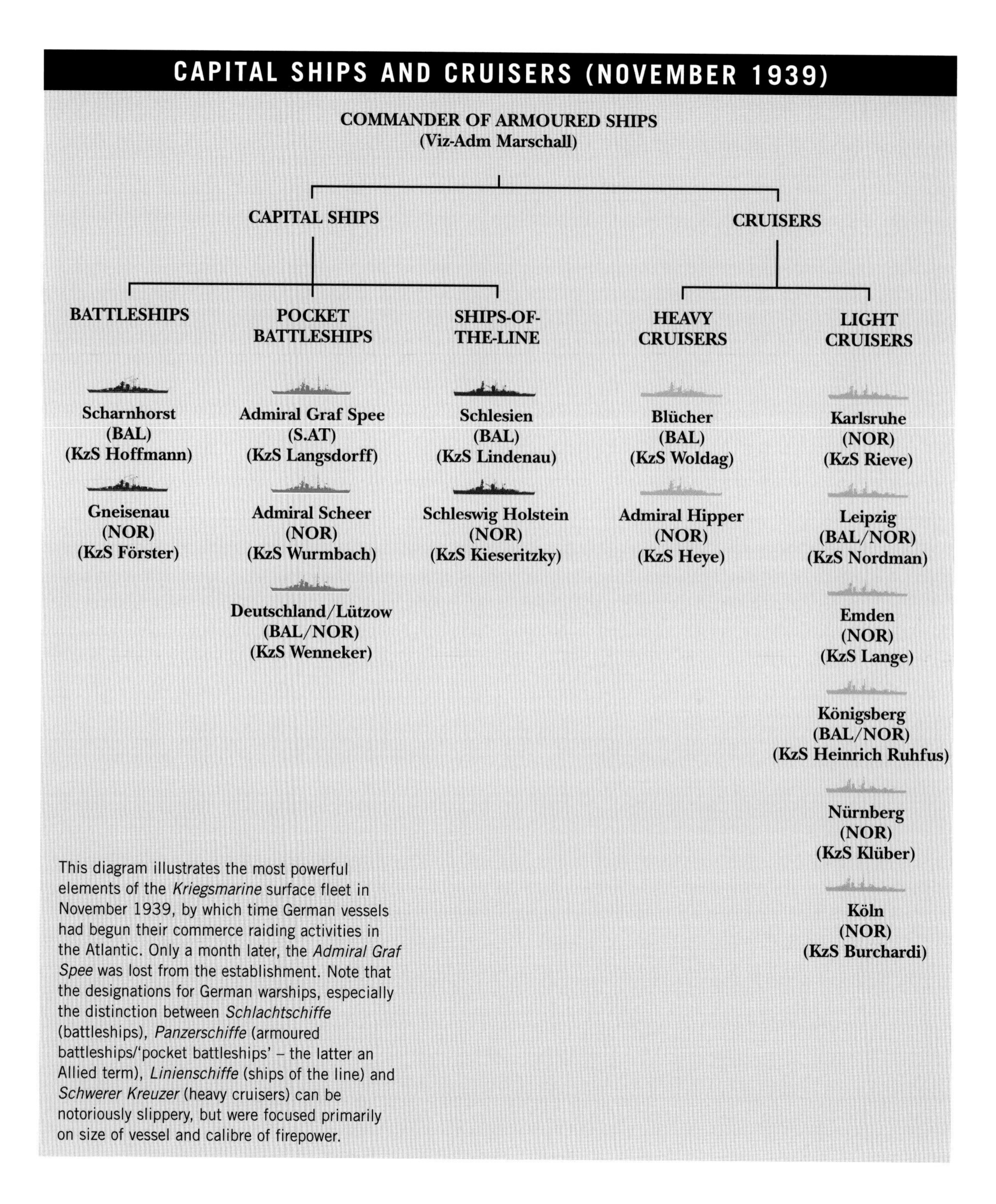

This diagram illustrates the most powerful elements of the *Kriegsmarine* surface fleet in November 1939, by which time German vessels had begun their commerce raiding activities in the Atlantic. Only a month later, the *Admiral Graf Spee* was lost from the establishment. Note that the designations for German warships, especially the distinction between *Schlachtschiffe* (battleships), *Panzerschiffe* (armoured battleships/'pocket battleships' – the latter an Allied term), *Linienschiffe* (ships of the line) and *Schwerer Kreuzer* (heavy cruisers) can be notoriously slippery, but were focused primarily on size of vessel and calibre of firepower.

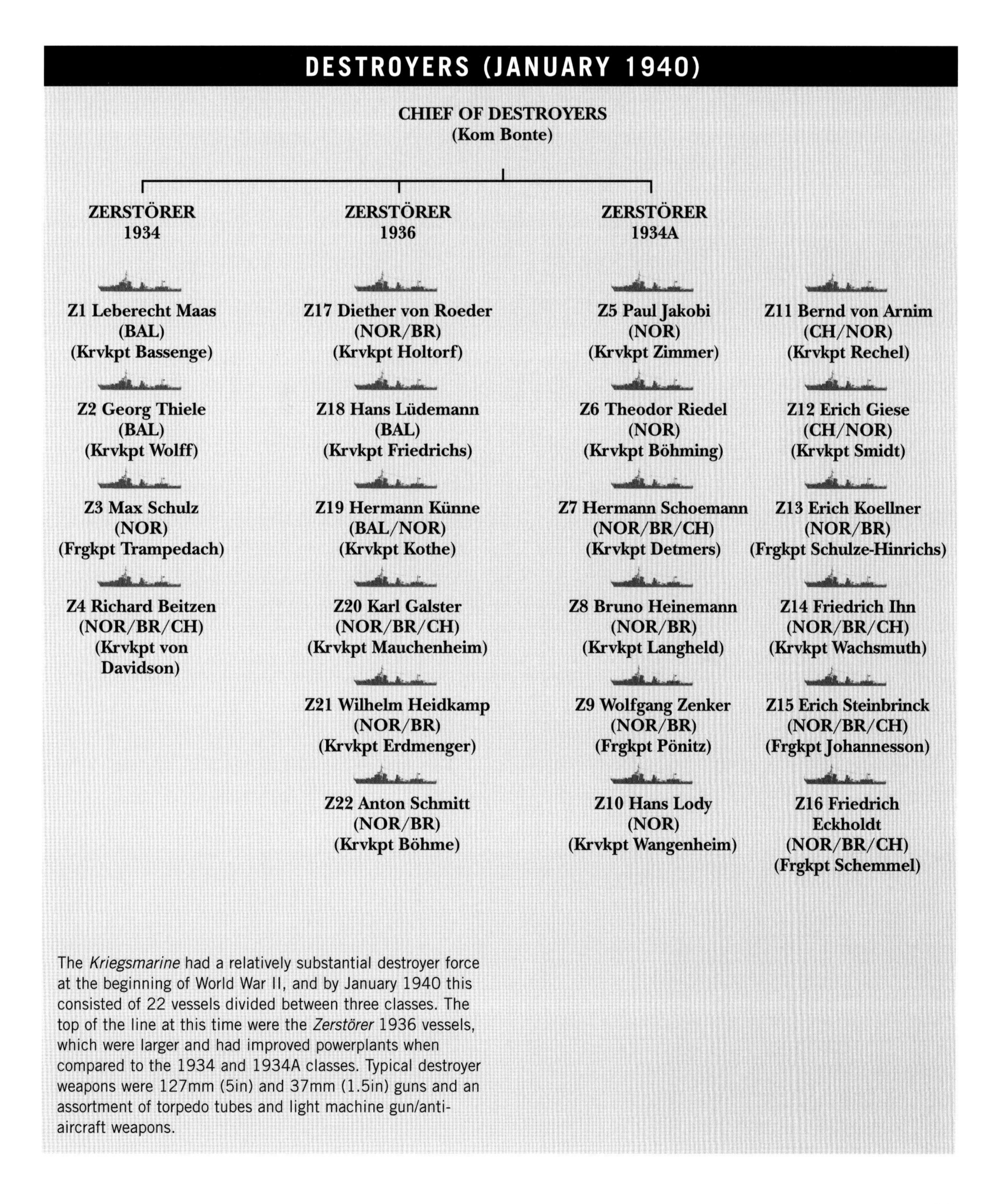

The *Kriegsmarine* had a relatively substantial destroyer force at the beginning of World War II, and by January 1940 this consisted of 22 vessels divided between three classes. The top of the line at this time were the *Zerstörer* 1936 vessels, which were larger and had improved powerplants when compared to the 1934 and 1934A classes. Typical destroyer weapons were 127mm (5in) and 37mm (1.5in) guns and an assortment of torpedo tubes and light machine gun/anti-aircraft weapons.

Norway 1940

The German war machine is not primarily remembered for its amphibious warfare capability. Yet in April 1940, only seven months after the Poland campaign, the *Kriegsmarine* launched a major amphibious action against Scandinavia.

During the late months of 1939, Hitler's concentration was mainly focussed at future operations in western Continental Europe, not up into the icy northern expanses. Raeder's naval perspective, however, convinced him that taking Norway and its neighbour was utterly critical if Germany were to protect its logistical interests and give the *Kriegsmarine* greater operational freedom.

By early 1940, the strategic imperative for Germany's invasion of Norway was indeed acute. The primary justification was to protect vital iron ore imports that flowed into Germany from Sweden via the Norwegian port of Narvik. Yet there were many other motivations, both offensive and defensive in nature. Not only would airbases in Norway provide the *Luftwaffe* with an operating platform to strike at northern mainland Britain, but Norwegian ports offered the *Kriegsmarine* the capability to range out against British ships in the North Sea, and make better transit into the North Atlantic.

Risk factor

Raeder had his work cut out. Many amongst the *Oberkommando der Wehrmacht* (OKW), such as the chief of the Army General Staff, *General der Artillerie* Franz Halder, felt the distant northern operation, which by its nature would be heavily reliant upon aerial and naval resupply, carried too much tactical and logistical risk. Yet by January 1940, Raeder had essentially convinced Hitler of the perils involved in waiting too long to implement the Norwegian invasion, and the *Führer* authorized planning of an operational study, codenamed *Weserübung*. The capture of the German supply ship *Altmark* in Norwegian waters on 14 February 1940 gave Raeder's arguments that Norway was vulnerable a more solid base. Following the Polish campaign, Britain was planning its first major strategic move, and the Germans became convinced that Norway could be the target. If Britain could control Norwegian waters, the operating capabilities of the *Kriegsmarine* could be severely limited by British mining of the coastal areas and entrance to the Baltic. Furthermore, not only would Britain be in a position to control Germany's iron ore imports, but it would also have a stronger platform for supporting Finland in its war against Russia – British merchant ships had already begun moving supplies to Finland through Norway in November 1939.

Time was of the essence. Raeder correctly argued that the Royal Navy was indeed a considerable threat to the German invasion force, but if the army, navy and air force were to establish themselves on Norway, then it would be extremely difficult for the British to prosecute a long-term campaign. On 21 February 1940, Hitler gave *Weserübung* the green light to go.

Separated into three task forces, a combined total of over 200 vessels, plus a major airborne assault to secure Norwegian airbases, would be used to deploy some six divisions of German troops around the Scandinavian coastline. The most critical part of the action was a major assault against Narvik and Trondheim in northern Norway. For this task, the ground forces were to be deployed from one cruiser (*Hipper*) and 14 destroyers, with *Gneisenau* and *Scharnhorst* operating as offshore support alongside submarine forces. Reinforcements and supplies were to be run in by 39 transport ships.

Launching *Weserübung*

The *Weserübung* invasion force set sail late on 6 April, in heavy weather, the northern group sailing first, followed by the invasion force destined for southern Norway and Denmark; this latter group included the pocket battleship *Lützow* and the heavy cruiser *Blücher*. On 8 April came the first major engagement, when the Royal Navy destroyer *Glowworm* was engaged by the German warships off Trondheim. It was an unequal

INVASION OF NORWAY: NAVAL FORCES

Here we see the primary naval forces for the invasion of Norway. At the heavier end of the scale were the *Scharnhorst* and *Gneisenau* battleships, the heavy cruiser/pocket battleship *Lützow* (ex-*Deutschland*), the two heavy cruisers *Admiral Hipper* and *Blücher* and the four light cruisers *Emden*, *Karlsruhe*, *Köln* and *Königsberg*. The *Kriegsmarine* also deploy a large percentage of its destroyer force as landing craft or amphibious support vessels, with 10 destroyers landing troops at Narvik, and the remaining four destroyers being used for deployments at Trondheim.

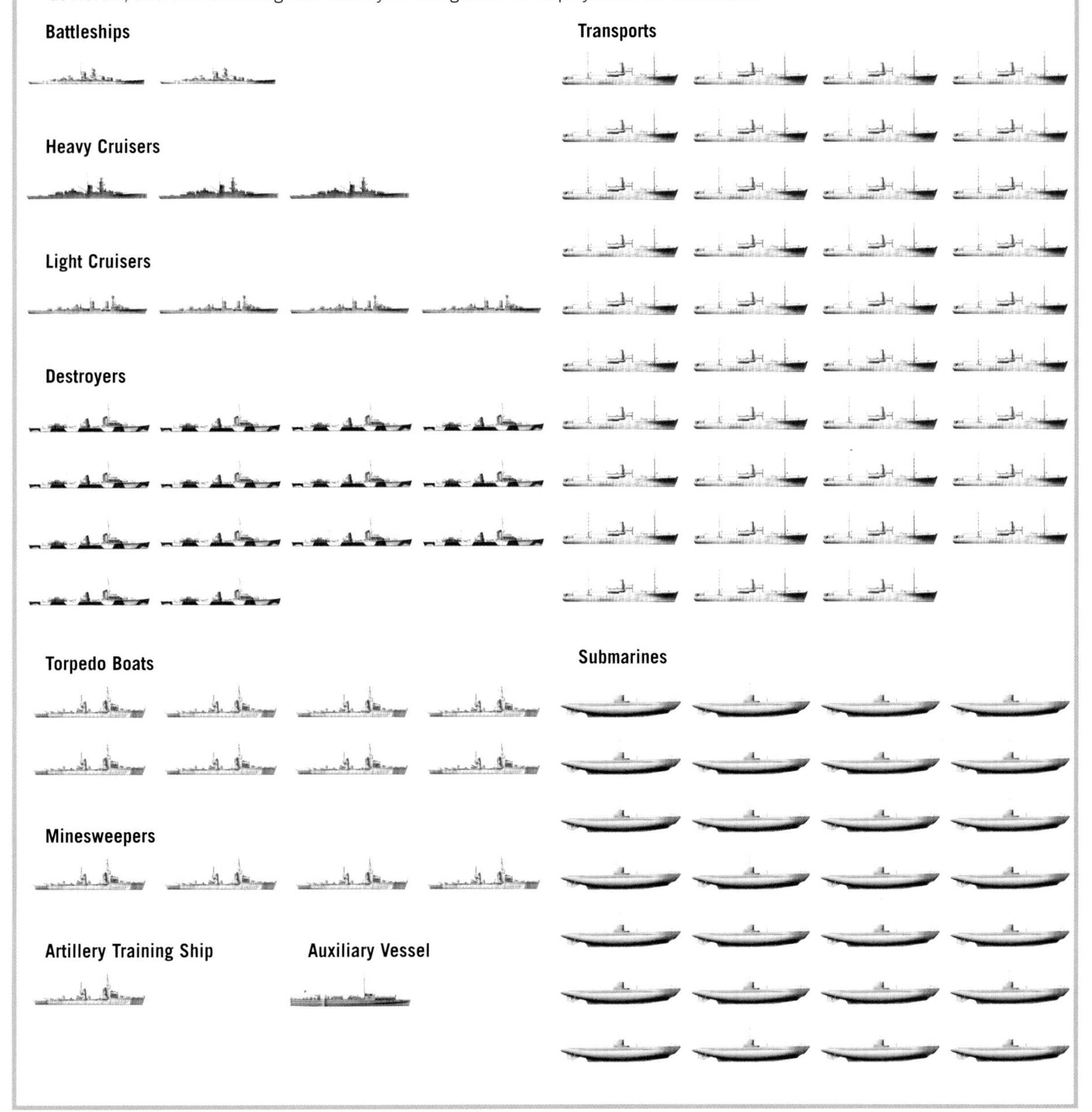

struggle: *Glowworm* was battered by 203mm (8in) gunfire from the *Hipper*. As a final act of defiance, *Glowworm* rammed the *Hipper* – leaving the heavy cruiser with a four-degree list – before she finally broke away and sank.

Landing forces

The sinking of the *Glowworm* was the first of several major engagements that took place prior to and during the actual invasion on 9 April. The Polish submarine *Orzel* sank the German troopship *Rio de Janeiro* on the 8th, and the next morning the big-gun ships clashed. A large British force of destroyers plus the battlecruiser *Renown* locked horns with the *Scharnhorst* and *Gneisenau* (although the combat was primarily with the British battlecruiser). The *Gneisenau* was hit by three 381mm (15in) shells during the prolonged engagement in truly appalling weather, crippling her fire-control system and one of her main turrets. The *Renown* was also hit with two shells, although neither exploded and hence caused only limited damage. Yet the *Gneisenau* and *Scharnhorst* were tasked not with engaging the British vessels, but with drawing them off to the northwest away from the landing force. This they achieved, and their impressive speed in the weather conditions meant that the large fleet of British destroyers was unable to catch them.

Shortly after this engagement, the German warships and troopships began their landings. Principal resistance came from coastal batteries, resulting in several damaged ships and one major loss – the *Blücher* went down in Oslo Fjord after shell and shore-launched torpedo strikes. Yet most of the shore batteries were quickly slammed into submission by heavy naval guns, and by the end of 9 April the Germans had successfully lodged themselves in Norway.

Battle for Narvik

The Norwegian port of Narvik became the *Kriegsmarine*'s nightmare over the course of two major engagements. These demonstrated terrible local vulnerabilities in German surface power when compared with the opposing Royal Navy.

The first stage of the invasion of Norway was over, but now came the period of real danger for the *Kriegsmarine*. Supply shipping had to be maintained against mounting Royal Navy pressure, and Raeder had to avoid the possibility of his warships being trapped in Norwegian ports, where they could be decimated by naval gunfire and air attacks.

Trapped in Narvik

Both German and British naval forces faced a significant tactical challenge regarding Narvik. The approach to the harbour was along the narrow confines of the Ofotfjord, a slender waterway punctuated by smaller fjords that formed offshoots. The initial invasion had faced some opposition from the Norwegian Navy during the run up the fjord, primarily from two antiquated Norwegian coastal defence ships, the *Norge* and the *Eidsvold*, both armed with heavy guns. Outwitted and outmanoeuvred by three German destroyers, the *Eidsvold* was torpedoed by the *Wilhelm Heidkamp* (Z21) and blew apart in an enormous explosion, while the *Norge* was dispatched in similar fashion by the *Bernd von Arnim* (Z11).

The Germans now had free access to Narvik. It was a bad place to be trapped, and a difficult place to attack. Nevertheless, the British attempted the latter at around 0430 on 10 April, in what became known as the First Battle of Narvik.

By 10 April, 10 German destroyers were crowded into the waters around the port. It hd been intended to refuel them rapidly from three oilers, so that they could sail out from Narvik back towards Germany. Only one oiler had reached Narvik, however – the two others had been intercepted by Norwegian patrol and torpedo

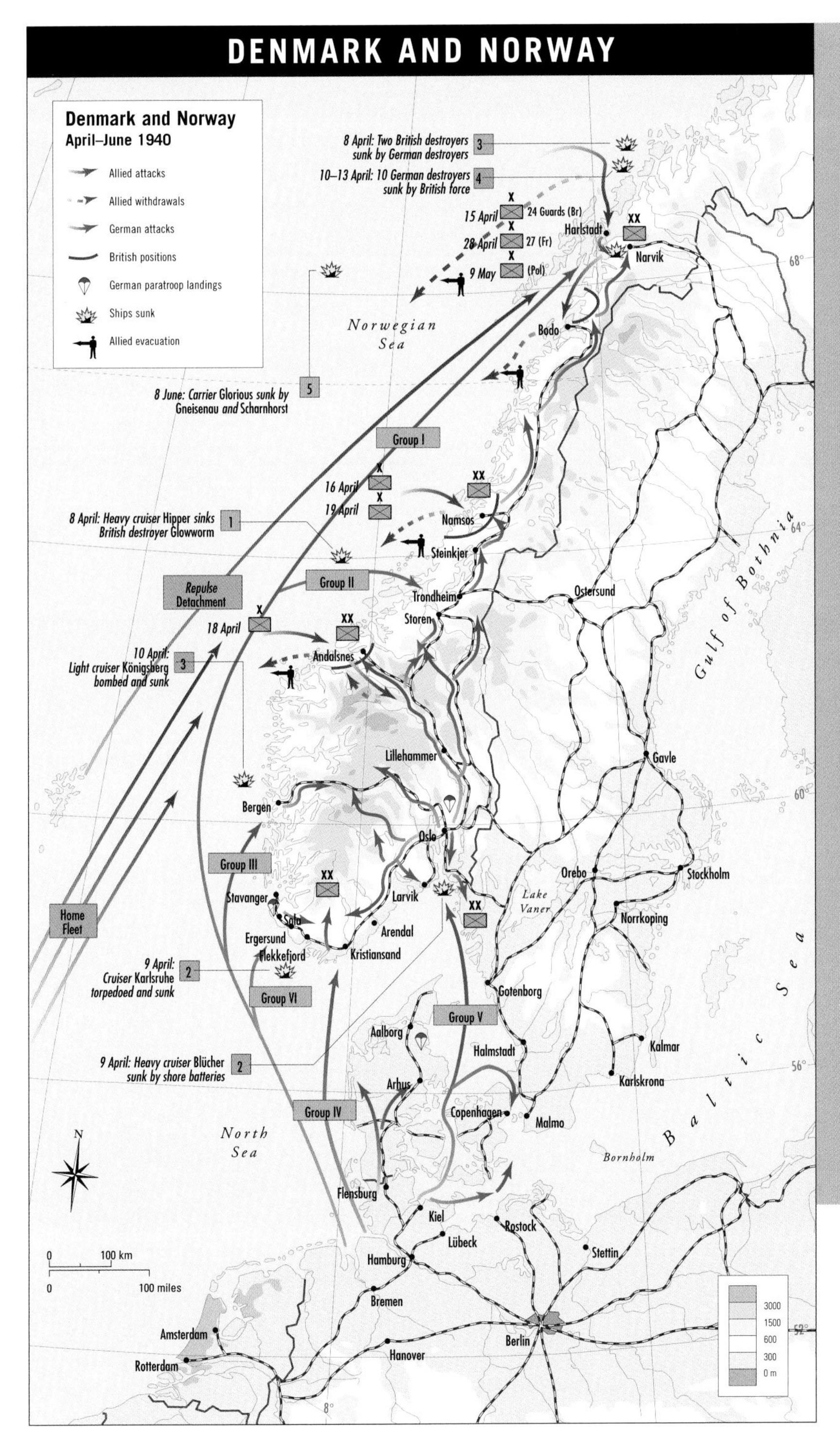

April–June 1940

At 0500 on 9 April, German *Fallschirmjäger* were dropped at the unused fortress of Masnedø in Denmark and then at Aalborg airport. At 0600, a battalion of infantry, which had been hidden in a merchant ship in Copenhagen harbour, emerged to seize the Danish king and his government.

Two divisions of the German XXI Infantry Corps crossed the border and moved into Jutland. Totally outmatched, the Danish Army put up little resistance except in North Schleswig, and there was a brief firefight for possession of the Royal Palace in Copenhagen.

At dawn on the same day, German troops were swarming ashore at Oslo, Bergen, Trondheim and even at Narvik, over 1610km (1000 miles) from Germany. German paratroops seized Sola airport near Stavanger and dropped later on to Fornebu airport near Oslo, while the *Kriegsmarine* ferried the army formations across the Skagerrak and Kattegat.

Allied landings and naval actions in the north around Narvik briefly reversed the tide of German success, but the British and French troops were withdrawn at the end of May after reverses in France meant that they were more urgently needed there.

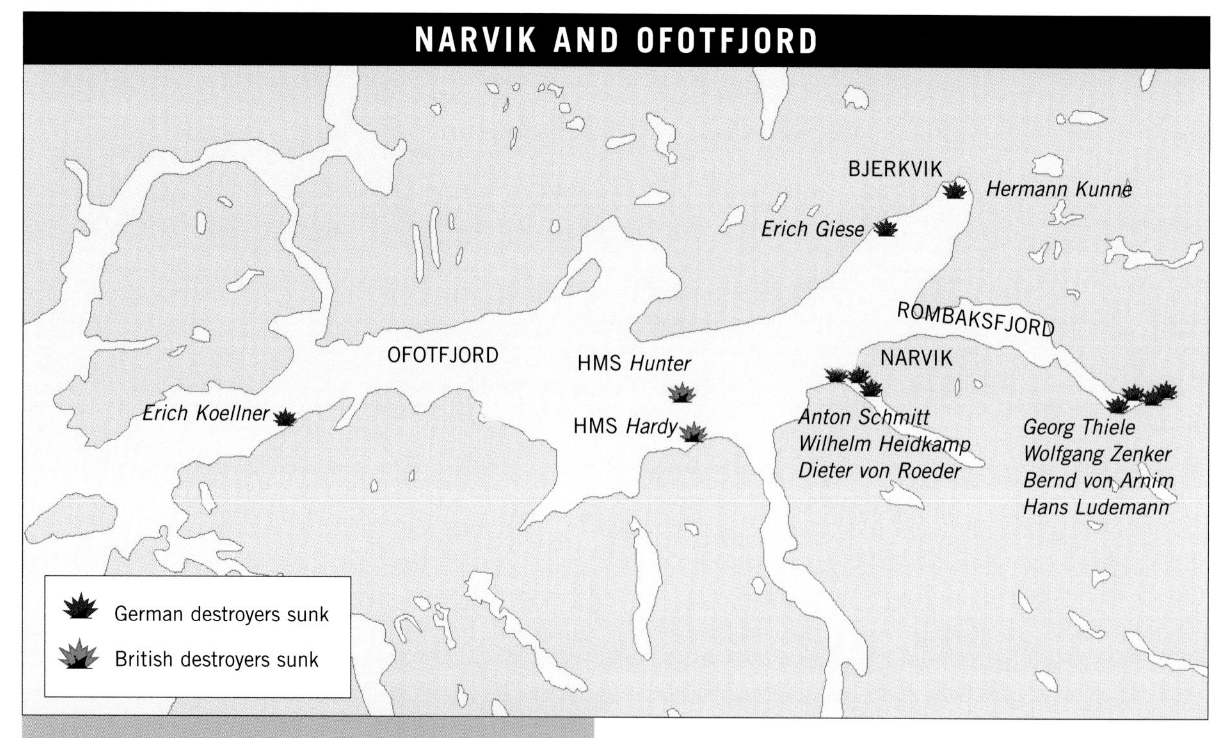

Battles around Narvik

The problems of both offensive and defensive operations around Narvik are clear from this map. Narvik is tucked well towards the back of the Ofotfjord, flanked to the south by the Belsfjorden and Skjomen fjords, and further west by Ballangen Bay, all capable of hiding defenders. Behind Narvik, the Herjangsfjord and Rombaksfjord provided additional anchorages. Although the geography of the area was good for hiding vessels, and was complicated for attackers to navigate, it could also turn into a trap for defenders caught by surprise, as they were on 9 April. As the map indicates, most of the engagements around Narvik occured around the harbour, in the Ofotfjord or in the Herjangsfjord and Rombaksfjord, showing how the Germans became unable to break out to open waters owing to refuelling failures and the tactical advantages held by the British at this stage of the campaign.

boats early in the operation. The result was extremely slow refuelling for the destroyers (only three had been refuelled by the morning of the 10th), and it was into this situation that the British decided to make their first major incursion.

Surprise attack

By early on the 9th, the British 2nd Destroyer Flotilla under Captain B.A.W. Warburton-Lee, composed of the five British H class destroyers (*Hardy, Hotspur, Havock, Hunter* and *Hostile*), had deployed to nearby Vestfjord, and at 1200 they received orders to advance and make an attack against German naval forces at Narvik. At this point there was much Allied confusion about the actual situation in Narvik, so the British destroyers largely sailed into the unknown, and into a snowstorm. The snowstorm made visibility limited for the British ships, but it also shielded their approach from the German destroyers around Narvik.

The first attack ran in at 0430 on the 10th, as *Hardy, Hunter* and *Havock* moved at speed into the harbour, firing patterns of torpedoes as well as opening up with gunfire. At anchor inside the harbour itself were five of the German destroyers and 23 merchant ships; the other German destroyers were distributed around the Ofotfjord (two were in Ballangen Bay, while the remaining three were further north in the Herjangsfjord). Such was the element of surprise that initially the Germans thought they were under air attack. The flagship *Wilhelm Heidkamp* was hit in the magazine by a torpedo hit and disintegrated in the resulting explosion, killing destroyer chief *Kommodore* Friedrich Bonte. *Anton Schmitt* was crushed in a welter of torpedo and gunfire, broken in half by explosions.

Now the tables turned on the British as the other five now alerted German destroyers swung into action.

FIRST BATTLE OF NARVIK (10 APRIL 1940): *KRIEGSMARINE* CASUALTIES

Name	Displacement	Speed	Guns	Torpedoes	Damage
DESTROYERS					
Wilhelm Heidkamp	3470 tonnes (3415 tons)	70km/h (38kn)	5x127mm (5in)	8x533mm (21in)	Sunk
Anton Schmitt	3470 tonnes (3415 tons)	70km/h (38kn)	5x127mm (5in)	8x533mm (21in)	Sunk
Bernd von Arnim	3241 tonnes (3190 tons)	70km/h (38kn)	5x127mm (5in)	8x533mm (21in)	Moderate
Erich Giese	3241 tonnes (3190 tons)	70km/h (38kn)	5x127mm (5in)	8x533mm (21in)	–
Erich Koellner	3241 tonnes (3190 tons)	70km/h (38kn)	5x127mm (5in)	8x533mm (21in)	–
Diether von Roeder	3470 tonnes (3415 tons)	70km/h (38kn)	5x127mm (5in)	8x533mm (21in)	Significant
Hans Lüdemann	3470 tonnes (3415 tons)	70km/h (38kn)	5x127mm (5in)	8x533mm (21in)	Light
Hermann Künne	3470 tonnes (3415 tons)	70km/h (38kn)	5x127mm (5in)	8x533mm (21in)	Light
Georg Thiele	3206 tonnes (3156 tons)	70km/h (38kn)	5x127mm (5in)	8x533mm (21in)	Moderate
Wolfgang Zenker	3241 tonnes (3190 tons)	70km/h (38kn)	5x127mm (5in)	8x533mm (21in)	–

DESTROYER FORCE AT NARVIK (10 APRIL 1940)

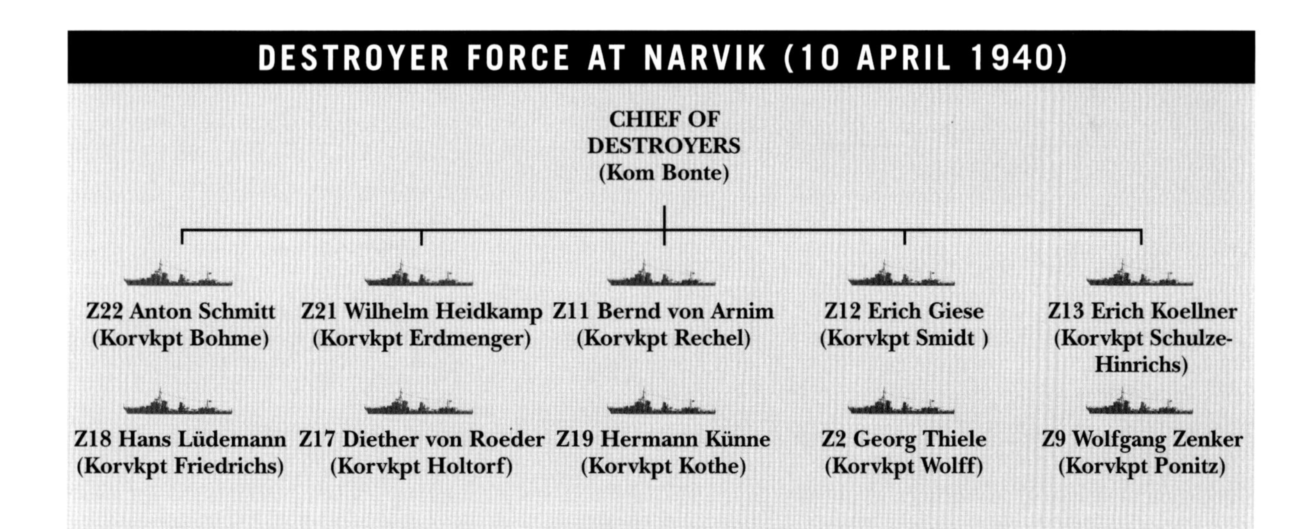

The hapless destroyer force at Narvik was commanded by *Kommodore* Friedrich Bonte, an experienced naval officer who had joined the German Navy in 1914 and received his commission in 1916. Bonte was one of the first Germans to be killed at the First Battle of Narvik, aboard his flagship *Wilhelm Heidkamp*. By the end of the campaign, all of these destroyers had been sunk, depriving the *Kriegsmarine* of a major component of its operational surface fleet.

Warburton-Lee finally broke off the harbour attack. The British vessels just made open water, but were caught between intense German salvos as the other destroyers, moving in from the peripheral waters around the Ofotfjord, closed in. In the following gun battle, *Hardy* and *Hunter* were sunk (Warburton-Lee was fatally wounded on *Hardy*) and *Hotspur* was damaged, although some British hits were registered on the German attackers before the First Battle of Narvik ended around 0700. Both the Germans and the British had lost two destroyers each, but a further five German destroyers had suffered major damage.

Second Battle of Narvik

The losses resulting from the First Battle of Narvik had delivered a major shock to the *Kriegsmarine*. Yet on 13 April, far worse was to come as the British attempted to finish off the German naval capability around the port.

In the aftermath of the battles on 10 April, the naval personnel around Narvik attempted to repair the damaged destroyers, although such was the destruction aboard the *Diether von Roeder* that she was essentially written off, and simply docked as a floating battery. Two destroyers, *Wolfgang Zenker* and *Erich Giese*, attempted a breakout under cover of darkness late on the 10th, but turned back when they spotted three British destroyers guarding the exits to the North Sea. The *Führer der Zerstörer* (Chief of Destroyers) was now *Kapitän zur See*

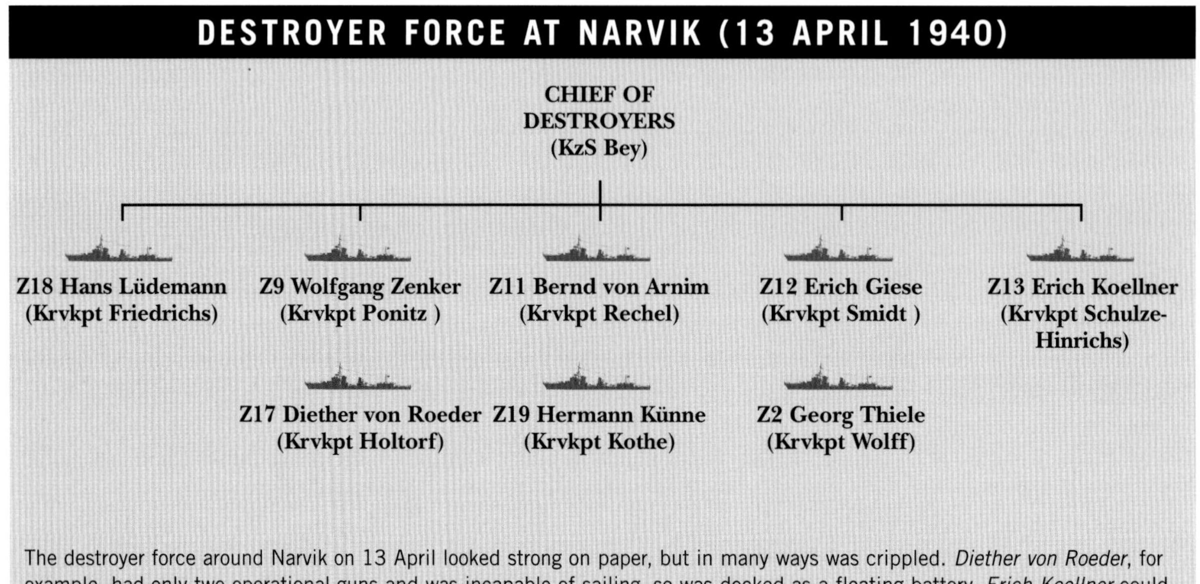

The destroyer force around Narvik on 13 April looked strong on paper, but in many ways was crippled. *Diether von Roeder*, for example, had only two operational guns and was incapable of sailing, so was docked as a floating battery. *Erich Koellner* could make only 13km/h (7 knots) and *Erich Giese* had damaged electrics and engines. Only the *Hermann Künne, Wolfgang Zenker* and *Bernd von Arnim* were essentially fully operational.

SECOND BATTLE OF NARVIK (13 APRIL 1940): *KRIEGSMARINE* CASUALTIES					
Name	**Displacement**	**Speed**	**Guns**	**Torpedoes**	**Damage**
DESTROYERS					
Bernd von Arnim	3241 tonnes (3190 tons)	59/km/h (33kn)	5x127mm (5in)	6x533mm (21in)	Sunk
Erich Giese	3241 tonnes (3190 tons)	9km/h (5kn)	5x127mm (5in)	8x533mm (21in)	Sunk
Erich Koellner	3241 tonnes (3190 tons)	13km/h (7kn)	5x127mm (5in)	2x533mm (21in)	Sunk
Diether von Roeder	3470 tonnes (3415 tons)	0/km/h (0kn)	2x127mm (5in)	8x533mm (21in)	Sunk
Hans Lüdemann	3470 tonnes (3415 tons)	70km/h (38kn)	4x127mm (5in)	4x533mm (21in)	Sunk
Hermann Künne	3470 tonnes (3415 tons)	70km/h (38kn)	5x127mm (5in)	8x533mm (21in)	Sunk
Georg Thiele	3206 tonnes (3156 tons)	50km/h (27kn)	4x127mm (5in)	6x533mm (21in)	Sunk
Wolfgang Zenker	3241 tonnes (3190 tons)	9km/h (5kn)	5x127mm (5in)	8x533mm (21in)	Sunk

Erich Bey, and he resisted making further escape attempts, not without incurring subsequent criticism by history. By the end of 11 April, Bey had eight destroyers at his disposal, most of them in some form of disrepair, with problems ranging from reduced firepower and speed through to a complete lack of seaworthiness.

Seizing the advantage

The British realized that they had bloodied the German nose at Narvik, but were still unclear about the amount of damage they had caused and the naval resources remaining around the port. Despite the uncertainty, the Royal Navy commanders decided to implement a follow-up attack. The first Admiralty response was to launch the light cruiser *Penelope*, backed by several destroyers, in an attack on 11 April, but this was called off after *Penelope* opened its hull on rocks off the coast. The next day, the Royal Navy adopted a different approach, launching Fairey Swordfish aircraft from the aircraft carrier HMS *Furious*, which had deployed with six destroyers and three cruisers around Lofoten. The air attack went in at 1600, and four bomb strikes on the German destroyers were reported, but the action was not tactically decisive.

Following the air attack, Admiral Sir Charles Forbes, the British naval commander around Norway, decided along with the Admiralty to make a more decisive deployment. Therefore, on the morning of 13 April, the battleship HMS *Warspite*, supported by nine destroyers, sailed into Ofotjord.

The scene was set for a massacre. First contact came at 1230, when patrolling spotter planes from *Warspite* bombed and sank the submarine *U-64* at the head of the Herjangsfjord. Shortly afterwards, the British destroyers and *Warspite* began exchanging fire with their German counterparts, some of which were desperately trying to raise enough steam to get under way. By 1350, one German destroyer had sunk – the *Erich Koellner*. Three British destroyers were damaged, but the Royal Navy force pressed on to the back of the Herjangsfjord and hunted in the waters off the Ofotjord.

Over the course of the next two hours, the British killed the German ships one by one, several falling to the firepower of *Warspite*'s 381mm (15in) guns. *Erich Giese* was battered to death by shellfire and *Hermann Künne* went down under a barrage of torpedoes from *Eskimo* and *Forester*. *Diether von Roeder*'s battery function was suppressed by fire from *Warspite* and two destroyers, although in response the German vessel achieved six hits on the destroyer *Cossack*. Her captain, *Korvettenkapitän* Erich Holtorf, was forced to scuttle his vessel, and the *Georg Thiele* was forced to run aground under horrifying shellfire, although not before she had seriously damaged the *Eskimo* with a torpedo attack. *Wolfgang Zenker* capsized and sank at 1545, and the *Hans Lüdemann* was sunk after being captured by British boarding parties.

By the time the gunfire ceased, the *Kriegsmarine* had, over the space of four-and-a-half hours, lost eight destroyers, for three British destroyers damaged.

Operation *Seelöwe*

With France securely in his grasp, Adolf Hitler delivered a clear statement of intent on 16 July 1940: 'I have decided to prepare a landing operation against England, and if necessary to carry it out.'

Events around Narvik had cast a long shadow over the *Kriegsmarine*. Not only had Raeder's force lost 10 destroyers in two separate attacks, but the results of supporting U-boat operations had been extremely disappointing (largely because of defective torpedoes), with only one British transport ship lost to submarine attack for the cost of four U-boats destroyed. (By 28 April, most U-boats had been deployed away from Norway in commerce raiding roles.) Nor was the *Kriegsmarine* able to prevent British and Allied counter-landings between 15 and 18 April. In fact, it was the rival *Luftwaffe* that posed the most substantial threat to Allied shipping. The German grip on Norway began to slip, but was eventually restored when the Allies pulled out of Norway, completing their withdrawal by 8 June, ultimately overwhelmed by the German land offensive and the need to counter a much more serious threat to the south. For on 10 May 1940, Hitler launched his invasion of France and the Low Countries.

Late losses

The *Kriegsmarine*'s experience in and around Norway had not been entirely discouraging, and morale was boosted by some late victories. Even as the Allies were withdrawing, a large German naval force consisting of *Scharnhorst, Gneisenau, Hipper* plus four destroyers, commanded by *Admiral* Wilhelm Marschall, made an aggressive sortie against the Allied shipping. On 8 June, the force sank a troop transport (empty), and later spotted the British aircraft carrier *Glorious*, escorted by two destroyers. At a

PROPOSED INVASION FORCE: OPERATION *SEELÖWE*

Commander	Ships	Base
CONVOY PROTECTION		
Kapitän zur See Erich Bey	2 destroyers	Le Havre
Kapitän zur See Hans Bütow	4 torpedo boats 3 motor torpedo boats	Cherbourg Zeebrügge, Flushing, Rotterdam
Vizeadmiral Karl Dönitz	27 U-boats	Kiel, Wilhelmshaven
TRANSPORT		
Vizeadmiral Hermann von Fischel	Transport Fleet 'B', Tow Formation 1	Dunkirk
Kapitän zur See Walter Hennecke	Transport Fleet 'B', Tow Formation 2	Ostend
Kapitän zur See Gustav Kleikamp	Transport Fleet 'C'	Calais
Kapitän zur See Werner Lindenau	Transport Fleet 'D'	Boulogne
Kapitän zur See Ernst Scheurlen	Transport Fleet 'E'	Le Havre
SUPPORT		
	3 minesweeping flotillas	
	2 anti-submarine flotillas	
	14 minelayers	various

range of 22.5km (14 miles), the *Scharnhorst* opened up with its guns and scored some early hits. Steadily, the *Glorious* was transformed into a blazing inferno, and was abandoned to its fate by its crew. The one comfort for the British was that a spread of torpedoes fired by the destroyer *Acasta* resulted in a hit on the *Scharnhorst*, causing major damage near the battleship's after turret.

Ultimately, the Norwegian campaign had cost the *Kriegsmarine* one heavy cruiser, two light cruisers, 10 destroyers and four submarines, plus a collection of auxiliary craft. On the Allied side, the losses, which included those to air attack, amounted to one aircraft carrier, two cruisers, nine destroyers and six submarines. In addition, a number of ships on both sides suffered serious damage.

Ironically, Raeder's original intention for Norway to act as the *Kriegsmarine*'s premier western base was somewhat qualified by developments in France, Belgium and the Netherlands. In an accomplished land and air campaign, Hitler had essentially conquered all of western Europe in less than two months, with France signing its surrender agreement on 22 June. The *Kriegsmarine*'s involvement in this campaign had been limited, both on account of its commitments in the north, and because of the dangers of deploying surface vessels against the massed British evacuation fleet around Dunkirk in late May and early June.

OPERATION *SEELÖWE*

Type	Commander	Base
Transport Fleet 'B'	Vizeadmiral Hermann von Fischel	Dunkirk
Tow Formation 1	Vizeadmiral Hermann von Fischel	Dunkirk
Tow Formation 2	Kapitän zur See Walter Hennecke	Ostend
Convoy 1	Kapitän zur See Wagner	Ostend
Convoy 2	Kapitän zur See Ernst Schirlitz	Rotterdam
Transport Fleet 'C'	Kapitän zur See Gustav Kleikamp	Calais
Convoy 3	Kapitän zur See Wesemann	Antwerp
Transport Fleet 'D'	Kapitän zur See Werner Lindenau	Boulogne
Transport Fleet 'E'	Kapitän zur See Ernst Scheurlen	Le Havre
Echelon 1a	Korvettenkapitän von Jagow	Le Havre
Echelon 1b	Kapitän zur See Ulrich Brockstein	Le Havre

Invading Britain

German ideas for an invasion of Britain had actually been formulated and considered as far back as November 1939, when plans were submitted to Raeder, as head of the German *Kriegsmarine*, giving various options as to how the operation might be conducted. Even the most cursory study, however, soon revealed that Britain would be a tough nut to crack. Its land forces were undeniably weaker than those of Germany, and following the depredations of the battle of France were in poor condition to resist *Blitzkrieg*. Instead, there were three other elements causing the German planners a headache – the English Channel, the Royal Navy and the Royal Air Force.

To invade Britain, German forces needed to make an amphibious crossing of the Channel, and to do that ran the risk of massacre at sea by the Royal Navy. Germany's numbers of combat-deployable U-boats were still limited at this stage of the war, and its amphibious capability was poor, even more so in light of operational losses in Norway. The *Luftwaffe* could be used in a maritime interdiction role; indeed Raeder insisted that this was a key part of the plan, but to do that it first had to achieve air superiority over the RAF, an outcome that was far from certain.

The invasion plan that was eventually conceived was codenamed Operation *Seelöwe*. It envisaged an initial landing of some 65,000 troops along the English south coast, as the Royal Navy were kept busy in the North Sea and Mediterranean by the *Kriegsmarine*, the Italian Navy and the *Luftwaffe*. Routes through Allied minefields in the Channel could be cleared by German minesweepers in the expectation that they would be free from interference from the RAF. The invasion was planned for September 1940, by which time it was assumed – and Göring would promise – that the RAF would have been destroyed by a sustained *Luftwaffe* air campaign. With the German troops safely ashore, they would push outwards into England, surround London, then drive north to complete the takeover.

Invasion doubts

Although the plan appeared robust on paper, and German forces began requisitioning barges and vessels from across the occupied territories (Germany had no specialized landing craft), doubt hung over the idea at the highest levels. Raeder himself stated a belief that 'a successful invasion of Britain depends on conditions that we can scarcely fulfil' – not inspiring rhetoric from the man effectively responsible for delivering the invasion force. The waters and harbours around southeast England were complicated and treacherous at the best of times, but making contested landings against a nation that still had one of the world's most powerful navies seemed almost suicidal. Furthermore, without dedicated landing craft, the *Kriegsmarine* had two options – acquire them from the conquered territories, or build them. In the end, both options were explored. Barges and coastal vessels were obtained from across Europe, but many were suitable for little more than river and coastal use, not for a potentially rough crossing of the perilous Channel. In terms of new-build vessels, the Germans put into production a range of fresh types. The *Marinefährprahm* (MFP) Type D, for example, was the most widely produced type, and had a total length of 47m (154ft) with a payload of 105 tonnes (103 UK tons). Although this vessel was never used in an invasion of Britain, it neverthless proved useful in several other theatres of war, such as the Mediterranean and around the coastal regions of the USSR.

For *Seelöwe* itself, however, the Germans estimated a total requirement of 1722 barges plus around 1300 motorboats and other transports. Many of the river barges would have to be towed across the Channel by a fleet of 471 tugs, making the landing particularly precarious. Although none of this looked realistically plausible, planning continued.

Hitler himself seemed to have some reticence in principal about invading Britain, possibly explained by his ill-formed desire to create an alliance between Germany and Britain. More convincingly, Hitler was by mid-1940 already thinking about turning his ambitions east into Russia, and the demands of Operation *Seelöwe* would affect those plans significantly. The final nail in *Seelöwe*'s coffin was the *Luftwaffe*'s failure to crush the RAF in the summer of 1940, and Raeder must have breathed a sigh of relief.

KRIEGSMARINE BASES (SEPT 1940)

ATLANTIC OCEAN
Narvik
Bergen
Kiel
Gotenhafen
Wilhelmshaven
Brest
Lorient

Expanded bases

The advantage bestowed on the *Kriegsmarine* by the fall of France is immediately apparent here, as the German Navy took over French ports and harbours on the Atlantic, Channel and North Sea coastlines. The bases further to the south, such as Lorient, were perfect for U-boat deployments, as they allowed the submarines to slip directly into Atlantic waters south of the UK and then swing northwest to intercept incoming supply convoys. The Channel bases were useful for fast-boat rescues of German airmen downed over the Channel, while those in Belgium and the Netherlands provided support for naval shipping operating in northern waters. Taken together, the new bases also made it far easier for the *Kriegsmarine* to threaten British naval supply routes, making it harder for Allied military shipping to have free movement and also limiting the amount of coastal supply traffic up and down southern and eastern Britain.

Western Waters: 1940

With new operating bases established on the far western coast of Continental Europe, the *Kriegsmarine* had greater opportunities to interdict British convoys and warships around the coast of Britain and further into the Atlantic.

Although the most important deployments along the French coastlines were those of the U-boat flotillas, the surface fleet of the *Kriegsmarine* also benefited from the conquests of May and June 1940. In September, ships of the 5th Torpedo Boat Flotilla, the 5th Destroyer Flotilla (consisting of five destroyers) and two ships of the 6th Destroyer Flotilla deployed to coastal France, the destroyers making their first combat sortie with a mining operation around Falmouth Bay on the 28th. Meanwhile, the torpedo boats of the 5th Flotilla (*Greif, Kondor, Falke, Seeadler* and *Wolf*) operated in an interdiction and harassment capacity around the English coast, backed by the various *Schnellboote* (Fast Boat; S-boat) flotillas – the 1st, 2nd, 3rd and 4th – which sailed out of Dutch, French and Belgian harbours.

SPECIFICATIONS	
Name	*Z4 Richard Beitzen* (Type 34 destroyer)
Commissioned	13 May 1937
Crew	315
Displacement	3210 tonnes (3160 tons)
Dimensions	Length: 119m (390ft); Beam:11.3m (37ft)
Range	8150km (5064 miles) at 35km/h (19 kts)
Armour	N/A
Main Armament	5 x 127mm (5in) guns; 8 x AA guns; 2 x quadruple 533mm (21in)torpoedo tubes; 60 mines
Powerplant	Two steam turbines: 52,199kW (70,000hp)
Performance	70km/h (38 kts)

Attack capability

The S-boats provided a useful fast-attack capability against vulnerable British shipping in the English Channel and the Bristol Channel. They could have posed one of the most significant threats to the British troop evacuation at Dunkirk, but they had not been available in sufficient numbers. In July 1940, S-boats operated in tandem with the *Luftwaffe* in coastal convoy interception missions, with some moments of resounding success. For example, on 8 August 1940 a convoy of 21 merchant ships passed through the Strait of Dover, but were caught by an attack from the 1st S-boat Flotilla, and 11 of the 21 ships were sunk or damaged. On 4 September, just four S-boats sank six freighters off Great Yarmouth.

The combined effect of the S-boat and *Luftwaffe* anti-shipping missions severely curtailed traffic along the British coastline, and the situation was balanced out only later in the year and in 1941, by which time the RAF had more control over coastal waters and the Royal Navy had

formed gunboat flotillas that could fight the S-boats on equal terms.

Coastal actions

The English Channel and the Western Approaches (the waters leading up to the wide 'mouth' formed between southwestern England and Brittany) were not suitable areas for *Kriegsmarine* deployment of capital ships and cruisers, but were more suited to the lighter, faster craft that could deploy quickly, make their attack and then return home at speed. A good example of a typical raid occurred off the Isle of Wight on 11 October 1940. Following a British naval bombardment of Cherbourg the night before by HMS *Revenge*, the five torpedo boats of the 5th Flotilla embarked on an aggressive coastal patrol of the Isle of Wight.

There they happened upon two armed trawlers, which they subsequently chased down and destroyed with 104mm (4.1in) gunfire. Within hours, they had also sunk two Free French submarine chasers, and satisfied

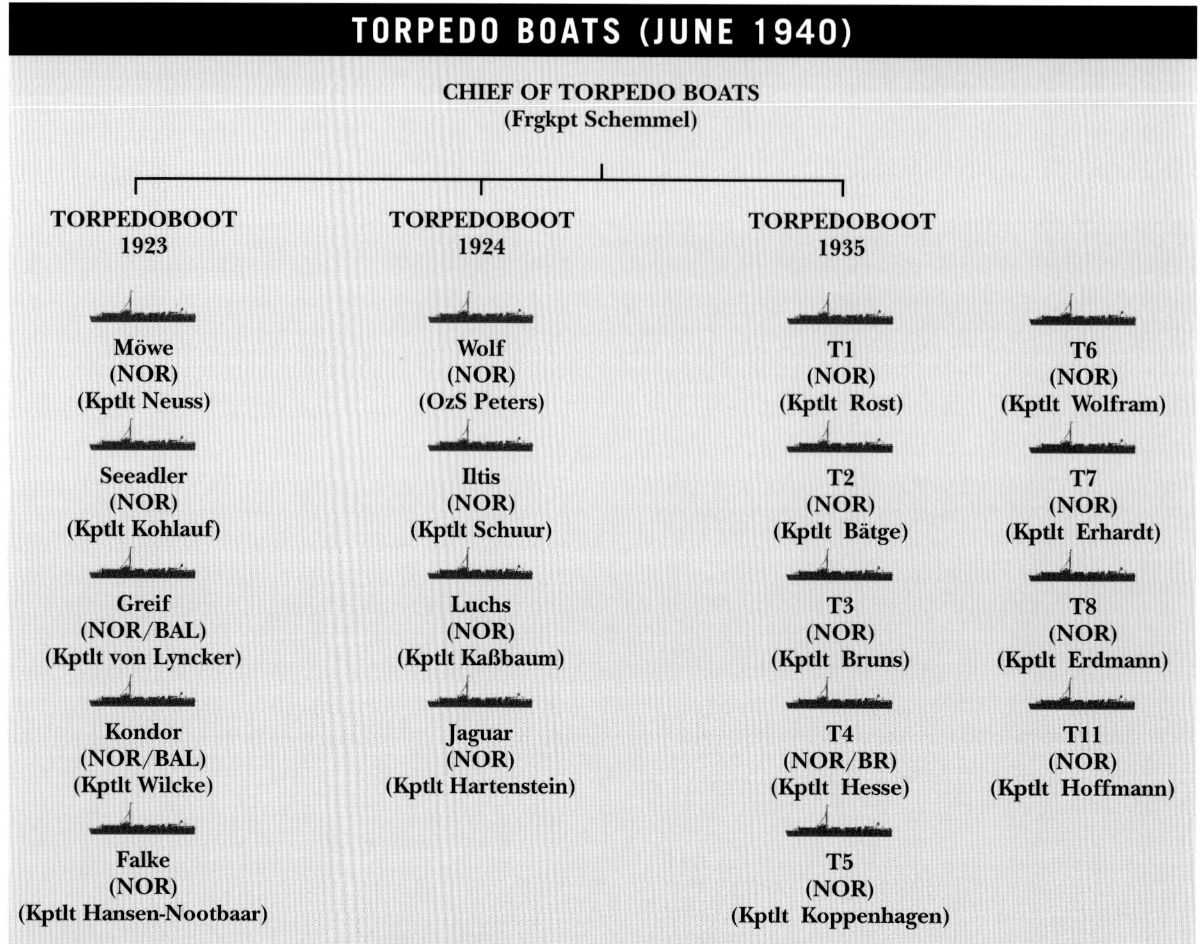

Although many of the older 1923 and 1924 torpedo boats were still in service by June 1940, the newer 1935 type was the largest single class; several of the later 1937 class had been launched but had yet to be commissioned. A typical 1935 class ship such as the T11 was armed with a 105mm (4.1in) gun and six 533mm (21in) torpedo tubes, 30 depth charges and 37mm (1.5in) and 20mm (0.79in) cannon.

DESTROYERS (JUNE 1940)

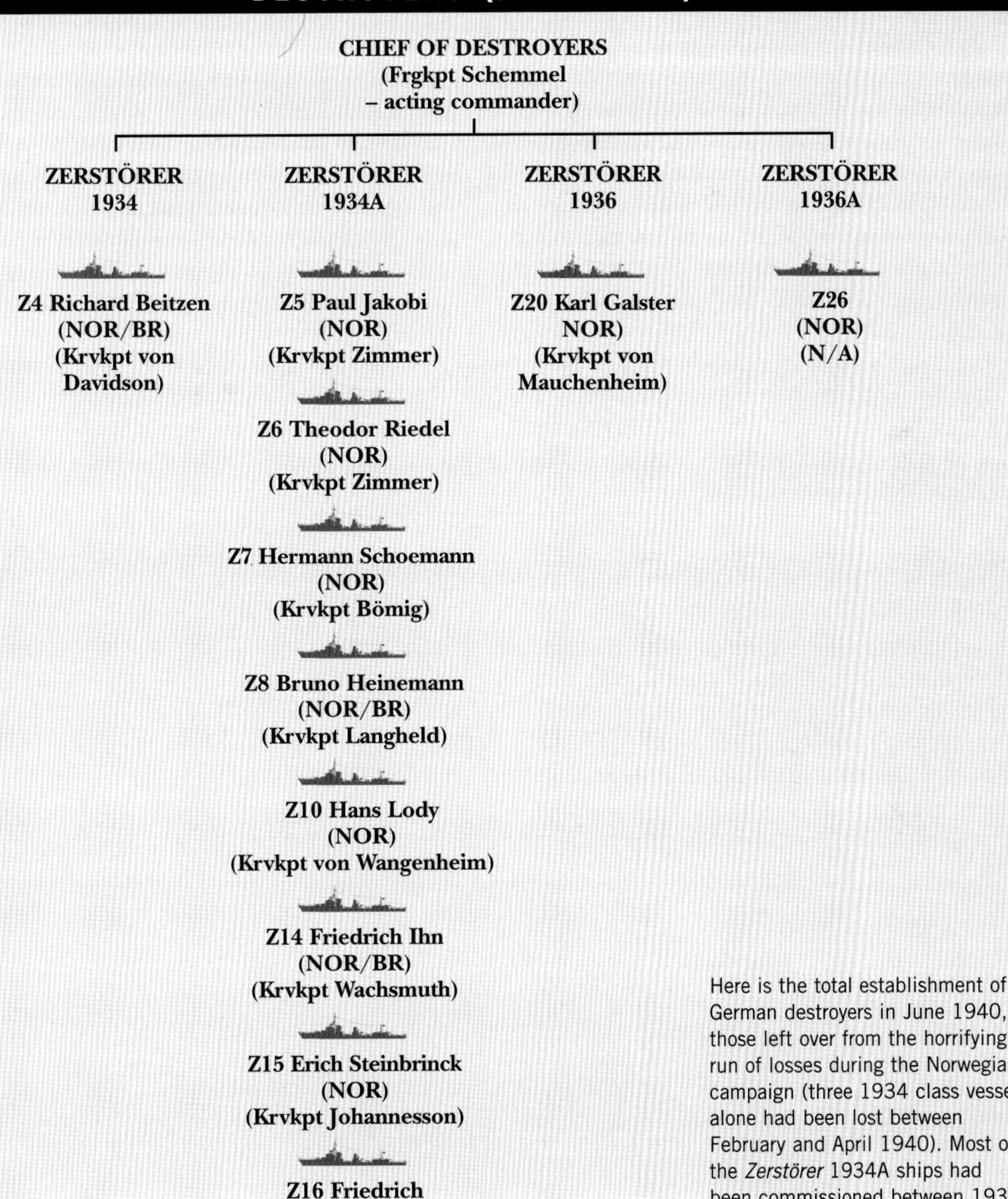

Here is the total establishment of German destroyers in June 1940, those left over from the horrifying run of losses during the Norwegian campaign (three 1934 class vessels alone had been lost between February and April 1940). Most of the *Zerstörer* 1934A ships had been commissioned between 1937 and 1940, and they still formed the most numerous type despite having lost four of their number on 13 April around Narvik. Z26 was the first of eight Type 1936A destroyers commissioned during the war.

with the day's work, they turned for home at 0220 on the 12th. On the way back, however, they encountered the British 5th Destroyer Flotilla, composed of five destroyers commanded by the legendary Captain Lord Louis Mountbatten. In rapid response, the German torpedo boats laid smokescreens and opened up the power in an attempt to lose the pursuing British ships. Mountbatten ordered to ships to open fire, but none of the shells struck home. In reply, two of the German vessels, *Falke* and *Wolf*, launched torpedoes at the British ships, but also did not achieve a hit. In the darkness, the torpedo boats managed to evade the destroyers, which at this point of the war were not equipped with effective short-range radar. All five German torpedo boats made home by 1025.

Just five days later, a similar action occurred in the Western Approaches, albeit on a larger scale. At 0403 on 17 October, six German destroyers – *Hans Lody, Friedrich Ihn, Erich Steinbrinck, Karl Galster* and *Theodor Riedel* – sailed out from the French coast to intercept a reported British convoy as it passed near to Brest. The plan did not begin smoothly.

A British reconnaissance plane spotted the ships and reported their location, and the *Theodor Riedel* suffered from engine troubles and had to return to port. In response to the sighting information, the British deployed their Force F, a rapid-response squadron on the southeast coast, consisting of the cruisers *Newcastle* and *Emerald* and five destroyers (*Jackal, Jupiter, Kashmir, Kelvin* and *Kipling*).

At 1407, Force F spotted the German vessels, and began firing. The commander of the German vessels, Erich Bey, ordered a smokescreen and an about-turn towards the home port of Brest, but the British began to

CHASE IN THE WESTERN APPROACHES (17 OCTOBER 1940)

Name	Displacement	Speed	Guns	Torpedoes	Damage
DESTROYERS					
Hans Lody	3241 tonnes (3190 tons)	70km/h (38kn)	5x127mm (5in)	8x533mm (21in)	Light
Karl Galster	3470 tonnes (3415 tons)	70km/h (38kn)	5x127mm (5in)	8x533mm (21in)	Light
Friedrich Ihn	3216 tonnes (3165 tons)	70km/h (38kn)	5x127mm (5in)	8x533mm (21in)	–
Erich Steinbrinck	3216 tonnes (3165 tons)	70km/h (38kn)	5x127mm (5in)	8x533mm (21in)	–

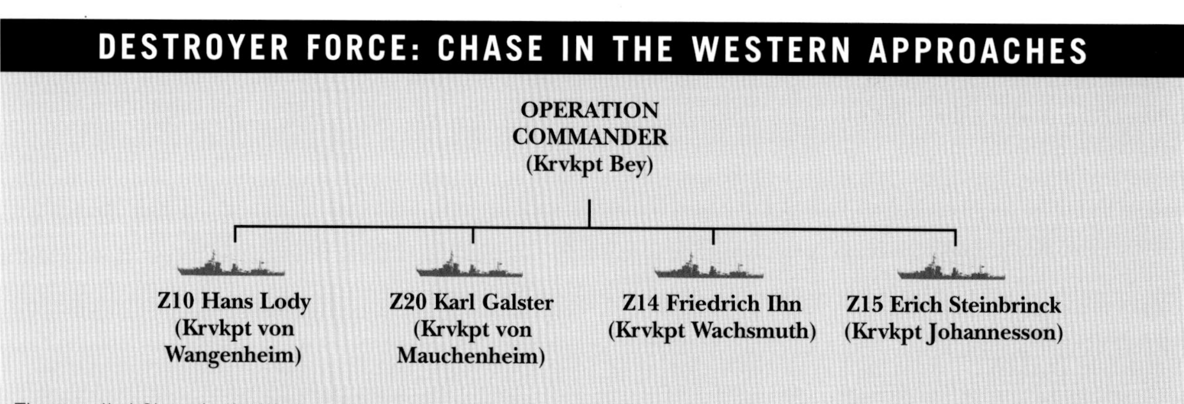

The so-called Chase in the Western Approaches of 17 October 1940 involved four German destroyers, three Type 1934A vessels (*Hans Lody, Friedrich Ihn* and *Erich Steinbrinck*) and one Type 1936 destroyer (*Karl Galster*). The formation was captained by *Führer der Zerstörer* Erich Bey, who led the 4th Destroyer Flotilla in Norway and who later went on to command the *Scharnhorst* during the Battle of North Cape in December 1943.

gain on the fleeing destroyers. In an attempt to disrupt the British pursuit, *Hans Lody*, *Erich Steinbrinck* and *Karl Galster* all made torpedo attacks, and they were helped by German air attacks from Dornier Do 17 bombers. The combination of aggressive action and the approaching evening finally allowed Bey's destroyers to give the enemy the slip. Two of the destroyers, *Hans Lody* and *Karl Galster*, had suffered very minor damage, which is acceptable considering that the British had fired well over 1000 rounds at the German vessels, a poor shell-to-hit ratio.

SPECIFICATIONS	
Name	Z26 (Type 36A destroyer)
Commissioned	11 January 1940
Crew	c.320
Displacement	3750 tonnes (3691 tons)
Dimensions	Length: 127m (417ft); Beam: 12m (39ft)
Range	3498km (2174 miles) at (19kts)
Armour	N/A
Main Armament	4 x 150mm (5.9in)guns; 13 a AA guns; 8 x 533mm (21in) torpedo tubes
Powerplant	Two steam turbines, 52,199kW (70,000hp)
Performance	71.3km/h (38.5kts)

Heavy guns

By the middle of December 1940, the *Kriegsmarine* heavy cruiser *Admiral Hipper* was operating in a commerce raiding role out in the North Atlantic, joining the *Admiral Scheer* in this role. *Hipper* found little in the northern waters except huge seas and dangerous storms, and on the 20th the captain, Wilhelm Meisel, gave the order for the cruiser to return to Brest.

Late in the evening on Christmas Eve, positioned some 1126km (700 miles) west of Cape Finisterre, *Hipper* detected a large British convoy, actually a massive Allied troop deployment destined for the Middle East. Meisel waited until dawn of Christmas Day to make his attack. He opened fire at 0639, by which stage he was aware that the British convoy had a powerful escort with it in the form of the heavy cruiser *Berwick* and two light cruisers, *Bonaventure* and *Dunedin*.

Two convoy ships were soon damaged by *Hipper*'s 203mm (8in) shells, but the British escort quickly responded and bore down on the solitary German vessel. Meisel was under orders not to become engaged in slugging matches with superior forces, so began pulling away and making evasive manoeuvres. At 0651, however, *Hipper* once again came into contact with the *Berwick*, itself armed with 203mm (8in) guns, and a major firefight evolved between the two ships. It was *Hipper* that would gain fire superiority, hitting the *Berwick* with four shells in quick succession, although only two of the shells actually exploded. The *Berwick* wisely decided to break off the action, and would subsequently spend six months out of action being repaired. *Hipper* escaped the other escorts, and arrived at Brest two days later unharmed, having also sunk a cargo ship on the journey home for good measure.

The presence of ships like the *Hipper* in the Atlantic undoubtedly unnerved the British Admiralty, and resulted in a beefed-up escort for most of the transatlantic convoys (a move also inspired by the U-boat depredations). Yet the isolated commerce raiders were themselves vulnerable. Despite their undeniable power, the coming years saw most of them either sunk or confined to port.

Surface War in the West: 1941–43

The years 1941–43 were a time of deep transition for the *Kriegsmarine* surface fleet. From a position of ascendancy in the Channel, North Sea and North Atlantic, the *Kriegmarine*'s capital vessels had become strategically impotent by 1943.

A dramatic view of the bow end of the *Bismarck*, seen from the deck of the heavy cruiser *Prinz Eugen*.

On 24 August 1940, a new battleship, striking in silhouette and menacing in its evident firepower, received its commission and entered the ranks of the *Kriegsmarine.* It was a battleship almost like no other in the Western world – its top speed was around 56km/h (30 knots), swifter than many destroyers, yet it carried into battle an armament of eight 380mm (15in) and 12 150mm (6in) guns. The *Bismarck* sent a justifiable ripple of fear through the Allied surface navies.

Strategic shift

The years 1941–43 were a curious period in the history of the *Kriegsmarine.* Raeder, still in charge after two years of war both traumatic and victorious, faced several strategic challenges in the application of his navy. One of the most intellectually taxing was what to do with his surface fleet. Warfare was steadily changing. The U-boat campaign had become by far the most successful strand of *Kriegsmarine* strategy, its massive drownings of merchant vessels far exceeding anything that the top surface commerce raiders could achieve. It seemed ironic to many that a U-boat with a crew of fewer than 70 men and armed with a few torpedo tubes could pose more of a threat to Allied shipping than a massive multi-turreted battleship with a complement of nearly 2000 men, but naval warfare was increasingly becoming about stealth and escape, rather than about blazing gunbattles.

It was also becoming more about air power. The *Kriegsmarine* was itself a beneficiary of this shift, as long-range *Luftwaffe* flights operating between southern France and Norway provided invaluable reconnaissance sweeps out into the Atlantic, then radioed convoy location data back to the U-boat bases and surface ships. It was only interservice rivalry that prevented this process from becoming more efficient; aircrew information was processed through three different layers of command before it reached the front-line ships, often resulting in outdated information by the time it reached wolf packs and commerce raiders.

On the flip side, aircraft were becoming more of a concern to the *Kriegsmarine,* particularly in the increased Allied use of escort carriers to protect convoys. The Germans had been amazed before by the sheer audacity of British Swordfish and Skua pilots, flying outdated aircraft that nevertheless managed to inflict serious damage on or even sink large German vessels. (A flight of 16 Skuas, for example, sank the *Königsberg* in Bergen harbour on 10 April 1940.) Developments within the Japanese and US Navies also suggested that naval thinking was shifting towards carrier power as its focal point. Increasingly, major surface vessels began to appear as burdens to be protected.

New raiders

It was into this changing environment that the *Bismarck* entered operational duty, followed on 25 January 1941 by the commissioning of her sister ship, the mighty *Tirpitz.* The design concepts for *Schlachtschiff* F (Battleship F), which ultimately became the *Bismarck,* actually dated back as far as 1935, and went through several subsequent upgrades to keep pace with changes in French and British warship design. The 1930s were still a time in which the international arms race was expressed partly in the scale of naval armament (although it was Hitler's prescient investment in new land and air warfare technology that largely gave his forces the edge during the early *Blitzkrieg* campaign). Both *Bismarck* and *Tirpitz* were laid down in 1936 and launched in 1939. The dates were important – when they were launched, the battleships could justifiably expect their influence on the high seas to be great, and were in keeping with Hitler's Z-Plan ambitions. Only two years later, however, things had changed, not least because from June 1941 Germany was involved in the war on the Eastern Front. It was increasingly recognized that the war would be won or lost in that theatre.

Maritime burden

There was no doubt that the Allies feared both battleships; if just one of them penetrated a convoy, the potential for massacre was very real. The two vessels therefore caused modifications to convoy policy – the bolstering of escort numbers and the power of those escorts. Yet both Raeder and Hitler were aware that in the event that the *Bismarck* and *Tirpitz* made combat strikes, the Allies would pull out all their considerable resources to destroy them, and their loss would be major both in military and propaganda terms. These humbling monsters of naval warfare were actually chained beasts.

The cruiser war

The term 'cruiser war' is not applied solely to *Kriegsmarine* cruiser operations but to all German commerce raiding activities during the early part of the war. It was a time of epic successes and equally magnificent defeats for the German Navy.

The year 1941 was very much a high point in the fortunes of the wartime *Kriegsmarine.* Not only was the U-boat campaign beginning to pay strategically significant dividends, but Raeder's surface fleet also appeared to be proving its worth in the commerce raiding role. Commerce raiding missions by *Admiral Scheer, Admiral Hipper, Gneisenau* and *Scharnhorst* leading up to April had sank a total of 264,057 tonnes (259,897 UK tons) of merchant shipping in Atlantic waters. In just one incident, on 11 February, the *Admiral Hipper* attacked an unescorted convoy out in the Atlantic, and sank seven of the 19 ships. It was expected that *Bismarck* and *Tirpitz* would soon increase the total victories exponentially, and they would be joined in their operations by the heavy cruiser *Prinz Eugen.*

Dented confidence

April 1941 saw some events, however, that altered Raeder's deployment options. A Royal Naval Air Service (RNAS) Bristol Beaufort torpedo-bomber on 6 April managed to penetrate Brest harbour and drop a single torpedo. Although the aircraft was subsequently shot from the skies, killing all its crew, its torpedo struck the docked *Gneisenau,* causing critical damage that was reinforced by four bomb strikes in a subsequent air attack on 10/11 April. Two weeks later, *Prinz Eugen* struck a mine and was put out of action for a fortnight.

Unsettled by the events, Raeder had to decide what ships he could deploy to the Atlantic and when. *Tirpitz* had been commissioned, but was still on trials and would not come into full operation until 1942. Therefore he decided to deploy the *Bismarck* and the repaired *Prinz Eugen* together. They conducted an exercise in the Baltic on 18 May, before turning westwards, heading for the Atlantic. Critically, Allied intelligence received reports of the *Bismarck* under sail by 20 May. In response, the British commander-in-chief of the Home Fleet, Admiral Sir John Tovey, not only increased aerial reconnaissance over the northern passages into the Atlantic, but also put together a pursuit task force consisting of the battleship *Prince of Wales,* the battlecruiser *Hood* and six destroyers. The 'Mighty' *Hood,* an Admiral class battlecruiser, was one of the prides of the British fleet, and its primary armament of eight 381mm (15in) guns made it well respected even within the German Navy.

Shadowing *Bismarck*

Unfortunately for the *Bismarck,* which was under the command of *Kapitän zur See* Ernst Lindemann (although the combined *Bismarck/Prinz Eugen* task force was commanded by *Admiral* Günther Lütjens), it was being monitored by Allied reconnaissance aircraft as it made its way from Scandinavian waters into the Atlantic. Tovey deployed his forces across the Denmark Strait and between Iceland and the Faeroes in attempt to prevent *Bismarck*'s breakout into the Atlantic.

On 23 May, the British heavy cruiser *Suffolk,* which had been patrolling the Denmark Strait with the heavy cruiser *Norfolk,* spotted the *Bismarck,* and began shadowing operations. *Suffolk* was soon joined by the *Norfolk,* and the two British cruisers maintained visual range, which also meant that the *Bismarck* spotted them and engaged at a range of 11,880m (13,000 yards). The proximity of the *Bismarck*'s 380mm (15in) shells meant that the two far less powerful cruisers were soon forced to retire beyond visual distance.

Radar technology, however, meant that the *Bismarck* and the *Prinz Eugen* could still be tracked, even at night, so Tovey's British fleet was soon a gathering storm against the German vessels. Meanwhile, the two German warships altered their positions, the *Prinz Eugen* taking the lead while *Bismarck* made repairs to her radar system (damaged by her own guns firing).

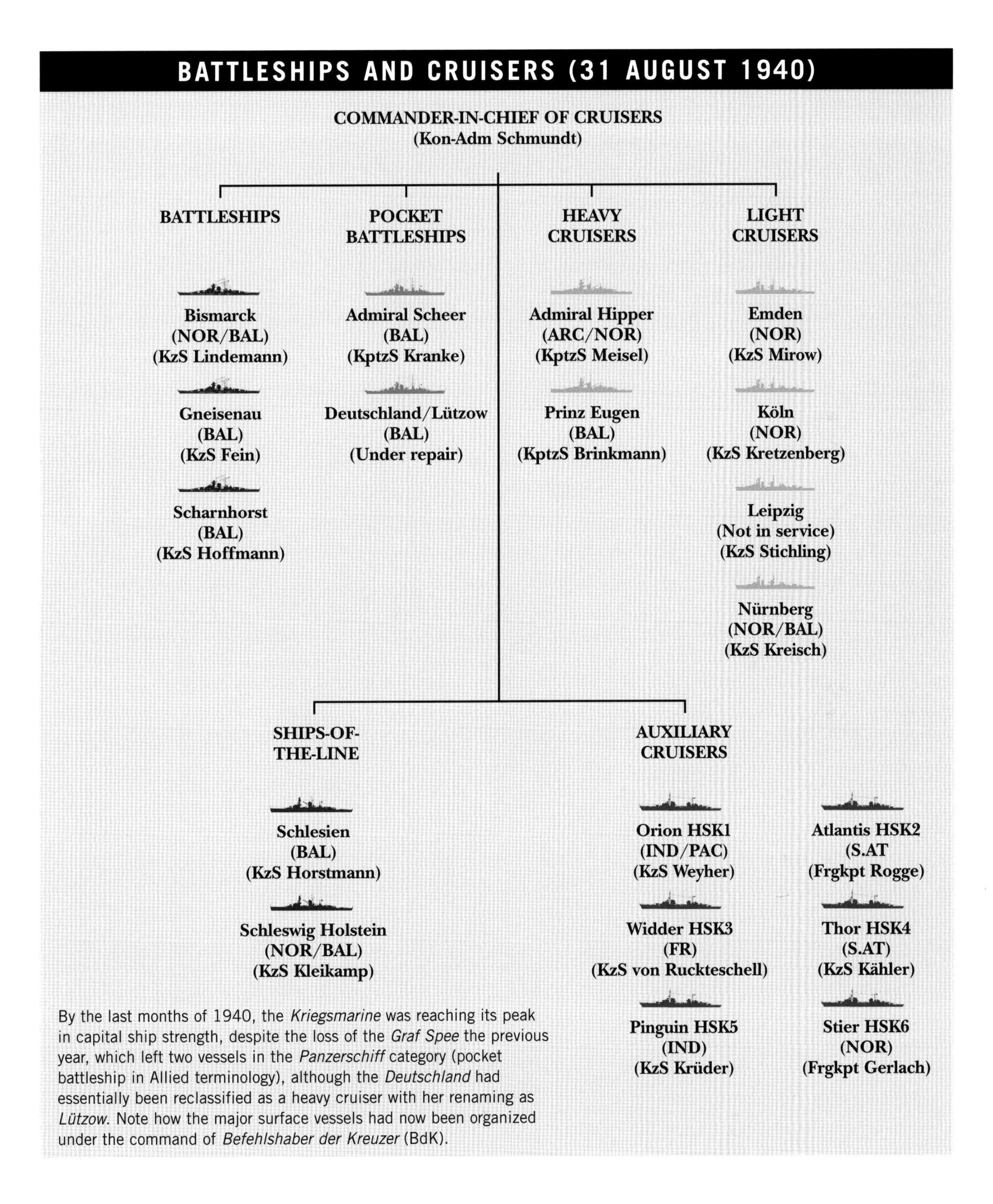

By the last months of 1940, the *Kriegsmarine* was reaching its peak in capital ship strength, despite the loss of the *Graf Spee* the previous year, which left two vessels in the *Panzerschiff* category (pocket battleship in Allied terminology), although the *Deutschland* had essentially been reclassified as a heavy cruiser with her renaming as *Lützow*. Note how the major surface vessels had now been organized under the command of *Befehlshaber der Kreuzer* (BdK).

Raider hunting

The hunting of the *Bismarck* illustrated both the power and the vulnerabilities of Hitler's maritime commerce raiders. Once located, she was unable to hide from the Allied task force seeking her destruction.

As the *Bismarck* pushed down through the Denmark Strait, its command was fully aware that the British were tracking the vessel. The *Bismarck*'s radio operators were monitoring Allied naval radio traffic, and were also aware of the *Suffolk*'s radar monitoring of their position. In fact, it was radar as much as anything that altered the status of the major *Kriegsmarine* capital ships operating in the Atlantic.

If *Suffolk* had not been fitted with radar just the month before, *Bismarck* probably could have made her escape in the low visibility conditions common in those waters. Lütjens knew that the British would soon close down on his two warships, and the anticipated engagement came on 24 May 1941, while the German ships were still in the Denmark Strait.

PRINZ EUGEN	
Name	*Prinz Eugen*
Commissioned	1 August 1940
Crew	1450
Displacement	18,695 tonnes (18,400 tons)
Dimensions	Length: 210m (690ft); Beam: 22m (72ft)
Range	11,587km (7200 miles) at 37km/h (20kts)
Armour	Belt: 70–80mm (2.75–3.1in); Deck: 12–50mm (0.5–2in); Turrets: 70–105mm (2.75–4.1in)
Armament	8 x 203mm (8in); 12 x 105mm (4.1in); 36 x AA guns; 12 x 533mm (21in) torpedo tubes
Performance	62km/h (33.4kts)

Destruction of the *Hood*

During the early hours of the 24th, the British ships maintained radio and radar silence while the *Hood* and *Prince of Wales*, commanded as a squadron by Vice-Admiral Lancelot Holland from the *Hood*, advanced at speed in an attempt to intercept. At 0537, with daylight just smudging the horizon, the opposing forces spotted each other and began a very long-range artillery duel. At a distance of 31km (19 miles), the four ships began trading shells. The German ships had the advantage of position – the *Hood*, leading the British squadron, was facing head on, halving the number of guns that could be brought to bear – and gunnery sophistication, as Germany's excellent stereoscopic rangefinders gave quick targeting data.

In almost their first salvos, the *Bismarck* and *Prinz Eugen* achieved hits on the *Hood*, and another salvo shortly afterwards saw a shell from the *Bismarck* puncture the battlecruiser's weak deck armour and ignite the magazine. In a cataclysmic explosion, the *Hood* blew to pieces, taking with her 1419 crew (only three survived). It was an extraordinary horror for the British, and an

DESTROYERS (31 MARCH 1941)

COMMANDER OF DESTROYERS
(Frgkpt Alfred Schemmel – acting commander)

ZERSTÖRER 1934

Z4 Richard Beitzen (NOR) (Krvkpt von Davidson)

ZERSTÖRER 1934A

Z5 Paul Jakobi (NOR/BAL) (Krvkpt Schlieper)

Z6 Theodor Riedel (NOR/BAL) (Krvkpt Riede)

Z7 Hermann Schoemann (NOR/BAL) (Krvkpt Wittig)

Z8 Bruno Heinemann (NOR/FRA) (Krvkpt Alberts)

Z10 Hans Lody (NOR) (Krvkpt Pfeiffer)

Z14 Friedrich Ihn (NOR/FRA) (Krvkpt Wachsmuth)

Z15 Erich Steinbrinck (NOR/FRA) (Krvkpt Johannesson)

Z16 Friedrich Eckholdt (NOR/BAL) (Krvkpt Menge)

ZERSTÖRER 1936

Z20 Karl Galster (NOR) (Krvkpt von Mauchenheim)

ZERSTÖRER 1936A

Z23 (NOR) (Frgkpt Böhme)

Z24 (NOR) (Krvkpt Salzwedel)

Z27 (NOR/ARC) (Frgkpt Smidt)

Z25 (NOR/ARC) (Krvkpt Gerlach)

Z26 (NOR/ARC) (Krvkpt von Berger)

Here is the establishment of commissioned German destroyers in the *Kriegsmarine* at the end of March 1941. At this point in the war, there was three principal destroyer flotillas: the 5th, 6th and 8th, formed in May 1940 (5th and 6th Flotillas) and December 1940 (8th Flotilla). Flotillas 1–4, which had been formed in 1938 and 1939, had all been disbanded in April 1940 following the disastrous losses in destroyers during the Norwegian campaign. A 7th Destroyer Flotilla was not operational.

DEUTSCHLAND/LÜTZOW	
Name	*Deutschland/Lützow*
Commissioned	1 April 1933
Crew	Up to 950
Weight	14,751 tonnes (14,519 tons)
Dimensions	Length: 212.5m (697ft); Beam: 22m (72ft)
Range	11,586km (7200 miles) at 37km/h (20kts)
Armour	Deck: 12–50mm (0.5–2in); Belt: 70–80mm (2.7–3in); Turrets: 70–105mm (2.7–4in)
Armament	8 x 203mm (8in); 12 x 105mm (4.1in); 45 x AA guns; 12 x 533mm (21in) torpedo
Powerplant	Three turbines, 101,320kW (136,000hp)
Performance	62km/h (33.5kts)

equally extraordinary victory for the *Bismarck*. On her first combat voyage, she had destroyed one of the great ships of the Royal Navy.

Cost of victory

The *Prince of Wales* was still in action, however. This brand-new ship – she was still in the process of working-up – was quickly battered by seven shell strikes from both German warships, causing serious casualties and damage. Her badly wounded captain, J.C. Leach, ordered the ship to turn around and escape under cover of smoke. Yet during the battle, *Prince of Wales* managed to score three strikes on the *Bismarck*, and Lütjens was forced to call off his combat operation and attempt to take the battleship back to dry dock at St Nazaire.

The sinking of the *Bismarck*

The *Bismarck*'s first combat operation had been a spectacular success, resulting in the sinking of the British battlecruiser HMS *Hood*. Yet, ironically, it was this very action that secured the *Bismarck*'s eventual destruction at the hands of a vengeful enemy.

The loss of the *Hood* was a tremendous blow to British public morale, and Prime Minister Winston Churchill gave his personal order that the *Bismarck* was to be tracked down and sunk with all available resources. Continuing radar contacts from the *Suffolk*, which indicated that the *Bismarck*'s speed had dropped to 44km/h (24 knots), plus physical evidence in the form of surface oil, informed Tovey that the *Bismarck* was probably damaged. Various Allied forces were redirected to intercept the *Bismarck*, including Force H sailing from Gibraltar with vessels that included the battleships *Rodney*, *Revenge* and *Ramilies* and the cruiser *Edinburgh*. The *Prinz Eugen* had already left the *Bismarck* on her own, to return safely to the coast of France.

Race for home

On the *Bismarck*, there were command disagreements between Lindemann and Lütjens. The former wanted to turn northwards and run back directly to Germany, whereas Lütjens ordered him to maintain a southwesterly course into the Atlantic to make a deep southern journey back to France. Lütjens' choice of

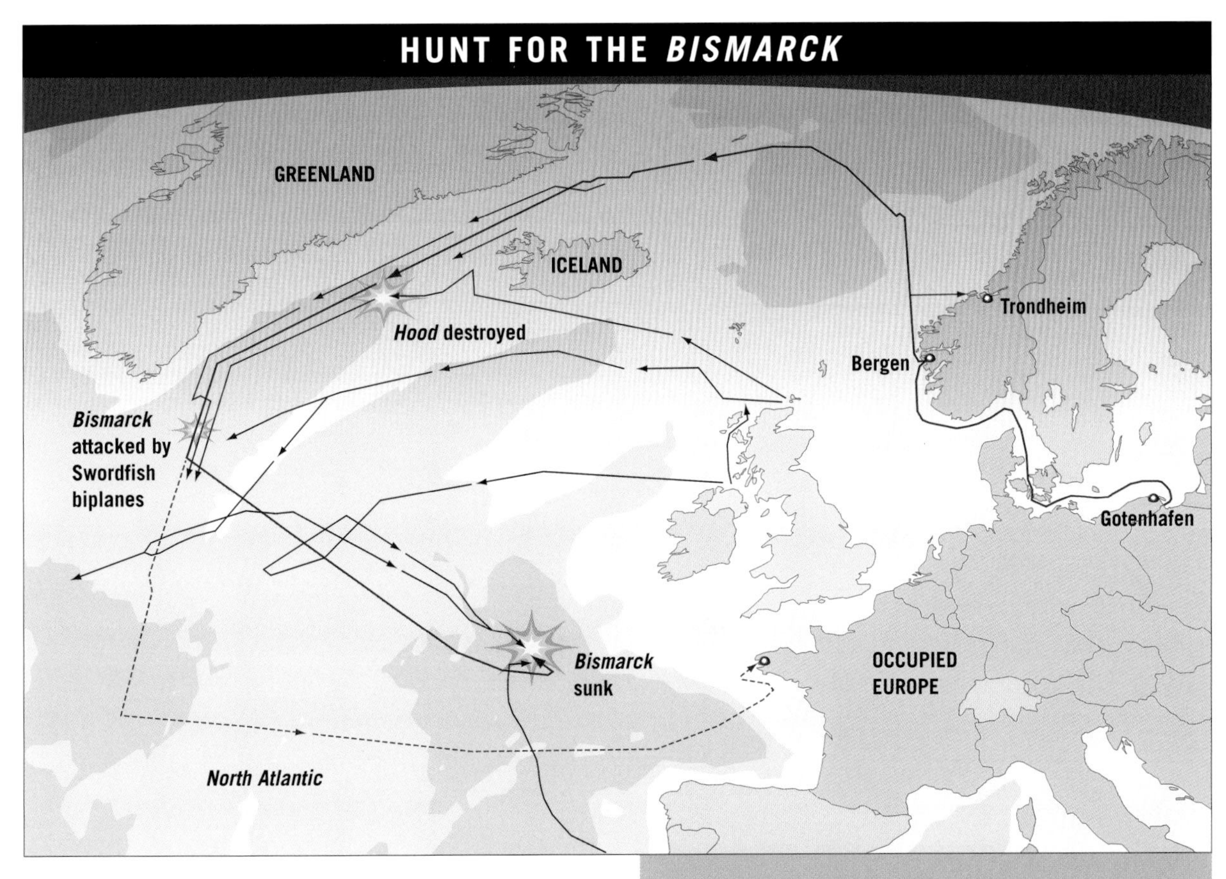

route was undoubtedly the longer one, but there was arguably a better chance of remaining undetected in the vastness of the Atlantic Ocean, rather than run the risk of battling back through narrow northern waters under pressure from the Royal Navy Home Fleet. Yet the *Bismarck* was losing fuel oil rapidly, and unless the battleship could take on more fuel from a tanker or submarine, there was a very real risk of running out of power in a hostile Atlantic.

The first British strike back at *Bismarck* came in the form of a raid by Swordfish aircraft from the carrier HMS *Victorious*, which attacked at around 1450 on 24 May. Through *Bismarck*'s massive anti-aircraft fire, one of the Swordfish achieved a torpedo strike, but it hit the ship's main 380mm (15in) belt armour and had no major effect. Furthermore, at 0300 the next day, the British lost contact with *Bismarck* as she made a bearing change to the southeast and headed for France.

Route to destruction

The problems of penetrating the North Atlantic for German capital ships are evident from this map, which depicts the course of the *Bismarck* from the exercise in the Baltic through to her sinking 480km (300 miles) west of Brest. The waters of the Baltic and around Norway provided plenty of discreet anchorages, but the narrow waterways also made spotting by Allied reconnaissance aircraft easier. To access the North Atlantic, the vessel also had to squeeze through the Denmark Strait between Greenland and Iceland, or between Iceland and northern Great Britain, the latter the location of the British Home Fleet.

With the introduction of radar and more effective maritime aerial reconnaissance, it became increasingly difficult for the German warships to move unnoticed through the Allied net. The only point at which *Bismarck* temporarily lost British tracking ships was when she turned southeast for Brest.

GÜNTHER LÜTJENS (1889–1941)

Günther Lütjens joined the *Kaiserliche Marine* in 1907, rising steadily through the officer ranks aboard a variety of cruisers and battleships.

- During World War I, he served as a torpedo boat commander, a position to which he returned in 1921 following several years in civilian transport shipping. He rose to become commander of the 3rd Torpedo Boat Flotilla, eventually becoming *Führer der Torpedoboote* in 1937, with the rank of *Konteradmiral.*

- In 1940 he took charge of the northern naval forces during the invasion of Norway, and in June became *Flottenchef* (Fleet Commander) of the *Kriegsmarine.* Promoted *Admiral* in September 1940, Lütjens perished aboard *Bismarck* on 27 May 1941.

For the best part of the day, *Bismarck* remained hidden from British radar contact, but then on the morning of the 26th, it was spotted by a Catalina reconnaissance aircraft and its coordinates, some 1297km (700nm) from Brest, were relayed back to Tovey. The ships of the Gibraltar Fleet were in the best position to launch an immediate attack, and the carrier *Ark Royal* sent out two flights of Swordfish, the first mistakenly (and thankfully without consequence) attacking their own cruiser *Sheffield,* while the second found *Bismarck* at 1910. The *Bismarck* was hit by two torpedoes, one slammed ineffectually into the belt armour, but the other struck and jammed the rudder in a 15-degree turn to port.

The *Bismarck* was now effectively doomed, turning helplessly in circles in the ocean, while British warships began to circle round like sharks. Lütjens knew the situation was hopeless, and broadcast a message back to the *Führer,* stating that the ship was no longer

BISMARCK	
Name	*Bismarck*
Commissioned	28 August 1940
Crew	2192
Displacement	50,957 tonnes (50,153 tons)
Dimensions	Length: 251m (824ft); Beam: 36m (118ft)
Range	13,035km (8100 miles) at 30km/h (16kts)
Armour	Belt: 320mm (12.6in); Deck: 50–120mm (2–4.7in); Turrets: 230–355mm (9–14in)
Armament	8 x 380mm(15in);12 x 150mm (6in); 44 x AA guns
Powerplant	3 x turbines, 102,810kW (138,000hp)
Performance	54km/h (29kts)

manoeuvrable but that he and the crew would fight to the end. Attempts by a nearby U-boat, *U-556*, to attract other submarines to a rescue attempt failed, and *U-556* itself was out of torpedoes.

Coup de grâce

As dawn broke on 27 May, *Bismarck* came under the combined naval bombardment of two battleships, *King George V* and *Rodney*, and the cruisers *Norfolk* and *Dorsetshire*. With her manoeuvrability so severely restricted, the *Bismarck* was essentially a sitting target, and British fire brought unimaginable destruction and slaughter to the decks of the great German battleship. Most of her main turrets were blasted out of action, but enough secondary batteries and two of the 380mm (15in) guns remained operational and fired occasional shells at the attackers, with little effect but to incite the British to heavier shelling. At one point, the British ships stood at just 3.2km (2 miles), pouring salvo after salvo into the burning ruin. Finally, torpedoes from the *Norfolk* and *Dorsetshire* finally caused the *Bismarck* to sink, with the loss of over 1800 men.

Consequences

The loss of the *Bismarck* had far-reaching repercussions for the *Kriegsmarine*. The deployment of surface warships as Atlantic commerce raiders was cancelled, as their survivability could no longer be predicted in an era of radar detection and maritime aviation. Furthermore, the German aircraft carrier *Graf Zeppelin* was cancelled mid-production. Put simply, it was deemed too risky for any surface ship to attempt a breakout into the North Atlantic, including a carrier. For this reason, mighty warships like the *Tirpitz* would be largely consigned to hidden anchorages, there to be pounded regularly by Allied air strikes.

Channel battles: 1942

During 1942, the English Channel formed a highly contested battleground between the *Kriegsmarine* and the Royal Navy. Following the sinking of the *Bismarck*, however, Hitler felt that the waters were not the place for his major warships.

At the beginning of 1942, the *Kriegsmarine* had a hefty percentage of its forces concentrated in harbours along the western French coastline. These not only included U-boats and S-boats, but also the battleships *Scharnhorst* and *Gneisenau* and the heavy cruiser *Prinz Eugen*. The large vessels threw their shadow over the English Channel, threatening British naval and commerce traffic, but for Hitler they posed more of a worry than an encouragement.

Base issues

The major problem for Hitler was the location of the big ships – Brest. Brest was useful for German naval operations in variety of ways. Its location was superb – the westernmost spur of France, it drove out into the Atlantic south of England, providing ready access to the open sea and the Atlantic hunting grounds. It was physically sheltered, giving safe anchorage for its vessels. Strategically, maintaining a strong naval presence at Brest meant that Britain had to divert resources, or physically divert convoys, to avoid potential interceptions launched from the port.

Yet Brest's location was its curse as well as its blessing. First, we should never forget that it was located in occupied territory, not in the German homeland. Although Germany's grip over France was secure, the maritime infrastructure still had to cope with the daily run of sabotage (minor and major), deliberate tardiness and other acts of defiance from indigenous workers, plus the perils that Resistance activity posed to resupply trains running across France from Germany. The combined effect was an added level of inertia to all maintenance activities, which in turn retarded the operational tempo of the ships. More serious, however, was the fact that Brest was in comfortable striking distance of Allied bombers. Both *Scharnhorst* and *Gneisenau* were damaged at Brest during air raids in 1941, and the port became a priority target for RAF Bomber Command until it was liberated in 1944. Furthermore, although the Germans could intimidate British shipping from Brest, the reverse was also true. Brest had the potential to be a trap for the major German warships, should the Royal Navy apply an effective blockade of the port.

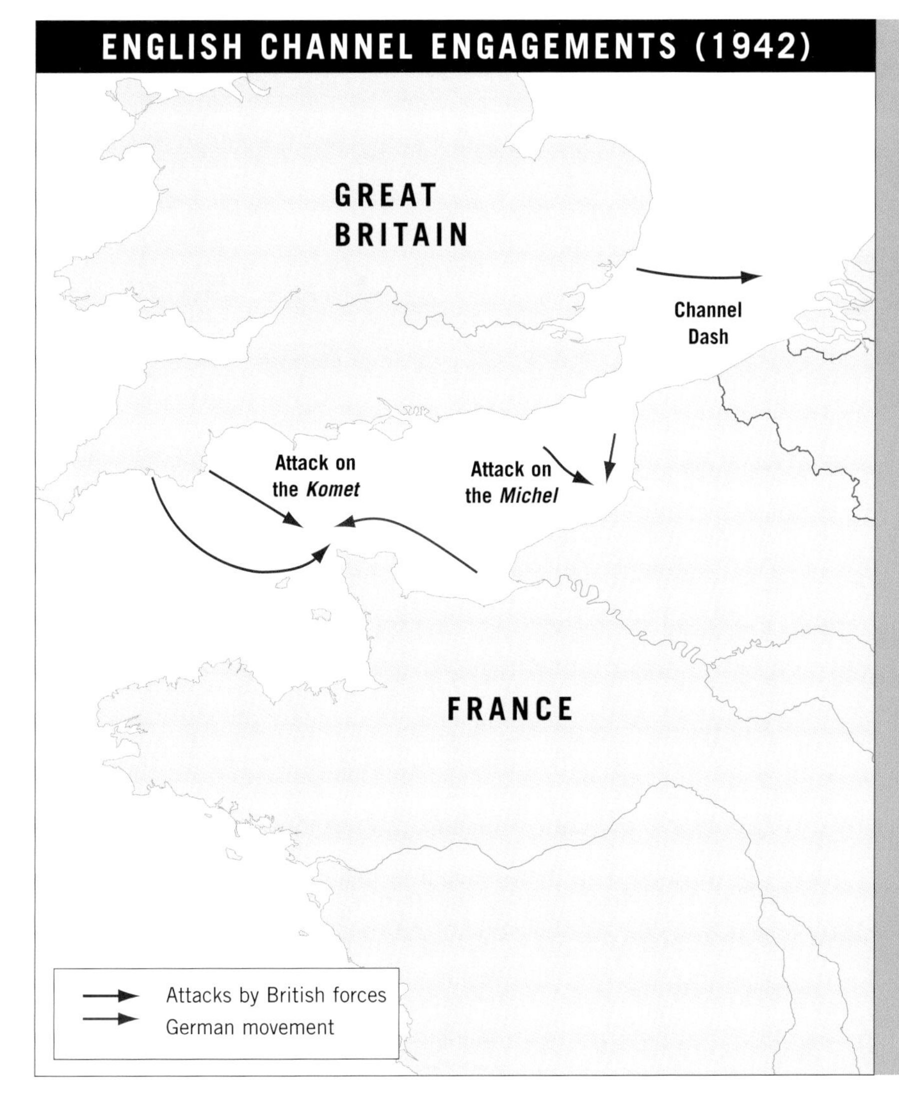

Channel engagements

The year 1942 was a busy one for Channel battles between British and German naval forces. There were numerous small-scale engagements between opposing fast patrol craft, and German S-boats made regular torpedo runs against British convoys in the North Sea.

The Channel Dash of 12 February involved the greatest movement of vessels, and an opportunity for the British to inflict major losses on the German surface fleet was lost.

In fact, the *Kriegsmarine* continued to make Channel runs throughout 1942, resulting in actions such as the largely unsuccessful British attack on the auxiliary cruiser *Michel* on 14 March as it attempted to break out into the Atlantic, and the attack on the *Komet* on 14 October, which resulted in the auxiliary cruiser being sunk.

S-boat deployments 1939–44

The S-boats (*Schnellboote*, or Fast Attack Craft; known to the Allies as E-boats) were deployed in four main operational areas: the English Channel/North Sea; the Baltic/Far North; the Black Sea; and the Mediterranean/Aegean. They were extremely useful craft, employed on maritime rescue (typically of downed *Luftwaffe* pilots), coastal patrol and reconnaissance and fast-attack missions.

During the war, a total of 14 S-boat flotillas were formed, the vast majority of these being sent to the first two theatres mentioned, while the Black Sea had only one flotilla. Note that almost all of the S-boat flotillas operated on an autonomous basis, except for the four flotillas (3, 7, 21, 24) in the Mediterranean/Aegean, which together comprised the 1.*Schnellbootsdivision*.

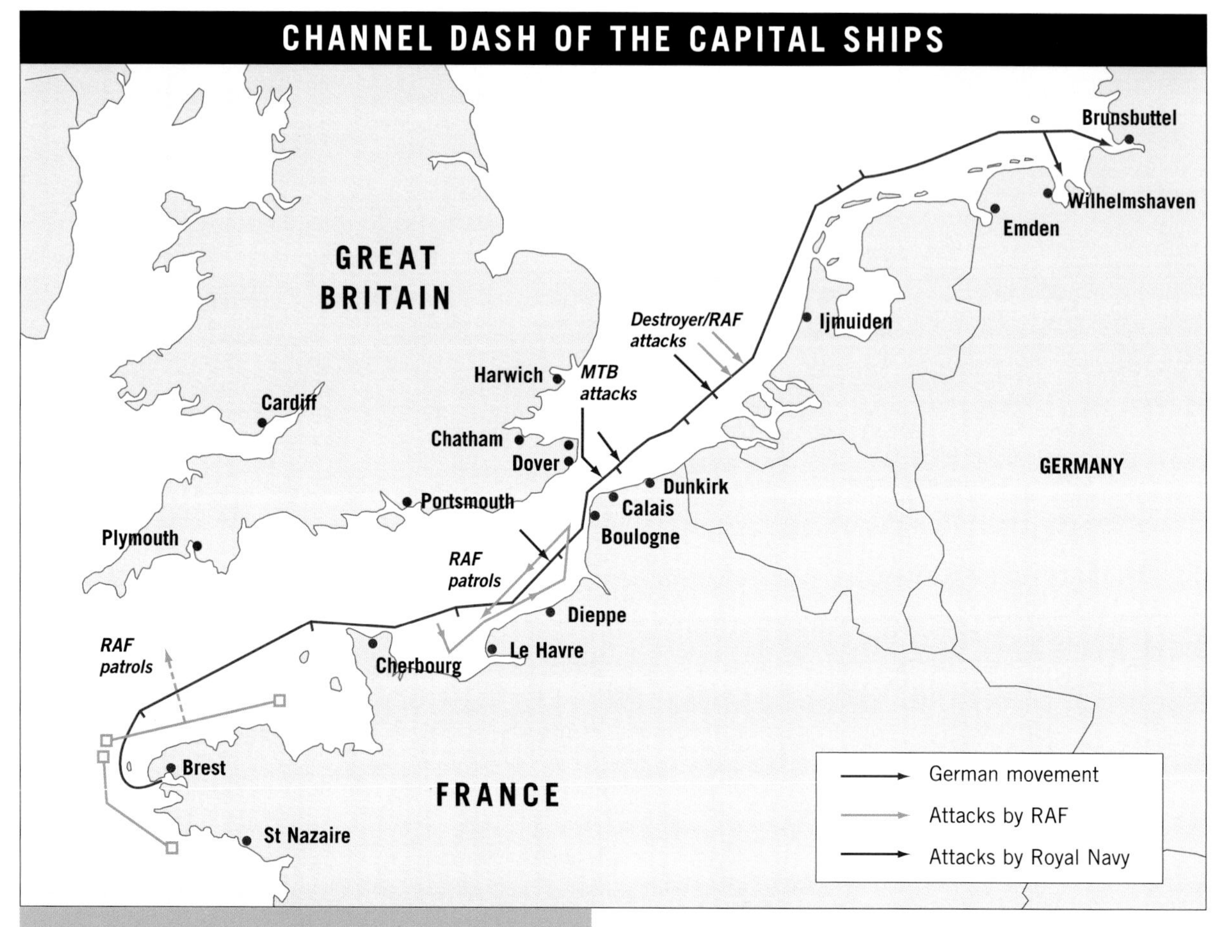

February 1942

The narrow waters between France and southern England provided a precarious route for warships moving to and from Germany. They were not only the most contested maritime areas in Europe, but navigation through the often shallow waters of the Channel required precision and care, particularly from the captains of major capital ships.

Nevertheless, for *Scharnhorst*, *Gneisenau* and *Prinz Eugen*, a journey to Germany through Atlantic waters was potentially far more dangerous, owing to the real possibility of encountering the British Home Fleet in strength on the open seas. Using a combination of air cover, successful jamming of British coastal radar, plus inefficiencies in the Royal Navy's tactical arrangements, the 'Channel Dash' was a well-conceived and well-executed operation.

Break for home

Requests to redeploy the German warships from Brest back to Germany had been made by *Kriegsmarine* coastal commanders in France as early as May 1941, and by the beginning of 1942 Hitler had bought into the idea, also motivated by his belief that a British invasion of Norway was looming, and more firepower was required in the far north. The chosen escape route was through the Channel itself, selected for being safer than Atlantic routes and because 50 per cent cuts in *Kriegsmarine* fuel quotas in December 1941 were beginning to bite. Nevertheless, British intelligence was aware of an impending Channel dash, and had prepared a powerful combined naval and aviation force to interdict the German vessels. (The Admiralty had no idea as to the actual launch date of the operation, just surmises about the ideal meteorological conditions for such an action.)

Moving off

Operation *Cerberus* began at 2245 on 11 February 1942, commanded by *Vizeadmiral* Otto Ciliax from the *Scharnhorst*. The German squadron was huge – in addition to the *Gneisenau*, *Scharnhorst* and *Prinz Eugen* there were six destroyers, 14 torpedo boats and 26 S-boats, plus air cover from more than 250 aircraft, courtesy of the *Luftwaffe*.

Incredibly, the squadron made some 480km (300 miles) of progress without detection. Many of the British response vessels had been stood down, and poor surveillance combined with night cover meant that the Germans were able to penetrate the Strait of Dover before they were engaged, unsuccessfully, by Dover's coastal batteries.

Making passage

Now the British response began to intensify. An attack by Swordfish torpedo aircraft at 1245 was beaten off with fighter cover and anti-aircraft fire; 42 aircraft were lost but only one patrol boat was sunk and two torpedo boats were damaged. More seriously, though, *Scharnhorst* hit a mine at 1432 and spent the next 20 minutes under repair, before pushing north once more.

By late afternoon, the German squadron was off the Dutch coast, progress that even an attack by over 200 Allied bombers had not been able to prevent (most of the bombers were unable to find their targets). At around 1545 came the British naval response – an attack by five British destroyers. The five ships closed in to attack and launched successive patterns of torpedoes in the face of massive defensive gunfire. None of the torpedoes struck home, and at 1550 the destroyer *Worcester* was smashed by two shell strikes, which left her helpless in the water. She subsequently took nine major hits, including two from 280mm (11in) guns. The British ship *Campbell* had also been hit, less seriously, on the bows. The British were saved from further punishment by poor weather and by Ciliax's need to keep pressing north.

The German Channel Dash had succeeded, and although *Scharnhorst* and *Gneisenau* both hit mines before reaching port, the ships made it safely home to Wilhelmshaven and Kiel. A combination of audacity, firepower and, admittedly, a poor British response had won the day for the *Kriegsmarine*.

Air power and auxiliaries: 1942

The Channel Dash was the high point of German transit operations through the English Channel, but was actually only one of many such voyages made by *Kriegsmarine* vessels through the Strait of Dover between 1941 and 1943.

Historically, the Channel Dash represents an ambiguous moment in *Kriegsmarine* strategy during World War II. From the German point of view, the redeployment of the capital ships to the north was a tactical success, but it also acknowledged the limitations of major surface vessels to air attack.

Air power

The proof of air power against maritime targets came over the weeks immediately following the Channel Dash. *Gneisenau* went to Kiel to undergo repairs, and on the night of 26 February the port came under major Allied air attack. One of the bombs dropped hit the battleship square on forecastle, penetrated through the deck and exploded in the ammunition magazine of one of the main gun turrets. A huge secondary detonation occurred, ripping the turret from its moorings and killing 100 of the ship's crew. Although not readily apparent at the time, this was effectively the end of the *Gneisenau*. She sailed to Gotenhafen for repairs and upgrading, the principal modification being changes in her main armament to the twin-turret 380mm (15in) arrangement seen on the *Bismarck* and *Tirpitz*. This work was still incomplete in July 1942 when Hitler ordered it stopped, and the battleship became a static dock facility for the remainder of the war, until she was sunk at Gotenhafen on 27 March 1945 as a blockship. Also during the first half of 1942, the *Tirpitz* endured several major air attacks at its anchorage in Norway, which increased the question marks over the value of these large and expensive vessels. As if to add insult to injury, on 23 February the heavy cruiser *Prinz Eugen* was torpedoed by a British submarine off Norway, losing its stern in the attack.

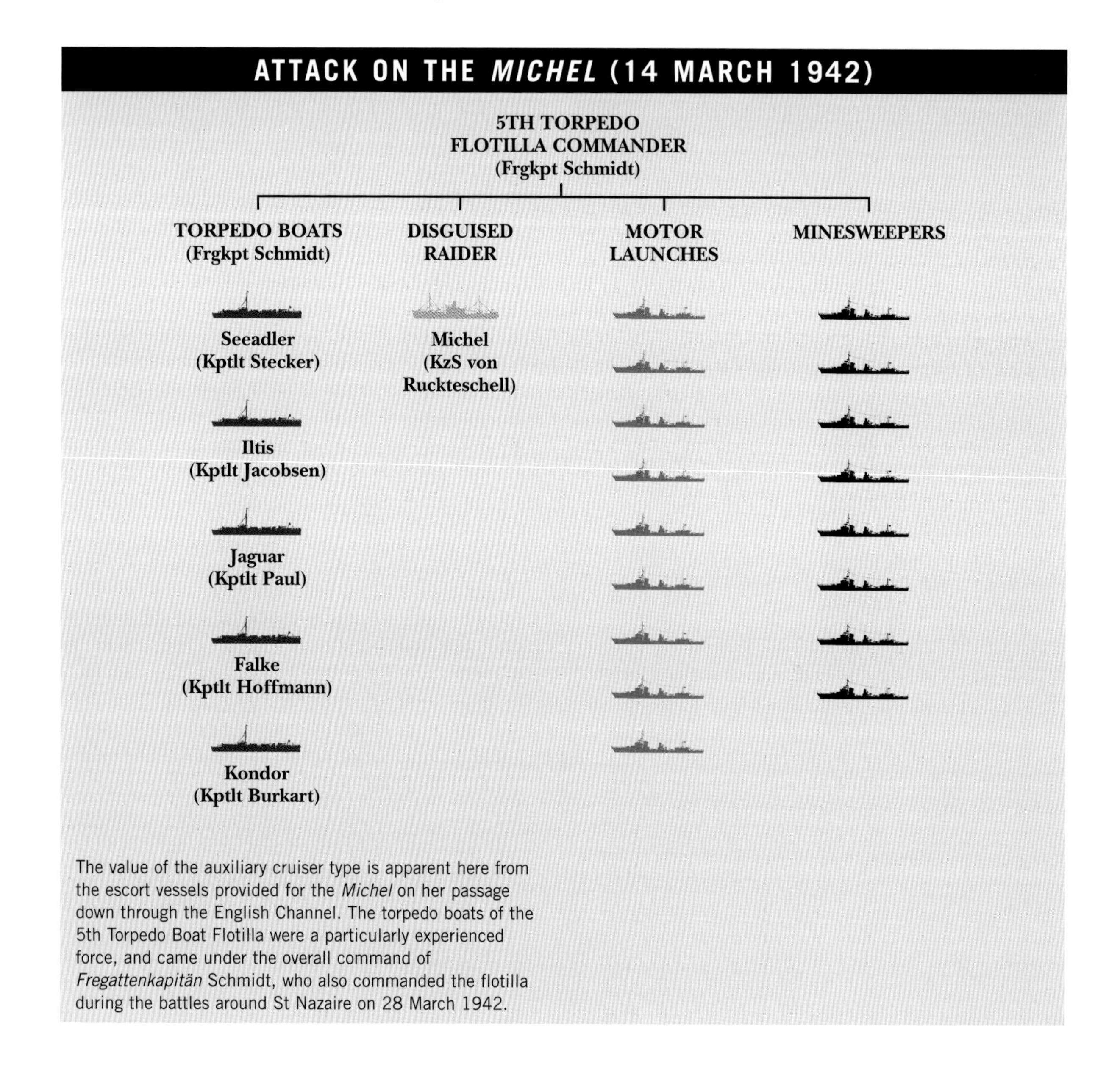

The value of the auxiliary cruiser type is apparent here from the escort vessels provided for the *Michel* on her passage down through the English Channel. The torpedo boats of the 5th Torpedo Boat Flotilla were a particularly experienced force, and came under the overall command of *Fregattenkapitän* Schmidt, who also commanded the flotilla during the battles around St Nazaire on 28 March 1942.

ATTACK ON THE *MICHEL* (14 MARCH 1942)					
Name	**Displacement**	**Speed**	**Guns**	**Torpedoes**	**Damage**
TORPEDO BOATS					
Seeadler	1310 tonnes (1290 tons)	59km/h (33kn)	3x105mm (4.1in)	6x533mm (21in)	–
Iltis	1341 tonnes (1320 tons)	61km/h (34kn)	3x105mm (4.1in)	6x533mm (21in)	–
Jaguar	1341 tonnes (1320 tons)	61km/h (34kn)	3x105mm (4.1in)	6x533mm (21in)	–
Falke	1310 tonnes (1290 tons)	59km/h (33kn)	3x105mm (4.1in)	6x533mm (21in)	–
Kondor	1310 tonnes (1290 tons)	59km/h (33kn)	3x105mm (4.1in)	6x533mm (21in)	–
DISGUISED RAIDER					
Michel	11,075 tonnes (10,900 tons)	29km/h (16kn)	1x105mm (4.1in)	6x533mm (21in) 6x150mm (6in)	Light

Maintaining movement

In essence, the northern ports would become the eventual graveyards of German battleships, as much as their operating bases. For the Allies, nevertheless, the presence of big-gun warships in the far north was a considerable cause for concern. Meanwhile, the *Kriegsmarine* was still making occasional runs up through the English Channel. One of the major sources of traffic were the *Hilfskreuzer* (auxiliary cruisers). These were essentially converted merchant ships, fitted out with guns and torpedoes to perform commerce raiding operations (main armament was six 150mm/6in guns). They retained the camouflage of merchant vessels, however, and to even trained observers might appear as nothing more than a passing trawler or supply ship. During the war, there were nine principal auxiliary cruisers in service: *Orion, Atlantis, Widder, Thor, Pinguin, Stier, Komet, Kormoran* and *Michel.* These vessels put in highly successful war service between them, sinking over 700,000 tonnes (688,944 UK tons) of shipping.

The *Michel*

Auxiliary cruisers operated largely undetected for much of 1941, but on 14 March 1942 their luck changed during one particular operation. The *Michel* had been commissioned on 7 September 1941, but her first operation did not come until the following March, when she sailed from Vlissingen in the Netherlands down through the English Channel. For her maiden voyage, she was heavily escorted by the five vessels of the 5th Torpedo Boat Flotilla plus eight minesweepers and nine *Räumbooten* (motor launches; R-boats) to clear her passage. As the squadron moved down through the Channel in the early hours of the morning, it was detected and the Royal Navy began to make Motor Torpedo Boat (MTB) and Motor Gun Boat (MGB) attacks from 0400 on. Two motor boat assaults were fought off by the German crews, but at around 0730 the British committed a heavier force, consisting of the destroyers *Walpole* and *Windsor* and the destroyer escorts *Blencathra, Calpe* and *Fernie.*

A thunderous gun and torpedo battle resulted, in which the *Michel* was obliged to drop all pretences to being a merchant ship and opened up with her main guns. *Michel* was peppered with splinters and anti-aircraft shells. Incredibly, in return the German vessels hit every British ship except the *Calpe.* The *Windsor* suffered major damage from a shell strike; the other vessels had mostly minor damage, but still enough to put them into dock for repairs.

Losing the auxiliaries

The *Michel* and her escort made Le Havre successfully, but the Germans' luck seemed to run out over subsequent weeks. On 27 September 1942, a similar run by the *Stier* resulted in the sinking of two of her escorts following a British MTB attack, and one of the cruisers would fall a month later. The *Komet* attempted a similar passage to that the *Michel*, but with an escort of only three torpedo boats and six R-boats, four of which were lost to mines off Dunkirk. Worse was to come. Having left Le Havre, the ships were spotted by British vessels off Cap de la Hague, and attacked by nine destroyer escorts and one MTB. Four R-boats were damaged and the *Komet* was sunk following shell and torpedo hits. It was a striking loss. All of a sudden, the passage down through the Channel looked increasingly obstructed to the German Navy, and with improved coastal defence there began the steady shift of Britain's position from weakness to dominance over its home waters.

ATTACK ON THE *KOMET* (14 OCTOBER 1942)					
Name	Displacement	Speed	Guns	Torpedoes	Damage
DISGUISED RAIDER					
Komet	7620 tonnes (7500 tons)	26.6km/h (14.8kn)	6x150mm (6in)	6x533mm (21in)	Sunk
TORPEDO BOAT					
T4	1105 tonnes (1088 tons)	63km/h (35kn)	1x105mm (4.1in)	6x533mm (21in)	Light
T10	1099 tonnes (1082 tons)	63km/h (35kn)	1x105mm (4.1in)	6x533mm (21in)	Significant
T14	1116 tonnes (1098 tons)	63km/h (35kn)	1x105mm (4.1in)	6x533mm (21in)	Light
T19	1116 tonnes (1098 tons)	63km/h (35kn)	1x105mm (4.1in)	6x533mm (21in)	Light

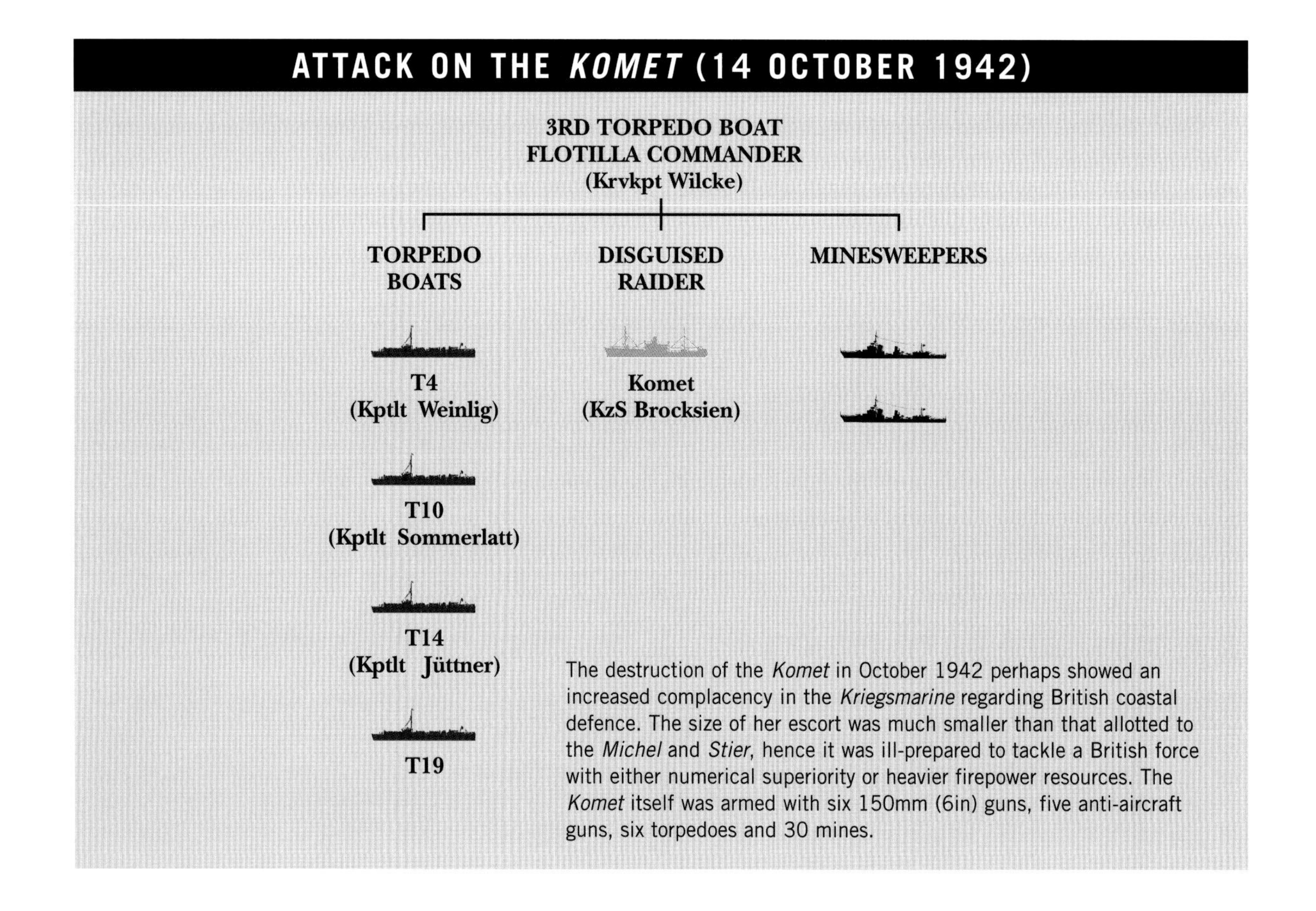

The destruction of the *Komet* in October 1942 perhaps showed an increased complacency in the *Kriegsmarine* regarding British coastal defence. The size of her escort was much smaller than that allotted to the *Michel* and *Stier*, hence it was ill-prepared to tackle a British force with either numerical superiority or heavier firepower resources. The *Komet* itself was armed with six 150mm (6in) guns, five anti-aircraft guns, six torpedoes and 30 mines.

Strategic changes: 1942–43

During 1942, Hitler began implementing major changes in the status and operational structure of the *Kriegsmarine*, mainly focused on the status of the *Kriegsmarine*'s battleships and cruiser types.

During 1942, there was an increased aggression on the part of the Allies in their maritime policy. The submarine war was intense, but this did not mean that the Allies stopped paying attention to the German surface fleet. Britain still feared that the battleships, particularly *Tirpitz*, would recommence raiding activities in the North Atlantic and other waters. This fear was the motivation behind the audacious combined British and Canadian raid against the massive dry dock at St Nazaire on 27/28 March 1942. The British theory was that if the *Tirpitz* was launched on combat operations, only the huge dock facilities at St Nazaire were capable of providing the vessel with a safe French port. The raid was aimed at preventing this and involved an amphibious attack by commandos on the port facilities, plus the destruction of the dry dock by detonating an explosive-filled destroyer, HMS *Campbeltown*, against the dock gates. Despite a terrible cost in Allied lives, the St Nazaire raid was actually a success – the dock would essentially remain out of commission until 1947. The major implication of the action for the *Kriegsmarine* was that capital ships such as the *Tirpitz* would have to make a long return journey to home waters after a raid, rather than being able to dock in western France.

LEBERECHT MAAS	
Name	*Leberecht Maas* (Type 34 class)
Commissioned	14 January 1937
Crew	315
Displacement	3210 tonnes (3160 tons)
Dimensions	Length: 119m (390ft); Beam: 11.3m (37ft)
Range	8150km (5064 miles) at 35 knots
Armament	5 x 127mm (5in); 2 x twin 37mm (1.5in) AA; 6 x 20mm (0.79in) AA; 2 x quadruple torpedo mounts; 60 mines
Powerplant	2 x steam turbines, 52,199kW (70,000hp)
Performance	70km/h (38kts)

Watershed

As we shall see in later chapters, the main focus of the surface war in 1942 was concentrated in the far north, as the *Kriegsmarine* attempted to intercept and destroy the Allied arctic convoys sailing across to northern Russia. The position of the large surface ships in these actions was an awkward one. Hitler, aware of how easy it was to lose a battleship after the *Bismarck* disaster of 1941, constantly cautioned that 'no unnecessary risks should be taken with the big-gun warships'. Yet the warships

were themselves nothing more than floating iron if they were not actually deployed in combat, so they made several forays out into arctic waters to intercept the convoys. Some missions were wildy successful, such as the massacre of convoy PQ17 in June–July 1942, in which 25 out of 36 Allied ships were sunk by either maritime action or *Luftwaffe* air attack.

Yet other operations were far less satisfactory, particularly for the major surface warships, and gradually Hitler's patience was running out. Matters came to a head during the Battle of the Barents Sea on 31 December 1942. During this inconclusive encounter, the two heavy cruisers *Admiral Hipper* and *Lützow*, backed by six destoyers, were unable to stop a convoy of 14 merchant ships plus escorts delivering a huge slab of supplies to the USSR.

The fact that both cruisers were severely damaged by fire from British destroyers, and were forced to retire through fear of torpedo attack, incensed a *Führer* already wearied by the collapse of his fortunes at Stalingrad and in North Africa. Hitler had had enough of his major warships, which to his mind seemed to tiptoe around the war zones of the world causing little damage and expending large volumes of fuel and other other supplies. It was time to trim the *Kreigmarine*'s sails.

Naval cull

Once Hitler had received the full report of the day's battle in the Barents Sea, he rounded furiously on Raeder and the wider German Navy. Accusing the service of everything from cowardice to timidity, he finally passed sentence – he ordered that every German warship larger than a destroyer in size was to be decommissioned and scrapped.

Although the severity of Hitler's order was ameliorated a little over the coming weeks, it was in essence the end of the *Kriegsmarine*'s war with large surface warships. The naval historian Vincent O'Hara has put the decision in its full perspective:

'While this order was never carried out as originally delivered, it nonetheless gutted the surface fleet as a fighting force. Before Barents Sea, the German Navy fought twenty-nine surface actions and a third involved cruisers or larger ships. After Barents Sea, the navy fought thirty-seven actions and only one involved a

Marinegruppenkommando Nord (Naval Group Command North) was formed from the earlier *Marinegruppenkommando Ost* (East) in October 1940, part of a general restructuring following the German military successes in western Europe. Its operational areas covered the Baltic Sea and German Bight plus the coastal waters surrounding Denmark and Norway. The command existed for four years until it was finally dissolved at the end of July 1944.

heavy unit.' (Vincent O'Hara, *The German Fleet at War, 1939–1945*)

The large warships after the Battle of the Barents Sea were consigned to humiliating operations either as floating anti-aircraft batteries or, in the case of ships such as the *Tirpitz*, a brief foray in shore bombardment roles. Others were utilized as training vessels, hospital or passenger ships, or even sunk as blockships across harbour entrances.

Hitler's cull of the surface fleet also had some major personnel repercusions. Greatest of them all was the resignation of Raeder as head of the *Kriegsmarine*. As with so many commanders within the Third *Reich*, Raeder had suffered from the poison chalice of an inexorably strengthening Allied power, combined with operational interference from Hitler as commander-in-chief of all Germany's armed forces.

Raeder's reputation was also plagued by the success of Dönitz in handling the U-boat arm. Hitler was fond of what he perceived as radical technologies, and U-boats increasingly seemed more persuasive instruments of war than the floating bomb targets that were battleships and cruisers. On 30 January 1943, Dönitz received his appointment as commander-in-chief of the German Navy, and a new era of naval operations began.

NAVAL GROUP COMMAND WEST (FEBRUARY 1943)

NAVAL GROUP COMMAND WEST
(Gen-Adm Marschall)

- **Naval Area Command Channel Coast (Adm von Fischel)**
- **Admiral Atlantic Coast (Adm Bachmann)**
- **Admiral South Coast (Kon-Adm Zuckschwerdt)**
- **Naval Command Italy (Viz-Adm Weichold)**

Formed in August 1939, *Marinegruppenkommando West* originally had operational responsibility for the German Bight, the North Sea and the Atlantic, although in 1940 its northern commitments passed to the newly created *Marinegruppenkommando Nord*. As with its northern counterpart, the naval command in the west was dissolved in 1944 following the D-Day invasion, becoming the *Marineoberkommando West*, essentially in charge of remaining coastal positions and related personnel.

NAVAL GROUP COMMAND SOUTH (SEPTEMBER 1943)

NAVAL GROUP COMMAND SOUTH
(Adm Schuster)

- **Commanding Admiral Adriatic (Viz-Adm Lietzmann)**
- **Commanding Admiral Aegean (Viz-Adm Lange)**
- **Commanding Admiral Black Sea (Viz-AdmKieseritzky)**

Marinegruppenkommando Süd was established in November 1941 with the increase in German naval responsibilities in the Mediterranean, Aegean and Black Sea areas (reflected in the sub-commands). Technically this command was subordinated to Italian control for the first years of the war, but this changed with the Italian surrender to the Allies in 1943. The command was dissolved in December 1944.

Command change: 1943

The ascent of Karl Dönitz to the positions of *Oberbefehlshaber der Kriegsmarine* (Commander-in-Chief German Navy) and *Großadmiral* (Grand Admiral) of the *Oberkommando der Marine* (Naval High Command) transformed the command relations of the *Kriegsmarine*, but it could not alter the swelling superiority of Allied naval power across almost all theatres.

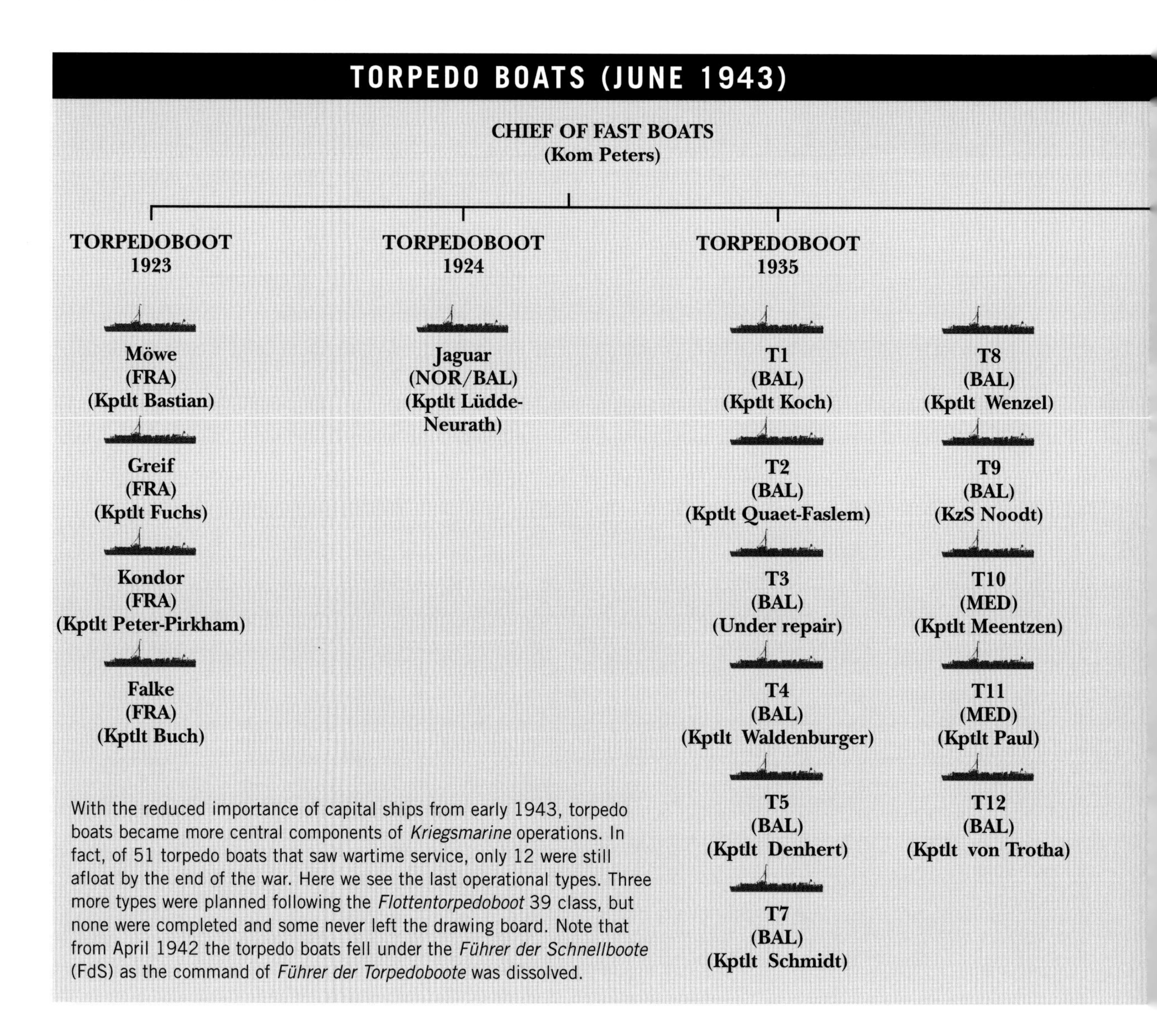

With the reduced importance of capital ships from early 1943, torpedo boats became more central components of *Kriegsmarine* operations. In fact, of 51 torpedo boats that saw wartime service, only 12 were still afloat by the end of the war. Here we see the last operational types. Three more types were planned following the *Flottentorpedoboot* 39 class, but none were completed and some never left the drawing board. Note that from April 1942 the torpedo boats fell under the *Führer der Schnellboote* (FdS) as the command of *Führer der Torpedoboote* was dissolved.

Dönitz was a remarkable, steady and intelligent naval officer. Through a combination of strong personality and a good grasp of character politics, he was able to walk the tightrope between defending the interests of his service, and placating Hitler's strategic imperatives. He was not entirely subservient to Hitler; he incurred the *Führer*'s wrath on more than one occasion. Yet his plain-spoken attitude, allied to his awareness of Hitler's cyclical mood swings, at least enabled him to avoid the persecution that dogged many land forces commanders in the latter years of the war.

Saving the navy

Dönitz had made his name as a U-boat man, but he was a representative of the broader navy, and worked to avoid implementing Hitler's order that the major surface warships be scrapped. Through a sequence of modifications, he managed to secure the survival of the

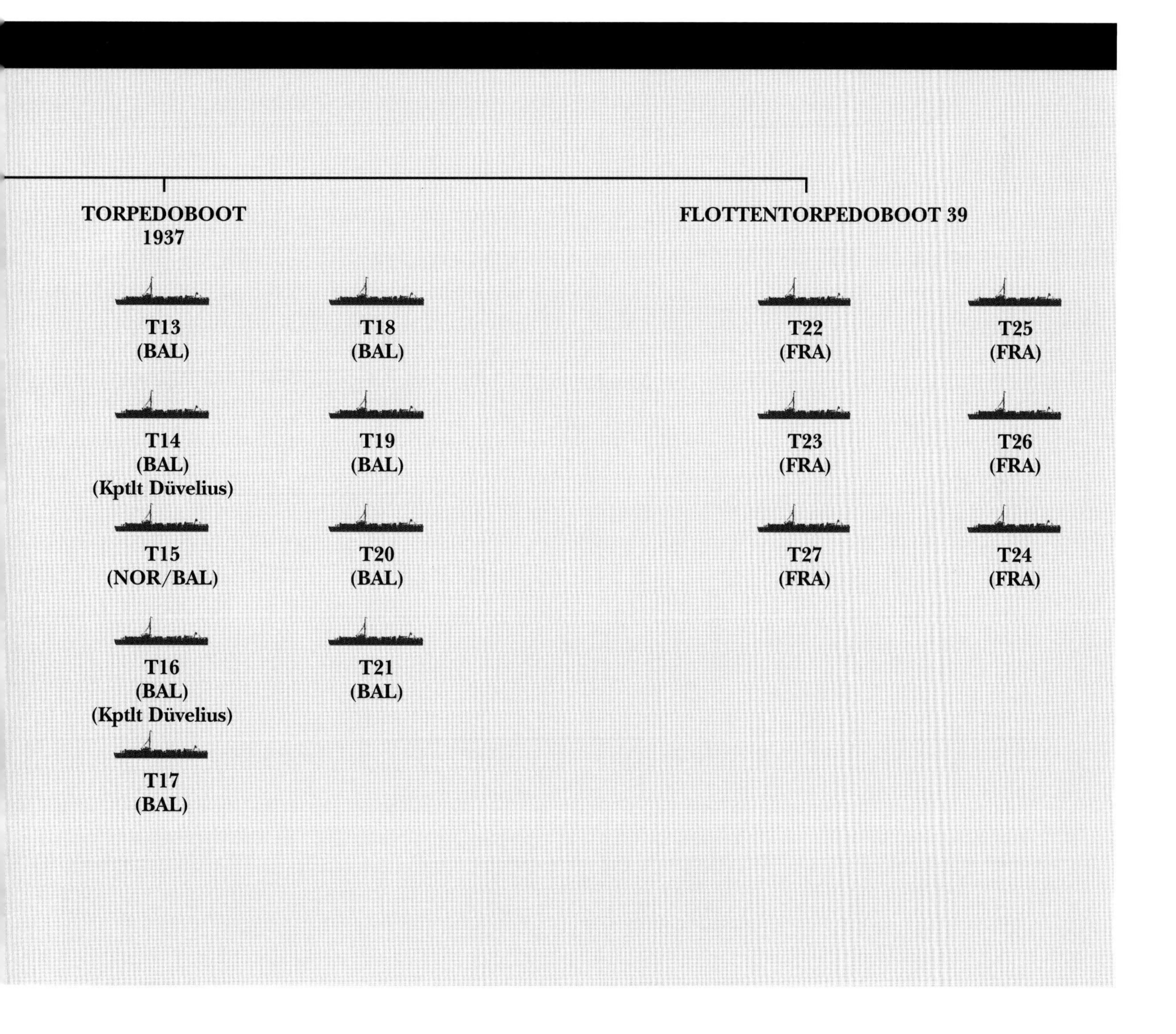

great warships as a 'fleet in being' – that is, a fleet that is essentially non-operational, but which has a strategic value purely in the fact of its existence as a deterrent or as a force of distraction for enemy resources. That the Allied air forces kept hunting the German warships at their anchorages was proof that the concept had value. Moreover, Dönitz pushed Hitler to allow operational use of the large warships should appropriate conditions arise. Specifically, Dönitz argued that the *Lützow, Prinz Eugen* and a clutch of light cruisers be retained in a training capacity, with the option of returning them to battle stations when needed. The *Tirpitz* and *Scharnhorst* would be kept up in Norwegian waters to act as a draw on Allied attention and resources, with the option of utilizing them for attacks on passing Arctic convoys when the opportunity presented itself.

The relegation of the battleships and cruisers to relatively unimportant duties was in many ways a reflection of the wider war for Germany. By early 1943, the Sixth Army had been lost at Stalingrad, the German forces in North Africa were in the process of being squeezed out of Tunisia, and the air war in all theatres was steadily turning against the *Luftwaffe*. Hitler's Third *Reich* was completely outclassed in the production war by the Soviet Union and the industrial monster of the United States. If cuts were to be made, the surface navy was an obvious candidate.

Continuing struggle

Although the age of great battles between capital ships was essentially over in the West, this did not mean that surface naval conflict ended. Around the English Channel and French coastal waters the struggle continued, fought by the multiplicity of smaller German craft, ranging from destroyers down to motor launches. For the *Kriegsmarine*, the combat revolved around two main priorities. First, to retain as much control over the Channel sea lanes and French coastal waters as possible.

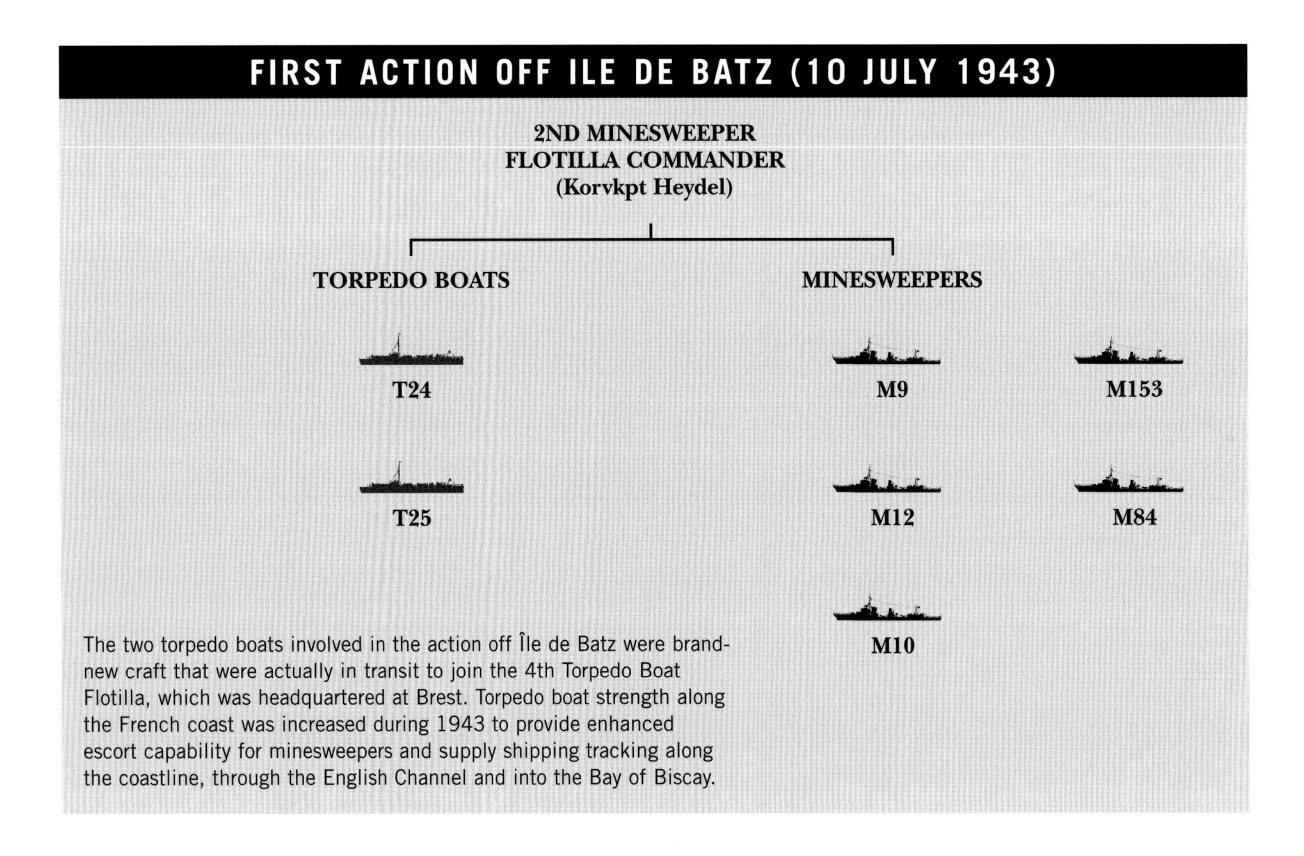

The two torpedo boats involved in the action off Île de Batz were brand-new craft that were actually in transit to join the 4th Torpedo Boat Flotilla, which was headquartered at Brest. Torpedo boat strength along the French coast was increased during 1943 to provide enhanced escort capability for minesweepers and supply shipping tracking along the coastline, through the English Channel and into the Bay of Biscay.

FIRST ACTION OFF ILE DE BATZ (10 JULY 1943)					
Name	Displacement	Speed	Guns	Torpedoes	Damage
TORPEDO BOAT					
T24	1782 tonnes (1754 tons)	59/km/h (33kn)	4x105mm (4.1in)	6x533mm (21in)	–
T25	1782 tonnes (1754 tons)	59/km/h (33kn)	4x105mm (4.1in)	6x533mm (21in)	Light
MINESWEEPER					
M9	888 tonnes (874 tons)	32km/h (18kn)	2x105mm (4.1in)	–	–
M12	888 tonnes (874 tons)	32km/h (18kn)	2x105mm (4.1in)	–	Moderate
M10	888 tonnes (874 tons)	32km/h (18kn)	2x105mm (4.1in)	–	–
M153	892 tonnes (878 tons)	32km/h (18kn)	2x105mm (4.1in)	–	Sunk
M84	892 tonnes (878 tons)	32km/h (18kn)	2x105mm (4.1in)	–	–

This objective was important not only to allow the free passage of German convoys up and down the coast, but also to provide a central precaution against a future Allied invasion of France, which was expected to cut directly through the English Channel. The second priority was to control British attempts to interdict both U-boats and surface traffic moving to the French coast through the Bay of Biscay. These priorities, combined with an increasingly aggressive Allied naval policy, improved Allied intelligence-gathering on maritime traffic and heavier use of air power in a anti-shipping role, actually made 1943 a lively year in terms of surface combat, although the actions concerned involved none of the headline-grabbing big ships.

Coastal actions

An example of a typical coastal action is provided by the night of 28 April 1943, when two Italian freighters attempted to move between Le Havre and Nantes, with an escort consisting of two *Unterseebootsjäger* (submarine hunter) and a single *Vorpostenboot* (patrol boat). Unfortunately for the German crews, British intelligence had reports of the convoy, and two destroyers, the *Goathland* and *Albrighton*, were dispatched to deal with it.

Shortly after midnight, the British ships found their mark in the Bay of Morlaix, and began a fast attack run-in with gunfire and torpedoes. One of the freighters, the *Butterfly*, was an immediate victim, being struck by torpedoes and catching fire quickly. The patrol boat was hit by shellfire, but then the *Kriegsmarine* crews managed to turn the tables somewhat. All available guns, however light, were brought to bear on the British ships. *Goathland* steered away with splinter damage, but *Albrighton* was badly shot up after her steering was temporarily put out of action and three German minesweepers also joined the action. The British destroyer finally regained her steering and escaped, leaving behind one submarine hunter that eventually sank from damage sustained during the fight, and a freighter effectively destroyed.

Such actions came thick and fast. On 10 July, for example, a force of five minesweepers (*M9*, *M12*, *M10*, *M153* and *M84*) was being escorted down the Breton coast by two torpedo boats – *T24* and *T25*. Off Ile de Batz, the convoy was surprised by three British destroyers (*Melbreak*, *Wensleydale* and *Glaisdale*), and a raging 90-minute gunbattle was the result. As so often happened during such engagements, the British superiority in absolute firepower was offset by fanatical but professional resistance by the German crews. Although the action left *T25* and *M12* damaged, and *M153* was sunk by a torpedo strike, all three of the British ships were also damaged.

Intensifying action

The battles described above were just two of many engagements that took place between January and October 1943. They proved that the surface war was far from over, and if anything the actions would increase in scale over the final months of the year.

Major actions: late 1943

The late months of 1943 brought some major surface engagements in Western waters between the *Kriegsmarine* and the Royal Navy, part of a general intensification of naval activity as the Allies steadily built up towards the D-Day landings the following year.

ERICH BEY (1898–1943)

Erich Bey began his naval career in June 1916 as a junior officer aboard destroyers, and he stayed in the *Reichsmarine* following World War I.

- Over the next 20 years, he rose up through the ranks, and in the Norway campaign of 1940 was commander of the 4th Destroyer Flotilla. Bey was involved in the disastrous battles of 10 April and 13 April around Narvik, but distinguished himself sufficiently to receive the Knight's Cross of the Iron Cross.

- Promoted to *Führer der Zerstörer* (Commander of Destroyers), Bey subsequently commanded the destroyer force during Operation *Cerberus*, the 'Channel Dash' of February 1942.

- Bey was promoted *Konteradmiral* in March 1943, and was killed aboard *Scharnhorst*, his flagship, on 26 December 1943 in the Battle of North Cape.

The naval actions in the English Channel and Bay of Biscay during late 1943 involved significant numbers of vessels, partly due to Britain's frustration at not being able to exert control over its sea lanes. In October 1943, the Royal Navy's Plymouth Command implemented Operation *Tunnel*, a programme of continuous offensive patrols designed to enforce a more thorough blockade of German traffic. It was not especially effective. On 4 October, off Les Triagoz, for example, four German torpedo boats damaged four British destroyers for no losses or damage. On 23 October, a force of five German torpedo boats had even greater success, sinking the cruiser *Charybdis*, with a main armament of only 114mm (4.5in) guns, and the destroyer escort *Limbourne*. The *Kriegsmarine* had not only developed an effective system of counter-tactics to *Tunnel*, but their better standards of training were paying off in the firefights.

Reversed fortunes

After a string of victories, the *Kriegsmarine* in the West suffered a major counterblow at the end of 1943. On 28 December, five German destroyers and six torpedo boats were attacked in the Bay of Biscay by two British cruisers, the *Glasgow* and *Enterprise*. The commander of the German squadron, *Kapitän zur See* Hans Erdmenger, issued confused instructions that resulted in his vessels dividing rather than concentrating their power. Therefore they became more vulnerable to the British cruisers' superior firepower, and in rough seas the German long-range torpedo attacks were ineffective. The final outcome of the engagement was one destroyer and two torpedo boats sunk, with no significant damage inflicted upon the British ships. Bearing in mind that this was also the month in which the *Scharnhorst* was sunk in the far north, it seemed that the *Kriegsmarine* surface fleet was again slipping in its authority and in its ability to control theatre waters.

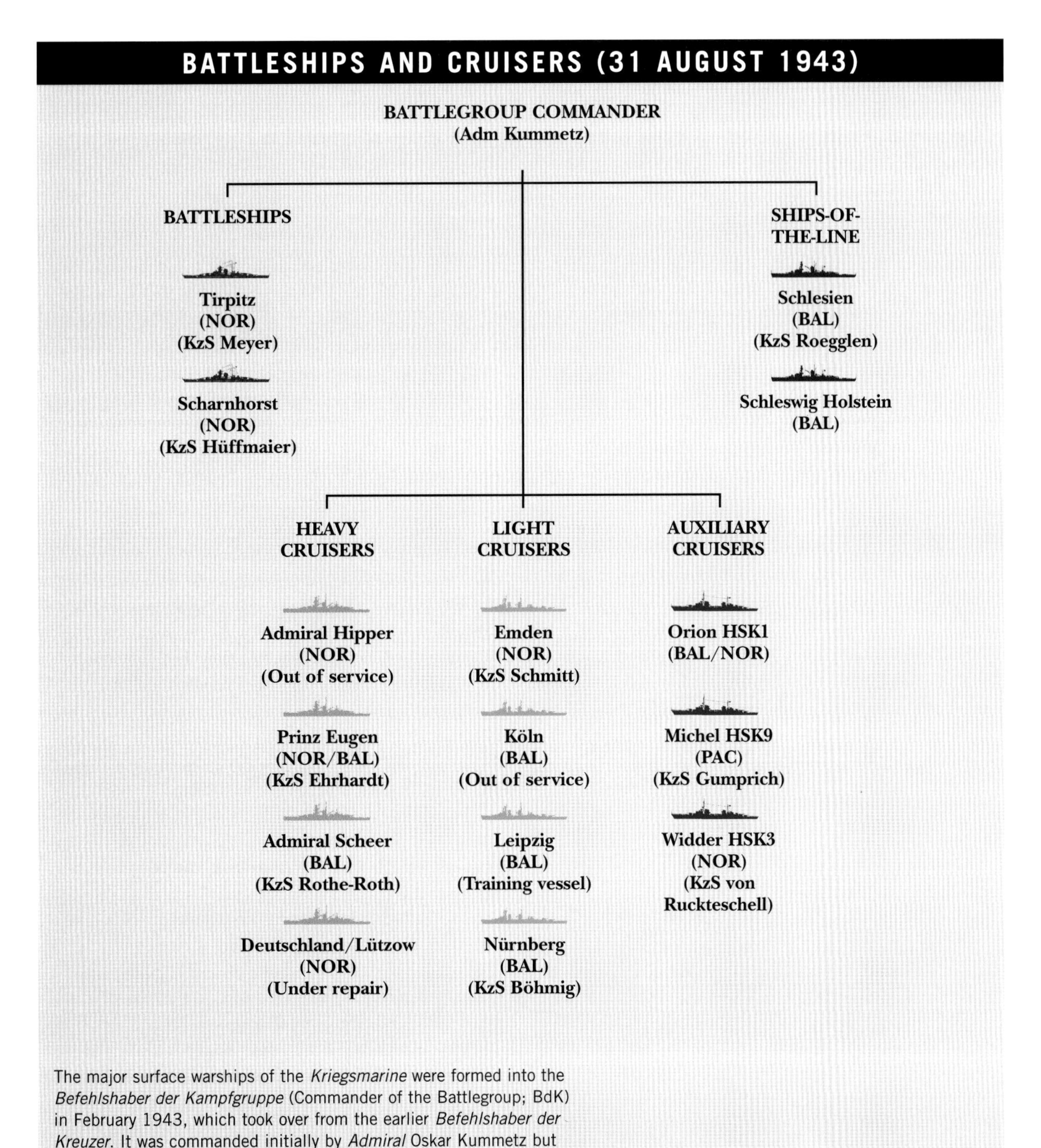

The major surface warships of the *Kriegsmarine* were formed into the *Befehlshaber der Kampfgruppe* (Commander of the Battlegroup; BdK) in February 1943, which took over from the earlier *Befehlshaber der Kreuzer*. It was commanded initially by *Admiral* Oskar Kummetz but then went through a further six commanders between November 1943 and October 1944, when it was finally dissolved.

The U-Boat War: 1939–41

The U-boat arm was the true cutting edge of the *Kriegsmarine* during World War II. On several occasions, it came close to severing the Allies' transatlantic lifeline but was eventually defeated at a terrible cost in vessels and crews.

A U-boat crew eat a meal on the deck of their submarine, relaxing in the sunshine off the French coast.

The interwar U-boat arm struggled, as did every other aspect of the *Kriegsmarine*, under the dictates of the Versailles Treaty. As a first condition in the immediate aftermath of World War I, U-boats and their related production and maintenance facilities had to be handed over to the Allies, including stocks of torpedoes. The treaty then denied Germany the right to build, buy or own submarines, regardless of whether they were for military purposes or not. By the early 1920s, therefore, it seemed as if the German Navy was destined for a future without combat submarines.

Regeneration

As it turned out, Germany was able to maintain its submarine development through an act of international sleight of hand. Between 1922 and 1935, Germany operated a bureau of U-boat designers, working from within a Dutch company in The Hague. Inside Germany itself, an *U-Abwehrschule* ('Anti-Submarine School') in Kiel was essentially a light cover for U-boat training and development, and from October 1933 this enabled the *Kriegsmarine* to disseminate tactical theory through its nascent U-boat crews.

By this point, it would have been apparent to all but the most naive foreign powers that Germany was resurgent, and in 1935 Hitler renounced the Versailles Treaty and put his country on the road to full rearmament. For the U-boat force, the Anglo-German Naval Agreement of 1935 (see chapter 'The Pre-War *Kriegsmarine*') was a watershed. It practically, if not verbally, gave Germany the power to construct a powerful military U-boat fleet. The problem for Hitler was that of manning the U-boats. The 'Anti-Submarine School' had produced a small body of trained submariners, but a commander was needed to rationalize recruitment, training and tactics. Such a person was found in Karl Dönitz, former commanding officer of the cruiser *Emden*. Dönitz was placed in charge of the first U-boat flotilla, *U-Flottille Weddigen*, in 1935, and quickly showed a passion and a talent for this still-emergent form of warfare. In January the following year, Dönitz was made *Führer der Unterseeboote* (FdU), and following the outbreak of war in 1939 his position was raised to *Befehlshaber der Unterseeboote* (BdU).

Transformation

With its new commander, the U-boat arm began to shape itself into a service capable of and ready for war. It would do so, however, against tough production limits and retrograde strategic thinking.

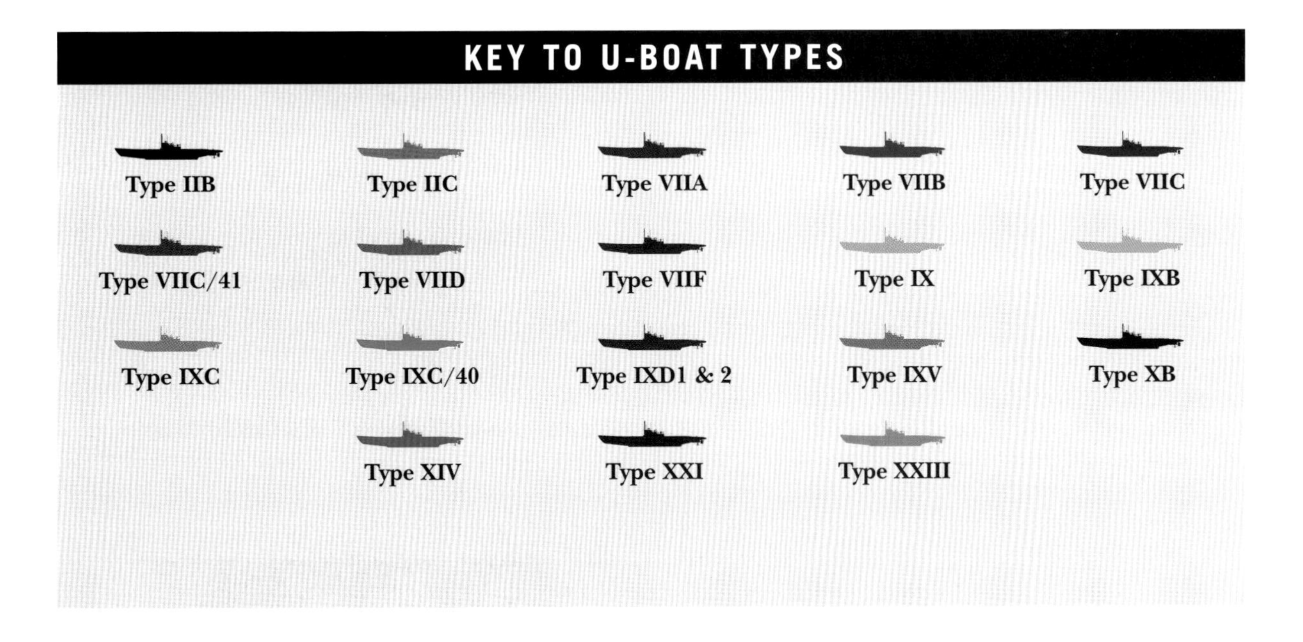

Ready for war: 1939

As we have seen, the *Kriegsmarine* entered World War II with limited numbers of U-boats available for combat operations. Dönitz's first challenges, therefore, were to raise U-boat production and make effective deployments with the resources at hand.

At the outbreak of war in September 1939, there were six combat *Unterseebootsflottillen* (U-boat flotillas) in operation, numbers 1–3 and 5–7. (Note that the U-boat flotillas which previously had names, e.g. *U-Flottille Weddigen*, were given regular formation numbers from 1939, hence *Weddigen* became 1.*Unterseebootsflottille*.) In terms of vessel, there were three main types available. The Type II submarines were short-range coastal types, and although they formed the largest percentage of the U-boat fleet at the beginning of the war, they were of least relevance to the forthcoming conflict. Far more useful were the limited numbers of Type VII and

1ST FLOTILLA (1 MAY 1940)

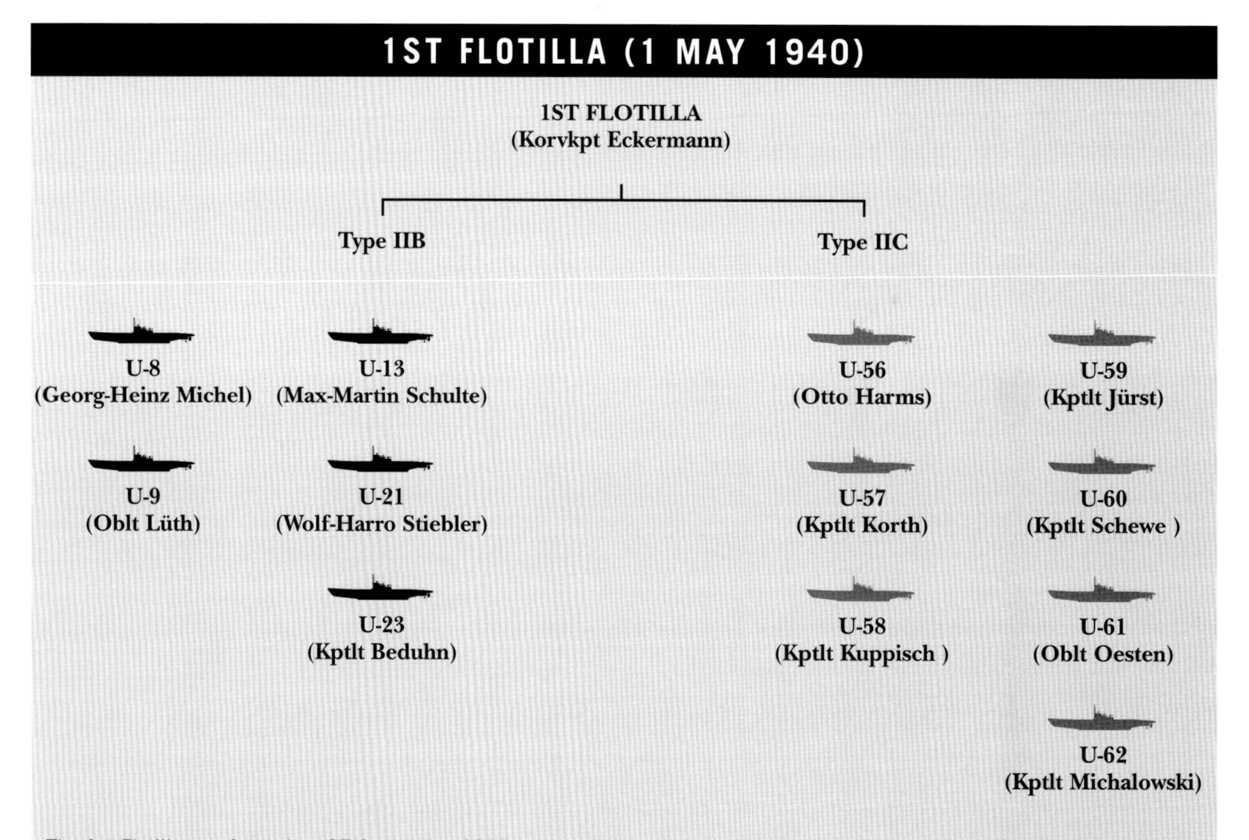

The 1st Flotilla was formed on 27 September 1935 and was originally called *U-Flottille Weddigen*, after Otto Weddigen, a successful World War I-era U-boat commander. For all of 1939 and the early months of 1940, it was equipped purely with Type II U-boats, but in early 1941 it began to receive Type VII submarines, giving it a viable Atlantic-operating capability.

Type IX vessels, both long-range boats with better performance characteristics and more powerful weapons fits. The Type VIIB, for example, had a surface range of 14,000km (8700 miles), a submerged speed of 15km/h (8 knots) and a weapons payload of 14 torpedos and a quick-firing 88mm (3.5in) deck gun with 220 rounds of ammunition. The Types IX and IXB had even greater range, speed and power, hence it was these types that were destined for Atlantic operations.

First deployments

Even before Germany invaded Poland in September 1939, the U-boats were beginning deployments in preparation for the forthcoming conflict. Ten Type II vessels stayed around the Baltic, waiting to counter any local naval responses to the action in Poland. Meanwhile, a total of 14 Type VII and Type IX U-boats headed out into the North Atlantic for potential operations against British supply ships, and over 20 more vessels were distributed from the North Sea down to the Bay of Biscay. In essence, the U-boats were putting a noose around Europe's neck.

***U-9* TIMETABLE**

Patrol Dates	Operational Area	Ships Sunk
25 Aug 1939 – 15 Sep 1939	Reconnaissance of English Coast	0
16 Jan 1940 – 22 Jan 1940	North Sea	2
5 Feb 1940 – 17 Feb 1940	North Sea	2
14 Mar 1940 – 20 Mar 1940	North Sea submarine hunting	0
4 Apr 1940 – 24 Apr 1940	Norwegian invasion	0
5 May 1940 – 30 May 1940	Low Countries	4

On 1 September 1939, Germany invaded Poland, and two days later Britain declared war on Germany. There quickly followed the first U-boat kill in the Atlantic. *U-30*, a Type VIIA submarine captained by *Kapitänleutnant* Fritz-Julius Lemp, torpedoed and sank the passenger liner *Athenia*, killing 112 people. The attack was a mistake – Lemp believed that the ship was an armed merchant cruiser – but the U-boat war had begun.

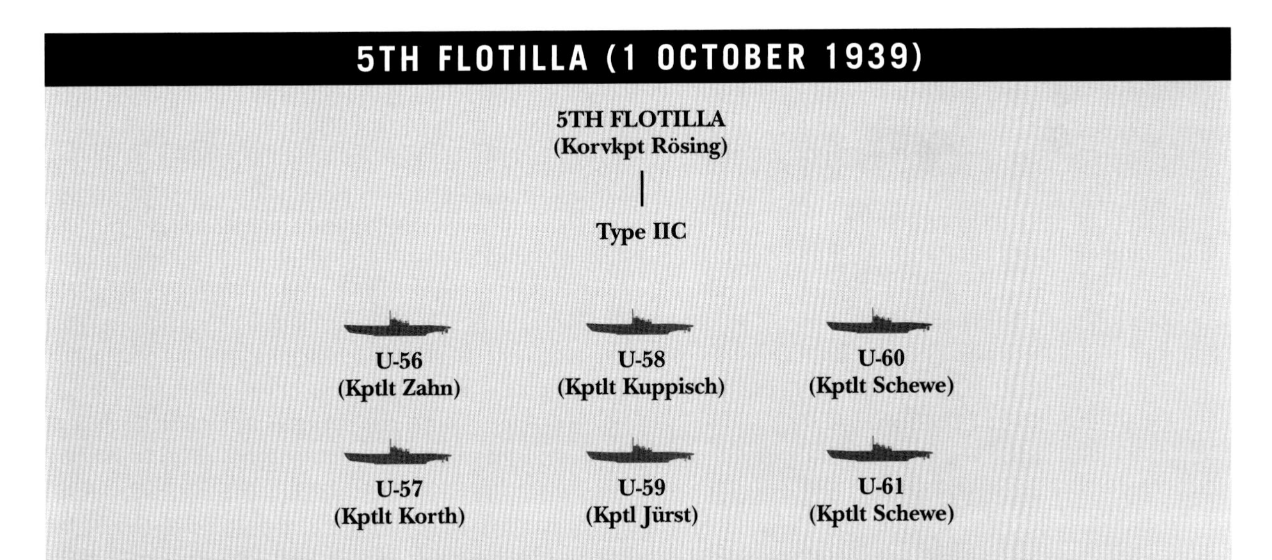

The *U-Flottille Emsmann*, so-called after World War I U-boat ace *Oberleutnant* Hans Joachim Emsmann, was founded on 1 December 1938, and was renamed the 5th Flotilla by the outbreak of World War II. It was a short-lived unit: it was disbanded in January 1940, after which its boats were transferred to the 1st Flotilla. Its commander, Hans-Rudolf Rösing, was one of the U-boat service's most experienced commanders at the beginning of the war.

Battle of the Atlantic: 1939–40

Within days of the opening of World War II, the U-boats in the Atlantic were beginning their first convoy attacks. Allied losses went from manageable to critical in the space of only 18 months.

The sinking of the *Athenia* caused outrage throughout the Western world, with headlines declaring that the sinking was against all the protocols of maritime warfare. Under the 1936 London Submarine Agreement, combat submarines were meant to stop and search merchant ships before sinking them, and indeed sink them only if they contained war supplies.

Although this nicety was soon lost in the horror of total war, Hitler initially gave a strict order that no passenger ships were to be sunk, only warships, convoys under armed escort or resisting vessels. The problem was that Britain quickly set about arming its merchant ships, or providing them with combat escorts, so obeying the protocols could easily get a submarine sunk. By 1940, they were effectively dropped, and any merchant vessel that bore an Allied flag became fair game. During the period September 1939 to March 1940, the U-boats primarily hunted alone, patrolling busy waters in the hope of spotting either convoy targets or military vessels. These operations brought some early and spectacular victories for Dönitz's men.

On 15/16 September, for example, the Type VIIA U-boat *U-31* was patrolling the Atlantic shipping lanes west of Liverpool, when it happened upon the outbound OB4 convoy, destined for New York. *U-31* attacked, and hit and sank the merchant ship *Aviemore* in the first U-boat convoy attack of the war.

First kills

Other U-boats acquired bigger prizes. On 17 September, *U-29* captained by *Kapitänleutnant* Otto Schuhart, torpedoed the British carrier *Courageous* in the Western Approaches. The great carrier sank, taking with it 515 sailors, and this sinking had the important effect of

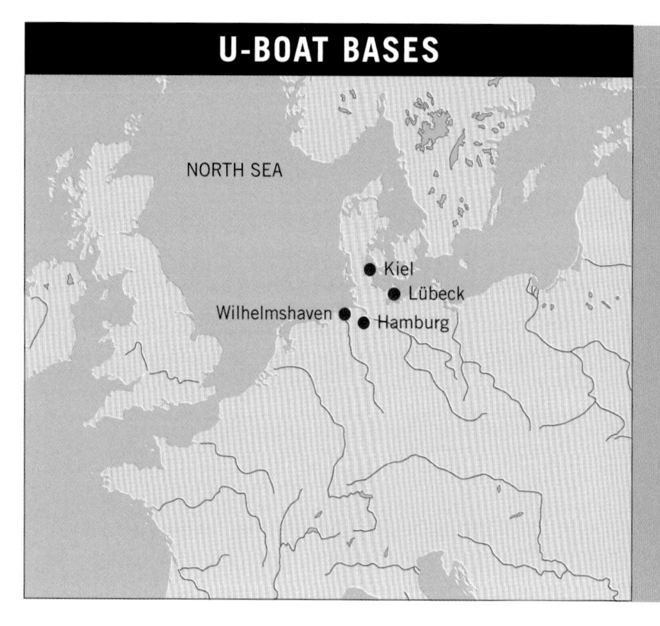

September 1939

At the beginning of World War II, the *Kriegsmarine*'s U-boat training facilities and operating bases were confined to the northern coastline of Germany. The primary centres were the Baltic port of Kiel, home to Dönitz's headquarters and five U-boat flotillas, and the North Sea naval base of Wilhelmshaven, headquarters for the 2nd Flotilla (established in September 1936). The U-boat school, which had previously worked out of Kiel, was moved to Neustadt near Lübeck, also on the Baltic. There were later further training bases at Hamburg and Wesermünde.

As the map makes clear, the problem with the geographical location of the bases in an operational sense was that they confined the U-boats within a limited pocket of water, and to break into the Atlantic involved a potentially perilous journey through the British-controlled North Sea or English Channel.

causing Britain to withdraw its major carriers from escort work in the Atlantic, opening the way for greater operational freedom for the U-boats.

The killing of the *Courageous* was an alarming blow to the British Admiralty, and the danger of the U-boats was bitterly reinforced just under a month later. On 13/14 October, under cover of darkness, *U-47*, commanded by the soon-to-be-legendary *Kapitänleutnant* Günther Prien, managed to work its way into the British Home Fleet harbour at Scapa Flow. There it put three torpedoes into the mighty battleship *Royal Oak*, which sank with the loss of 833 crew.

The successes against military ships were reinforced by continuing results against merchant shipping. In fact, from September 1939 to March 1940, the U-boats sent 222 merchant ships totalling 777,038 tonnes (764,766 tons) to the bottom of the sea. The numbers could have been higher, but for the early part of the war the *Kriegsmarine* was plagued with batches of defective torpedoes, which would often strike the target with a resounding clang, but fail to detonate.

The early U-boat operations were not conducted with impunity. The first U-boat combat loss came on 14 September 1939, when *U-39* was sunk by escort vessels after making an unsuccessful attack on the aircraft carrier *Ark Royal*. Further losses would come regularly over the following months, to mines, Allied aircraft and escort guns and depth charges.

Losses and limits

By March 1940, some 18 U-boats had been destroyed. These figures were small compared with the losses later on in the war, but considering that Germany produced only 58 submarines in the whole of 1939, including a large percentage of short-range types, they constituted a significant depletion.

In fact, at the end of September 1939, Churchill declared that the Royal Navy had effectively crushed the U-boat menace after a string of sinkings. As history would subsequently show, that declaration was woefully premature: the Allies were not to gain the upper hand for at least another three years.

6TH FLOTILLA (30 SEPTEMBER 1939)

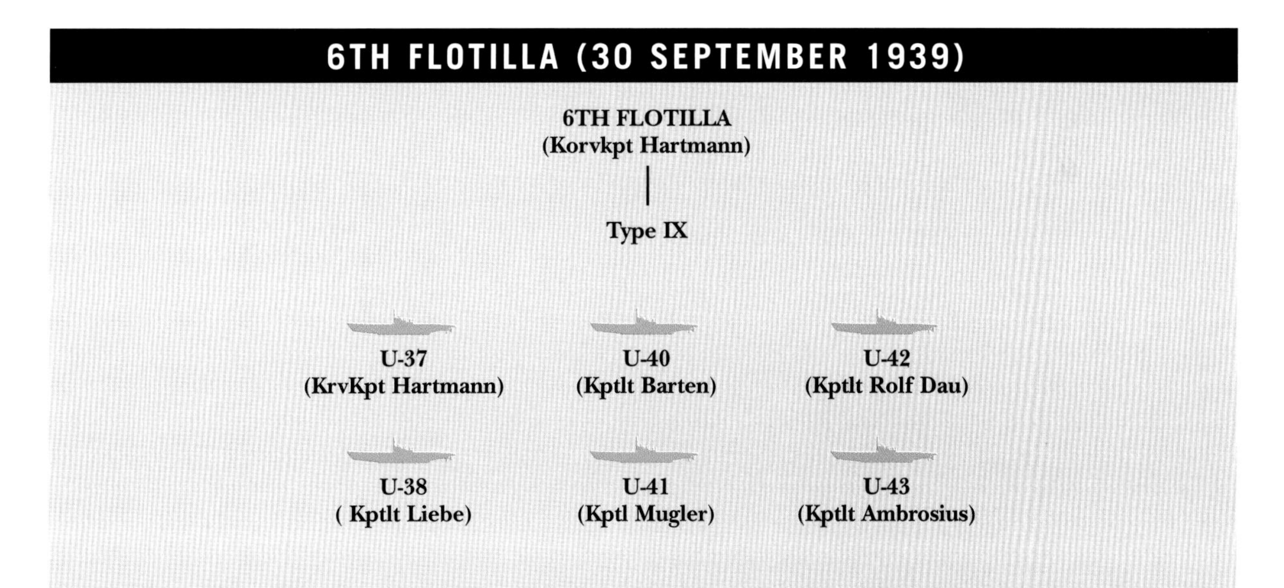

The 6th Flotilla was initially term *U-Flottille Hundius*, again after a famous World War I U-boat captain. It was established on 1 October 1938 and was equipped purely with the long-range Type IX U-boat. It was disbanded in December 1939, but reactivated as the 6th Flotilla in July 1941, headquartered in Danzig. The 6th Flotilla would contribute over 90 U-boats to the campaign by the time it was finally disbanded in August 1944.

U-37 TIMETABLE		
Patrol Dates	**Operational Area**	**Ships Sunk**
19 Aug 1939 – 15 Sep 1939	West of the Iberian Peninsula	0
5 Oct 1939 – 8 Nov 1939	Central Atlantic	8
28 Jan 1940 – 27 Feb 1940	Southwest of Ireland	8
30 Mar 1940 – 18 Apr 1940	Escorting raider Faeroes/Shetlands	3
15 May 1940 – 9 Jun 1940	Northwest of Cape Finisterre	10
1 Aug 1940 – 12 Aug 1940	Transit from Wilhelmshaven to Lorient	1
17 Aug 1940 – 30 Aug 1940	West of the British Isles	6
24 Sep 1940 – 22 Oct 1940	West of the British Isles	6
28 Nov 1940 – 7 Jan 1941	West of Spain/West of Africa	6
30 Jan 1941 – 18 Feb 1941	Central Atlantic off Freetown	3
27 Feb 1941 – 22 Mar 1941	North Atlantic	2

U-BOATS THAT TRAINED WITH THE 4TH FLOTILLA	
Type	**Boats ordered**
Type IX, IXC	U-37, U-38, U-129, U-130, U-153, U-154, U-155, U-156, U-157, U-158, U-159, U-160, U-161, U-162, U-163, U-164, U-165, U-166, U-171, U-172, U-173, U-174, U-175, U-176, U-504, U-505, U-506, U-507, U-508, U-509, U-510, U-511, U-512, U-513, U-514, U-515, U-516, U-517, U-518, U-519, U-520, U-521, U-522, U-523, U-524
Type IXC/40	U-167, U-168, U-169, U-170, U-183, U-184, U-185, U-186, U-187, U-188, U-189, U-190, U-191, U-192, U-193, U-194, U-525, U-526, U-527, U-528, U-529, U-530, U-531, U-532, U-533, U-534, U-535, U-536, U-537, U-538, U-539, U-540, U-541, U-542, U-543, U-544, U-545, U-546, U-547, U-548, U-549, U-550, U-801, U-802, U-803, U-804, U-805, U-806, U-841, U-842, U-843, U-844, U-845, U-846, U-853, U-854, U-855, U-856, U-857, U-858, U-865, U-866, U-867, U-868, U-869, U-870, U-877, U-878, U-879, U-880, U-881, U-883, U-889, U-1221, U-1222, U-1223, U-1234
Type IXD1, 2	U-177, U-178, U-179, U-180, U-181, U-182, U-195, U-196, U-197, U-198, U-199, U-200, U-847, U-848, U-849, U-850, U-851, U-852, U-859, U-860, U-861, U-862, U-863, U-864, U-871, U-872, U-873, U-874, U-875, U-876
Type VIIC	U-78, U-131, U-290, U-351, U-370, U-475, U-579, U-676, U-821, U-822, U-901, U-906, U-925, U-926, U-927, U-928
Type VIIC/41	U-317, U-318, U-319, U-320, U-321, U-322, U-323, U-324, U-325, U-326, U-327, U-328, U-929, U-930, U-1025, U-1301, U-1302, U-1303, U-1304, U-1305, U-1306, U-1307, U-1308
UA	UA (ex-Turkish)
Type XB	U-118, U-119, U-219, U-220, U-233
Type XIV	U-459, U-460, U-461, U-462, U-463, U-464, U-487, U-488, U-489, U-490
Type XXI	U-3001, U-3002, U-3003, U-3004, U-3005, U-3006, U-3007, U-3008, U-3009, U-3010, U-3011, U-3012, U-3013, U-3014, U-3015, U-3016, U-3017, U-3018, U-3019, U-3020, U-3021, U-3022, U-3023, U-3024, U-3025, U-3026, U-3027, U-3028, U-3029, U-3030, U-3031, U-3032, U-3033, U-3034, U-3035, U-3037, U-3038, U-3039, U-3040, U-3041, U-3044
Type XXIII	U-2321, U-2322, U-2323, U-2324, U-2325, U-2326, U-2336, U-2339, U-2343, U-2346, U-2347, U-2348, U-2349, U-2350, U-2351, U-2352, U-2353, U-2354, U-2355, U-2356, U-2357, U-2358, U-2359, U-2360, U-2361, U-2362, U-2363, U-2364, U-2365, U-2366, U-2367, U-2368, U-2369, U-2370, U-2371

Securing the French bases

The German conquest of France and the Low Countries in May–July 1940 was not only a major triumph for Hitler's land forces. It also provided Dönitz with more direct access to the Atlantic hunting grounds.

The signficance of the capture of the French ports to the U-boat service cannot be overstated. Previously, the U-boats had to negotiate the troubled northern waters, which the Allies had not only mined extensively but which were also more accessible to British naval and air control. Furthermore, precious volumes of fuel were used in making the transit through the arctic seas to the North Atlantic, increasing the U-boats' logistical burdens and decreasing their operational ranges.

Opening the sea lanes

The use of bases such as Lorient, Brest and St Nazaire following the conquest of France changed everything. First, the bases gave the U-boats direct access straight into the Atlantic, bypassing the precarious northern routes entirely. The waters of the Bay of Biscay were largely free of Allied mining, so the transit to the hunting grounds was far less costly in itself. To patrol the waters directly off the French coast was too risky for the Royal Navy because of *Luftwaffe* air operations and the local strengths of the *Kriegsmarine* surface navy, so the U-boats essentially had (initially at least) secure deployment routes.

Allied bombers

The biggest threat was, in fact, Allied bombing raids on the bases themselves, which necessitated the construction of massive ferro-concrete pens that were largely immune to the effects of mainstream Allied bomb munitions.

Incidentally, a by-product of the attention from Allied air raids was that the ports became extremely heavily defended by anti-aircraft guns and associated crews, and these centres of resistance would cause some intense

U-BOAT BASES (JAN 1941)

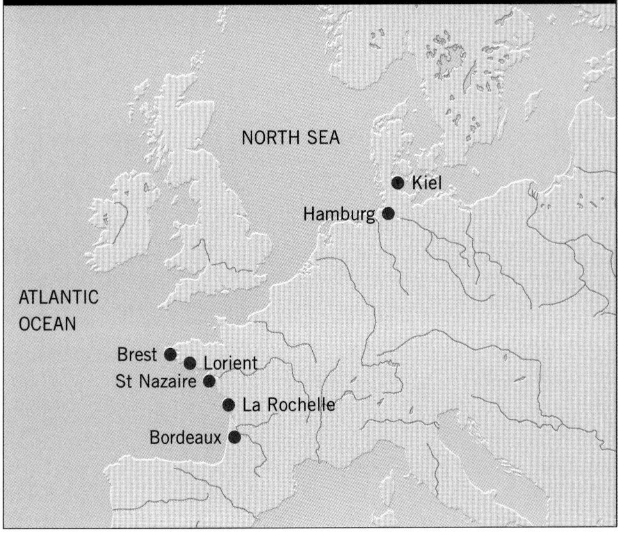

NORTH SEA
Kiel
Hamburg
ATLANTIC OCEAN
Brest
Lorient
St Nazaire
La Rochelle
Bordeaux

French advantage

The bases that became available to the *Kriegsmarine* after the fall of France offered a much more protected environment for the U-boats than they had previously enjoyed in the northern waters of the Baltic and North Seas – at least in terms of deployment routes.

The U-boats first began operating from these bases by July 1940, and they continued to do so until December 1944 in some cases, and even until the end of the war itself at La Rochelle/La Pallice.

As the map shows, the primary value of the French coast as an operating platform was its direct access into Atlantic waters. Not only did this make deployment less hazardous and costly in resources, it also meant that the U-boats could now influence more readily the British shipping routes into the Western Approaches and up from the South Atlantic.

problems for British and American ground forces following the D-Day invasion of France in June 1944.

Strategic effects

The other critical advantage of the French bases was to be found at a strategic level. Previously the Allies had relied upon the Western Approaches for the flow of their convoy shipping, but now that these waters were directly under the noses of the U-boats, many of the convoys had to divert to routes north of Ireland. Delivering shipping supplies here increased the logistical strains in terms of both the handling at overstretched northern harbours and the supply distribution around inland Britain, as the largest urban areas lay much further to the south.

A further problem for Britain was that its shipping lanes from the South Atlantic, Mediterranean and Indian Ocean also crossed the mouth of the Bay of Biscay. From now on, convoy routes became more convoluted and lengthy, not an ideal situation for a country that relied squarely on timely maritime supplies for its very survival.

Another strategic effect of the fall of France was that the French fleet was no longer capable of contributing to convoy escort duties. The Royal Navy's commitments increased commensurately, stretching escort resources to the maximum and thereby reducing the danger to the U-boats during their attacks. All told, the U-boat war was about to intensify for the Allies.

The bases

The fall of France resulted in the immediate appropriation of five principal bases: Lorient, Brest, St Nazaire, La Rochelle and Bordeaux. Note also that a base much further south at Toulon was established in 1943 to provide support for operations in the Mediterranean.

The Lorient base was in use by isolated U-boats by 7 July 1940, but over time it became the largest and most industrious of the French U-boat bases. (Indeed, such was its importance that Dönitz moved his headquarters here from Paris in November 1940, although it was moved back again in 1942 following the British raid on St Nazaire.) It became home to the 2nd and 10th U-boat Flotillas, and was also a major centre for the repair of damaged submarines – in total, 492 U-boats would receive overhauls at Lorient. The first Allied air raids hit Lorient in September 1940, and

U-2 (TYPE IIA)	
Commissioned	25 July 1935
Crew	22–24
Displacement	364 tonnes (358 tons) submerged
Dimensions	Length: 43.9m (144ft); Beam: 4.8m (16ft)
Range	Surfaced: 2575km (1600 miles) at 15km/h (8kts); Submerged: 56km (35 miles) at 7.4km/h (4kts)
Armament	3 x 533mm (21in) torpedo tubes; 1 x (later 4) 20mm (0.79in) AA gun
Powerplant	Surfaced: diesels 522kW (700hp); Submerged: electric motors 306kW (410hp)
Performance	Surfaced: 24km/h (13kts); Submerged: 13km/h (6.9kts)

1ST FLOTILLA, STRENGTH 1941	
Type	**Boats on strength**
TYPE	
Type IIB	14
Type IIC	8
Type IID	13
Type VIIB (after 1941)	3
Type VIIC (after 1941)	81
Type VIIC/41 (after 1941)	2
Type XB (after 1941)	2

1ST FLOTILLA STAR COMMANDERS		
Commander	**Patrol**	**Ships Sunk**
Großadmiral Karl Dönitz	None	None
Korvettenkapitän Adalbert Schnee	12	21
Kapitänleutnant Rolf Mützelburg	7	19
Kptlt Friedrich Guggenberger	10	14

consequently the *Kriegsmarine* constructed bomb-proof Keroman shelters, some of which had roofs 7.4m (24ft) thick in places.

Brest and St Nazaire

Brest was occupied by the 1st Flotilla from June 1941, and the 9th Flotilla from the following October. The 1st Flotilla boats arriving at Brest moved straight into a massive pre-constructed bunker system that covered 52,000 sq m (559,723 sq ft)with roof protection more than 6m (19.6ft) thick.

Only when British bombers dropped the massive 5454kg (12,000lb) Tall Boy bombs in August 1944 was this structure finally penetrated. Brest was abandoned by the U-boats a month later.

The 6th and 7th Flotillas had their base at St Nazaire, the latter occupying the base in the first half of 1941, while the former moved in during February 1942. (U-boats actually began using the harbour from September 1940, however.) St Nazaire's massive bunker system was completed by June 1941. It was highly effective – during 1942 the Allies lost over 60 aircraft attacking St Nazaire, but the pen was never penetrated. The British raid of

GÜNTHER PRIEN (1908–1941)

Günther Prien was one of World War II's greatest U-boat aces. He joined the *Reichsmarine* in the early 1930s after service in the merchant marine, moving from surface ships to U-boats in 1935 and taking part in submarine patrols during the Spanish Civil War.

- In December 1938, Prien took command of *U-47*, a Type VIIB boat, and on the outbreak of war sank the British steamer *Bosnia* on his first Atlantic patrol.

- Prien hit the headlines for his daring sinking of the Royal Navy battleship *Royal Oak* at Scapa Flow on the night of 13/14 October 1939, for which action he became the first winner of the Knight's Cross.

- Prien went on to be a scourge of Allied shipping in the Atlantic, sinking a total of 30 merchant ships, totalling 162,769 gross registered tons (GRT), and receiving the Oak Leaves to his Knight's Cross.

- Around 7 March 1941, Prien went down with *U-47* in the Atlantic, possibly through destroyer attack or stray torpedo strike. The cause was never confirmed.

U-106 TIMETABLE		
Patrol Dates	**Operational Area**	**Ships Sunk**
4 Jan 1941 – 10 Feb 1941	Northwest of Rockall	2
26 Feb 1941 – 17 Jun 1941	Central Atlantic	8
11 Aug 1941 – 11 Sep 1941	Southwest of Ireland	0
21 Oct 1941 – 22 Nov 1941	North Atlantic	1
3 Jan 1942 – 22 Feb 1942	US Coast	5
15 Apr 1942 – 29 Jun 1942	Gulf of Mexico	5
25 Jul 1942 – 28 Jul 1942	Damaged by aircraft in Bay of Biscay	0
22 Sep 1942 – 26 Dec 1942	Gulf of St Lawrence/Central Atlantic	1
17 Feb 1943 – 2 Aug 1943	Azores/Canaries	0
19 Mar 1944 – 5 Apr 1944	Sunk off northern Spain	0

2ND FLOTILLA (1 DECEMBER 1940)

The 2nd Flotilla's home base for much of the war (July 1940–August 1944) was Lorient, although prior to its move there it had been based in Kiel and at Wilhelmshaven. It was originally formed as *U-Flottille Saltzwedel* on 1 September 1936. During its lifespan a total of 91 boats were assigned to the flotilla, with most being the long-range types seen above.

March 1942 on St Nazaire, mentioned above, also had only a limited effect on the U-boats, as the U-boat pen and its vessels were not a priority target for the British and Canadian raiders.

3rd Flotilla

La Rochelle/La Pallice was home to just one German U-boat flotilla, the 3rd, which moved into the base in October 1941 (although from September 1940 the harbour was also used by Italian submarines). From April 1941, construction of a new U-boat bunker began, and work was completed within the year. Incredibly, U-boats would continue operating out of La Rochelle right up until the end of the war, although with limited combat duties, and the base was defended by its garrison until 8 May 1945.

Bordeaux bunker

The Bordeaux base received the 12th Flotilla in October 1942, although by this time it was already in use with the Italian Navy for its submarine operations, and they would continue to operate alongside the German boats until September 1943.

The port at Bordeaux was actually situated 96km (60 miles) inland, but this location did not mean it lacked protection, and it received a major ferro-concrete bunker just like the other bases. U-boats began operating out of the bunkers in January 1943. The Bordeaux base specialized in deploying very long-range U-boats such as the Type IXD2, and the Type XIV *Milchkuh* (Milk Cow).

As already noted, the Toulon base was a later addition to the network of U-boat bases. Submarines of the 29th Flotilla, escaping from vulnerable bases in Italy, were transferred to Toulon from March 1943, the 29th's headquarters moving there the following August. Unlike the other U-boat ports, Toulon had no specially constructed bunkers. It paid for this decision once the British and US air forces started to pay the base attention from November 1943. Between November 1943 and August 1944, nine U-boats were destroyed in 12 air raids, and many other were damaged. Enough was enough – Toulon was abandoned. For Dönitz, securing the French bases meant that the Battle of the Atlantic could start in earnest.

The one issue that still dogged his mind, however, was numbers of submarines. Despite his best efforts, U-boat production was still dragging. In 1940, only 68 new submarines rolled off the assembly lines. Given the massive amount of sea freight rolling across the Atlantic, much would have to change.

U-29 (TYPE VIIA)	
Commissioned	16 November 1936
Crew	42–46
Displacement	745 tonnes (733 tons) submerged
Dimensions	Length: 64.5m (212ft); Beam: 5.9m (19ft)
Range	Surfaced: 9978km (6200 miles) at 18km/h (10kts); Submerged: 151km (94 miles) at 7.4km/h (4kts)
Armament	5 x 533mm (21in) torpedo tubes; 1 x 88mm (3.5in) deck gun
Powerplant	Surfaced: diesels 1588kW (2130hp); Submerged: electric motors 559kW (750hp)
Performance	Surfaced: 31.5km/h (17kts); Submerged: 14.8km/h (8kts)

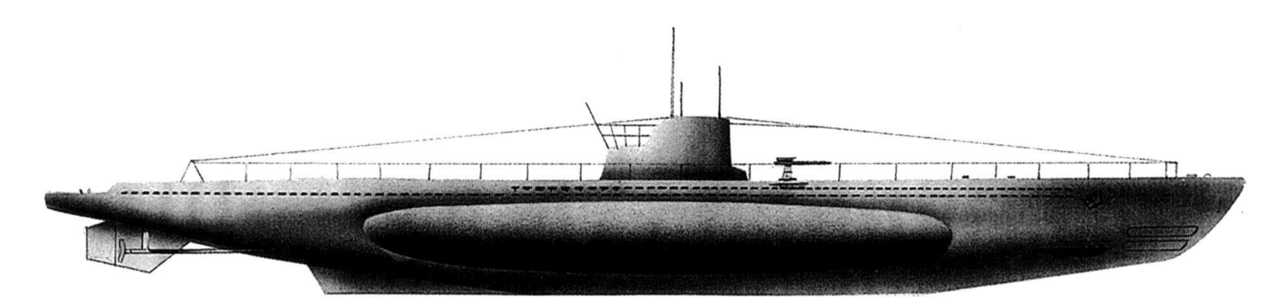

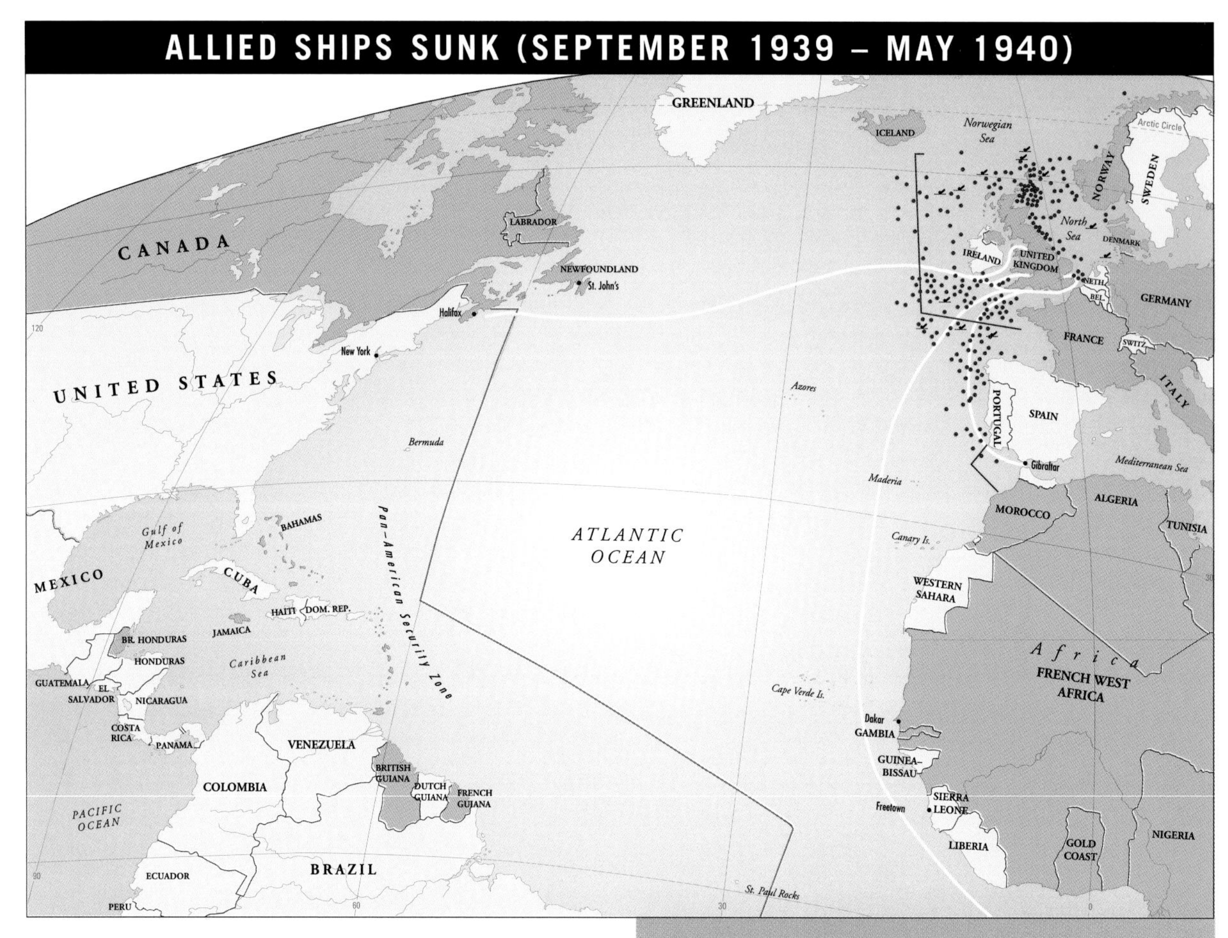

September 1939 – May 1940

- Limit of US merchant responsibility
- Extent of air escort cover
- Major convoy routes
- Allied merchant ships sunk by U-boats
- U-boats sunk
- Territory under Allied control
- Territory under Axis control
- Neutral territory

Early sinkings

In 1939 *Konteradmiral* Karl Dönitz had only 56 U-boats in service, of which only 22 were ocean-going types. Initially, however, pickings for the U-boat commanders were rich, as their boats sank merchantmen returning individually to Britain.

Even when convoys were established almost immediately after the outbreak of war, they could be escorted only through 15 degrees of longitude at either end of the transatlantic route due to a lack of suitable escorts. Even so, the U-boats were little more than a nuisance – until the fall of France and the acquisition by Germany of strategically important bases.

This map indicating U-boat merchant kills between September 1939 and May 1940 clearly illustrates the main U-boat hunting grounds.

The first 'Happy Time'

The expression 'Happy Time' was the grim coinage of U-boat crews to describe the period from mid-1940 to roughly mid-1941. It was a time during which tactics were refined and thousands of tonnes of Allied shipping went to the bottom of the Atlantic.

The year 1940 was the period in which the German U-boat force began to come into its own in the Atlantic. The early part of the year had seen modest successes in the Atlantic, but also problems closer to home during the German invasion of Norway in April. During that operation, Dönitz had been unable to prevent the massacre of 10 German destroyers, even though he had some 30 submarines deployed in either Norwegian or coastal British waters. A large part of the failure there was due to sea conditions; the low-floating submarines simply could not spot their enemies in high northern seas and freezing snowstorms. Defective torpedoes also played a part (see below), the submarines either scoring hits on British warships but with no torpedo detonation, or having the torpedoes explode prematurely, bringing the escorts down on their heads.

The result was that four submarines were lost during the Norway campaign, and Dönitz looked to make amends for this tactical failure in the Atlantic and the seas around Britain.

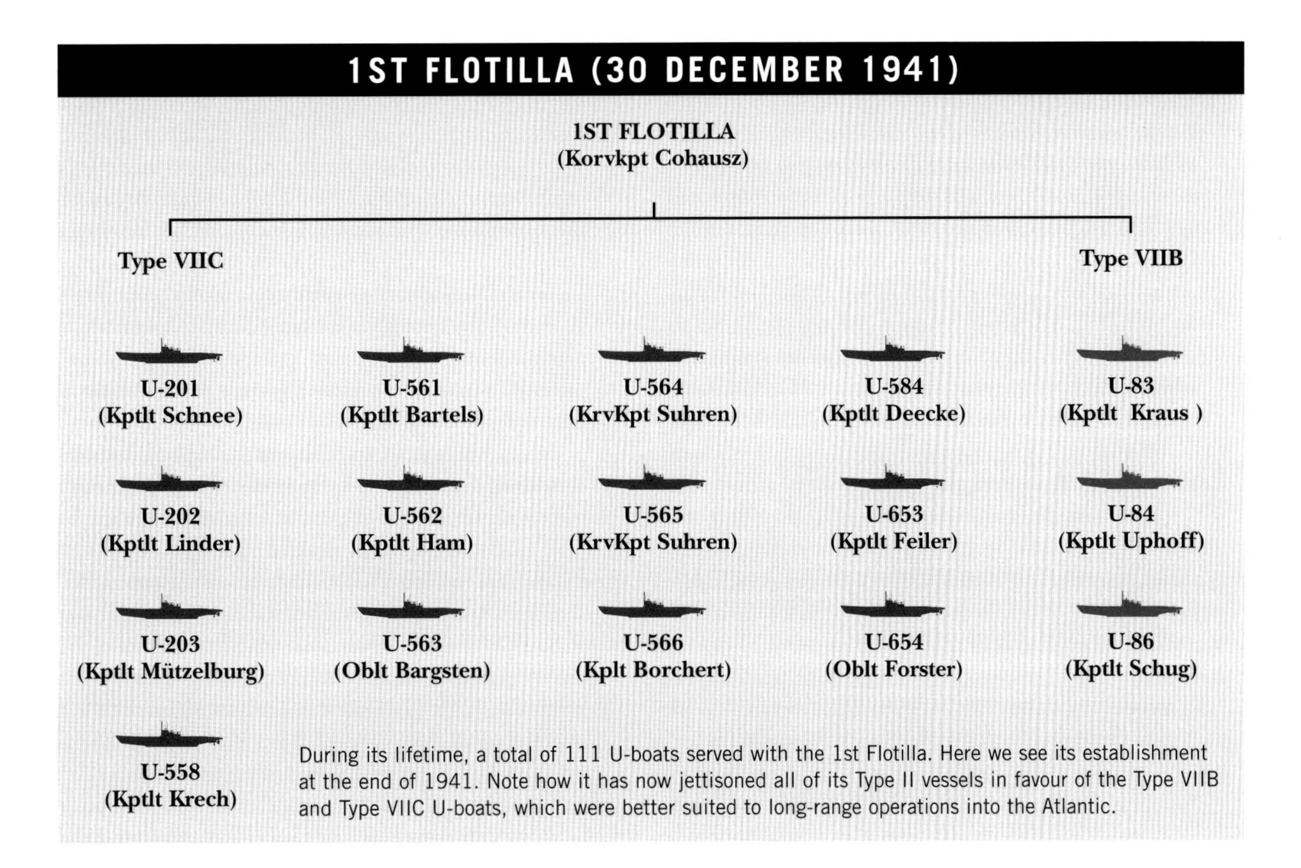

During its lifetime, a total of 111 U-boats served with the 1st Flotilla. Here we see its establishment at the end of 1941. Note how it has now jettisoned all of its Type II vessels in favour of the Type VIIB and Type VIIC U-boats, which were better suited to long-range operations into the Atlantic.

The 'Happy Time' was a product of various factors aligning themselves in favour of the German U-boat crews. Many of these factors have been noted above in relation to the German advantages in bases that came with the fall of France.

Yet the U-boats were also learning at a tactical level. Previously the U-boat skippers might have launched submerged daytime attacks, but now many commanders realized that far better gains could be had from faster surfaced night-time attacks. With its low silhouette, a U-boat was fiendishly difficult to spot in the choppy Atlantic waters at night. Bold commanders would sometimes actually slip their submarines directly in amongst the Allied convoys, then hit the target vessel with a single torpedo at close range, instead of firing spreads of long-range shots.

U-BOATS THAT TRAINED WITH THE 5TH FLOTILLA

Type	Boats ordered
Type IIB	U-11
Type VIIB	U-86
Type VIIC	U-91, U-92, U-134, U-135, U-208, U-210, U-211, U-221, U-224, U-225, U-226, U-227, U-228, U-229, U-230, U-231, U-232, U-235, U-236, U-237, U-238, U-239, U-240, U-241, U-242, U-243, U-244, U-245, U-246, U-247, U-248, U-249, U-250, U-257, U-258, U-259, U-262, U-301, U-333, U-336, U-337, U-348, U-353, U-354, U-355, U-360, U-364, U-365, U-366, U-374, U-375, U-380, U-381, U-382, U-384, U-385, U-386, U-387, U-388, U-389, U-390, U-391, U-392, U-393, U-394, U-396, U-397, U-398, U-399, U-400, U-403, U-407, U-408, U-409, U-410, U-435, U-436 , U-439, U-440, U-441, U-442, U-454, U-455, U-466, U-467, U-468, U-469, U-470, U-471, U-472, U-473, U-475, U-476, U-477, U-478, U-479, U-480, U-481, U-482, U-483, U-484, U-485, U-486, U-578, U-579, U-580, U-581, U-582, U-583, U-584, U-600, U-601, U-602, U-603, U-604, U-605, U-606, U-607, U-608, U-609, U-610, U-611, U-612, U-617, U-618, U-619, U-626, U-627, U-628, U-629, U-630, U-631, U-632, U-633, U-634, U-635, U-636, U-637, U-638, U-639, U-640, U-641, U-642, U-643, U-644, U-645, U-646, U-647, U-648, U-649, U-650, U-654, U-656, U-659, U-660, U-661, U-662, U-663, U-665, U-666, U-667, U-668, U-669, U-670, U-671, U-672, U-673, U-674, U-675, U-676, U-677, U-678, U-702, U-705, U-706, U-708, U-709, U-710, U-711, U-714, U-715, U-716, U-717, U-718, U-719, U-749, U-750, U-754, U-755, U-759, U-904, U-951, U-952, U-953, U-954, U-955, U-956, U-957, U-958, U-959, U-960, U-961, U-962, U-963, U-964, U-965, U-966, U-967, U-968, U-969, U-970, U-971, U-972, U-973, U-974, U-975, U-976, U-977, U-978, U-979, U-980, U-981, U-982, U-983, U-984, U-985, U-986, U-987, U-988, U-989, U-990, U-991, U-992, U-993, U-994, U-1051, U-1052, U-1053, U-1054, U-1055, U-1056, U-1057, U-1058, U-1131, U-1132, U-1161, U-1162, U-1195, U-1207, U-1210
Type VIIC/41	U-320, U-828, U-995, U-997, U-998, U-999, U-1001, U-1008, U-1063, U-1064, U-1065, U-1105, U-1108, U-1110, U-1168, U-1274, U-1275
Type VIID	U-213, U-214, U-215, U-216, U-217, U-218
Type VIIF	U-1059, U-1060, U-1061, U-1062
Type IXA	U-38
Type XB	U-234
Type XVIIA, B	U-792, U-793, U-794, U-795, U-1405, U-1406, U-1407
Type XXI	U-3501, U-3502, U-3503, U-3504, U-3505, U-3506, U-3507, U-3508, U-3509, U-3510, U-3511, U-3512, U-3513, U-3514, U-3515, U-3516, U-3517, U-3518, U-3519, U-3521, U-3522, U-3523, U-3524, U-3525, U-3526, U-3527, U-3528, U-3529, U-3530
Type XXIII	U-2332, U-2333, U-4701, U-4702, U-4703, U-4704, U-4705, U-4706, U-4707, U-4709, U-4710, U-4711, U-4712
British H class	UD-1 (ex-Dutch)
O 21 class	UD-3, UD-4 (ex-Dutch)
Aurore class	UF-2 (ex-French)

U-201 TIMETABLE		
Patrol Dates	**Operational Area**	**Ships Sunk**
22 Apr 1941 – 18 May 1941	Transit from Kiel to Brest	2
18 May 1941 – 19 Jul 1941	Central North Atlantic	0
14 Aug 1941 – 25 Aug 1941	West of Ireland/West of Portugal	3
14 Sep 1941 – 30 Sep 1941	West/Southwest of Ireland	5
29 Oct 1941 – 9 Dec 1941	West of Ireland	0
24 Mar 1942 – 21 May 1942	US East Coast	3
27 June 1942 – 8 Aug 1942	Central Atlantic southeast of the Azores	6
6 Sep 1942 – 26 Oct 1942	Central Atlantic/Caribbean	3
27 Dec 1942 – 29 Dec 1942	Returned after developing fault	0
3 Jan 1943 – 17 Feb 1943	North Atlantic	0

U-boat crews were also improving their understanding of British anti-submarine tactics, which were weakened by their general lack of escort vessels. Such was the British desperation to plug this gap that in September Britain bought 50 ageing destroyers from the United States in exchange for US airbase rights at various key locations around the British Empire. Maritime reconnaissance also improved. With the conquest of France, maritime elements of the *Luftwaffe* also acquired bases on the French coast. The *Luftwaffe* used these to make long-range reconnaissance flights using Condor aircraft, which swept out over the Atlantic west of Ireland before tracking back up to bases in Norway. If any convoys were spotted, the coordinates were relayed back to naval stations in France, and the information was then passed on to hunting U-boats in the Atlantic.

Technologies

While external factors played a great part in the successes of the U-boats, the technology of the submarines themselves was also critical to their ascendancy. The endurance of a typical Type VII boat was formidable. It could hover around the Atlantic sea lanes for several weeks without refuelling, upping its chances of acquiring a good convoy target. The Type IXB had a range of 19,312km (12,000 miles) on the surface at a steady pace of 18.5km/h (10 knots).

The German submarines also carried on board excellent hydrophone detection equipment. This essentially consisted of a pair of microphones, set some distance apart on the submarine, that picked up the sound of distant ship propellers. Because of the distance between the two microphones, the hydrophone operator was able to triangulate the position of the source of the noise, giving a bearing to the target. From a submerged depth of around 30.5m (100ft), a U-boat could detect the churning screws of a convoy out to a distance of 100km (62 miles).

Of course, once it had detected a convoy, the submarine then had to attack it. The two principal types of torpedo between 1939 and 1942 were the gas/steam-powered G7a and the electrically powered G7e. Both were 533mm (21in) weapons and carried explosive warheads of 280kg (616lb), enough to punch a ship-threatening hole in the largest vessel. Ranges extended from 5000m (5468 yards) up to 12,500m (13,670 yards), depending on the speed of the submarine at launch and, in the case of the G7e, on whether the batteries had been pre-warmed before launch.

There was no homing or programmable element to these early torpedoes (these improvements came later), so the key to their successful use was the talent of the U-boat commander, who would either fire spreads of torpedoes at long-range or multiple targets, or single shots at close range, usually on the surface. The defective design of torpedo detonation pistols, which worked by either direct contact or by magnetic influence, was a major problem during the early years of the war, one that was steadily rectified but at the cost of many missed opportunities.

The pay-off in the improved strategic and tactical situation of the U-boat arm quickly became apparent. Consider the following figures, which show the tonnage of Allied merchant vessels sunk in the South Atlantic between January and May 1940:

January	217,948 tonnes (214,506 tons)
February	230,561 tonnes (226,920 tons)
March	108,726 tonnes (107,009 tons)
April	160,756 tonnes (158,218 tons)
May	290,480 tonnes (285,893 tons)

These tonnage totals were the result of 339 merchant ships being sunk, all in a period when the U-boats had limited numbers and had no access to operating bases along the French coastline. Now look at the figures from June to October 1940:

June	513,563 tonnes (505,453 tons)
July	370,932 tonnes (365,074 tons)
August	358,668 tonnes (353,004 tons)
September	409,978 tonnes (403,504 tons)
October	424,975 tonnes (418,264 tons)

The jump in tonnage totals is readily apparent, the result of 506 merchant sinkings. Even the introduction of the US destroyers shows no effect on the actual numbers of ships lost.

What is even more striking is that these results were achieved with so few U-boats actually on station. From June to November 1940, for example, the typical number of U-boats on station at any one time was only 16. This was not an ideal situation by any means, and it meant that enough convoys still slipped through the U-boat net to keep Britain functioning in its resistance.

The numbers of on-station U-boats dropped further between November 1940 and January 1941, plunging to around 4–6. This reduction was due partly to U-boat losses – the *Kriegsmarine* lost 23 submarines throughout 1940 – and partly to inadequate U-boat production. The decline in numbers of available submarines could not have come at a worse time. During the same period, the British increased the efficiency and number of their coastal maritime air patrols, with larger numbers of

U-BOAT CREW

German rank	British equivalent
Kommandant	Commander
Leitender Ingenieur (LI)	Chief engineer
Wachoffizier	Watch officer, exec officer
Obersteuermann	Chief quartermaster
Obermaschinist	Warrant machinist
Bootsmann	Chief boatswain
Seemännisches Personal	Nautical personnel
Technisches Personal	Technical personnel
Zentrale-Personal	Control room personnel
Funk-Personal	Radio personnel
Torpedo-Personal	Torpedo personnel
Artilleriemechaniker-Personal	Gunnery mechanical personnel
Koch, 'Smutje'	Cook
Bordarzt, Sanitätsmaat	Doctor
Flak Personal	Anti aircraft personnel
PK-Leute	War correspondent
Meteorologe	Meteorologist
B-Dienst	Intelligence personnel

Allied vulnerabilities

The Allied convoy routes depicted on this map show how U-boat commanders and German naval intelligence could with some degree of certainty predict the general areas through which convoys would be passing. The main areas of concentration were out to sea from the northeast coast of the United States and off the northwest coast of England and Scotland, the British limiting the number of convoys through the vulnerable Western Approaches.

There was also a prominent 'gap' in the middle of the Atlantic that could not be covered by Allied air patrols until the introduction of the very long-range B-24 Liberator in 1943, and surface escorts also had limits to range, depending on the type of ship. When the U-boats managed to patrol this gap more successfully, it resulted in a major surge in sinkings.

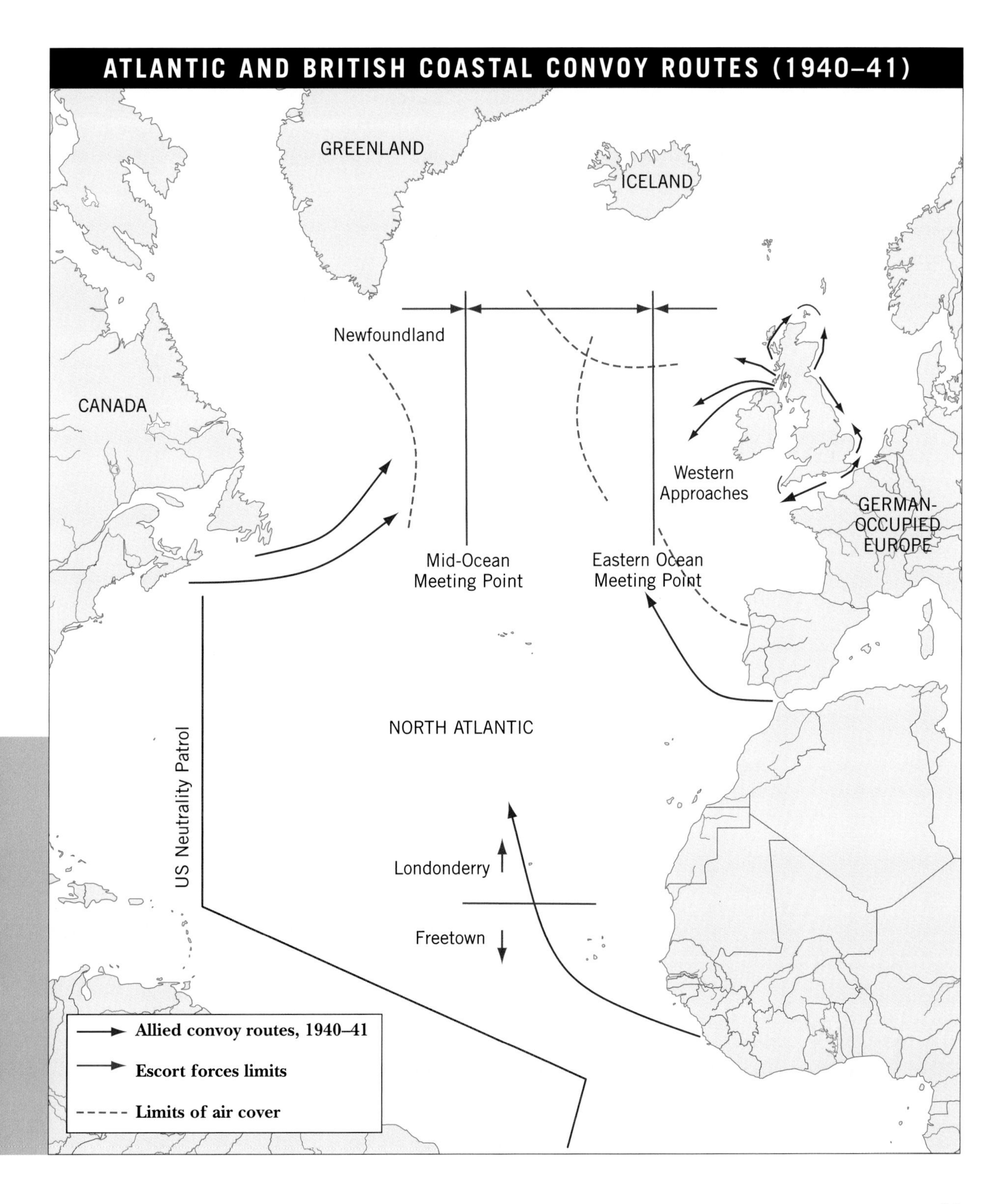
ATLANTIC AND BRITISH COASTAL CONVOY ROUTES (1940–41)
GREENLAND
ICELAND
Newfoundland
CANADA
Western
Approaches
GERMAN-
OCCUPIED
EUROPE
Mid-Ocean
Meeting Point
Eastern Ocean
Meeting Point
NORTH ATLANTIC
US Neutrality Patrol
Londonderry
Freetown
Allied convoy routes, 1940–41
Escort forces limits
Limits of air cover

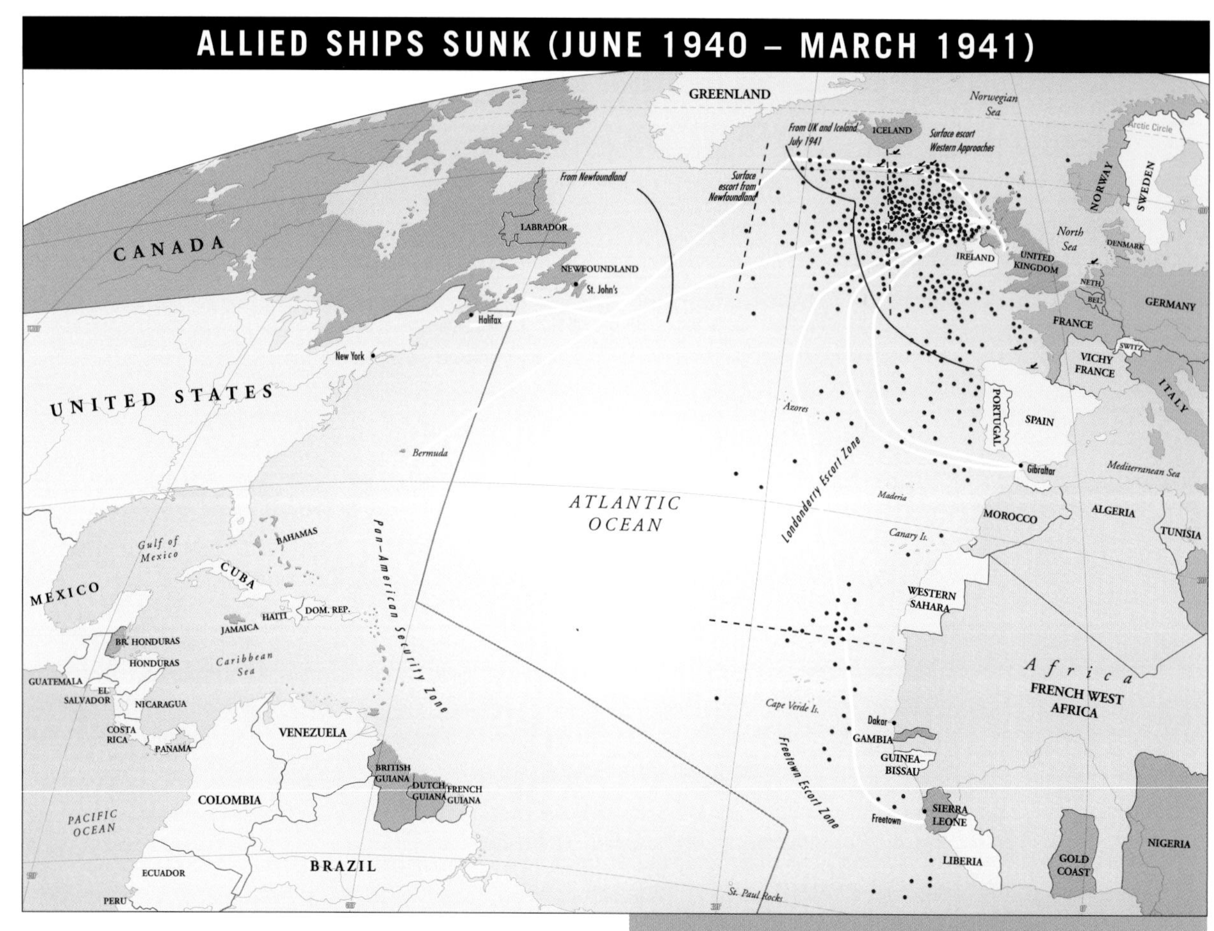

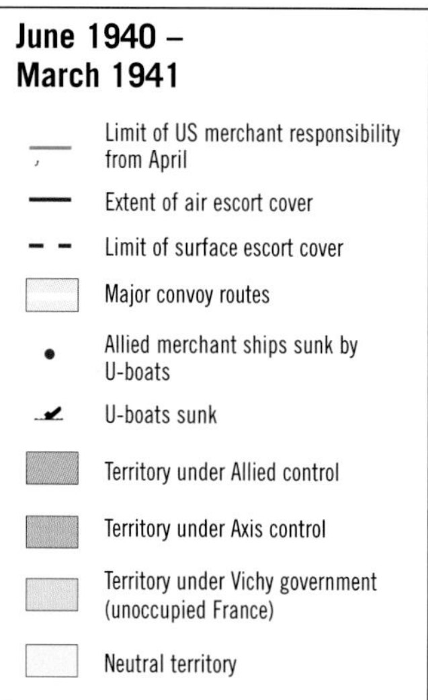

'Happy Time' sinkings

This map of merchant ship sinkings for the second half of 1940 and the first months of 1941 shows a clear pattern of development when compared with the map for the early months of the war (page 80).

While that map showed the main cluster of sinkings around the Western Approaches and northeastern Scotland, by now the wolf pack tactics were concentrated around the waters to the north and the northwest of Ireland, with further smaller clusters to the south of Ireland and off the west coast of Africa.

A total of 136 merchant vessels were sunk in March 1941 alone, helping to make up a total of 973 ships lost during the period here described. Note at this point that the Pan-American Neutrality Agreement prevented sinkings around the US coastline.

aircraft released following the victory of the RAF over the *Luftwaffe* in the Battle of Britain. This air cover forced the U-boats to move further away from coastal Britain into more open waters, where there was an increased chance of a convoy slipping through the net. The effect of these changes was evident in the tonnages of merchant vessels sunk. In November 1940 these dropped from the 424,975 tonnes (418,264 tons) of the previous month down to 298,772 tonnes (294,054 tons), a total of 86 vessels sunk compared with 99 in October.

On the plus side, the numbers of sinkings of U-boats were staying fairly constant. The sinkings from January to December in the Atlantic, Arctic and the Baltic were as follows:

January	2	February	4
March	3	April	2
May	1	June	0
July	2	August	3
September	0	October	1
November	2	December	0

These figures reflect the growing experience of the U-boat crews, and the lack of anti-submarine expertise on the part of the Allies. There was also the reality that the U-boat arm was not big enough to see very heavy losses. Nevertheless, a way had to be found of increasing the efficiency of this small but important service.

Tackling the convoys

The convoy system was the foundation of the British maritime strategy in the Atlantic. It was based upon a statistical calculation. Ships could be sent one at a time across the Atlantic, making a small individual target; but if a U-boat missed one vessel, there would be another along shortly after – one that was almost certainly operating without an escort. If a U-boat failed to encounter a convoy, by contrast, then a large volume of supplies would slip through in one go, aided by a stronger escort.

Dönitz therefore had to find improved methods of both detecting the convoy movements and increasing the number of kills if a convoy were attacked. The key to success, he realized after close discussions and debriefings with all his commanders, was to deploy his U-boats in groups that hunted together, rather than singly. This was the foundation of the wolf packs.

Wolf packs

The wolf pack was the defining tactic of the U-boats during World War II. By hunting together in mutually supporting groups, the U-boats could up their chances of spotting a convoy, and could deliver greater destruction when they did.

Allied convoys presented the juiciest of targets to any ambitious and ruthless U-boat commander, yet they also raised problems. If the convoy was reasonably well escorted, as they increasingly were during the second half of 1940 and into 1941, then attacking it would bring a fast and brutal response. From the first launch of his torpedoes, the commander was essentially preparing to dive to avoid the inevitable counterattack, which limited the time available to do damage to the convoy. Furthermore, while the escorts were attempting to destroy the attacking submarine, they were essentially drawn away from the convoy, leaving it more exposed. With only one submarine present in the attack, therefore, an opportunity to exploit the escort's distraction was lost. What was needed was some way of maximizing the effects of the first strike against the convoy, and of hitting the convoy again while the escorts were looking the other way.

Developing the wolf packs

The idea of the wolf packs, as Dönitz labelled them, was straightforward. In essence, U-boats would no longer work solitary patrols looking for enemy convoys. Instead, they would work in a group, hunting the sea lanes together and making attacks in a coordinated fashion. At first these wolf packs were necessarily small owing to limited overall numbers of submarines – often around three or four vessels. By mid-1942, however, wolf packs numbering over a dozen craft were patrolling large expanses of ocean, and sinking huge volumes of merchant traffic.

The development of the wolf packs was assisted in many regards by the simple increase of U-boat production following 1940. In 1940, as we have noted, German industry produced 68 new U-boats. In 1941, however, Hitler recognized the value of the submarine to his war campaign, and production jumped to 129 boats. In the following three years, before the epic collapse of Germany's resistance in 1945, production figures were:

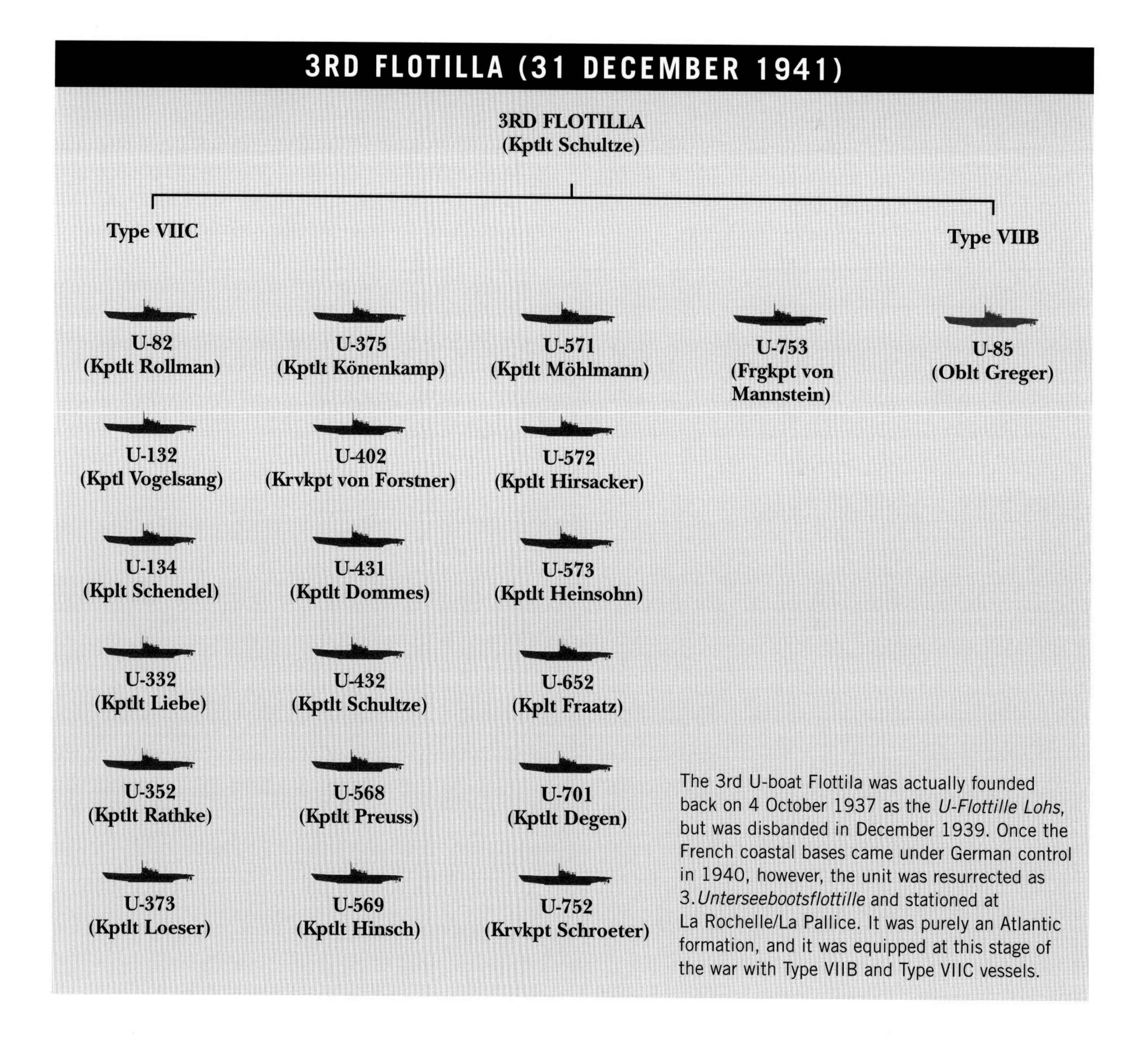

The 3rd U-boat Flottila was actually founded back on 4 October 1937 as the *U-Flottille Lohs*, but was disbanded in December 1939. Once the French coastal bases came under German control in 1940, however, the unit was resurrected as 3.*Unterseebootsflottille* and stationed at La Rochelle/La Pallice. It was purely an Atlantic formation, and it was equipped at this stage of the war with Type VIIB and Type VIIC vessels.

1942	282
1943	207
1944	258

Even in 1945, with Germany descending into apocalypse, some 139 new U-boats still rolled out onto the seas, more than were produced in 1940. In total, Germany built and launched 1141 submarines between 1939 and 1945. By comparison, bear in mind that the United Kingdom produced only 167 submarines in total between those same dates, and the United States only 203. In fact, the total Allied output of submarines during the war years was a mere 422 vessels, a low number reflecting the lack of Axis surface targets in Western waters, plus the greater importance of air power in Allied thinking.

The increases in U-boat numbers, although still below what was actually needed at a strategic level, made the wolf pack a viable tactical prospect. If it was deployed coherently across the Allied convoy routes, as Dönitz envisaged, the volume of supplies crossing the Atlantic could be cut dramatically.

There was one other important factor behind the development of the wolf packs. As we shall see, these groups required good long-range radio communications to provide the means for coordinated action. Prior to the fall of France, the distances were often simply too great to allow radio transmitters based in Germany or Norway to reach the Atlantic hunting grounds. The invasion of France not only brought with it U-boat bases but also sites for powerful coastal radio transmitters, broadcasting encoded messages that could reach submarines deep in the mid-Atlantic.

Tactical principles

At a tactical level, the wolf packs operated along the following general principles. The group of U-boats would be strung out over a recognized Allied shipping route, waiting on station for a convoy to appear. If one of the submarines spotted a convoy, its first action was not to attack, but instead it would shadow the convoy and report its position back to the BdU. The BdU would in turn relay the convoy position to all the other U-boats in the wolf pack. The 'shadower', as the first submarine was known, would stay out of visual range of the convoy, and its commander would wait until he was joined by enough members of the wolf pack to make an attack.

Attacks were usually launched at night to maximize confusion amongst the merchant ships and their escorts. Once the order to attack was given, the U-boats would

3RD FLOTILLA BASE LOCATIONS

ATLANTIC OCEAN

Kiel

La Rochelle/La Pallice

Move to France

The 3rd Flotilla was one of several U-boat flotillas that were re-formed to operate out of French coastal bases secured from June 1940. The flotilla was originally based up in Kiel, from where it carried out four months of combat operations between September and December 1939. Before the move, it was equipped purely with Type IIB and Type IID coastal submarines, but at La Rochelle/La Pallice it was equipped Type VIIB and Type VIIC craft.

The unit's actual move to the French bases came in September 1941, although it had been re-formed into the 3rd Flotilla the previous March. In total, the 3rd Flotilla deployed over 100 boats to the base at La Rochelle/La Pallice. Some of its submarines carried the distinctive turtle unit badge, although the rather meek nature of this creature meant that not all commanders were eager to display it.

swarm around the convoy at different angles and distances, firing patterns of torpedoes into the midst of the convoy.

The multiplicity of attack patterns made the escort response extremely difficult. The Germans added to the confusion further by maintaining rolling attacks as other submarines joined the wolf pack, although they tended to stay quiet during the more vulnerable daylight hours, when the escorts were better able to spot torpedo wakes or a periscope cutting through the water.

Convoy destruction

The effects of the wolf packs were utterly traumatic for those convoys caught by them. On 24 and 25 August 1940, for example, three U-boats (*U-48, U-57, U-124*) intercepted convoys HX65 and HX65A near the Hebrides. Despite the low number of U-boats involved in the attack, they still managed to sink six merchant ships totalling 37,882 tonnes (37,284 tons). On 20–22 September, nine U-boats (*U-29, U-32, U-43, U-46, U-47, U-48, U-65, U-99, U-100*) consigned 11 ships from convoy HX72 to the deep, and damaged three others.

A paticularly horrifying example of an effective wolf pack attack was that against convoy SC7 between 16 and 19 October 1940. SC7 was an eastbound convoy sailing between Sydney in Nova Scotia and Liverpool in the United Kingdom. In total it comprised 35 merchant ships, and the only escort for 75 per cent of its journey was HMS *Scarborough*, a 10-year-old sloop with limited armament to protect such a large convoy.

The merchant crews were nervous crossing the Atlantic with such low-level protection, and rightly so.

Biscay operations

The Bay of Biscay was a key war zone for the U-boat arm between 1939 and 1943, as it was a transit area for missions deeper into the Atlantic, plus an interception zone for U-boats picking up Allied convoys heading up from the South Atlantic.

Yet by 1943 the bay became known as the 'Valley of Death' to the U-boat crews. The reason was that once the Allies had gained air supremacy over the area, British maritime air patrols, using aircraft such as the B-24 Liberator and the Short Sunderland, flew backwards and forwards across the mouth of the bay, killing submarines as they passed through the flight paths (indicated here in blue). In total, 65 U-boats were destroyed in this way.

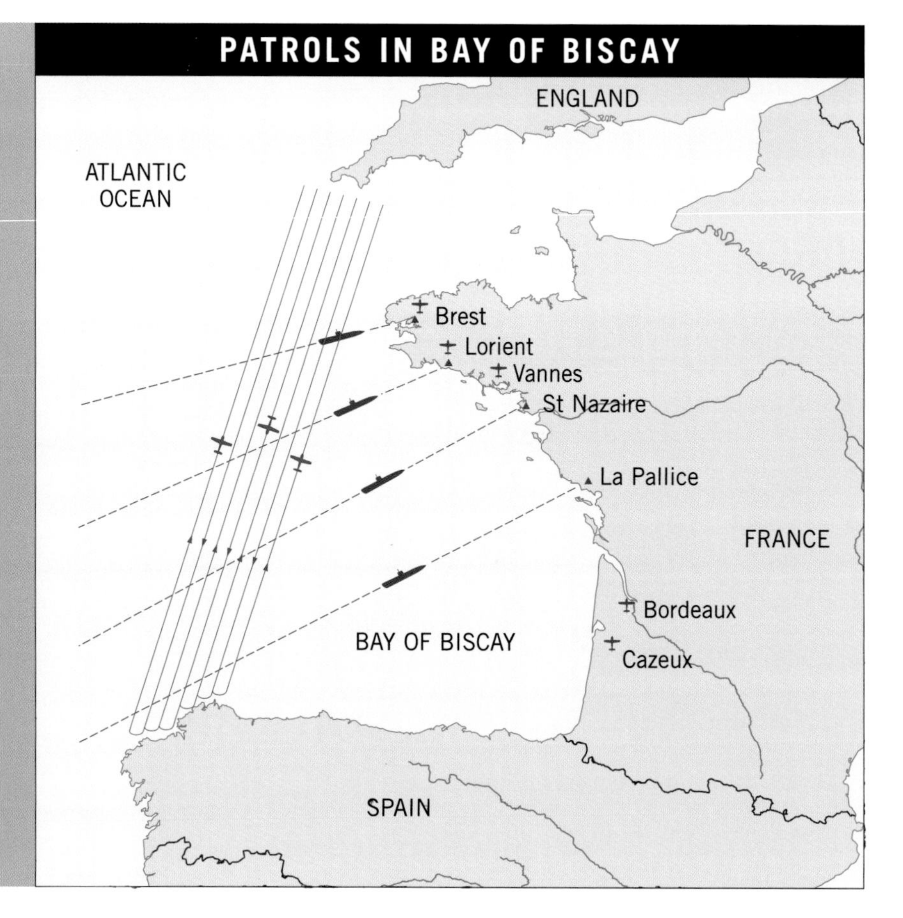

A U-boat wolf pack was steadily closing in on the convoy as it moved through the second half of its journey. In total, the wolf pack would consist of eight boats: *U-38, U-46, U-48, U-99, U-100, U-101, U-123* and *U-124*. Radio coordination for the attack came direct from Lorient, and the first kill was made on the 16th. By this time, rough Atlantic weather had caused some of the merchant ships to separate out from the convoy. One of them, the SS *Laker*, was spotted on the 16th and sunk by *U-123*, and the following day the SS *Aenos* went down, courtesy of *U-38*.

Thus, by the time the convoy entered the Western Approaches on the 17th, two ships were already lost. For the U-boats, though, these kills had been opportunistic strikes at isolated targets. Now, however, the wolf pack tactics came fully into play, despite the fact that in the Western Approaches SC7 received a slightly beefed-up escort in the form of the sloops *Fowey* and *Leith* and the corvettes *Bluebell* and *Heartsease*.

A brief attack on the convoy by the ever-eager *U-38* resulted in damage to the merchant ship SS *Carsbreck*, and *Heartsease* was deployed to escort the individual ship home, dropping away from the convoy. The main thrust of the wolf pack attack came on the night of the 18th/19th, when five U-boats worked their way up to and into the convoy. Many of the submarines actually sailed in formation with the convoy, using the cover of darkness to line up attacks at near point-blank range. The escorts were thrown into confusion as torpedoes began to slam with distressing regularity into the merchant ships. By the end of 19 October, 20 ships of SC7 had been sunk.

ALLIED SHIPPING LOSSES BY CAUSE, JAN–DEC 1941

Cause	Number Lost	Gross Tonnage
Submarine	222	777,300 tonnes (765,000 tons)
Mine	129	436,900 tonnes (430,000 tons)
Warship	16	62,700 tonnes (63,000 tons)
Aircraft	30	38,000 tonnes (37,000 tons)
Other	5	8128 tonnes (8000 tons)

ALLIED SHIPPING LOSSES BY LOCATION, JAN–DEC 1941

Location	Number Lost	Gross Tonnage
North Atlantic	75	377,000 tonnes (371,000 tons)
South Atlantic	8	49,800 tonnes (49,000 tons)
UK waters	319	897,000 tonnes (883,000 tons)

U-boat aces

The SC7 action constituted one of the worst convoy attacks of the entire war from the Allies' standpoint. From the *Kriegsmarine*'s point of view, it added further mystique to some of the rising stars of the U-boat arm. The kill rates of individual submarines during those terrible few hours were impressive. *U-46*, captained by Engelbert Endrass, sank three ships, as did *U-100* under Joachim Schepke. The *U-101* took out four merchant ships under its captain, Fritz Frauenheim.

The true stand-out name of the engagement was Otto Kretschmer, captain of *U-99*. Kretschmer had entered the U-boat service in 1936, and became a U-boat commander the following year. His first merchant ship sinking came on 12 January 1940, when as captain of *U-23* he sank the Danish tanker *Danmark*. It was the first of a prodigious run of kills, most of them made in the *U-99* submarine he commanded with such deadly effect against convoy SC7. During that single operation, he sank seven Allied ships, and over his 16-patrol career, he sent 44 ships to the bottom, totalling 266,629 gross registered tons.

Unlike many U-boat commanders, however, Kretschmer did not end his days in a U-boat. In March 1941, his vessel was forced to the surface by a depth charge during a battle with a British destroyer. Kretschmer was captured, along with the bulk of his crew. After the war he stayed in the navy, rising to the rank of *Flottillenadmiral* in the *Bundesmarine*, from which he retired in 1970.

Another U-boat ace, Erich Topp (35 ships sunk in 12 patrols), also rose to high rank in the postwar *Bundesmarine*. Not all of the other U-boat aces were as

WOLF PACK GROUP WEST

This particular wolf pack is seen as it was composed in June 1941. It was created from boats of the 1st and the 7th Flotillas and contained some of the *Kriegsmarine*'s latest submarines, including a Type IXC. The wolf pack deployed itself in waters to the southeast of the Grand Banks, spreading itself out across the Central Atlantic in the hope of encountering a convoy. On 23 June *U-203* spotted convoy OB336, and attacked and sank two merchant ships. Poor weather, however, meant that the rest of the wolf pack could not coordinate its attack, and the convoy was lost to sight in heavy fog. Poor weather also meant that the wolf pack was unable to intercept convoy OG66 later in the month.

Type VIIB

U-46

U-48

U-73

U-75

U-101

Type VIIC

U-77

U-204

U-553

U-557

U-558

U-751

Type IXA

U-43

Type IXB

U-108

U-111

Type IXC

U-66

lucky. The number two ace in Kretschmer's 7th Flotilla, Joachim Schepke (36 ships sunk in 14 patrols), died on 17 March 1941 when *U-100* was rammed and depth-charged in an attack by two British destroyers. The ace Günther Prien, as already noted, went down with *U-47* in March 1941.

The deaths of two top U-boat commanders in 1941, during the so-called 'Happy Time', proved that commanding a U-boat remained a dangerous business. In 1941, a total of 35 U-boats were destroyed in action, an ominous climb from the 24 boats that sunk the previous year.

Biting point

The wolf packs were paying off. In the first six months of 1941, the U-boats destroyed a total of 2,468,343 tonnes (2,429,340 tons) of British shipping, the type of figures that gave Churchill and the British Admiralty nightmares. The ultimate goal for the *Kriegsmarine*, in cooperation with *Luftwaffe* anti-shipping missions, was to

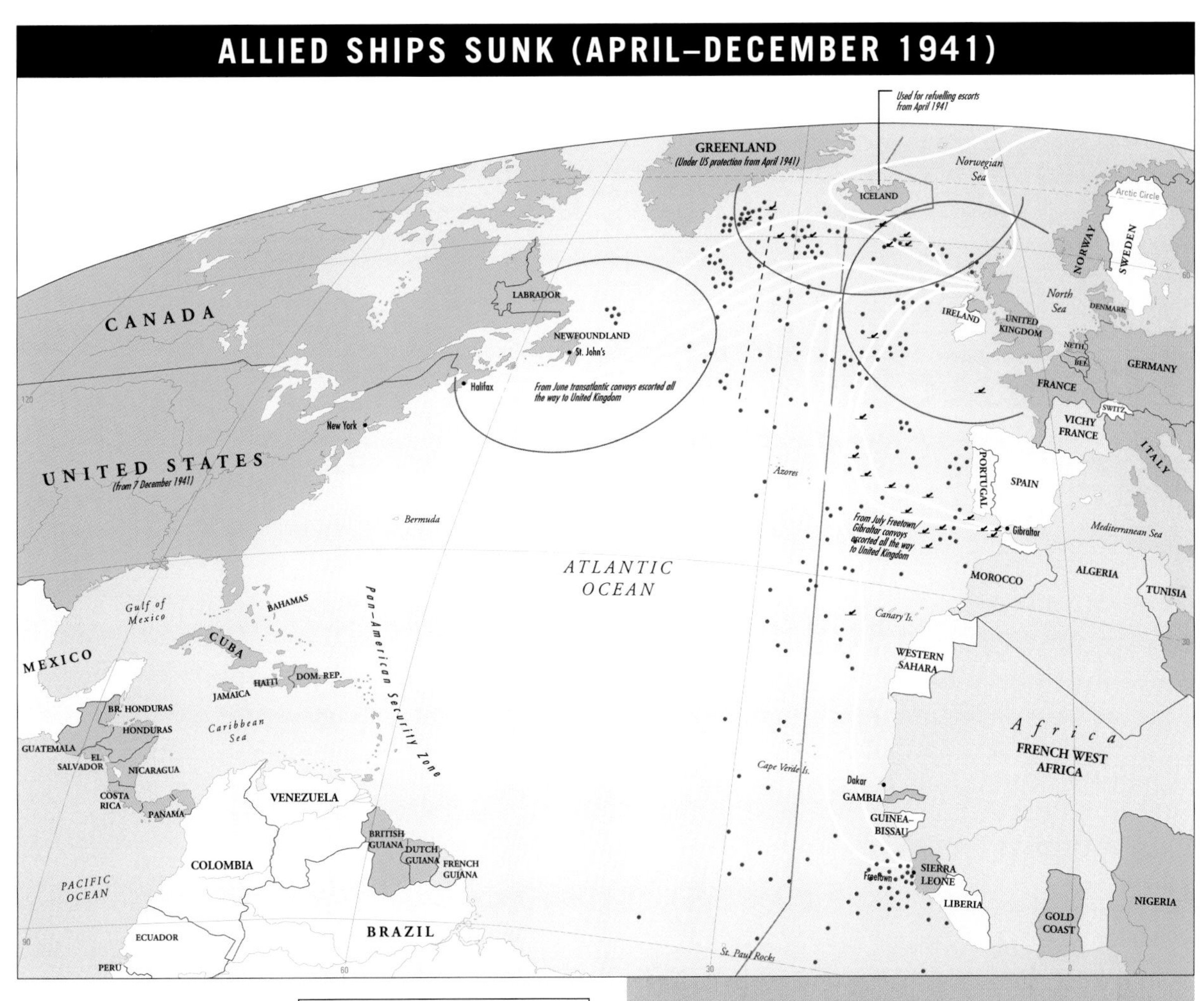

April–December 1941

- Limit of US merchant responsibility from April
- Extent of air escort cover
- Limit of surface escort cover
- Major convoy routes
- Allied merchant ships sunk by U-boats
- U-boats sunk
- Territory under Allied control
- Territory under Axis control
- Vichy French Territory
- Neutral territory

Air Cover Effects

During the second half of 1941, there was a noticeable spreading out across the Atlantic of merchant ship kills by U-boats. Note in particular, compared with earlier maps, how the waters directly around Britain and Ireland have become much safer for Allied merchant shipping, largely due to the improvement in anti-submarine air patrols.

Kill rates in the mid-Atlantic air gap and in the more southerly Atlantic waters, however, remained high, although it was often more problematic for U-boats to track down the convoys in these huge expanses of water. In essence, and with some periods of reversal, the Battle of the Atlantic was now starting to turn against the *Kriegsmarine*.

sink a total of 762,000 tonnes (750,000 tons) of shipping every month. It was believed that if this kill rate was achieved, Britain would inevitably be starved into submission, as the sinkings would far outstrip production of new vessels. Certainly, the situation was dire for the Allies. In the whole of 1941, the United States and United Kingdom between them produced 2,345,508 tonnes (2,308,465 tons) of new merchant ships, and the total sinkings for that year exceeded this figure by nearly a million tonnes.

Yet it was not a time for German complacency. The heavy losses meant that the Allies were now giving the war against the U-boats top priority. The 'Happy Time' would soon be over.

The effects of Allied intelligence

It is hard to exaggerate the importance of Allied intelligence gains over U-boat communications traffic in 1941. From being completely ignorant of the submarines' whereabouts, the Allies now had direct insight into their deployments.

By early 1941, the position of Britain in the supply war could hardly have been bleaker. The military historian Robert Jackson notes how the war in the Atlantic was directly affecting life in UK society:

'At the beginning of 1941, food stocks in Britain were dangerously low: there was enough wheat for 15 weeks; meat for only two weeks; butter for eight weeks on ration; margarine for three weeks on ration; and bacon for 27 weeks on ration. There were no longer any stocks of imported fruit.

All this added up to the grim fact that, unless merchant ship sinkings could be reduced, Britain would starve before new merchant vessels could be built fast enough to maintain imports at the level needed for her survival.' (Robert Jackson, *The German Navy in World War II*).

Radio traffic

What was needed to turn the tables against the German submarine arm was more than additional escort vessels for the convoys. Instead, a method had to be found to gain tactical superiority over the U-boats from the very moment they were deployed, avoiding confrontations rather than engaging in them. In short, intelligence would be the key. The Allies had long been aware of the buzz of communications traffic between U-boats and with their shore bases. The problem was cracking the high-grade enciphering system used by the *Kriegsmarine*. A good deal of the German communications were put through the now famous 'Enigma' machine, an encoding device that scrambled a message to a virtually impenetrable degree for those who did not have a receiving Enigma machine.

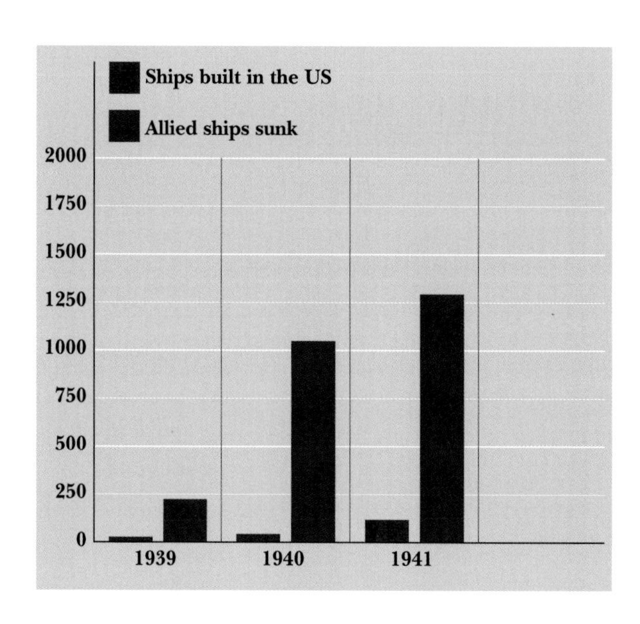

Right: The gross disparity between the numbers of merchant ships built in the US and the volumes sunk by the U-boats was a cause for huge Allied concern between 1939 and 1941.

The code settings for the machines were changed on a daily basis, meaning that yesterday's code-breaking solutions could become operationally redundant in a single night.

During the late 1930s, the Poles were actually reading some Enigma traffic, but by the early stages of World War II the German intelligence community had altered the settings of Enigma once more, putting the messages out of reach.

Between 1939 and early 1941, the Allies were largely in the dark about German data traffic, until a seminal event on 8 May 1941. On that day, the British destroyer

7TH FLOTILLA (1 DECEMBER 1940)

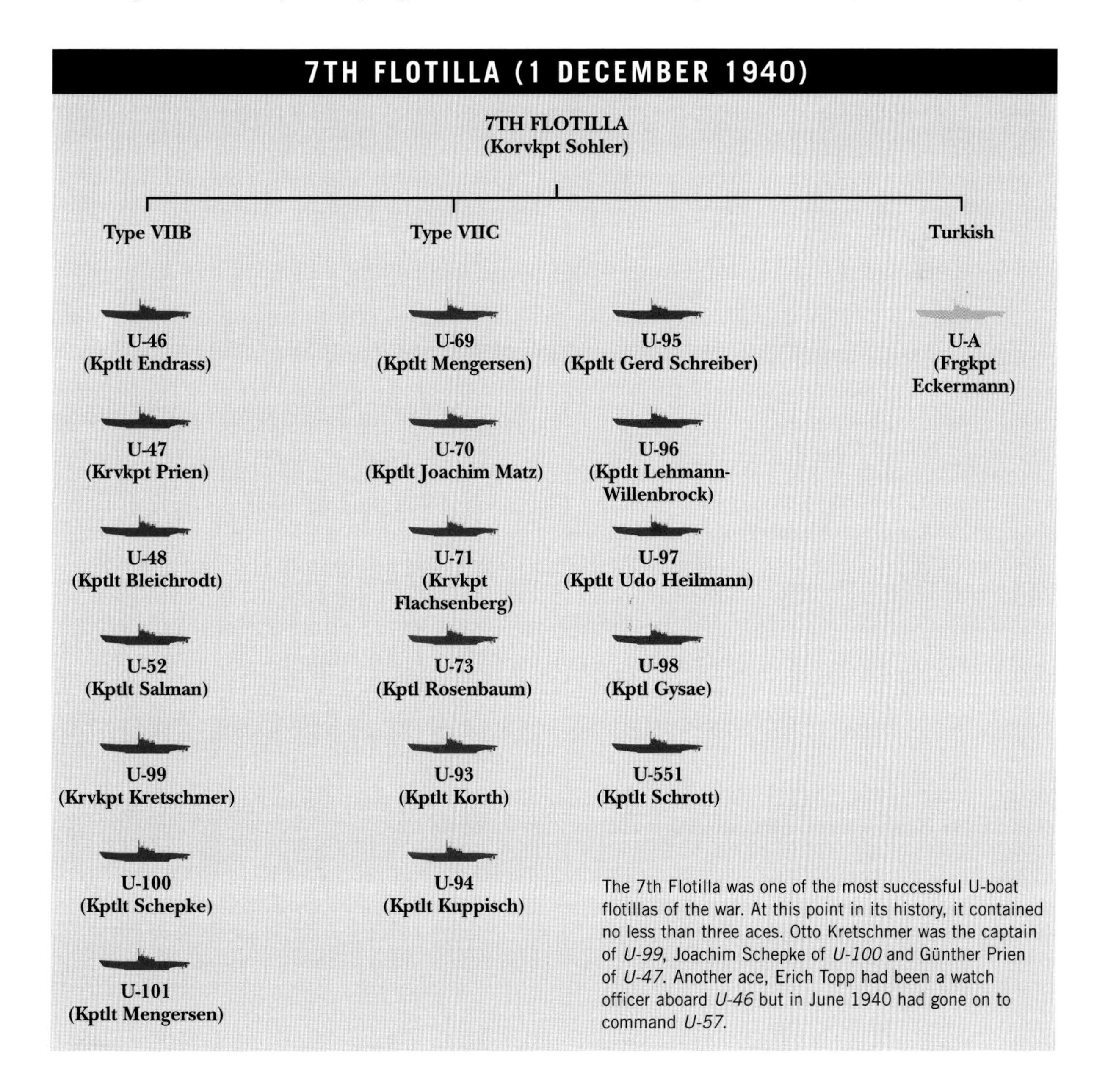

The 7th Flotilla was one of the most successful U-boat flotillas of the war. At this point in its history, it contained no less than three aces. Otto Kretschmer was the captain of *U-99*, Joachim Schepke of *U-100* and Günther Prien of *U-47*. Another ace, Erich Topp had been a watch officer aboard *U-46* but in June 1940 had gone on to command *U-57*.

U-48 TIMETABLE		
Patrol Dates	**Operational Area**	**Ships Sunk**
19 Aug 1939 – 17 Sep 1939	West of Biscay	3
4 Oct 1939 – 25 Oct 1939	West of Finisterre	5
20 Nov 1939 – 20 Dec 1939	Orkneys/Channel approaches	4
24 Jan 1940 – 26 Feb 1940	Channel approaches	4
3 Apr 1940 – 20 Apr 1940	Norway	0
26 May 1940 – 29 Jun 1940	West northwest of Finisterre	7
7 Aug 1940 – 28 Aug 1940	West southwest of Rockall	5
8 Sep 1940 – 25 Sep 1940	West of British Isles	8
5 Oct 1940 – 27 Oct 1940	Northwest of Rockall	7
20 Jan 1941 – 27 Feb 1941	South of Iceland	2
17 Mar 1941 – 8 Apr 1941	South of Iceland	5
22 May 1941 – 21 Jun 1941	West of St Nazaire (supporting *Bismarck*)/North of the Azores/ Central Atlantic	5
Jun 1941 – 1945	Served with 26 and 21 Flotillas as a training boat	0
Oct 1943	Decommissioned: used by 3. *Unterseeboots-Lehrdivision*	–
3 May 1945	Scuttled at Neustadt	–

MERCHANT SHIP LOSSES: ALL THEATRES								
	British		**Other Allied**		**Neutral**		**Total**	
Date	**Number**	**Gross Tons**	**Number**	**Gross Tons**	**Number**	**Gross Tons**	**Number**	**Gross Tons**
1939 (Sep–Dec)	158	498,000	17	90,000	148	347,000	323	935,000
1940	728	2,725,000	201	822,000	416	1,002,000	1345	4,549,000
1941	892	3,047,000	344	1,299,000	183	347,000	1419	4,693,000
1942	782	3,695,000	987	4,394,000	90	249,000	1859	8,338,000
1943	361	1,678,000	388	1,886,000	63	82,000	812	3,646,000
Total	2921	11,643,000	1937	8,491,000	900	2,027,000	5758	22,161,000

Bulldog attacked the U-boat *U-110* , which had been shadowing an Allied convoy, and forced it to the surface with depth charges. The ship was captured, along with an Enigma machine and its short-range code books. This was an event of seismic importance in the war against the U-boats.

Breaking into Enigma

It enabled the code-breakers at the Government Code and Cypher School, particularly those in the Bletchley Park mansion in Buckinghamshire, to read the *Kriegsmarine* short-range U-boat sighting reports and weather report transmissions. From this they were able to build up to reading more important codes, such as those intended for officers only, and by the August of 1941 they were reading most of the 'Home Waters' communications traffic of the German Navy.

The intelligence produced by the breaking of the Enigma code, plus intelligence from several other code-breaking activities, was known as 'Ultra', and it would

change the fate of many U-boat crews in the South Atlantic, at least in terms of their war-winning potential.

Allied survival

Once it fed into the system from July 1941, the effect of the Ultra intelligence was visible. It gave the Allies details of U-boat deployments and whereabouts, although the coordinates where often not exact. Most important was that convoys could be routed away from zones in which U-boats were known to be waiting.

Payback from this intelligence was instant and dramatic. Looking at the May–August 1941 figures, we see that in May and June a total of 869,531 tonnes (851,799 tons) of British merchant shipping was sunk. The figure for July 1941, however, dropped to just 114,892 tonnes (113,078 tons), and in the August it fell still further to 105,112 tonnes (103,452 tons).

The figures wobbled during the remainder of the year, peaking at 258,859 tonnes (254,761 tons) in September but dropping to a low of 86,872 tonnes (85,500 tons) in November. (The September rise was on account of renewed difficulties in deciphering the coordinates of the U-boat wolf packs, but these problems were solved by the following month.)

German frustration

The obstacles for the U-boats were increased by the fact that RAF Coastal Command air patrols had become so efficient that the U-boats had to push outwards into the deeper, wider waters of the North and mid-Atlantic beyond aircraft range. Although these areas were safer, they were also much more challenging in terms of finding convoys, so the Allies' evasive routing tactics were even more effective.

U-333 (TYPE VIIC)	
Commissioned	25 August 1941
Crew	44–52
Displacement	871 tonnes (857 tons) submerged
Dimensions	Length: 66.5m(218ft); Beam: 6.2m (20.3ft)
Range	Surfaced: 15,750km (9785 miles) at 18.5km/h (10kts); Submerged: 150km (93 miles) at 7.4km/h (4kts)
Armament	5 x 533mm (21in) torpedo tubes; 1 x 88mm (3.5in) deck gun; 1 x AA gun
Powerplant	Surfaced: diesels 2089kW (2800hp); Submerged: electric motors 559kW (750hp)
Performance	Surfaced: 32.4km/h (17.5kts); Submerged: 12.7km/h (6.9kts)

For the U-boat crews, and for Dönitz in particular, the second half of 1941 was a time of intense frustration. The wolf packs covered thousands of kilometres, yet often returned from their patrols with no kills. Even with 80 boats on station, more than in any previous year, kill ratios had dropped substantially.

Incredibly, the Germans were never aware that it was the Enigma machine that had been compromised. Another important advantage held by the Allies in the Atlantic in 1941 was that from September increasing numbers of U-boats were filtered off into the Italian theatre, moved there to support a failing Italian Navy and to prey on the Allied shipping convoys fuelling the war in North Africa (see below). The first 'Happy Time' was over, but the breathing space for the Allies was in fact only temporary. For the U-boat crews, the second 'Happy Time' was just round the corner.

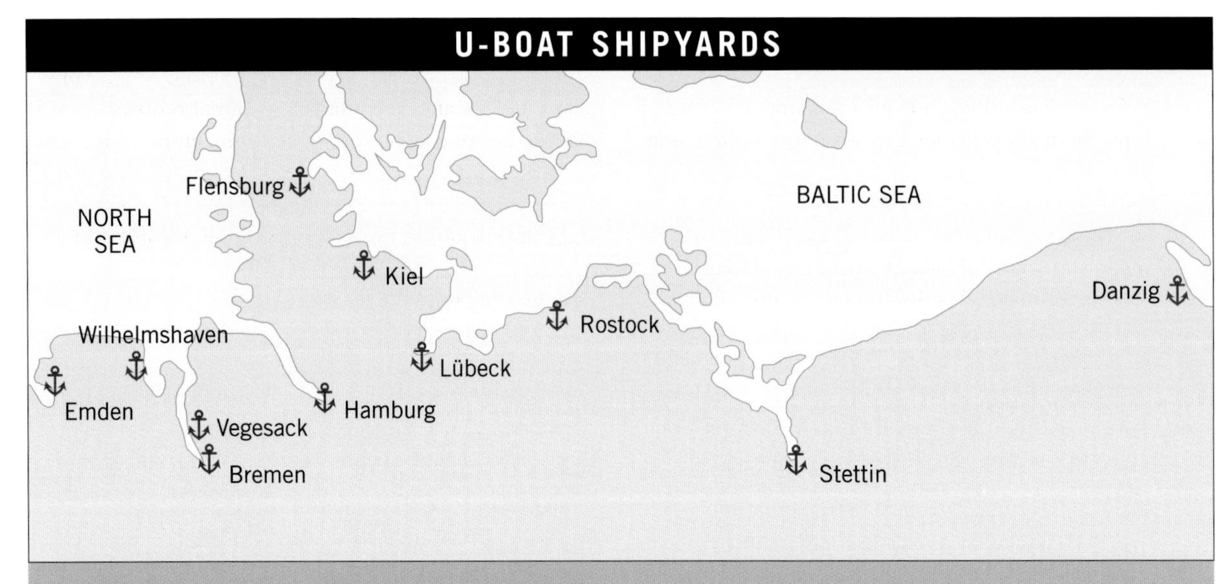

U-boat construction, 1939–45

U-boats were produced at a total of 19 shipyards, situated in 11 cities along the German coastal territories. The cities were (beginning in the west): Emden, Wilhelmshaven, Bremen, Vegesack, Hamburg, Flensburg, Kiel, Lübeck, Rostock, Stettin and Danzig. The most productive centre of all was Hamburg, where four shipyards (including the great Blohm und Voss) produced a total of 394 U-boats during the war years, while in second place came Kiel with 231 U-boats produced.

The Neptun Werft AG at Rostock, by contrast, produced only 10 U-boats between 1939 and 1945. The peak year for U-boat production was 1942, when the combined efforts of all these shipyards yielded 282 submarines, and they made 200-plus such vessels every year until 1945.

Long-range operations

The U-boat war in the Atlantic was not only carried out in the shipping lanes between North America and the United Kingdom. Other very long-range U-boats penetrated deep into the South Atlantic, preying on ships off the coast of Africa.

The U-boats used for South Atlantic operations were almost always Type IXs. These had been developed with ultra-long range in mind, and by the end of 1940 that range had grown very long indeed. The basic Type IX boat had a surfaced range of 16,897km (10,500 miles), a fine range in itself but one that was far exceeded by the subsequent versions of this type. The following figures give the surfaced ranges for the main subsequent Type IXs, all of which were in production by the end of 1940:

Type IXB	19,311km (12,000 miles)
Type IXC	21,645km (13,450 miles)
Type IXC/40	22,289km (13,850 miles)
Type IXD	38,140km (23,700 miles)

These prodigious range capabilities meant that Type IX patrols were soon preying on British shipping moving out of West Africa, although Dönitz was initially none too happy about his precious U-boats being pulled away from their main hunting grounds further north.

Yet there was no denying that the West African areas could, with a bit of luck, be massively profitable. In fact, the war's most successful U-boat patrol was actually conducted against British shipping sailing out of Freetown. Between March and July 1941, the U-boat commander *Kapitänleutnant* Günther Hessler hunted Allied merchant shipping off Africa in *U-107*. During the course of this patrol, the submarine sank 14 ships totalling 88,090 tonnes (86,699 tons), an incredible achievement for a single craft.

Resupplying

The seemingly endless distances between coastal France and the waters off West Africa made resupply a particular headache for the U-boat crews. Initially, they were supplied by surface vessels, either merchant ships working out of neutral ports or German warships. Also, the U-boats made moderate use of the Canary Islands as resupply ports, taking advantage of Spain's Axis-leaning tendencies during the war.

During the second half of 1941, however, the British became much better at hunting down these lone vessels through a combination of air and naval patrols. Furthermore, diplomatic pressure from the Allies on Spain, pointing to an apparent breach of its neutrality, meant that the Canary Islands were obliged to close their doors to German U-boats. Another solution had to be found to keep these distant ships on station.

The answer was the resupply submarine. The first of 10 Type XIV *Milchkuh* (Milk Cow) submarines was commissioned in November 1941 and went on patrol for the first time the following March. The type had no significant weaponry but was designed to carry not only spare fuel for another submarine, but also other essential stores, such as food, clothing, ammunition and replacement parts. As long as they could meet up with the resupply submarine on a fairly regular basis, then the U-boats could remain on station almost indefinitely.

New hunting grounds

Looking at the patterns of Allied ship sinkings between 1940 and September 1943, we see an inexorable spread of sinkings down into the Atlantic passages off West Africa and Brazil, including the intervening waters directly between these points. When conditions for the U-boats became much tougher later in 1942, the South Atlantic offered somewhat safer hunting grounds, beyond the scope of Allied air cover. Furthermore, at the very end of the war some U-boats here were able to make their escape to South America.

U-107 (TYPE IXB)	
Commissioned	8 October 1970
Crew	48–56
Displacement	1178 tonnes (1159 tons)
Dimensions	Length: 78.5m (258ft); Beam: 6.7m (22ft)
Range	Surfaced: 19,311km (12,000 miles) at 18.5km/h (10kts); Submerged: 103km (64 miles) at 7.4km/h (4kts)
Armament	4 x 533mm (21in) torpedo tubes; 1 x 105mm (4.1in) deck gun; 2 x AA guns
Powerplant	Surfaced: diesels 3281kW (4400hp); Submerged: electric motors 745kW (1000hp)

The U-Boat War: 1942–45

On 11 December 1941, Adolf Hitler declared war on the United States. It was a fateful decision, and one that ultimately accelerated Germany's final defeat. In the short run, however, it brought the second 'Happy Time' to the U-boat crews.

'Milk Cow' submarines head out on resupply operations, working to keep combat U-boats on station.

In 1941 the war seemed to be turning against the U-boats in the Atlantic. The Allies had gained an intelligence advantage through cracking a significant percentage of naval communications codes, resulting in a major drop in merchant sinkings. New convoy escort weapons were also coming into service (see below), creating a more lethal environment for the submariners. Allied anti-submarine air patrols were steadily extending their ranges, pushing the U-boats further and further out into the Atlantic. Soon Germany and the U-boats would have another concern on their minds – war with the largest industrial power on earth.

Increasing tensions

For over two years, Hitler had been tiptoeing around the United States, much to Raeder's chagrin. During these years the United States was not a declared combatant, but there was no doubt as to whose side it was on. Not only had it supplied the UK with 50 destroyers as additional escorts back in 1940, but it was also the major producer of the merchant ships that carried supplies in convoy across the Atlantic. The Atlantic Charter agreement, signed by Churchill and President Franklin D. Roosevelt at the Placentia Bay conference in August 1941, included the commitment by the United States to preserve the freedom of the seas for commercial traffic, a commitment squarely aimed at a warring Germany and an increasingly belligerent Japan in the Far East. Even before this, in October 1939, the United States had established the Pan-American Security Zone around its eastern coastal waters. This zone, in which the United States forbade acts of war, extended in some places for thousands of kilometres from the US coast, and in the north ran up to, and later beyond, the Icelandic approaches, a key staging post for Allied convoys. Within the zone, US destroyers provided escorts for British and Canadian convoys, including alerting them to the presence of U-boats when spotted.

Hitler was deeply unhappy about this arrangement, but initially gave orders for his U-boat crews to avoid incidents that might lead to direct confrontation. That situation changed entirely in December 1941.

U-BOAT BASES (JUNE 1943)

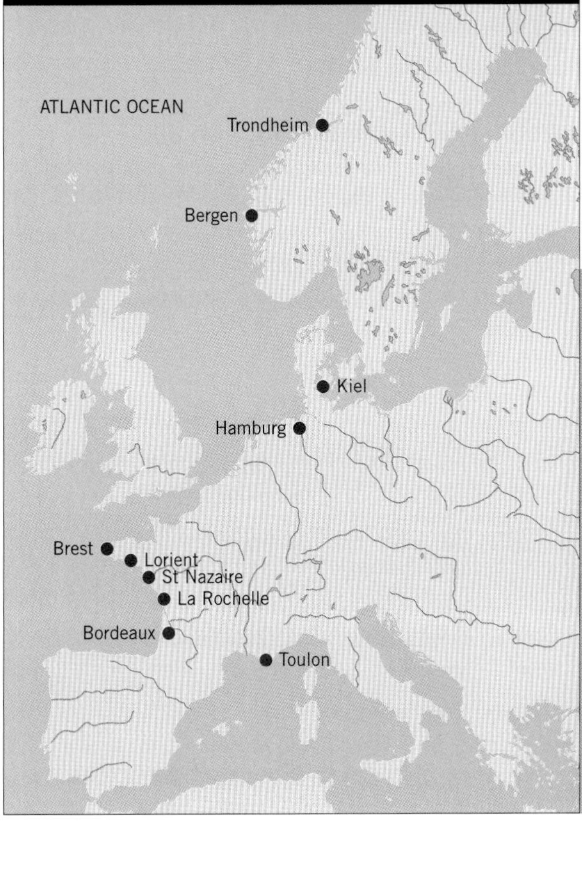

Broad deployments

This map shows the principal U-boat bases by June 1943, at which point the Battle of the Atlantic was turning irrevocably against Germany. Dönitz, who in January 1943 became commander-in-chief of the *Kriegsmarine*, had been particularly aggrieved when valuable U-boat resources were sent up to Norway in late 1941, arguing that they would sink far more Allied shipping if they were retained in the Atlantic. No one disagreed, but the German high command feared an Allied invasion of the north, so kept some U-boats on station in that region.

The Mediterranean also drew U-boats away from the Atlantic campaign, and to a far greater extent, with Toulon as the principal U-boat station serving that theatre. In both the naval and the land war, Hitler was frequently guilty of attempting to spread forces too thinly to cope with the demands of multiple fronts.

Enter the United States

Once the United States entered the war, the U-boats had a whole new stretch of water in which to hunt. Combined with a a tightening of their communications encryption, this resulted in the second 'Happy Time'.

WOLFGANG LÜTH (1913–45)

Wolfgang Lüth was second only to Otto Kretschmer in terms of Allied merchant tonnage sunk. His navy career began in 1933, and he transferred to U-boats in 1937, becoming a U-boat commander in December 1939.

• Lüth's deployments took him from the North Atlantic to the Indian Ocean. From 1939 to 1944, he sank 46 merchantmen (225,204 GRT). He also made the war's second-longest U-boat patrol (205 days), in *U-181*.

• In January 1944, he became commander of the 22nd Flotilla, a training formation, then head of the *Marineschule* from July.

• On 13 May 1945, with Germany already surrendered, Lüth was shot and killed by a nervous German sentry outside the *Marineschule*.

Even before the United States entered World War II, following the Japanese attack on Pearl Harbor on 7 December 1941, the U-boats were already coming to blows with US ships. Admittedly, this friction was more by accident than design, and resulted from the simple fact that the U-boats were hunting the very convoys to which the US fleet was giving some level of protection. Hitler had given a direct order that under no circumstances were the U-boats to attack US warships, unless the U-boats were attacked themselves.

'Accidental' clashes

Inevitably, this tense situation would lead to direct engagements between US escorts and the U-boats. On 4 September 1941, for example, *U-652* was detected shadowing a convoy by a British patrol aircraft, which subsequently dropped four depth charges while the US destroyer USS *Greer* closed in on the U-boat. The U-boat's captain, Georg-Werner Fraatz, may have believed that the detonations were from the destroyer, and fired a torpedo at it. It missed, and there followed a two-hour battle in which both sides attacked without success. Although there was no ultimate military cost for either side, the diplomatic fall-out was intense, with each side accusing the other of escalating the conflict.

The result was that tension increased, and the U-boat crews became far less willing to accommodate the supposed US neutrality. US destroyers now began to use their depth charges more frequently, and the U-boats responded in kind, damaging a US destroyer escort in early October with a torpedo attack.

Matters came to a head on 31 October, during an attack by *U-552* on convoy HX156. During the action, the U-boat torpedoed a destroyer escort, which subsequently blew up, killing two-thirds of the crew. The hapless ship turned out to be the USS *Reuben James*, and she was the first US ship to be destroyed in combat

***U-333* TIMETABLE**		
Patrol Dates	**Operational Area**	**Ships Sunk**
27 Dec 1941 – 9 Feb 1942	Transit from Kiel to La Pallice via North Atlantic	3
30 Mar 1942 – 26 May 1942	US coast off Florida	3
11 Aug 1942 – 24 Aug 1942	Central Atlantic – returned after damage	0
1 Sep 1942 – 23 Oct 1942	Central Atlantic – returned damaged	0
20 Dec 1942 – 2 Feb 1943	North Atlantic	0
5 Feb 1943 – 13 Apr 1943	North Atlantic	1
2 Jun 1943 – 31 Aug 1943	Central Atlantic	0
21 Oct 1943 – 1 Dec 1943	Off Spanish coast – returned damaged	0
10 Feb 1944 – 12 Feb 1944	North Atlantic – returned with mechanical fault	0
14 Feb 1944 – 20 Apr 1944	North Atlantic	0
6 Jun 1944 – 13 Jun 1944	Channel invasion front	1
23 Jul 1944 – 31 Jul 1944	English Channel	0

3RD FLOTILLA (1 AUGUST 1942)

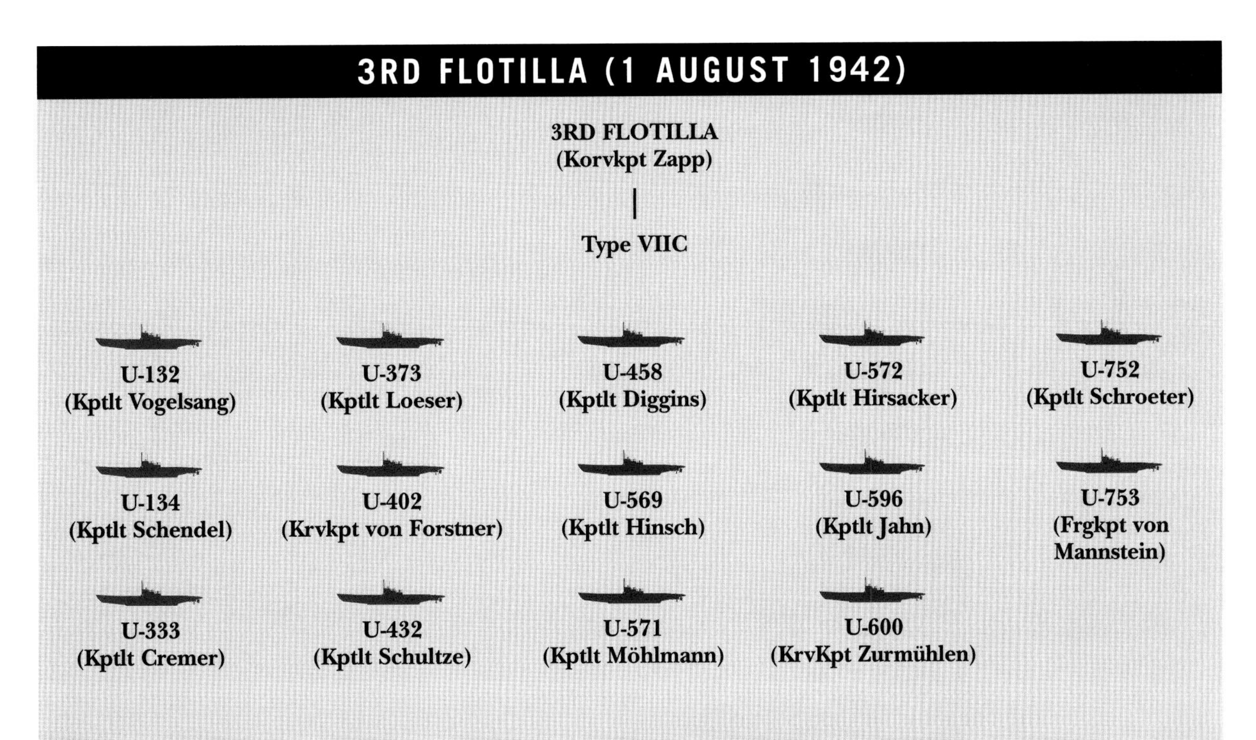

By August 1942, the 3rd Flotilla was on its fifth and final commander, in the form of the great *Korvettenkapitän* Richard Zapp. Although Zapp was an ace, the fact that the flotilla was re-formed after the first 'Happy Time' meant that the unit was generally low-scoring when compared with some of the true transatlantic U-boat flotillas. In total, the flotilla had 90 Type VIIC submarines during its lifetime, and also utilized four captured submarines in its ranks.

during World War II. Many more would follow over the next months.

Fresh targets

The entry of the United States into war against Germany had the immediate effect of rendering the Pan-American Security Zone void. The U-boats now had new hunting opportunities, which included not only the regular convoys as soon as they moved out of US ports, but also the American coastal traffic plying up and down the eastern seaboard. Dönitz had actually been planning for this moment for some time. Back in September

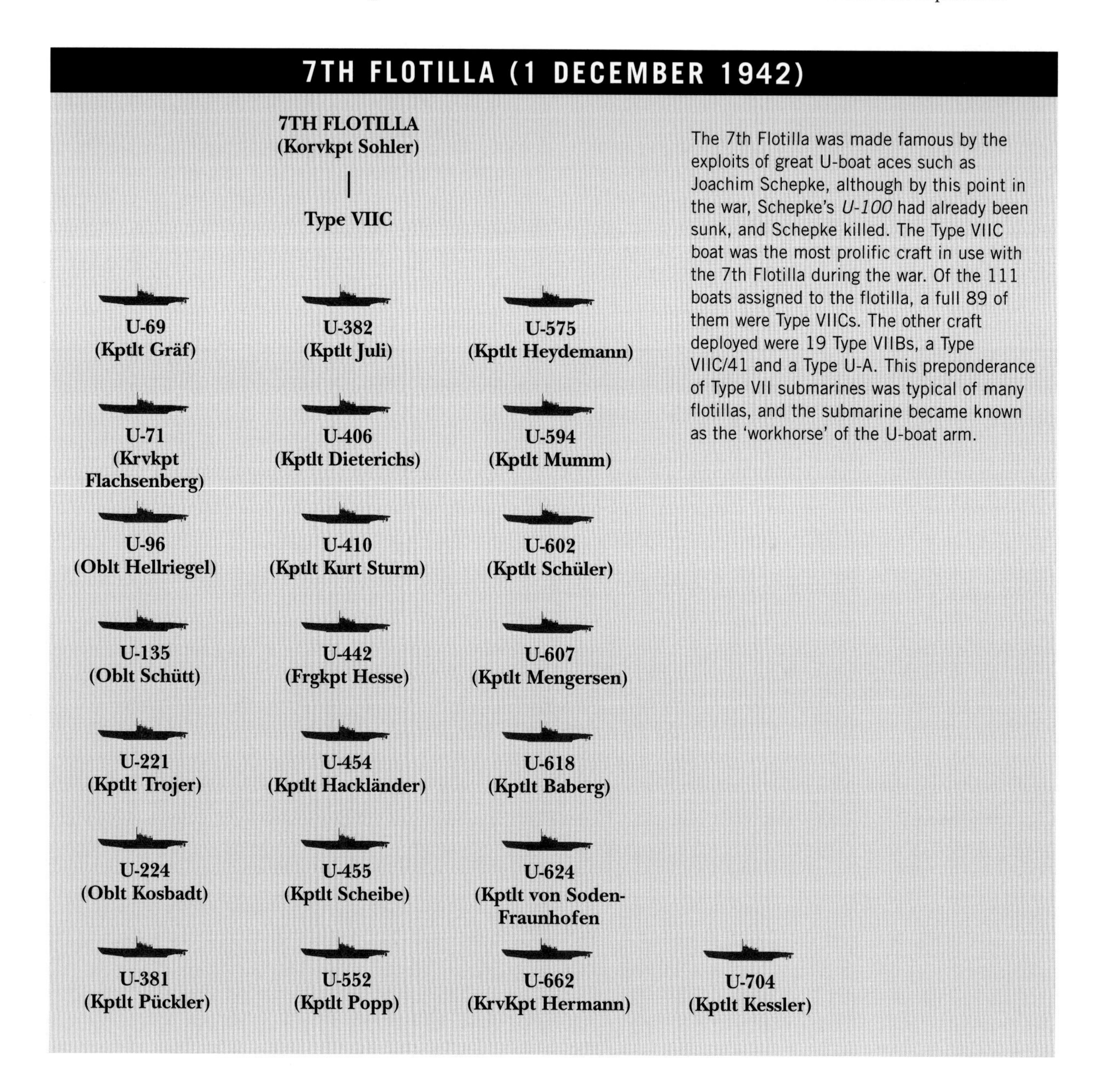

The 7th Flotilla was made famous by the exploits of great U-boat aces such as Joachim Schepke, although by this point in the war, Schepke's *U-100* had already been sunk, and Schepke killed. The Type VIIC boat was the most prolific craft in use with the 7th Flotilla during the war. Of the 111 boats assigned to the flotilla, a full 89 of them were Type VIICs. The other craft deployed were 19 Type VIIBs, a Type VIIC/41 and a Type U-A. This preponderance of Type VII submarines was typical of many flotillas, and the submarine became known as the 'workhorse' of the U-boat arm.

1941, he began designing what he would label Operation *Paukenschlag* (Drumbeat), a U-boat campaign directly within the eastern coastal waters of the United States. The Type VII U-boats simply did not have the range for these operations, especially as the use of surface tankers was no longer viable.

Long-range Type IXC

To this end, Dönitz requested the building of 12 Type IXC submarines. He was to be disappointed, as in the end he could shake out only five such vessels from the German high command. (Six Type IX craft were retained in the Mediterranean.)

Dönitz was highly disappointed, as he correctly believed that the hunting would be good. The United States was unprepared for an intensive U-boat campaign. Its escort tactics and weapon systems were inadequate, and the element of surprise would be significant. Furthermore, there were many prize targets sailing US waters, including huge tankers and merchant vessels that displaced more than 10,160 tonnes (10,000 tons).

Dönitz compensated for the lack of U-boats by selecting five of his most experienced commanders for the operation. These were *Fregattenkapitän* Richard Zapp (*U-66*), *Kapitänleutnant* Heinrich Bleichrodt (*U-109*), *Kapitänleutnant* Reinhard Hardegen (*U-123*),

12TH FLOTILLA (1 DECEMBER 1942)

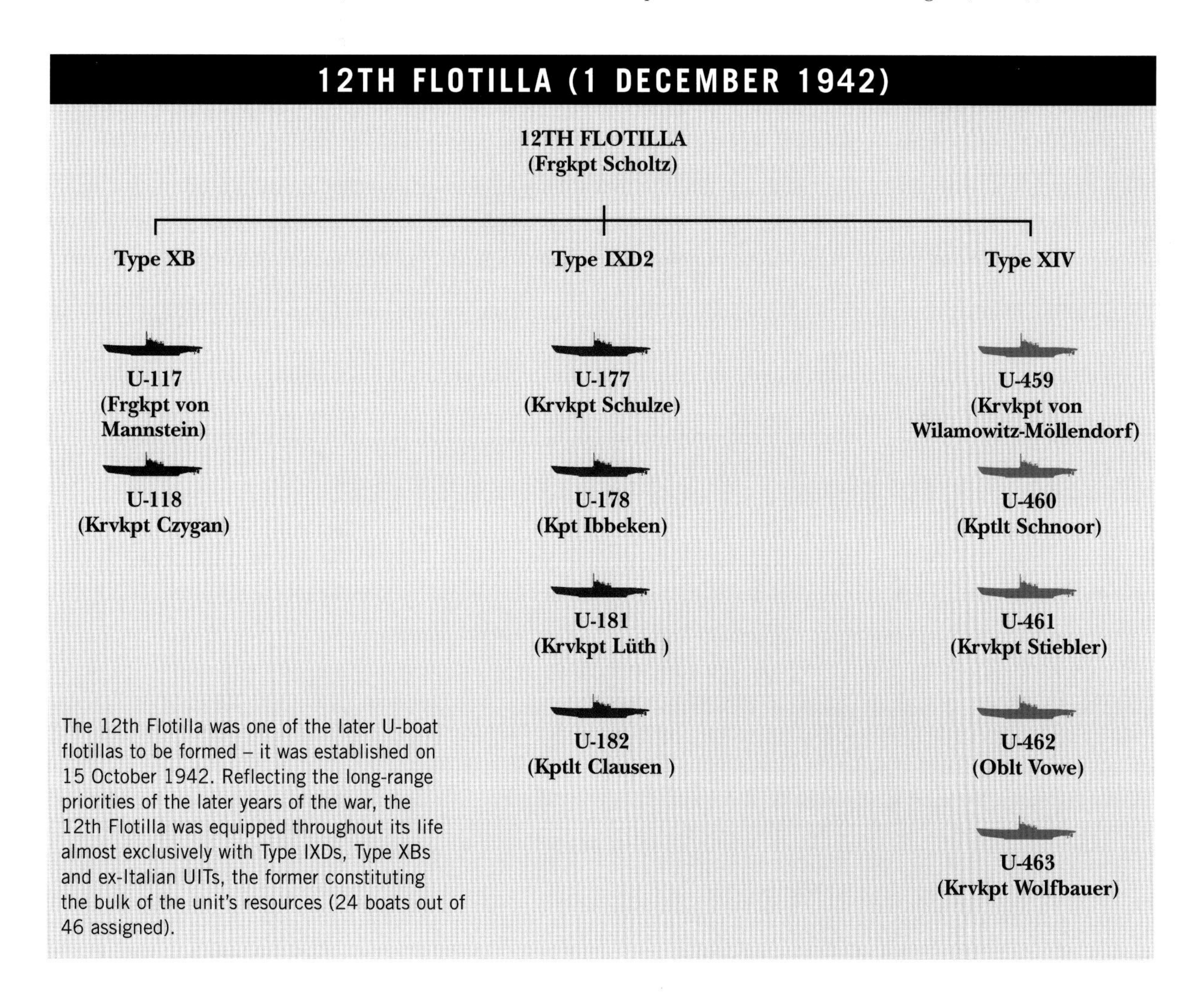

The 12th Flotilla was one of the later U-boat flotillas to be formed – it was established on 15 October 1942. Reflecting the long-range priorities of the later years of the war, the 12th Flotilla was equipped throughout its life almost exclusively with Type IXDs, Type XBs and ex-Italian UITs, the former constituting the bulk of the unit's resources (24 boats out of 46 assigned).

SHIPS SUNK BY GERMAN OR ITALIAN SUBMARINES	
Date	**Allied ships sunk by Axis submarines**
1939	147
1940	520
1941	457
1942	1155
1943	452
1944	125
1945	63
Total	2919

Kapitänleutnant Ulrich Folkers (*U-125*) and *Fregattenkapitän* Ernst Kals (*U-130*). On 18 December 1941, these five commanders and their vessels left France, loaded to the maximum possible extent with fuel, food and ammunition. They were headed for the waters off New York, but had few navigational charts, and even had to rely on tourist maps to give them an idea of what features were to be found along the coastline.

Despite the challenges of sailing across the entire width of the Atlantic Ocean, the five boats had settled themselves on station off the coast of North America by mid-January 1942. They straddled positions ranging from the waters off North Carolina up to Nova Scotia, waiting for targets to appear.

Opening salvos

The first ship to fall to *Paukenschlag* was the British freighter *Cyclops* on 12 January, and a further five ships were claimed over the next five days, all of them around the sea lanes extending outwards from New York. This was actually a disappointing return for Dönitz, and in response he gave the U-boats more leeway to patrol further afield.

It was a sound move, and in total between 21 January and 6 March 1942 the five Type IX boats sent another 19 merchantmen to the ocean floor. To reinforce the effect further north, there were also 12 Type VIIC U-boats operating off Grand Banks from 8 January, and by 12 February alone these had sunk 21 merchant ships. Another eight Type VIIC craft sank a further nine vessels off the eastern seaboard during a similar period.

Gradually, the war against US shipping was starting to hot up, and the U-boat commanders were once again enjoying high kill rates. The year would, however, get much worse for the Allies.

The second 'Happy Time'

By mid-1942, numbers of merchant ships sinking in the Atlantic had reached record levels. The U-boats were sinking millions of tons of Allied vessels and it seemed once again that the *Kriegsmarine* was potentially a war-winning force.

Once the U-boat crews fell into their full operational rhythm off the US coast, the massacre they unleashed was of breathtaking proportions. The following are the gross tonnages of merchant vessels sunk in the Atlantic between January and June 1942. They give a chilling indication of how effective the 1942 offensive was and what an impact it had on the Allied war effort:

January	300,888 tonnes (296,136 tons)
February	448,065 tonnes (440,989 tons)
March	571,359 tonnes (562,336 tons)
April	501,734 tonnes (493,810 tons)
May	655,174 tonnes (644,827 tons)
June	662,957 tonnes (652,487 tons)

These were incredible kill rates for the U-boats, which in just May and June achieved about half their success rate for the whole of the previous year. The monthly tonnages of Allied merchant vessels sunk would, furthermore, stay at more than 508,023 tonnes (500,000 tons) for the rest of the year apart from December. This was truly the second 'Happy Time' for Dönitz's men.

So what were the factors that gave the U-boats this renewed period of influence? First, the US merchant navy and the US Navy itself persisted, often against the pleading advice of the British Admiralty, in using outdated tactics. They would deploy ships singly rather than in convoy, and worse still, the ships followed regular routes on which the U-boats would simply sit and wait for their next victim to come along.

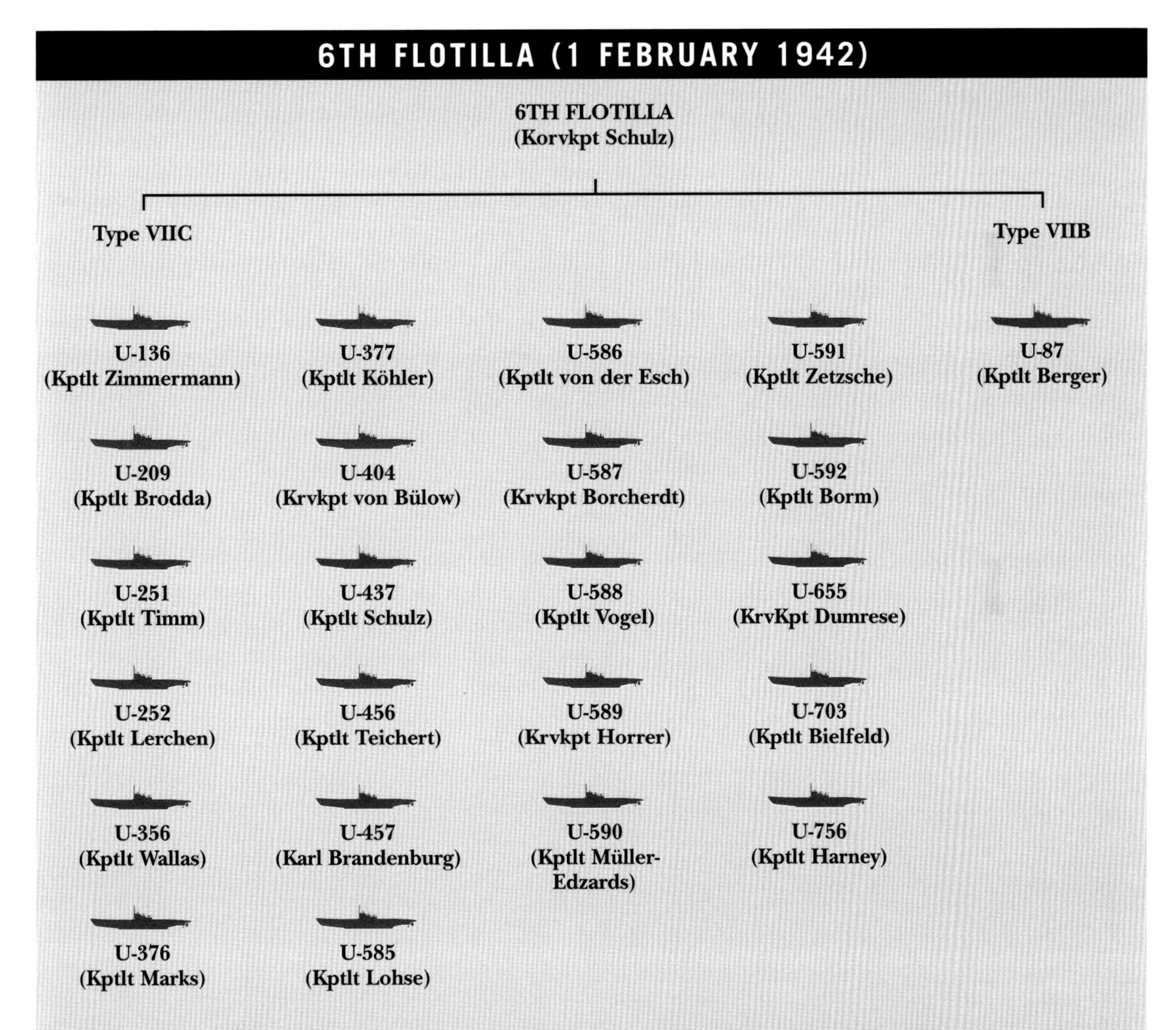

The 6th Flotilla was another of the prewar U-boat flotillas, and was formed at Kiel on 1 October 1938. As with many other prewar formations, its original name, *U-Flottille Hundius,* harked back to a World War I U-boat ace. *Hundius* was disbanded in December 1939, but then re-formed as the 6th Flotilla in July 1941, based initially at Danzig before moving down to St Nazaire in February 1942.

U-404 (TYPE VIIC)	
Commissioned	6 August 1941
Crew	44–52
Displacement	871 tonnes (857 tons) submerged
Dimensions	Length: 66.5m (218ft); Beam: 6.2m (20.3ft)
Range	Surfaced: 15,750km (9785 miles) at 18.5km/h (10kts); Submerged: 150km (93 miles) at 7.4km/h (4kts)
Armament	5 x 533mm (21in) torpedo tubes; 1 x 88mm (3.5in) deck gun; 1 x AA gun
Powerplant	Surfaced: diesels 2089kW (2800hp); Submerged: electric 559kW (750hp)
Performance	Surfaced: 32.4km/h (17.5kts); Submerged: 12.7km/h (6.9kts)

Second, US merchant ships often sailed close to the coastline, against which they were starkly highlighted by the lights of major coastal towns and cities, providing an easy target for the U-boat commander. Many people living on the coast of the United States were thus awed by the sight of tankers and other merchant ships erupting at night just a few kilometres off shore, then were faced with the grim job of reclaiming the bodies of Allied sailors from their beaches the next day. Finally, the lack of a consistent escort policy meant that U-boats could prey on smaller, unarmed vessels simply by surfacing and destroying the craft at close range with the deck gun.

Intelligence failure

The inadvisable tactics of the US maritime services were not the only causes of the dramatic leap in ship sinkings during 1942. In February 1942, the Allied code-breakers working in both the United States and the United Kingdom noted with growing horror that the German intelligence community had introduced a new cipher into its naval communications traffic.

This code was called 'Triton', and it was expressly designed for use by U-boats operating in the Atlantic, not for general naval traffic. The complexities of the Triton code were formidable. Essentially it worked by adding a fourth encoding wheel to the Enigma machine, thereby multiplying to an alarming extent

U-404 TIMETABLE		
Patrol Dates	**Operational Area**	**Ships Sunk**
17 Jan 1942 – 1 Feb 1942	Transit from Kiel to St Nazaire	0
14 Feb 1942 – 4 April 1942	Central Atlantic/US coast	4
6 May 1942 – 14 July 1942	US Atlantic coast/Bermuda	6 + 1 destroyer
23 Aug 1942 – 13 Oct 1942	West of Ireland/Newfoundland	1
21 Dec 1942 – 6 Feb 1943	North Atlantic	0
21 March 1943 – 3 May 1943	North Atlantic/South of Greenland	3
24 July 1943 – 28 July 1943	Transit through Bay of Biscay	0

the mathematical complexity of decryption. Such was the scale of this problem, that it would take the Allies almost the whole year to crack the code. During this time, the evasive routing intelligence was effectively lost for most of the period, with the result that the convoys were able to once more sail straight through wolf pack hunting grounds. Consequently, sinkings rose horrifically across the Atlantic, not just off the coast of the United States.

B-Dienst

Yet it was not only failures in Allied code-breaking that were giving the *Kriegsmarine* the edge in the intelligence war in 1942. The German *Beobachtungs-Dienst* (Observation Service; *B-Dienst*) was the *Kriegsmarine*'s own cryptanalysis organization, dedicated to trying to break the British and American naval codes. In this enterprise, it had enjoyed a real measure of success.

Having first broken the Royal Navy's basic administrative code in 1939, it was reading up to 50 per cent of all naval communications traffic by mid-1940. Not all of this was of tactical significance, but it gave the German Navy in general a deeper insight into military and merchant shipping movements.

German code-breaking success

The Allies began to suspect that their codes had been broken, and changed the encryption systems several times over the coming months. Yet the Naval Cypher No 3, introduced in June 1941 as a specific cipher for transmissions between Allied naval vessels making convoy runs in the Atlantic, was emphatically broken by the *B-Dienst* by February 1942, coinciding with the other factors working in the U-boats' favour at this point in time.

When combined with the fact that the Germans had also broken the code of merchant ships, this breakthrough meant that up to 80 per cent of all Allied naval communications in the Atlantic were being read by mid-1942. This information was then relayed to German submarines, who could take advantage of up to a day's warning about an approaching convoy.

New threats: 1942

Although 1942 was a time of great success for the U-boat arm of the *Kriegsmarine*, this did not mean that they operated in a risk-free environment. New Allied defensive technologies and practices were starting to destroy larger numbers of U-boats.

The wolf pack convoy attacks of 1942 reached new heights of ferocity and aggression. A dark example comes from convoy SC94, a convoy of 36 ships sailing between Nova Scotia and the UK in August 1942, accompanied by six Canadian and British escorts (one destroyer and five corvettes). On 5 August it was spotted by *U-593*, one of a large group of U-boats forming a North Atlantic wolf pack. Straightaway *U-593* made an attack, hitting and sinking a merchant vessel before being driven off by the escorts.

The day after, the U-boats once again tried to get close to the convoy, but by this time the escorts were alert. Two U-boats are damaged and had to return home and one more was sunk, but the wolf pack was growing with the arrival additional boats, swelling to eight submarines in total. U-boat attacks continued, and on 8–10 August the sinkings began in earnest. During those two days, the swarming U-boats sank a further 10 merchant vessels, a tremendous toll for three days' work. In return, the escorts sank *U-379* and delivered enough firepower to disrupt further attacks on the convoy, saving hundreds of lives.

Although 1942 was certainly a time of real success for the U-boat service, there was also no denying that the Allies were becoming better at killing enemy submarines. Since the war began, a number of anti-

ALLIED SHIPS SUNK (JANUARY 1942–SEPTEMBER 1943)

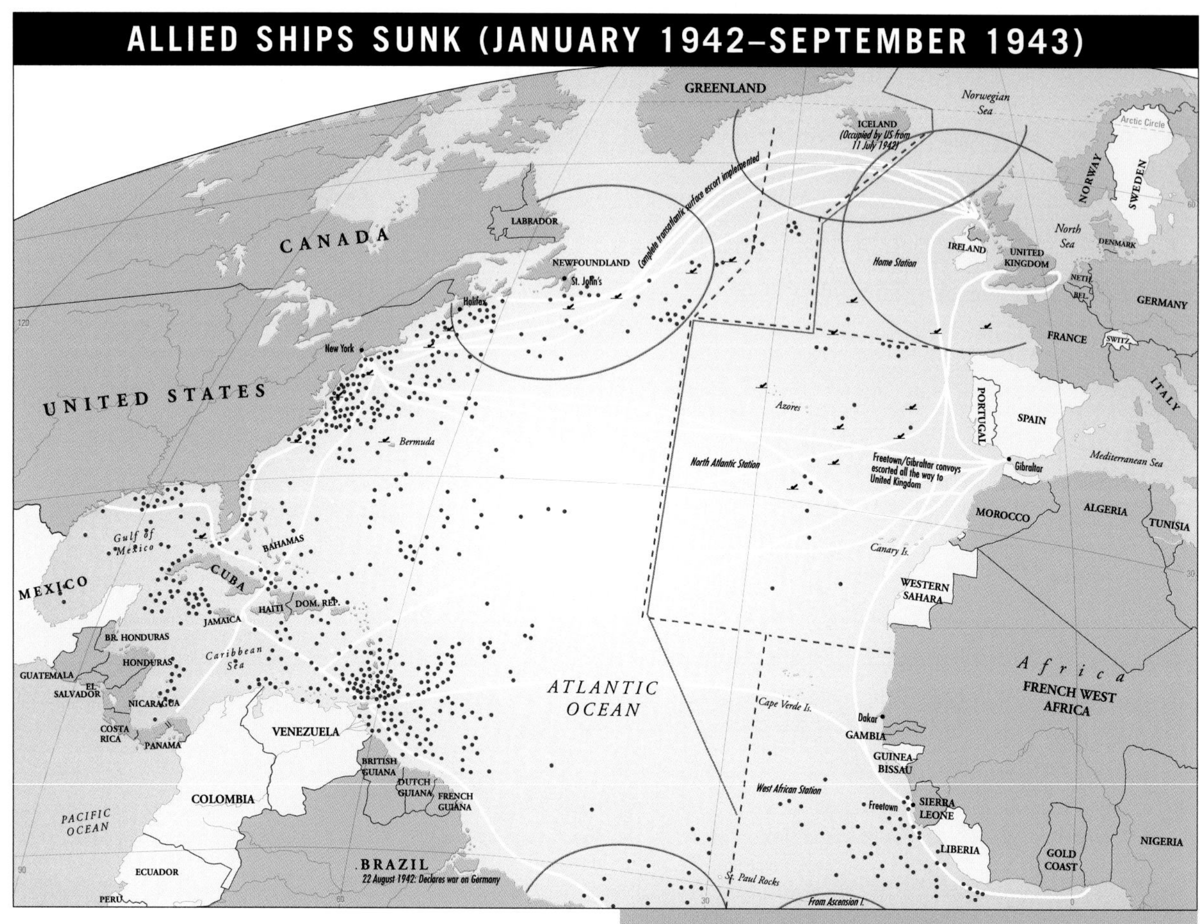

January 1942 – September 1943

- Change of operational control from UK to US, August 1942
- Extent of air escort cover
- UK escort stations to July 1942
- Major convoy routes
- Allied merchant ships sunk by U-boats
- U-boats sunk
- Territory under Allied control
- Territory under Axis control
- Neutral territory

The second 'Happy Time'

The consequences of the United States entering World War II are strikingly illustrated in this map. The number of sinkings in the eastern half of the Atlantic Ocean dropped dramatically during 1942, while sinkings in the western ocean, particularly around the coastal United States, rose equally precipitously.

Note how deep down into the Atlantic the attacks extended, from the eastern coast of Canada down to the waters off Brazil, testimony to the way that the wolf packs went wherever there was good hunting available (often based on areas where the Americans were still resisting adopting the convoy system).

Air escort cover over the waters in the north was steadily improving, although the large mid-Atlantic air gap still existed.

submarine technologies had been refined and developed, and were making life seriously dangerous for U-boat crews. On the detection side of the war, the Allies relied on three main onboard technologies. The first was High Frequency Direction Finding (HF/DF), more popularly known by the nickname 'Huff-Duff'. In a similar way to the U-boat's hydrophone, the HF/DF consisted of radio monitoring equipment that could triangulate a submarine's rough position from its radio transmissions.

1ST FLOTILLA (1 APRIL 1943)

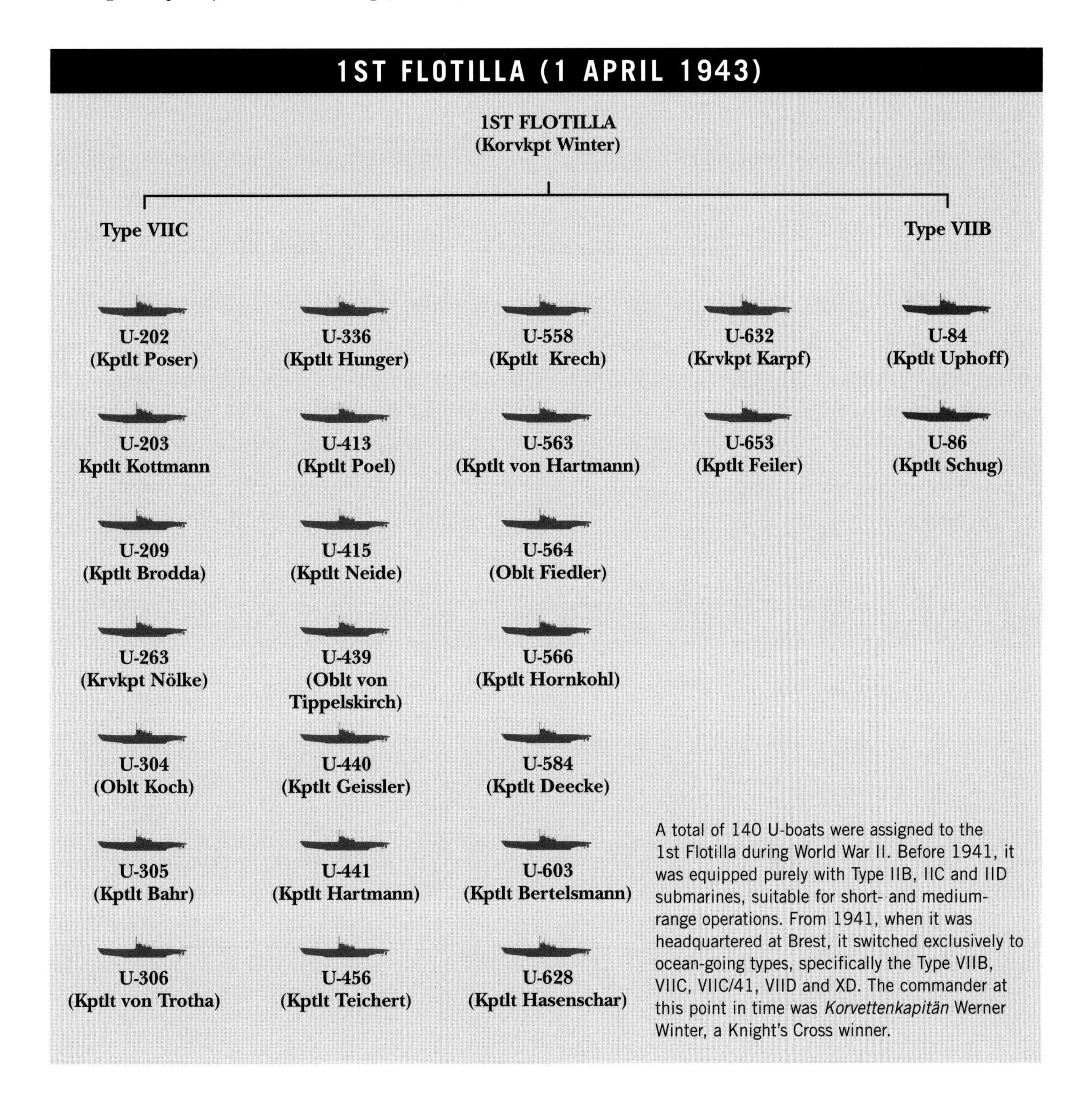

A total of 140 U-boats were assigned to the 1st Flotilla during World War II. Before 1941, it was equipped purely with Type IIB, IIC and IID submarines, suitable for short- and medium-range operations. From 1941, when it was headquartered at Brest, it switched exclusively to ocean-going types, specifically the Type VIIB, VIIC, VIIC/41, VIID and XD. The commander at this point in time was *Korvettenkapitän* Werner Winter, a Knight's Cross winner.

Before 1942, much HF/DF detection work was performed from powerful coastal installations, but during 1942 the system was also installed on merchant ships and warships, giving them a fast submarine location from even a short burst transmission. The great value of HF/DF to the Allies was that it could detect a U-boat at over-the-horizon ranges and transmit the location information immediately to anti-submarine aircraft. If they were lucky, they might catch the submarine still on the surface, and destroy it with depth charges or through strafing attacks.

While HF/DF was a passive system of detection, the Allied navies also came to rely on more active technologies. The two key tools were ASDIC and centimetric radar. ASDIC, short for Allied Submarine Detection Investigation Committee(the body responsible for its initial development), was a system for detecting a submerged submarine (it was essentially

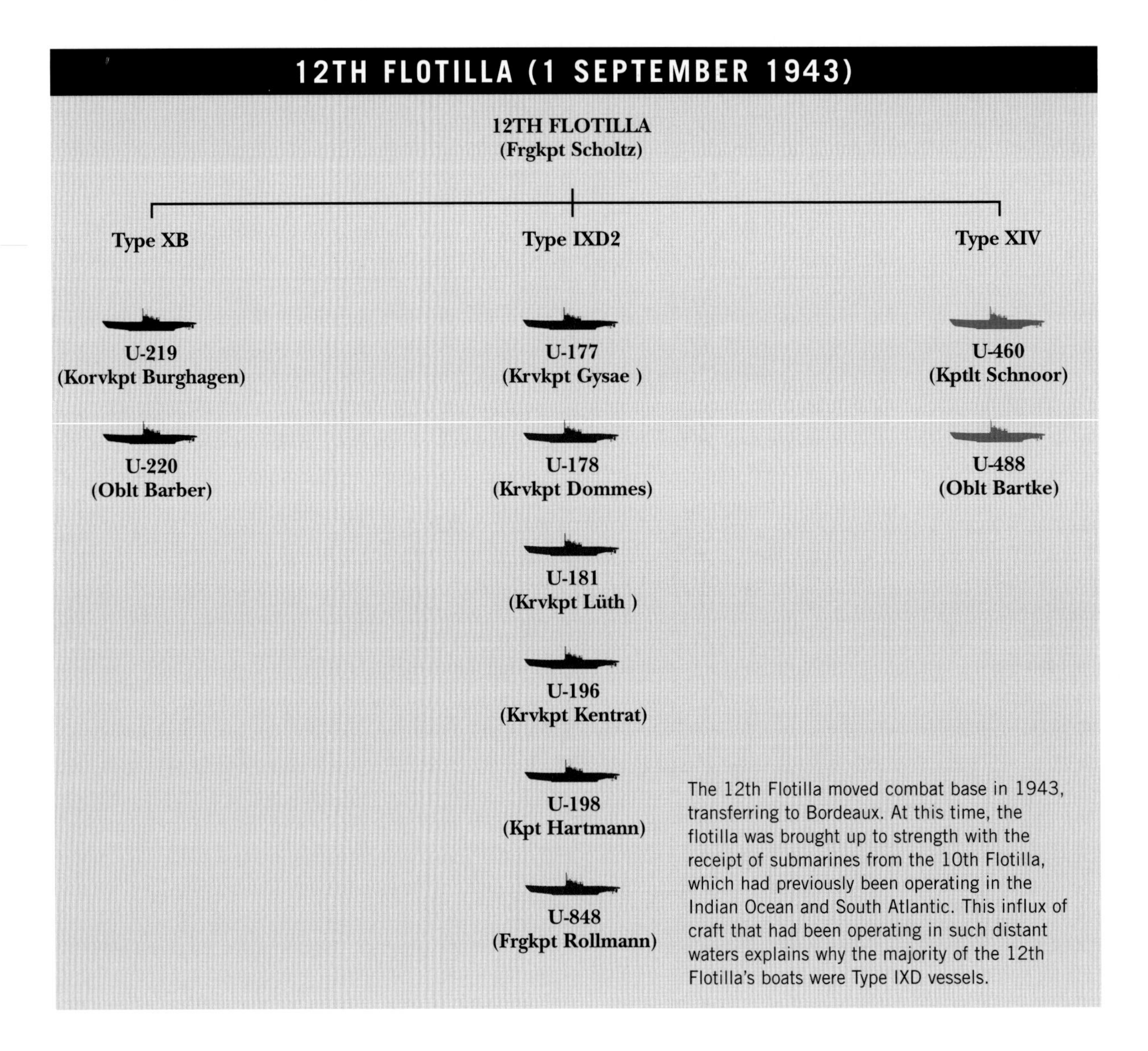

The 12th Flotilla moved combat base in 1943, transferring to Bordeaux. At this time, the flotilla was brought up to strength with the receipt of submarines from the 10th Flotilla, which had previously been operating in the Indian Ocean and South Atlantic. This influx of craft that had been operating in such distant waters explains why the majority of the 12th Flotilla's boats were Type IXD vessels.

U-BOATS THAT TRAINED WITH THE 8TH FLOTILLA	
Type	**Boats ordered**
Type VIIC	U-88, U-89, U-90, U-212, U-222, U-223, U-242, U-250, U-253, U-254, U-255, U-256, U-260, U-261, U-263, U-264, U-265, U-266, U-267, U-268, U-269, U-270, U-271, U-272, U-273, U-274, U-275, U-276, U-277, U-278, U-279, U-280, U-281, U-282, U-283, U-284, U-285, U-286, U-288, U-289, U-290, U-291, U-302, U-303, U-304, U-305, U-306, U-307, U-308, U-309, U-310, U-311, U-312, U-313, U-314, U-315, U-334, U-335, U-338, U-339, U-340, U-341, U-342, U-343, U-345, U-346, U-347, U-348, U-349, U-357, U-358, U-359, U-361, U-362, U-363, U-370, U-378, U-379, U-383, U-405, U-406, U-411, U-412, U-413, U-414, U-415, U-416, U-417, U-418, U-419, U-420, U-421, U-422, U-423, U-424, U-425, U-426, U-427, U-428, U-429, U-430, U-438, U-443, U-444, U-445, U-446, U-447, U-448, U-449, U-450, U-458, U-465, U-475, U-479, U-481, U-593, U-594, U-595, U-596, U-597, U-598, U-599, U-613, U-614, U-615, U-616, U-620, U-621, U-622, U-623, U-624, U-625, U-637, U-657, U-658, U-664, U-676, U-679, U-704, U-707, U-708, U-712, U-713, U-717, U-731, U-732, U-733, U-734, U-735, U-736, U-737, U-738, U-739, U-740, U-741, U-742, U-743, U-744, U-745, U-760, U-761, U-762, U-763, U-764, U-765, U-766, U-767, U-825, U-826, U-921, U-958, U-1102, U-1191, U-1192, U-1193, U-1199, U-1200, U-1201, U-1202, U-1203, U-1204, U-1205, U-1206, U-1207, U-1208, U-1209, U-1210
Type VIIC/41	U-292, U-293, U-294, U-295, U-296, U-297, U-298, U-299, U-300, U-827, U-828, U-1000, U-1001, U-1103, U-1104, U-1105, U-1106, U-1107, U-1108, U-1109, U-1110, U-1163, U-1164, U-1165, U-1166, U-1167, U-1168, U-1169, U-1170, U-1171, U-1172, U-1271, U-1272, U-1273, U-1274, U-1275, U-1276, U-1277, U-1278, U-1279
Type VIID	U-218
Type IXB	U-108
Type XVIIA, B	U-792, U-793, U-794, U-795, U-1405, U-1406
Type XXI	U-2501, U-2504, U-3501, U-3502, U-3503, U-3504, U-3505, U-3506, U-3507, U-3508, U-3510, U-3511, U-3512, U-3513, U-3514, U-3515, U-3516, U-3517, U-3518, U-3519, U-3520, U-3521, U-3522
Type XXIII	U-2339

useless against surfaced U-boats) by using sound pulses projected from beneath a ship's hull. If the pulse hit a submarine, it bounced back to the broadcasting ship and gave the ASDIC crew a range and bearing to the enemy boat (although not a depth), and this information would be passed to weapons crews to aid the effective laying of depth charge patterns.

In addition to ASDIC was centimetric radar. During 1942, microwave radar sets such as the Type 271 (a British radar) were fitted to escort ships, giving them search detection capabilities out to 25km (15.5 miles) – although this range was more suited to finding a large battleship, and not a small submarine.

Nevertheless, such radar detection equipment combined with ASDIC and HF/DF meant that the *Kriegsmarine*'s U-boats were increasingly struggling to find places to hide, particularly once they had given away their presence through launching an attack against merchant shipping.

Weapons technologies

The weapons actually used by the Allies to sink the U-boats had essentially changed little since the beginning of the war. The main offensive weapon was the depth charge, essentially a drum of explosives fitted with a hydrostatic pistol that could be set to detonate the explosives at a certain depth.

Depth charges were usually dropped in circular patterns over the suspected location of the U-boat, the location having been narrowed down by ASDIC or through interpretation of possible attack patterns. If a depth charge detonated within 10m (32ft) of a submarine, the resulting shock wave was enough to split open the U-boat's hull. Even if the submarine was not destroyed in a depth charge attack, the thunderous explosions and the possibility of rapid death would be psychologically hard on every submariner.

Furthermore, the explosions could force the submarine to remain at depth, and therefore prevent it from making another attack run. A significant problem with depth charges when used in combination with ASDIC was that ASDIC lost contact in the final 180m (590ft) of an attack run, thereby giving a U-boat a window to take fast evasive action. One counter-weapon to this problem was the 'Hedgehog' launcher. This system featured 24 projectiles that were fired ahead of the ship in a circular pattern about 40m (130ft) in diameter. The bombs sank through the water, and because of the fact that they were contact- rather than depth-detonated, an explosion usually signified a hit on the enemy submarine.

It was such technologies, plus the talents of anti-submarine aircrews, that enabled the Allies to kill submarines in respectable numbers, although more success was required to end the 'Happy Time'.

2ND FLOTILLA (1 DECEMBER 1943)

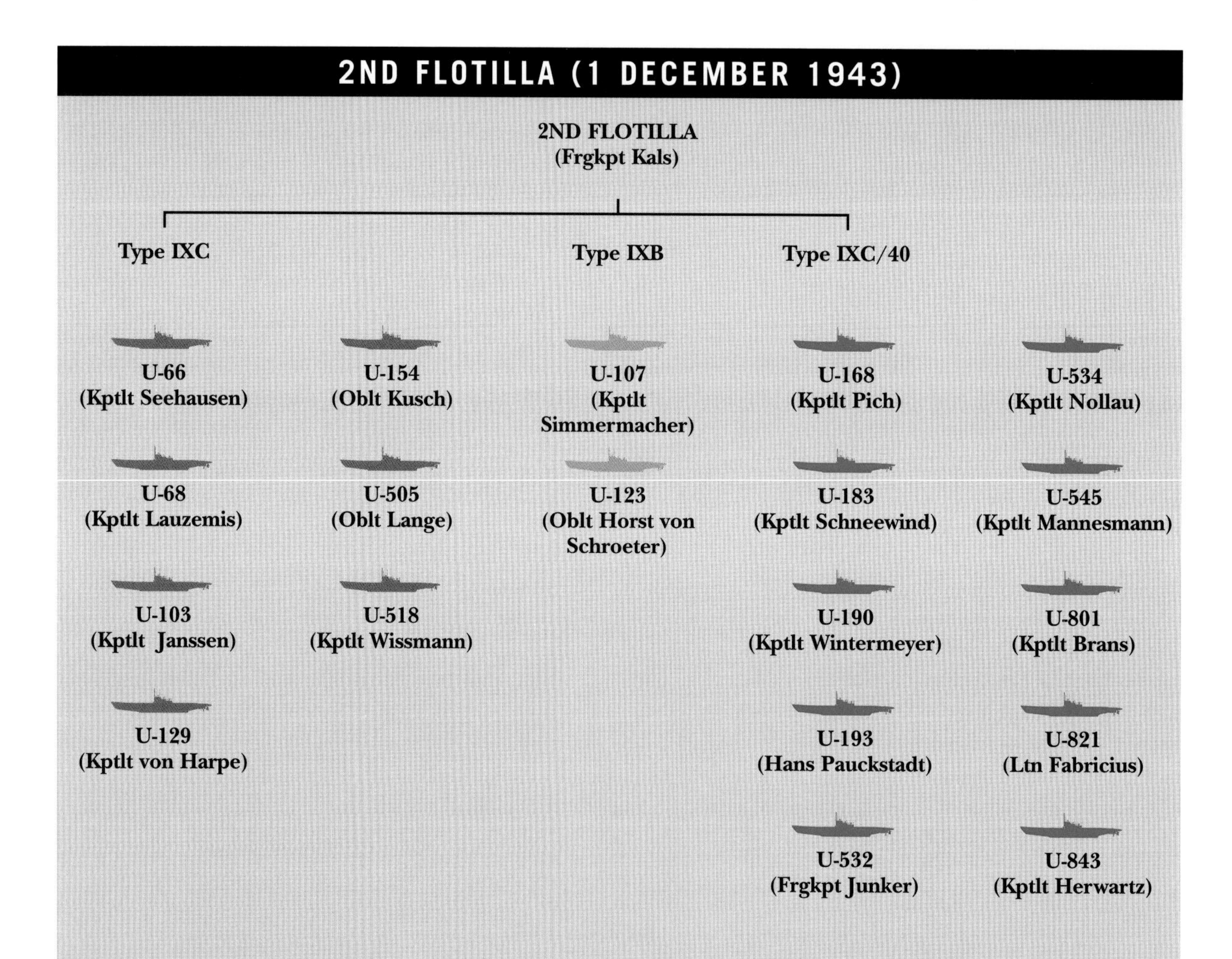

Here we see the composition of the 2nd Flotilla at a time when the Battle of the Atlantic had swung decisively against the U-boats. The experience of *U-843* was typical of this period. It was commissioned in March 1943 and began operational patrols in the following October. During its combat life, it managed to sink only one enemy merchant ship, and spent much its time in transit between theatres. It was sunk in the Kattegat on 9 April 1945 by air attack.

Tipping point in the Atlantic: 1943–44

In 1943 the whole complexion of the war in the Atlantic altered, and altered for good. The U-boats' status changed from that of the hunter to that of the hunted, although the *Kriegsmarine*'s submarines retained the capacity to impose terrible destruction.

The figures speak for themselves. In 1942, the *Kriegsmarine* lost 87 submarines in all theatres. The following year, by stark contrast, the number of U-boats destroyed in action rose to 237, and the year after to 242. The U-boat service began to operate under a dark cloud, with crews facing the near certainty of death a long way from home and many tens of metres beneath the cold Atlantic waters.

The reasons for the dramatic shift in fortunes of the U-boats in the Atlantic are primarily to do with improved Allied anti-submarine practices, rather than any deficiencies in the U-boats' tactics. The fact remained that the U-boats did still manage to sink appreciable amounts of Atlantic merchant shipping – a total of 2,205,238 tonnes (2,170,410 tons) in total in 1943. Yet this was still a dizzying drop from the

CONVOY TM1 TIMETABLE

Date	Event
29 Dec 1942	*U-124* sights a part of the convoy heading for an assembly point
3 Jan 1943	*U-514* locates the convoy and leaves one tanker abandoned and adrift. The hulk is sunk by *U-105* three weeks later. Dönitz, realizing that such a large tanker convoy is likely to be heading direct for North Africa to support the victorious Allied offensives, orders his boats to ignore convoy GUS2, which a wolf pack had been preparing to attack, and to move instead against TM1
4 Jan	Dönitz establishes Group Delphin, which with some other boats sets up a patrol line in the Central Atlantic
8 Jan	*U-381* sights the convoy. *U-436, U-571* and *U-575* head towards it. *U-436* attacks in the evening, sinking a tanker and damaging another, before being damaged and driven off by the escort. *U-571* and *U-575* are unable to penetrate the screen
9 Jan	*U-575* damages two tankers and newly arrived *U-442* hits another. *U-181* and *U-134* are driven off, the latter damaged by depth charges. *U-620* has also arrived, and shadows the convoy. At nightfall, *U-522* finishes off two damaged tankers, while *U-442* and *U-436* sink another. Meanwhile, *U-511* sinks an independent ship not belonging to the convoy
10 Jan	*U-522* damages a tanker, which is given the coup de grâce by *U-620*
11 Jan	*U-571* attacks but fails to sink the two surviving tankers
12 Jan	*U-511* is driven off by the escort
13 Jan	The escort is reinforced by the destroyer HMS *Quentin* and the corvettes HMS *Penstemon* and HMS *Samphire*. Air cover also arrives
14 Jan	The two surviving tankers arrive at Gibraltar

6,249,033 tonnes (6,150,340 tons) that Germany's submarines had claimed the previous year.

Losing the battle

There is no single reason for the shift against the U-boats, but instead their losses are a combination of multiple Allied advantages coalescing into a truly lethal anti-submarine campaign. The improvements in Allied anti-U-boat technologies already outlined were certainly very significant, particularly as the escort crews became more familiar with the technologies and optimized their tactics to suit them. Using HD/DF, ASDIC and centimetric radar, the escort vessels could throw a highly effective screen around a convoy.

This screen was improved on a strategic scale in December 1942, when the Allies cracked the Triton code for the Enigma machine. Once again, the convoys could be rerouted away from the U-boat wolf packs. The results were dramatic – in January and February the combined gross tonnages sunk in the Atlantic were

7TH FLOTILLA (1 DECEMBER 1943)

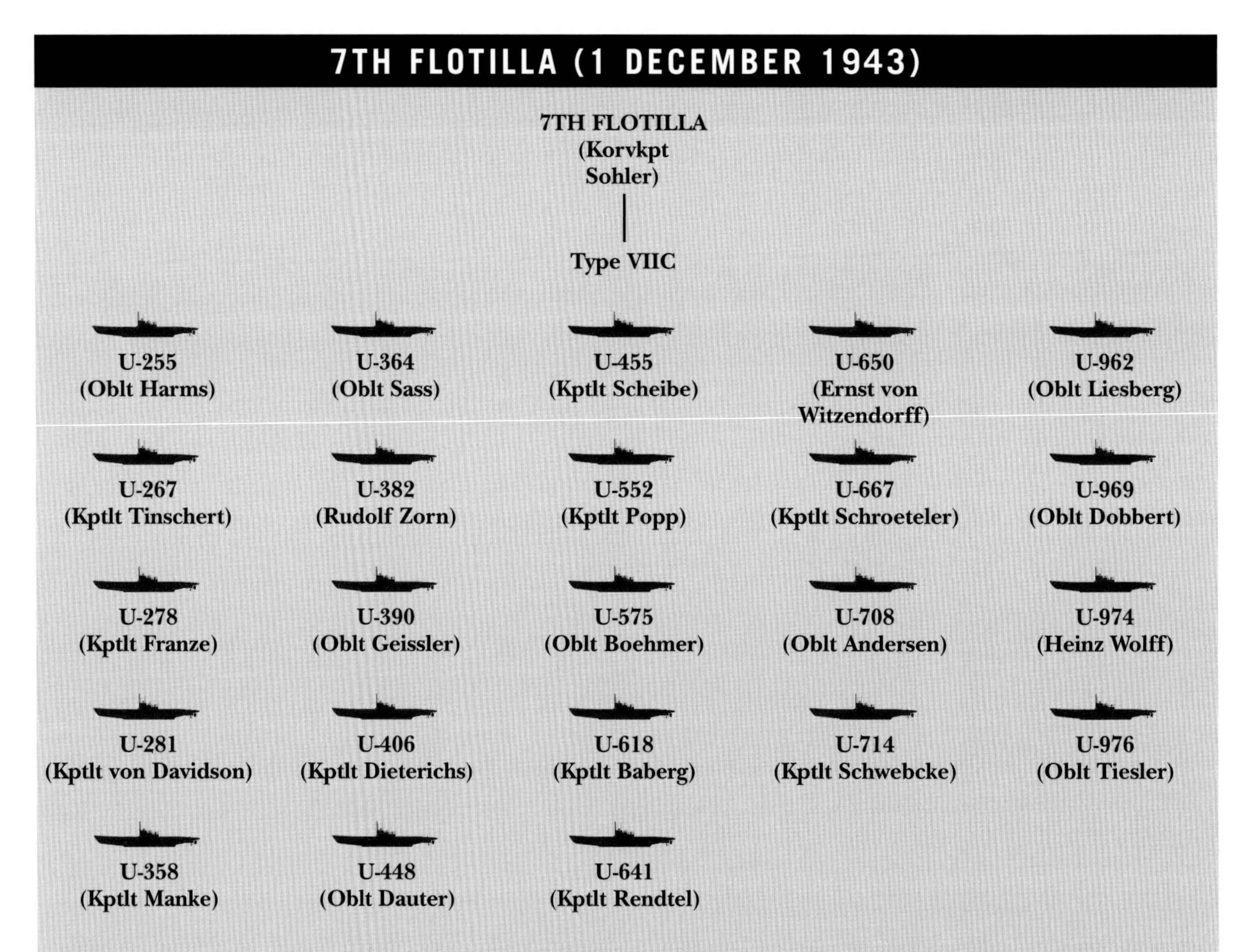

In December 1943, the 7th Flotilla was commanded by *Korvettenkapitän* Herbert Sohler, the flotilla's longest-standing commander (he was in charge from September 1940 to February 1944). At this point the flotilla, which was still based at St Nazaire, was about to enter its last year of war service before it was officially disbanded in August 1944. *U-255* remained operational until 7 May 1945.

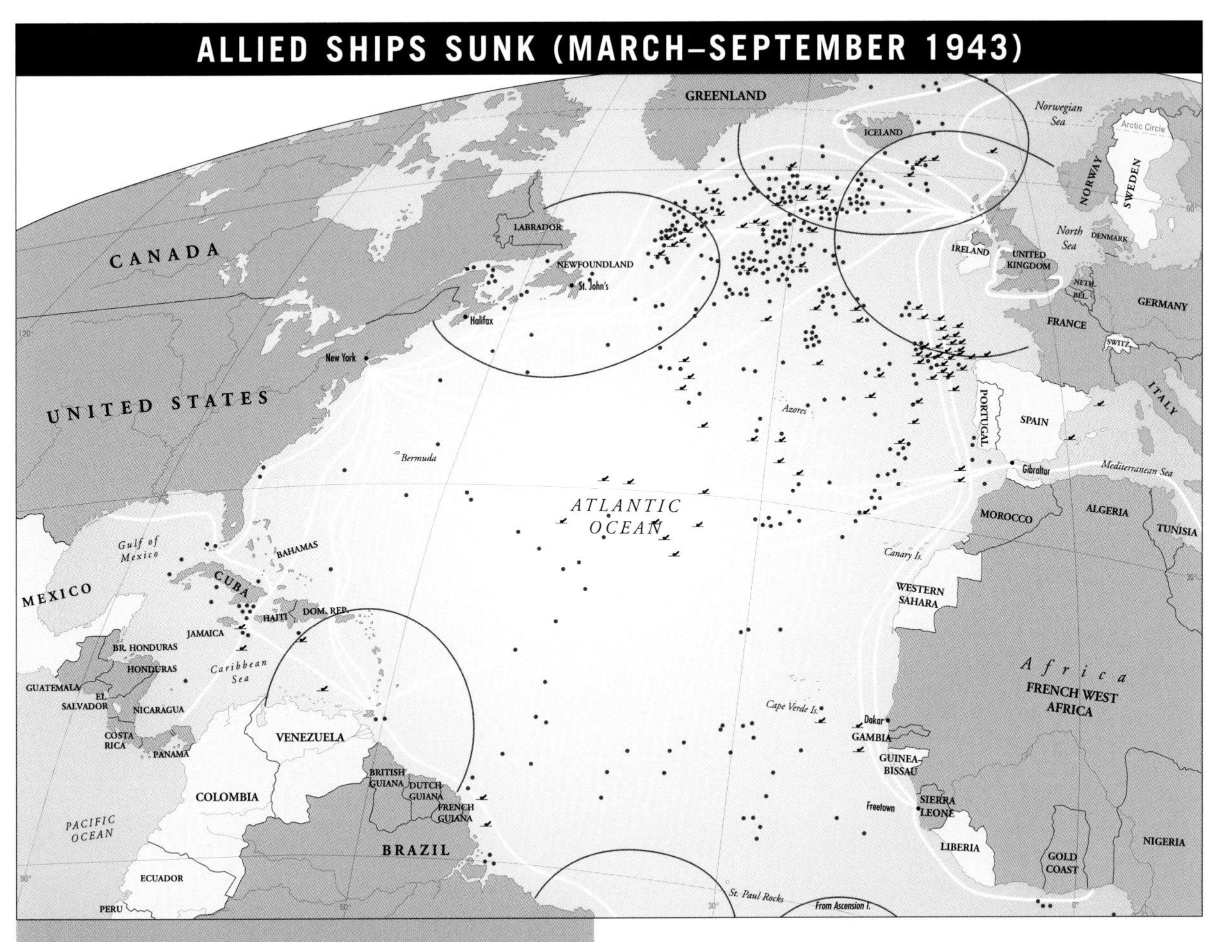

Plugging the air gap

Many of the Allied ships sunk by U-boats between March and September 1943 went down in the mid-Atlantic air gap, the zone which as yet Allied escort aircraft could not reach. Elsewhere, such was the efficiency of British and American anti-submarine aircraft that to venture into an area covered by air patrols became increasingly suicidal.

Yet before the end of the year, this air gap too would be closed, by very long-range aircraft such as the Consolidated B-24 Liberator and the Boeing B-17 Flying Fortress. As a result the beleaguered U-boats would be forced into ever remoter parts of the Atlantic Ocean, where their success rates fell to levels well below those enjoyed from 1941–43. More U-boat deployment time was spent in transit, and therefore less on active hunting duties.

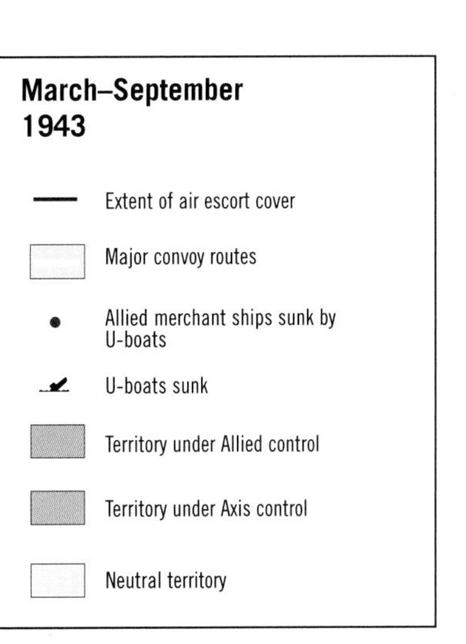

528,173 tonnes (519,832 tons). Yet the next month, March, saw Allied cryptanalysts lose the code again for roughly a four-week period, with the consequence that U-boats sank 108 merchant ships totalling 547,339 tonnes (538,695 tons). During April, by which time the Allies were back on top of the intelligence issues, the tonnages sunk once again fell, to 256,585 tonnes (252,533 tons).

Structural changes on both sides of the conflict would also have a significant impact upon the Battle of the

9TH FLOTILLA (1 FEBRUARY 1943)

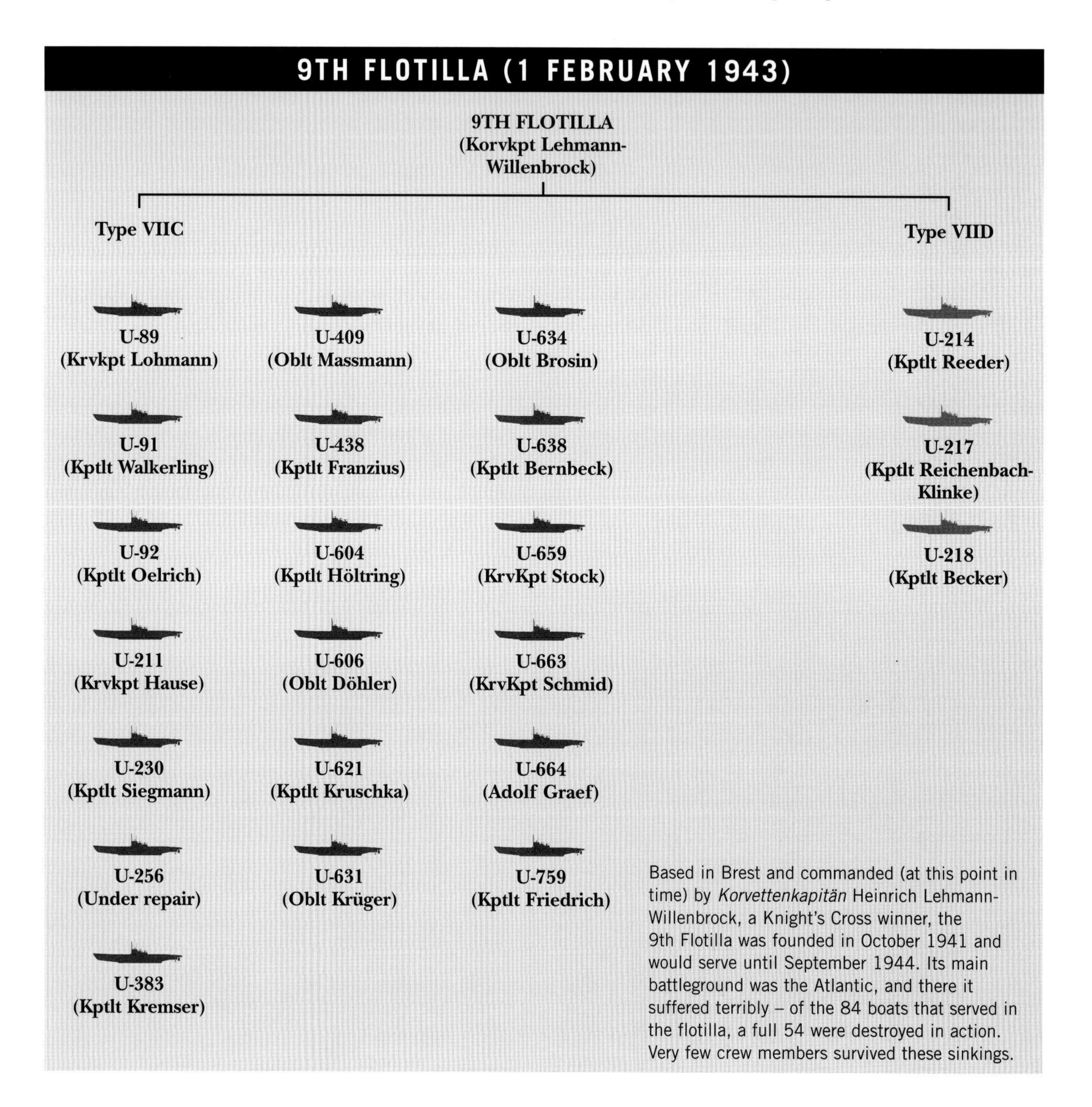

Based in Brest and commanded (at this point in time) by *Korvettenkapitän* Heinrich Lehmann-Willenbrock, a Knight's Cross winner, the 9th Flotilla was founded in October 1941 and would serve until September 1944. Its main battleground was the Atlantic, and there it suffered terribly – of the 84 boats that served in the flotilla, a full 54 were destroyed in action. Very few crew members survived these sinkings.

Atlantic. On the German side, Dönitz became commander-in-chief of the *Kriegsmarine* in January 1943. Raeder, his authority blunted by the maladies facing the German Navy's surface fleet, had resigned, and now Dönitz could express his concept of U-boat warfare more fully. He also appeared to have the numbers of U-boats necessary for a decisive campaign. Operational U-boat numbers had climbed over the 400 mark, so Dönitz could now put some 100 U-boats on station in the Atlantic at any one time.

The Allies were also changing their game plan. During the Atlantic Convoy Conference of March 1943, the Allied navies divided up their responsibilities between them. The US would focus on escorting tanker convoys between the UK and West Indies, while the British and the Canadians took charge of escorting the North Atlantic convoys between them. Furthermore, the conference led to the creation of special naval Support Groups, powerful combat formations that would escort convoys through vulnerable parts of the journey, and which acted aggressively as submarine-hunting packs.

Air war

The presence of an escort carrier in one of these groups meant that air power, by now the U-boat's greatest fear, could be deployed within minutes of picking up contacts from radar or HF/DF. In fact, it was air power almost more than anything that changed the balance of power

10TH FLOTILLA (1 SEPTEMBER 1943)

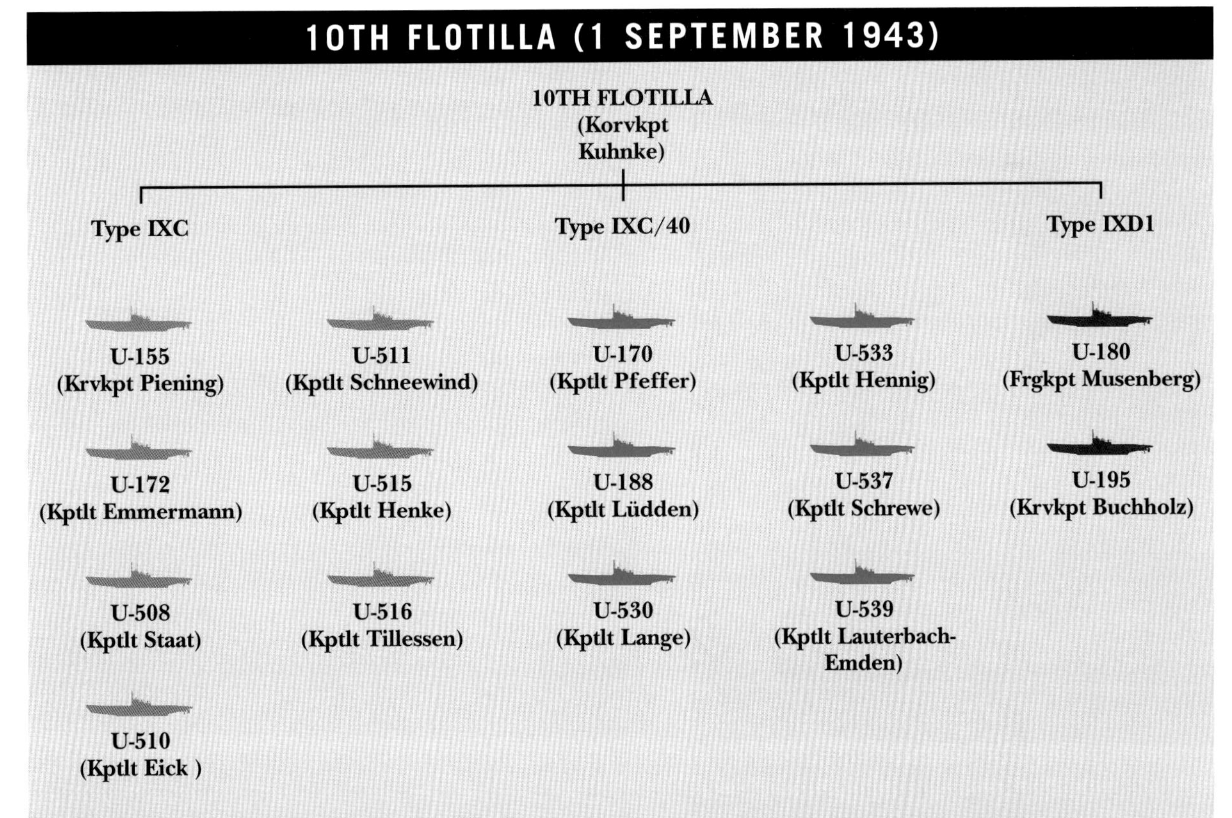

The 10th Flotilla was unusual in that it was commanded by the same man, *Korvettenkapitän* Günther Kuhnke, for the entire duration of its existence – he actually sailed on the very last 10th Flotilla U-boat out of Lorient on 27 August 1944. Because it was exclusively equipped with long-range submarine types, the flotilla was called upon to undertake missions as far apart as Greenland, South America and Southeast Asia.

U-459 (TYPE XIV)	
Name	*U-459* (Type XIV)
Commissioned	15 November 1941
Crew	53–60
Displacement	1932 tonnes (1901 tons)
Dimensions	Length: 64.5m (212ft); Beam: 5.9m (19ft)
Range	Surfaced: 19,874km (12,350 miles) at 18.5km/h (10kts); Submerged: 56km (35 miles) at 7.4km/h (4kts)
Powerplant	Surfaced: diesels 522kW (700hp); Submerged: electric 306kW (410hp)
Performance	Surfaced: 27.5km/h (14.9kts); Submerged: 11.5km/h (6.2kts)

6TH FLOTILLA BOATS ASSIGNED	
Type	**Number assigned**
Type IXA	8
Type VIIB	1
Type VIIC	81
Type VIIC/41	1

in the Atlantic. Throughout the war, aircraft steadily went from being a minor irritant to U-boat crews to being the premier threat they faced. If we look at statistics for the causes of U-boat sinkings between 1939 and 1945, attacks from the air using depth charges or torpedoes make up the largest grouping, at 290 kills. In second place come attacks by surface vessels using depth charges or gunfire, at 246 kills.

During the early years of the war, air patrols were mainly consigned to coastal waters, but the use of long-range aircraft steadily extended ranges out into the Atlantic. A large air gap existed, however – created by the points at which coastal aircraft, typically Sunderlands, Catalinas and Hudsons, had to turn for home on account of fuel shortages.

Yet in 1943, the introduction of very long-range Liberator and B-17 bombers finally closed the air gap for good. When this was combined with the addition of more escort carriers from May 1943, the effect was that the Germans had no hiding place from air power. Allied aircraft would now accompany convoys for the duration of their voyages, and they were equipped with their own centimetric radar systems so that they could autonomously hunt and destroy U-boats, as well as work in cooperation with surface vessel detection systems. The U-boats were consequently fitted with radar detection antennae, but these proved to be of limited use against the full spectrum of Allied radar technologies.

Massacre at sea

The combined effect of the Allies' improved intelligence, air power and escort tactics was fatal for the U-boats. Fifty-two U-boats were sunk by air attack between January and May 1943, from a total of 96 destroyed. May 1943 was indeed the critical month in the whole Atlantic conflict. During that month, the Germans sank a respectable 208,897 tonnes (205,598 tons) of enemy shipping, but in the process lost 37 U-boats. Compare this with the losses of U-boats for January–April – 4, 15, 13, 14 – and it was clear that the war in the Atlantic had turned. Nearly 70 more U-boats were lost over the next 3 months, while the volume of merchant ships sunk plunged by more than half.

Dönitz later wrote that this was the point at which 'We had lost the battle of the Atlantic.' The Atlantic U-boat fleet was thereafter pulled back to safer waters away from the major convoy routes. The attempt to cut the Allies' maritime lifeline had failed.

Convoy battles in the Arctic

From August 1941, the Allies began routing convoys from the UK and Iceland to Soviet bases in an attempt to help fuel Stalin's war against Germany. Not until a year later did the *Kriegsmarine*'s attempts to interdict this supply line begin in earnest.

By the end of the summer of 1941, it became clear to the world that the war on the Eastern Front was to be a conflict like no other. In the opening months of Operation *Barbarossa*, the Soviet forces had lost literally millions of men, dead, wounded or captured, and the German armoured spearheads were maintaining their momentum, with some strategic deviations, towards the Russian capital, Moscow.

Although the Soviet Union did have immense industrial capability, it was evident to the Western Allies that Stalin was going to need as much material assistance as possible if his forces were to ride out the catastrophic losses. So it was that from August 1941 Britain began seaborne supply runs to the Soviet Union, travelling through Arctic waters mainly to the ports of Archangel, Murmansk and Molotov. These runs combined with the US Lend-Lease Agreement supplies meant that in total the Allies would ship 4,501,087 tonnes (4,430,000 tons) of matériel to the Soviet Union through the frozen waters of the north. The contents of the shipments included aircraft, tanks, trucks, boots and telecommunications equipment, and they became increasingly vital to the Soviet war effort, particularly in terms of maintaining its offensive mobility.

Taking interest

Besides deploying a small U-boat force north, for most of 1941 and the early months of 1942, the *Kriegsmarine*

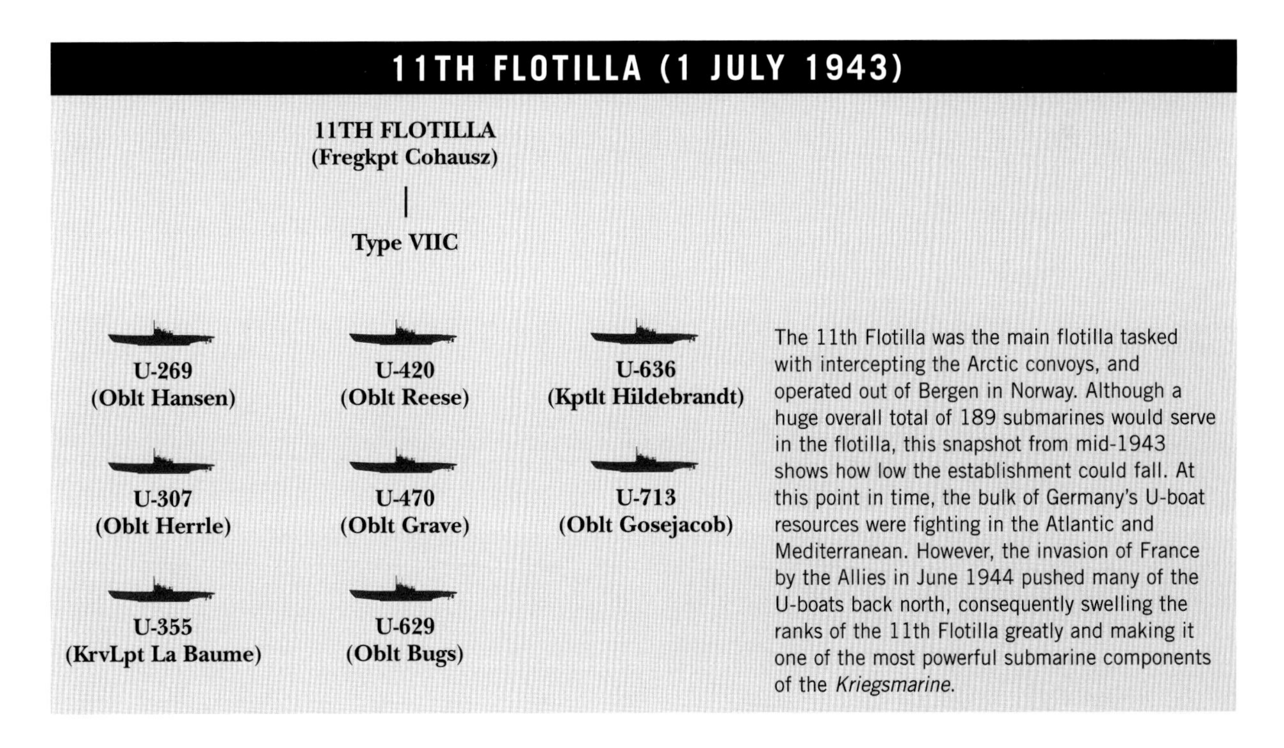

The 11th Flotilla was the main flotilla tasked with intercepting the Arctic convoys, and operated out of Bergen in Norway. Although a huge overall total of 189 submarines would serve in the flotilla, this snapshot from mid-1943 shows how low the establishment could fall. At this point in time, the bulk of Germany's U-boat resources were fighting in the Atlantic and Mediterranean. However, the invasion of France by the Allies in June 1944 pushed many of the U-boats back north, consequently swelling the ranks of the 11th Flotilla greatly and making it one of the most powerful submarine components of the *Kriegsmarine*.

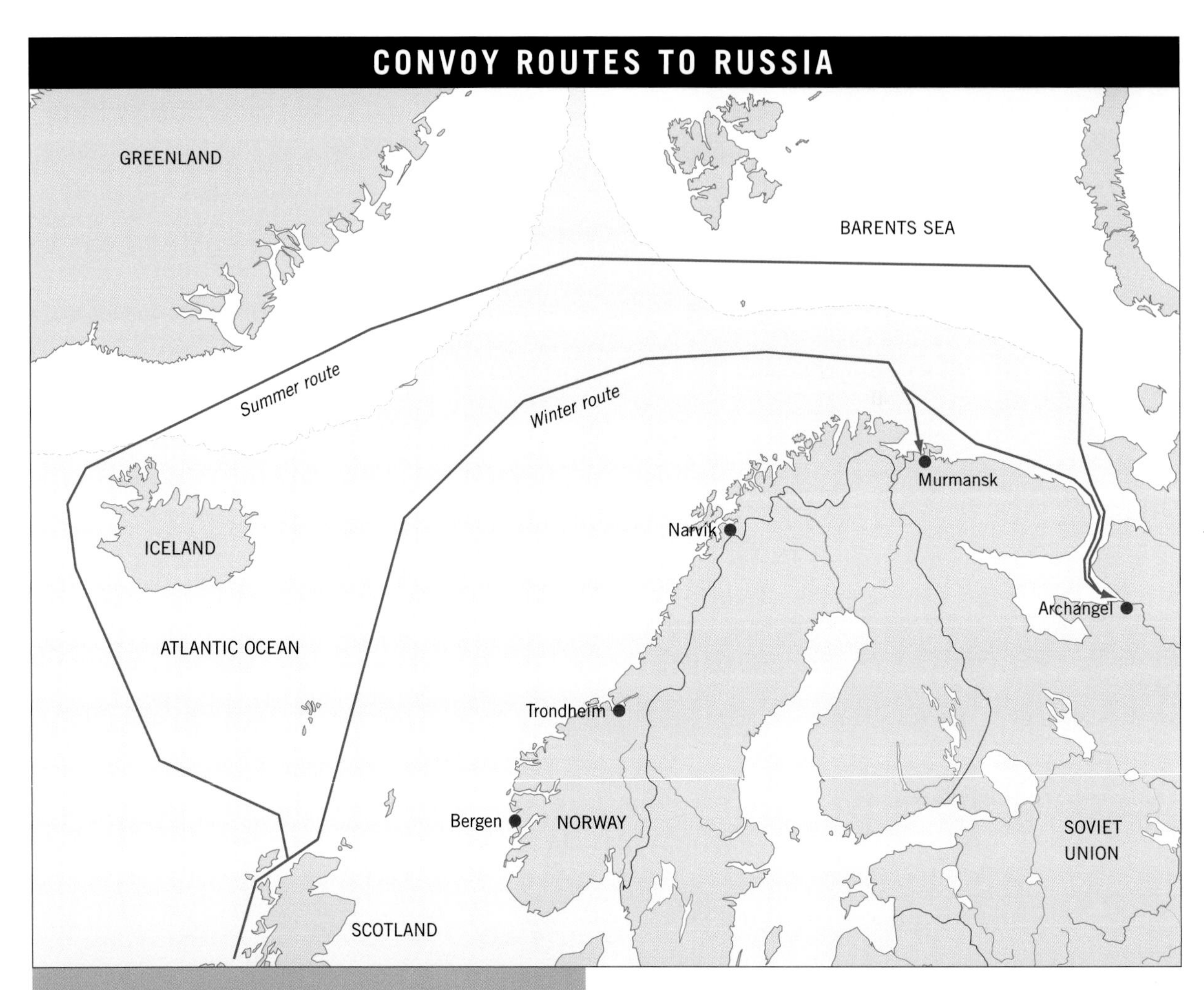

Arctic convoys

The Arctic convoys faced danger at multiple levels during their journeys to and from the northern Soviet Union. The extreme northern latitudes meant regular, furious Arctic storms in sub-zero temperatures. Ships would become locked in ice en route, and frostbite and hypothermia were constant and potentially lethal perils. Any crewmember that found himself in the water following a ship sinking was lucky to last a matter of minutes if he could not find his way to a liferaft.

The other danger was that the *Kriegsmarine* and *Luftwaffe* could operate at short range from bases in occupied Norway, using a combination of anti-ship aircraft, surface warships, submarines and minefields.

paid little attention to what was happening in the far north. It initially appeared as if *Barbarossa* was going to be a sweeping success, and if that was the case then the Allies' Arctic convoys were a futile attempt to prevent the inevitable. By mid-1942, however, the strategic picture had changed. The German offensive to take Moscow had failed, German logistics were struggling in the endless Russian and Ukrainian hinterlands, land forces losses were heavy and Soviet resistance was thickening. It was now apparent that the war against Stalin was not going to be a short-run thing, and so the *Kriegsmarine* was tasked with cutting the Allied convoy system to the north. Although the scale of the war in Arctic waters would not approach that which occurred

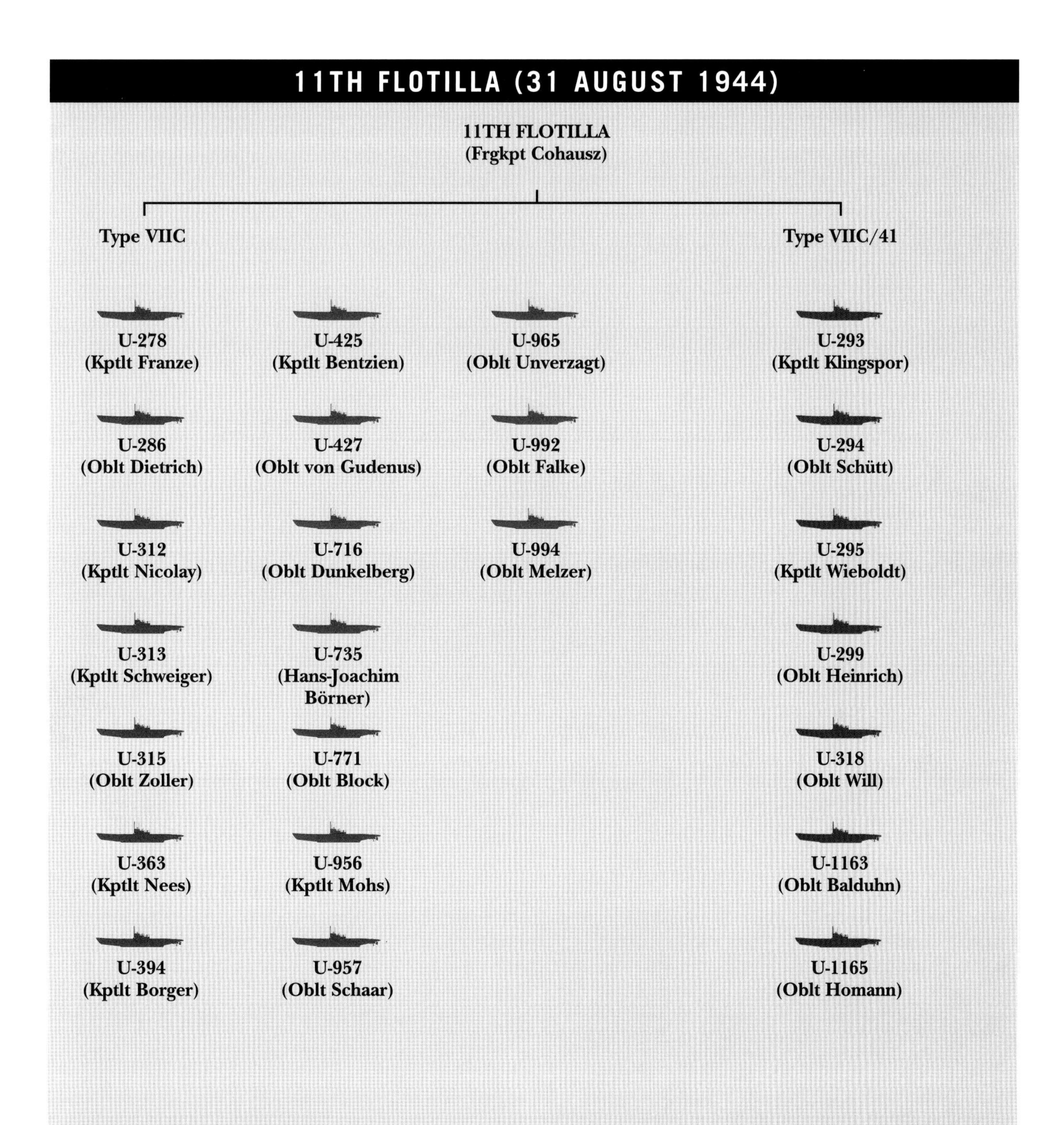

Compared with the previous diagram on page 121, the 11th Flotilla has now received a dramatic boost in numbers following the Allied invasion of France, which threatened or captured the *Kriegsmarine*'s bases on the French coast. The major part of the flotilla's strength increase was from force redeployments rather than new-build ships, the bulk of the vessels coming from the 3rd, 5th, 6th, 8th, 9th and 31st Flotillas.

ERNST KALS (1905–79)

Ernst Kals was a high-scoring U-boat ace who went on to become a much-respected U-boat flotilla commander. He joined the German Navy in 1924, transferring to the U-boat arm in October 1940.

- Kals proved to be a courageous and daring man in action, and was one of the five commanders deployed to the coast of the United States for Operation *Drumbeat* in early 1942. His performance there and in the Caribbean resulted in his being awarded the Knight's Cross.

- Kals then went on to give impressive service further east, sinking three merchant ships in one day alone off the coast of Morocco. By the end of his combat career, Kals had sunk 17 merchant ships with a total tonnage of 111,249 gross registered tons, and had also sent three auxiliary warships to the bottom.

- In February 1943, Kals was promoted to the rank of *Fregattenkapitän*, by which time he had been made commander of the 2nd U-boat Flotilla at Brest. He served three years in French captivity after the war.

in the Atlantic, it still developed into a major maritime campaign with heavy losses on both sides and some massive convoy battles, such as that which occurred around convoy PQ17 (see table page 129).

Combined offensive

Although we will discuss the *Kriegsmarine*'s Arctic campaign primarily in terms of U-boats, the Arctic offensive embraced multiple aspects of the German war machine. We have already noted something of the involvement of the *Kriegsmarine* surface fleet in the north, including the deployment of its major battleships and cruisers, and we will look at this aspect in more depth in later chapters. The role of the *Luftwaffe* was also substantial. The major *Luftwaffe* formation in the far north was *Luftflotte* 5. By 1942, *Luftflotte* 5 patrolled a territory that included the whole of Norway and wrapped around to incorporate Finland. It was primarily a maritime formation, its units tasked with coastal and long-range naval support operations – mainly reconnaissance (the intelligence being relayed to the *Kriegsmarine*) and anti-ship strikes. It used a diverse range of aircraft types to satisfy its role requirements – in July 1942 it included Bf 109 and Fw 190 aircraft in the fighter roles and Ju 88s and Ju 87s in reconnaissance and anti-shipping roles. The Ju 87s were useful for making precision strikes against merchant ships, although they were woefully vulnerable to retaliation by Allied fighter escorts. In addition to the above-mentioned types, *Luftflotte 5* also flew Fw 189s, Hs 126s, He 115s and Ju 52 floatplanes for coastal interdiction. The U-boats had much to gain from close cooperation with the *Luftwaffe*, as the aircraft could tackle Allied anti-submarine aviation while also aiding in convoy location. Yet the problem for *Luftflotte* 5 was its position on the periphery of the *Reich*'s war zone. As emergencies flared up elsewhere in the world, the *Luftflotte*'s aircraft were often creamed off by other formations.

U-BOAT LOSSES 1943	
Month	**Boats lost**
January	U-337, U-164, U-224, U-507, U-553, U-301, U-519
February	U-265, U-187, U-609, U-624, U-442, U-529, U-620, U-225, U-69, U-201, U-205, U-268, U-562, U-623, U-606, U-443, U-522, U-649
March	U-83, U-87, U-156, U-633, U-432, U-444, U-130, U-163, U-5, U-384, U-524, U-665, U-469, U-169, U-77, U-416
April	U-124, U-635, U-167, U-632, U-644, U-376, U-526, U-175, U-602, U-189, U-191, U-710, U-203, U-174, U-332, U-227
May	U-465, U-109, U-439, U-659, U-638, U-125, U-192, U-438, U-531, U-630, U-209, U-447, U-663, U-528, U-89, U-186, U-456, U-753, U-237, U-640, U-176, U-266, U-182, U-463, U-128, U-646, U-657, U-273, U-954, U-258, U-303, U-381, U-569, U-752, U-414, U-467, U-436, U-304, U-755, U-440, U-563
June	U-418, U-105, U-202, U-521, U-308, U-594, U-217, U-417, U-118, U-334, U-564, U-97, U-388, U-119, U-194, U-200, U-449
July	U-126, U-628, U-535, U-951, U-232, U-514, U-435, U-590, U-409, U-506, U-561, U-487, U-607, U-160, U-135, U-509, U-759, U-67, U-513, U-558, U-662, U-527, U-598, U-613, U-459, U-622, U-359, U-159, U-404, U-647, U-614, U-43, U-375, U-461, U-462, U-504, U-591, U-199
August	U-383, U-454, U-106, U-572, U-706, U-489, U-34, U-84, U-117, U-615, U-664, U-468, U-525, U-604, U-403, U-197, U-670, U-458, U-134, U-185, U-523, U-847, U-639, U-634
September	U-669, U-760, U-983, U-617, U-511, U-341, U-338, U-346, U-229, U-161, U-221
October	U-279, U-389, U-422, U-460, U-336, U-419, U-610, U-643, U-402, U-470, U-533, U-844, U-964, U-540, U-631, U-841, U-378, U-420, U-101, U-431, U-274, U-566, U-220, U-282, U-306, U-584, U-732
November	U-405, U-340, U-848, U-226, U-842, U-707, U-966, U-508, U-280, U-718, U-211, U-536, U-648, U-600, U-849, U-542, U-86
December	U-172, U-391, U-593, U-73, U-850, U-284, U-345, U-645

Structuring: 1939–45

As we have already seen, the U-boat arm was divided into separate flotillas, all with their own bases and their own distinctive ethos. As the war progressed, however, the flotillas were increasingly mixed and mingled.

During the war, the U-boat flotillas were separated into two distinct types: *Ausbildungsflottillen* (Training Flotillas) and *Frontflottillen* (Combat Flotillas). The names are fairly explanatory – combat flotillas were deployed directly in fighting roles, while the training flotillas trained new crews for their future combat duties. The distinction must not give the impression, however, that life in the training flotillas was safe. Training crews ran risks from weather, mines, Allied air attack and technical failure, and as the war progressed many training craft were also sent out on operational patrols, where dozens were sunk.

In total, 15 combat flotillas were deployed during the war: 1, 2, 3, 6, 7, 9–14, 23, 29, 30 and 33. There were also 15 training flotillas: 4, 5, 8, 18–27 (including the re-formed 23rd), 31 and 32. Boats would often serve in several flotillas as they redeployed to different theatres. The training units were based principally on the Baltic.

11TH FLOTILLA (1 MARCH 1945)

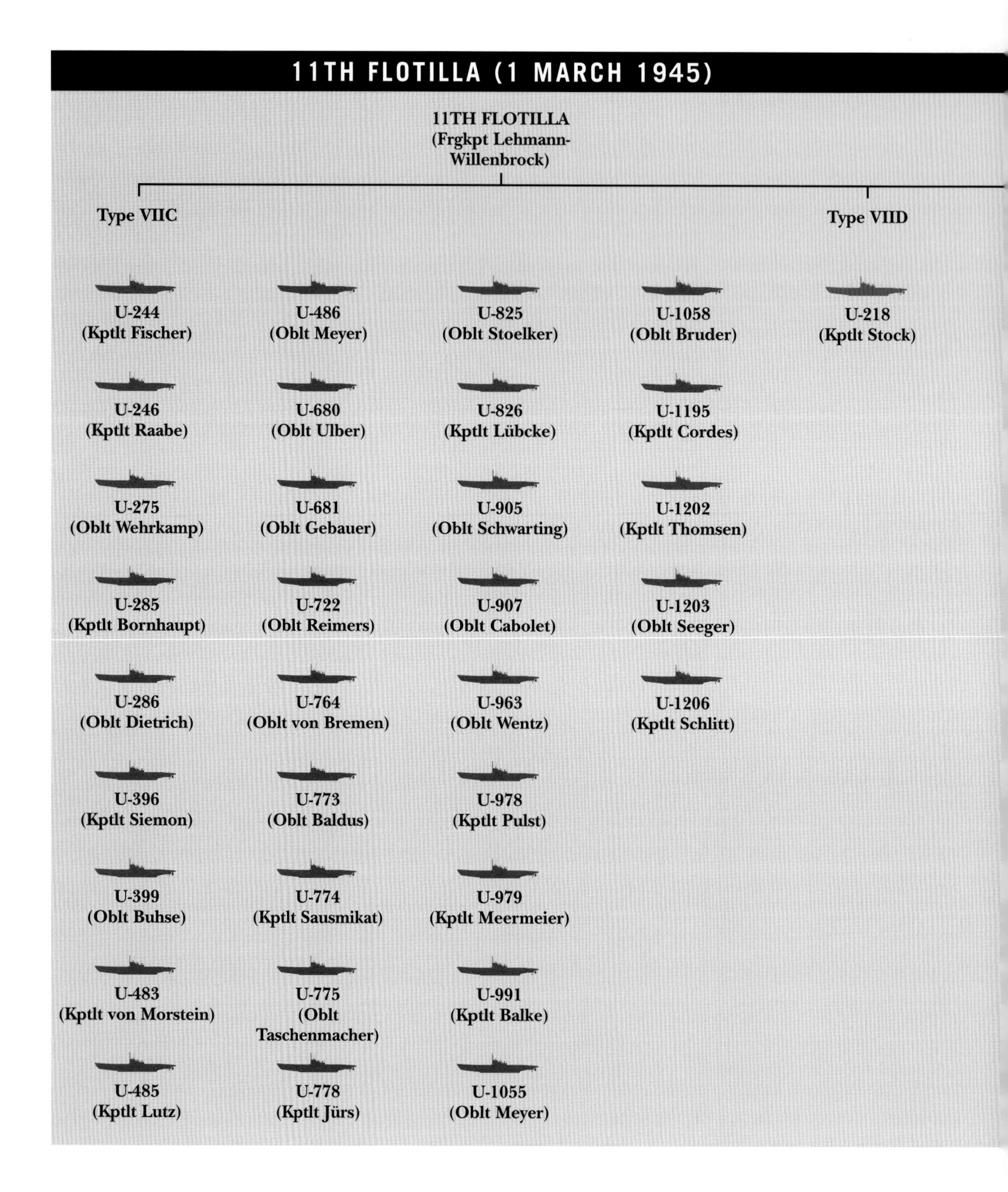

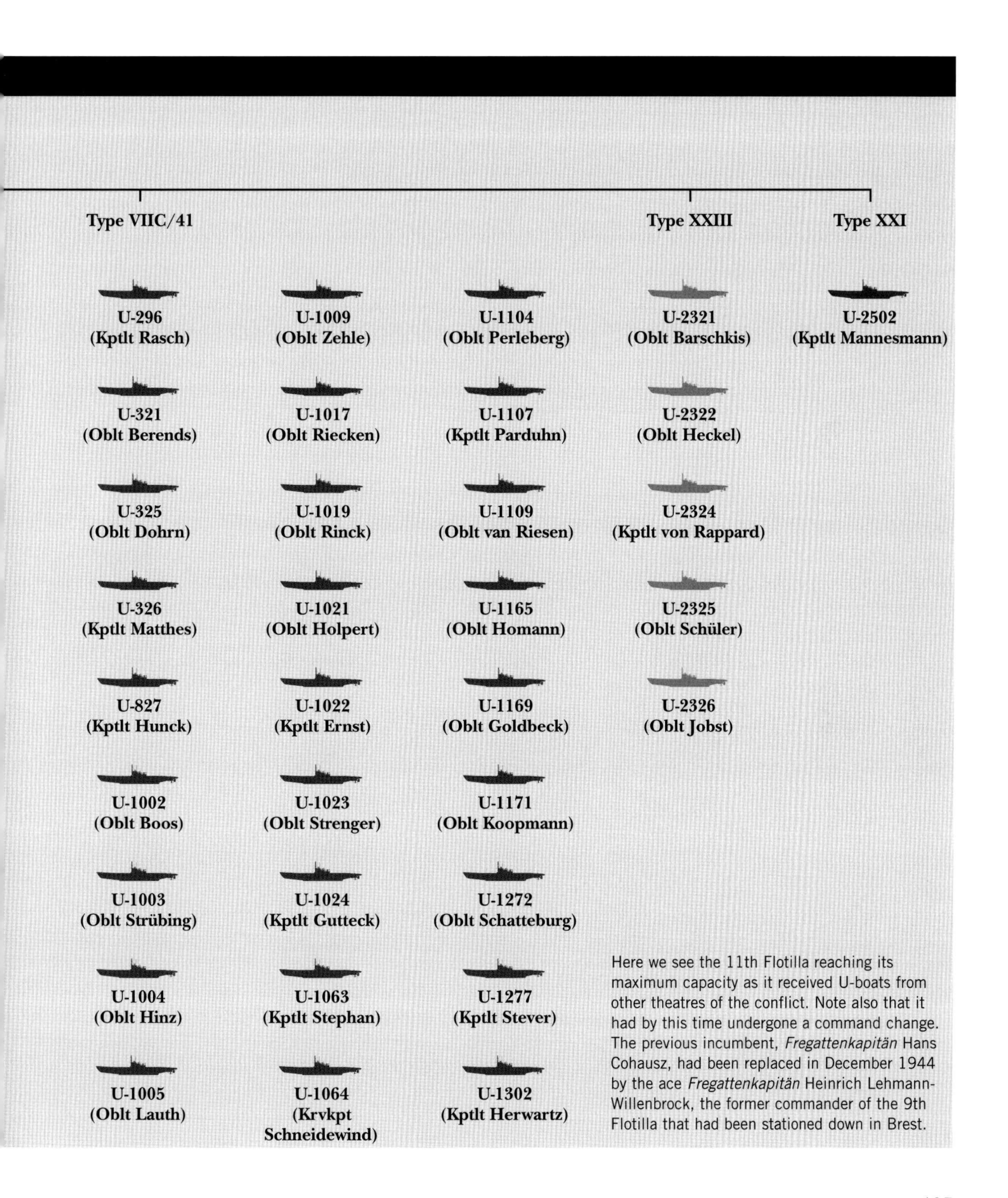

Here we see the 11th Flotilla reaching its maximum capacity as it received U-boats from other theatres of the conflict. Note also that it had by this time undergone a command change. The previous incumbent, *Fregattenkapitän* Hans Cohausz, had been replaced in December 1944 by the ace *Fregattenkapitän* Heinrich Lehmann-Willenbrock, the former commander of the 9th Flotilla that had been stationed down in Brest.

Convoy attacks: 1941–42

The first of the Allied Arctic convoys set out for the Soviet Union on 21 August 1941, carrying a supply of Hurricane fighter aircraft plus a variety of raw materials for war production. It took another four months before the U-boats began hitting the convoys, chipping away at the merchant vessels in relatively small numbers until the combined maritime/aviation strike against convoy PQ17 in July 1942.

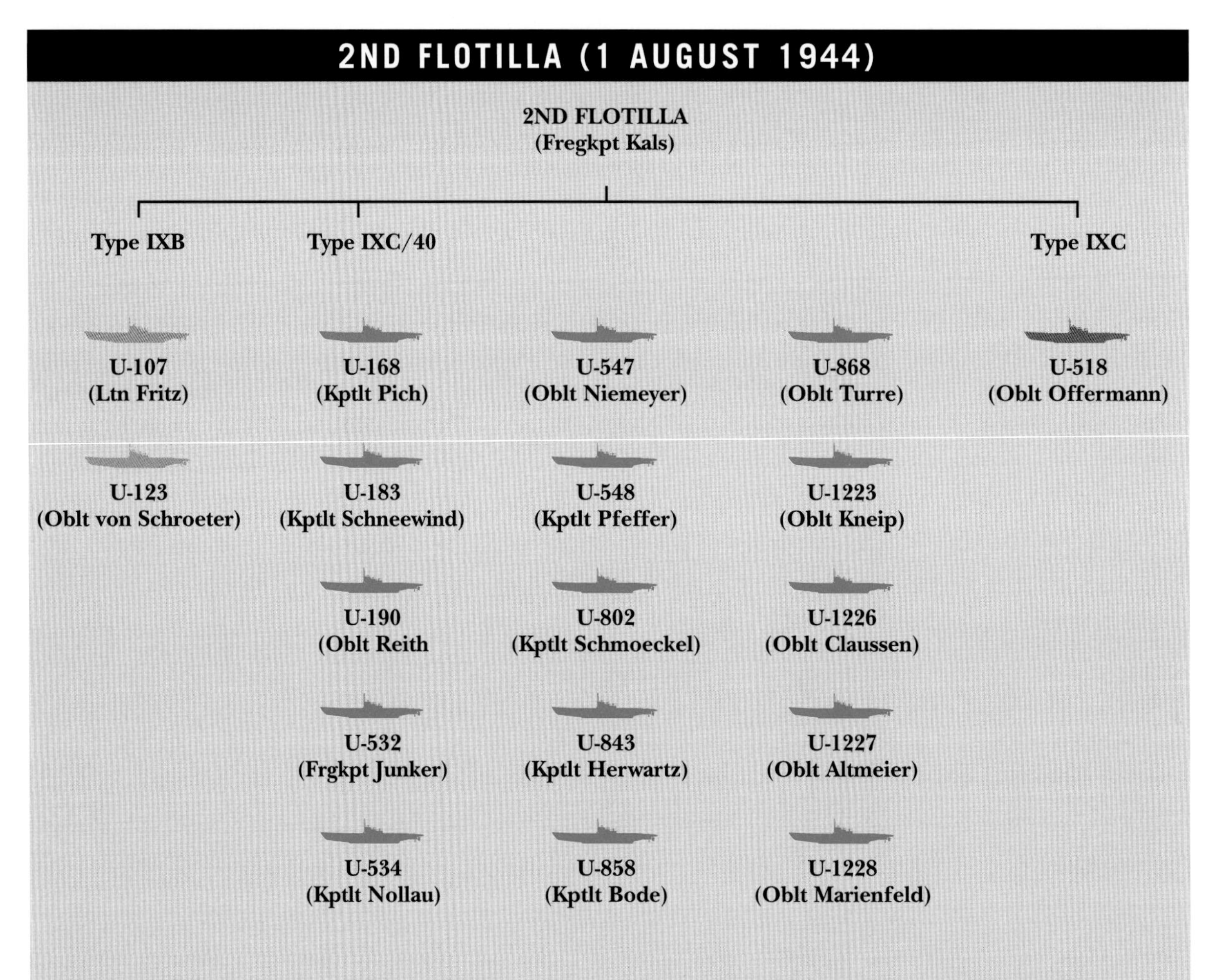

Fregattenkapitän Ernst Kals' 2nd Flotilla is seen here as it stood in August 1944, the month of its transfer from its long-standing base down in Lorient up to Norwegian waters. This transfer was effectively the end of the flotilla, as its U-boats were absorbed into various other combat and training units, and were used in operations in the far north. Many of the U-boat crews who survived the trip to the north also survived the war.

CONVOY PQ-17 TIMETABLE	
Date	**Event**
27 Jun 1942	At 1600, the ships of convoy PQ17 leave their anchorage in Hvalfjordur, Iceland, and head northwards. The convoy consists of 35 ships and is heavily loaded with 297 aircraft, 594 tanks, 4246 lorries and gun carriers and 158,503 tonnes (156,000 tons) of cargo. (This was enough to equip an army of 50,000 men and was valued at $700 million at the time.) Shortly after leaving, one ship runs aground and returns to port
29 Jun	The convoy encounters heavy drift ice. Four merchantmen are damaged, with one having to return to port. This leaves 33 ships en route to Russia
1 Jul	The convoy is spotted by *U-255* and *U-408*. *U-456* joins the other boats and begins tracking the convoy. Further reconnaissance information is provided by Bv 138 flying boats of the *Luftwaffe*
2 Jul	A number of U-boats attempt attacks on the convoy, but to little effect. They are joined in the evening by the first in a series of *Luftwaffe* torpedo attacks
3 Jul	U-boats and *Luftwaffe* torpedo planes continue to attack without success. However, British intelligence receives reports that a powerful German surface force is leaving Norwegian waters and heading northwards. The Admiralty calculates that Tirpitz, Hipper, Scheer and Lützow would intercept the convoy on the evening of 4 July
4 Jul	Two ships are sunk by *U-457* and *U-334*. At around 2200, the British Admiralty, fearing that Tirpitz and her consorts are about to strike, and knowing that the battleships of the Home Fleet are too far away to intervene, orders the escorts to run westwards and the convoy to scatter and ships to proceed independently towards Russia
5 Jul	Even though the German surface forces have not left port, the scattered merchantmen are vulnerable to U-boats and air attack. The slaughter begins almost immediately. *Luftwaffe* aircraft sink six ships, while the U-boats account for a similar number (*U-88* and *U-703* sinking two each, while *U-334* and *U-456* sink the others)
6 Jul	Two more vessels are lost, one to the *Luftwaffe* and one to *U-255*
7 Jul	The *Luftwaffe* sinks another ship, while *U-255*, *U-457* and *U-355* account for three more
8 Jul	*U-255* sinks her third ship
10 Jul	*U-251* and *U-376* each sink one merchantman
13 Jul	*U-255* sinks a derelict merchant ship that has been adrift since being struck by *Luftwaffe* bombs on 5 July

British Artic convoys were classified according to whether they were outgoing journeys or return journeys, and also according to their destination. Each convoy, as in the Atlantic system, was identified by the Allies using a system of letters and numbers. While the numbers simply designated the convoy number in a mainly sequential system, the letters marked the destination. The letters 'PQ' related to convoys sailing from Iceland to Russia, while the reverse 'QP' letters identified the return convoy. 'PK' convoys were destined for Petsamo-Kirkenes in Finland; 'RA' indicated the journey from Kola Fjord, Russia, to Loch Ewe, UK ('JW' was the outgoing journey); 'BD' was a Soviet coastal convoy between Archangel and Dikson. Between August 1941 and May 1945, there was a total of 78 Arctic convoys, made by 1400 ships.

The convoys presented various challenges for the U-boat arm, not the least of which was spotting them in the horrendous weather that dogged all shipping in northern waters. Air escorts accompanied the convoys as far as possible, and the naval escorts consisted of either British or US destroyers and, in the earlier days of the campaign, a separate cruiser group. Occasionally, Soviet naval vessels would also accompany the convoys, although their presence was a minor element within the overall campaign.

BOATS ASSIGNED TO 10TH FLOTILLA	
Type	**Number assigned**
Type IXC	26
Type IXC/40	41
Type IXD1	2
Type IXD2	4
Type XB	1
Type XIV	6

The campaign against the Arctic convoys would not begin in earnest until 1942, but Raeder was beginning to react to their presence at the end of 1941. In December of that year, he ordered the formation of a small U-boat hunting group codenamed 'Uhlan' *(U-134, U-454* and *U-584)* and its deployment across the stretch of water between Spitsbergen and northern Norway, there to lie in wait to passing convoys.

First kill for the northern group came on 2 January 1942, when *U-134* intercepted PQ7A heading east, torpedoing and sinking the steam merchant *Waziristan.* Just over two weeks later, on 17 January, it was *U-454*'s turn, when it sank one merchant ship and damaged another from convoy PQ8. On 30 March 1942, two British ships and one US merchantman went down following a three-U-boat attack *(U-376, U-435* and *U-456),* the numbers of U-boats deployed to the theatre having increased with Hitler's paranoia about a potential Allied invasion of Norway.

All such kills were celebrated by the individual U-boat crews, but on a grand strategic scale they were relatively ineffective. The U-boats were managing to sink only a handful of ships each month, and many of those craft were of small tonnages. This situation was unsatisfactory for Raeder, who was restless over Hitler's decision to keep significant numbers of U-boats around Norway when they would be better employed elsewhere. The fact remained that the Arctic convoys were simply not as regular, and often not as large, as the Atlantic convoys, so the tonnages sunk would always be smaller. Periodically, this fact would persuade Hitler to send some Norwegian-based boats elsewhere, such as south into the Mediterranean.

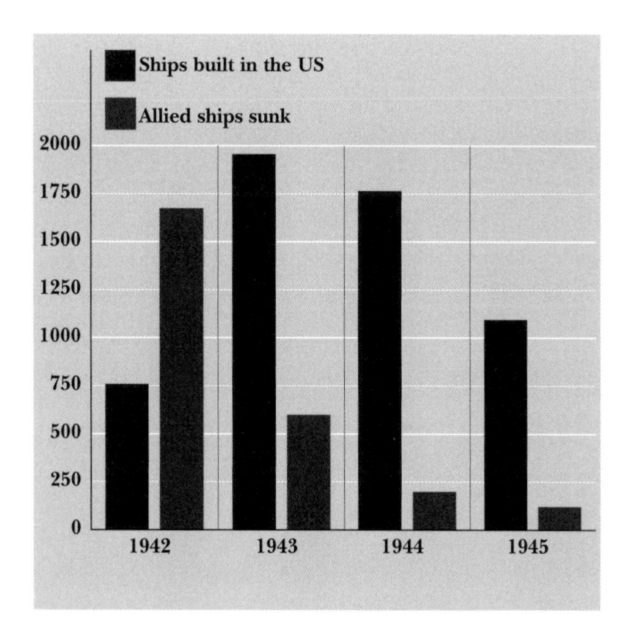

Left: By 1943, US ship production had far outstripped the ability of the U-boats to sink Allied shipping.

PQ 17

The high point of the Arctic campaign for the *Kriegsmarine*, and the incident that transformed the Allied approach to its northern convoys, was the attack on convoy PQ17 during the first two weeks of July 1942. This operation illustrated what success could be achieved if U-boats operated in conjunction with other elements of the *Kriegsmarine* fleet and also the *Luftwaffe* maritime strike forces. PQ17 has already been mentioned above, but a closer look will reveal more about the capabilities of the German submarines and other maritime vessels.

PQ17 was a convoy of 35 ships that left Iceland on 27 June. It was carrying a hefty and valuable cargo, which included nearly 300 aircraft, 594 tanks, over 4200 vehicles and thousands of tons of additional cargo.

By this time, the Allies had had enough bad experiences with the Arctic convoys to provide a respectably powerful escort. (During the earlier PQ16 convoy in late May, massed *Luftwaffe* attacks resulted in five ships sunk and four damaged, out of the 30 that sailed.) A significant core escort force was accompanying the convoy, which included four cruisers, three destroyers and two British submarines, and up to the North Cape point another 12 British warships provided additional security (this included two battleships and the aircraft carrier *Victorious*).

Yet they were sailing into dangerous waters. Not only was there the threat from the U-boats and the *Luftwaffe*, but on 4 July British intelligence revealed that the *Tirpitz*, *Hipper*, *Admiral Scheer* and *Lützow* were also deployed around Norway, alongside multiple destroyers, ready to overwhelm the convoy escort then turn on the convoy itself. The Germans did indeed know the convoy was on its way, and Raeder and his staff had devised Operation *Rösselsprung* (Knight's Move, referring to the move in chess) in response. Nine U-boats were deployed – three positioned across the Denmark Strait as an early warning line, while six others, known as the *Eisteufel* (Ice Devil) group, patrolled across the Norwegian Sea.

The powerful surface warships coalesced around Altenfjord on the 4th, just as Allied intelligence had revealed, but here the British response changed the fortunes of PQ17.

Alarmed by the news of the German warship group, Admiral Sir Dudley Pound, the British First Sea Lord, ordered the convoy's vessels to split up and rely on solitary seas for their protection. Now the U-boats and the *Luftwaffe* forces massed against the convoy could go to work in their ideal conditions, working against isolated, unarmed merchant vessels that were deprived of their escorts. (Although in fairness, had the convoy proceeded onwards together, with the Home Fleet escort vessels, then the destruction could have been worse if the German surface fleet attacked.) The results, as history now knows, were catastrophic. From 4–13 July, 25 merchant vessels from the convoy were sunk. The causes behind the sinkings are noteworthy. Sixteen of the 25 were sunk directly by submarine attack, and the remainder were critically damaged by air attack (bombs and torpedoes), but then finished off by the submarines. U-boats and aircraft then claimed another three victims during the convoy's return journey later in the month.

The rough handling of PQ17 was a great victory for the northern U-boats, and a shocking tragedy for the Allies. Such was the scale of the defeat that Churchill actually cancelled Arctic convoys for the next nine weeks, demonstrating the strategic power of the U-boat.

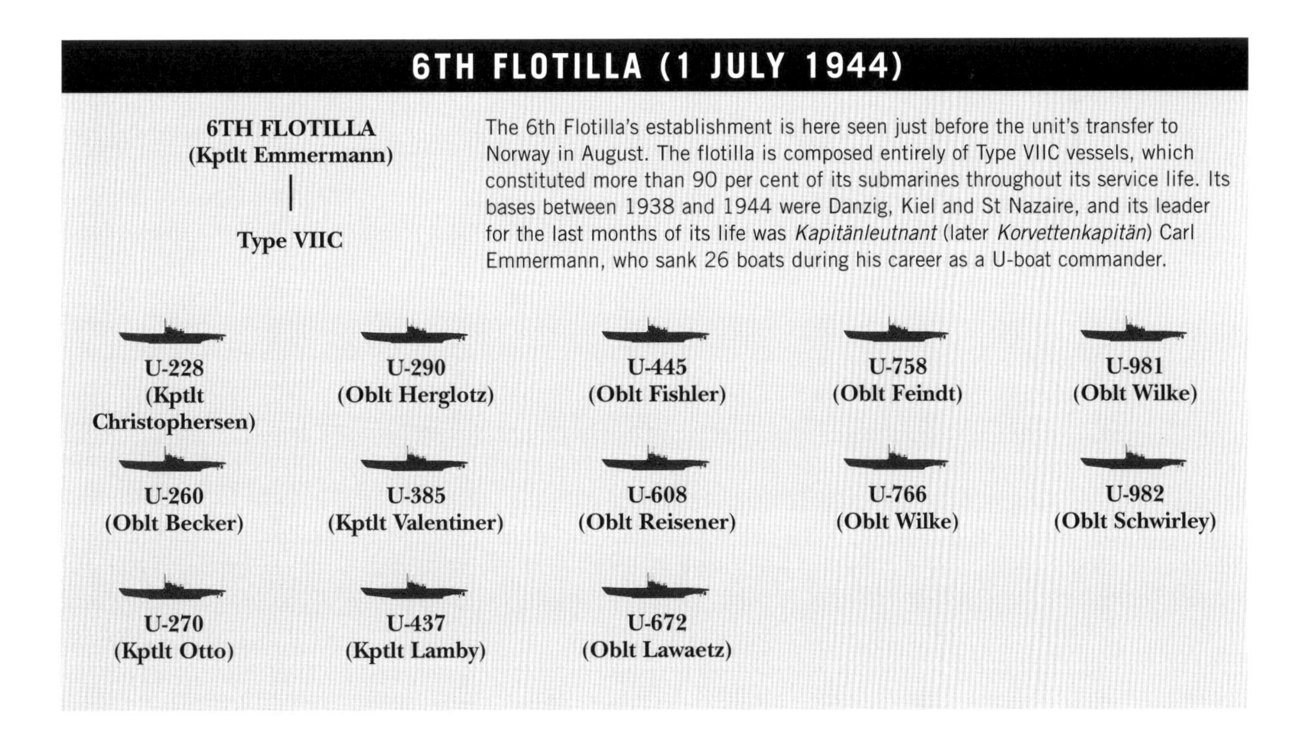

The 6th Flotilla's establishment is here seen just before the unit's transfer to Norway in August. The flotilla is composed entirely of Type VIIC vessels, which constituted more than 90 per cent of its submarines throughout its service life. Its bases between 1938 and 1944 were Danzig, Kiel and St Nazaire, and its leader for the last months of its life was *Kapitänleutnant* (later *Korvettenkapitän*) Carl Emmermann, who sank 26 boats during his career as a U-boat commander.

Losing the Arctic: 1942–44

The near destruction of convoy PQ17 was, for the U-boat service at least, the high point of the Arctic war, although the performance of the *Kriegsmarine*'s surface fleet had been disappointing.

After the PQ17 disaster, the Allies took stock of the situation with the Arctic convoys. By this stage of the war, the Battle of the Atlantic had taken a horrific turn against the Allies (see above), and Britain and the United States could not afford to see similar disasters repeated in the northeastern waters.

The key lesson to come out of PQ17 for the Allies was that convoy escorts had to be improved dramatically to provide a guard against both the U-boats and the *Kriegsmarine*'s surface fleet, should it intervene again. Furthermore, the threat posed by the *Luftwaffe* had to be if not neutralized then at least managed by the provision of solid air escorts. The proof of the new practices would come from 2 September 1942, when convoy PQ18 departed Loch Ewe in Scotland bound for the port of Archangel.

Redesigned convoys

PQ18, a convoy containing 44 merchant ships, was a completely different proposition for the *Kriegsmarine* U-boats in the Arctic. The commander-in-chief of the British Home Fleet, Admiral Sir John Tovey, had completely rearranged the escort both in terms of its magnitude and its tactics. Tovey created a large Fighter Destroyer Escort (FDE), 12–16 ships strong, that would form a permanent escort for the convoys, but added to that were two anti-aircraft gunships, four corvettes and, significantly, the escort carrier *Avenger*. A force of RAF

13TH FLOTILLA (1 OCTOBER 1943)

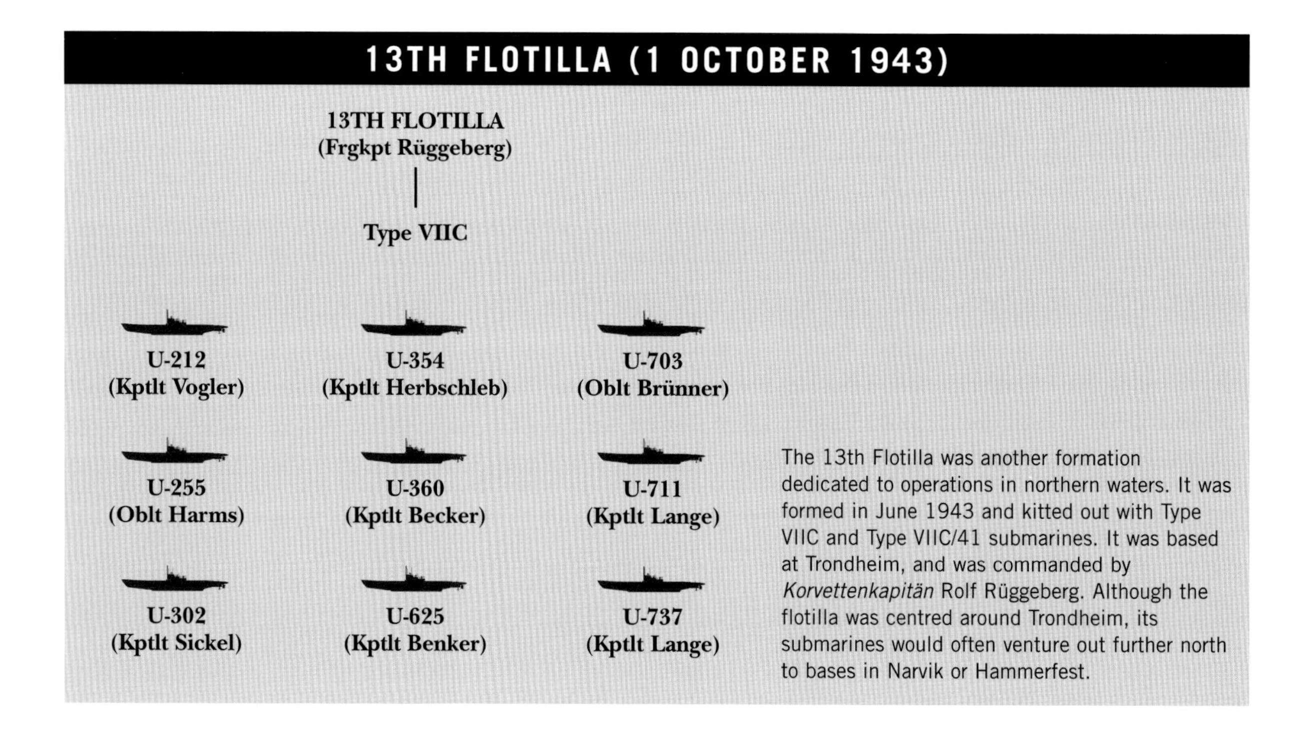

The 13th Flotilla was another formation dedicated to operations in northern waters. It was formed in June 1943 and kitted out with Type VIIC and Type VIIC/41 submarines. It was based at Trondheim, and was commanded by *Korvettenkapitän* Rolf Rüggeberg. Although the flotilla was centred around Trondheim, its submarines would often venture out further north to bases in Narvik or Hammerfest.

and Royal Australian Air Force (RAAF) Catalinas and Hampdens were also sent to Vaenga airbase near Murmansk, to provide additional air cover. Further away, the British Home Fleet had several battleships and cruisers at the ready in case the *Kriegsmarine* rolled out its big-gun warships.

Greater challenge

The strength of the convoy escort was a real tactical headache for the U-boats, as it not only threatened them at a direct attack level, but it also meant that the *Luftwaffe* would be less effective as a distraction force. By 8 September, *Luftwaffe* flights had detected the approaching convoy and 12 U-boats had deployed themselves in groups of three across the contested sea lanes. Raeder, it should be noted, had cancelled surface operations against the convoy by *Tirpitz* and the other large warships, noting the threat posed to his capital ships by the escort carrier, which in turn became the *Luftwaffe*'s number one target.

It quickly became evident to the U-boat crews that there was going to be no repeat of PQ17. On the 12th, *U-88* was sunk ahead of the convoy by the destroyer *Faulkner*. An air attack later that day sank eight Allied merchant ships, but over the course of the next few days the combination of heavy anti-aircraft fire and the use of the escort carrier's assets controlled the worst of the *Luftwaffe*'s actions. By the time the convoy reached its

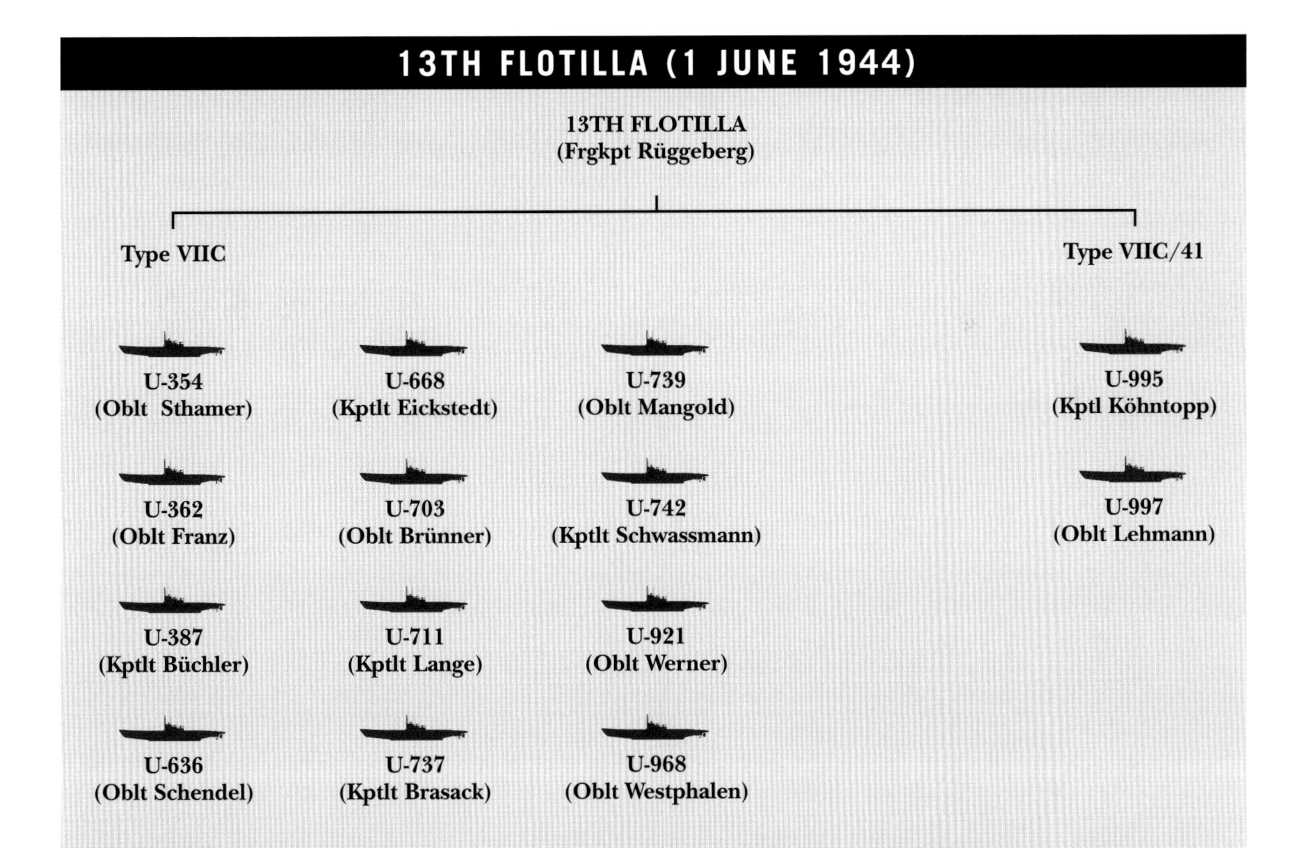

By June 1944, the 13th Flotilla had two Type VIIC/41 submarines on its establishment. These were essentially the same as the Type VIIC, but had specially strengthened hulls that allowed them to achieve greater dive depths. In total, the flotilla received a total of eight Type VIIC/41s, compared with 47 of the regular Type VIICs.

WOLF PACKS *KEIL* AND *DONNER*

The wolf packs known as *Keil* and *Donner* were assembled in March 1942 to intercept Arctic convoys, with patrol areas off Bear Island. The major attack made by the combined groups came on 30 April 1944, when the U-boats attacked convoy RA59. The action proved to be a nightmare for even such a strong force of U-boats. Although *U-711* did manage to penetrate the extremely strong escort screen and sink a large American freighter, the escort retaliation over the next three days saw *U-277, U-959* and *U-674* all sunk without the wolf pack's inflicting extra cost on the convoy. Such high rates of attrition amongst the U-boats became common during the last two years of the war.

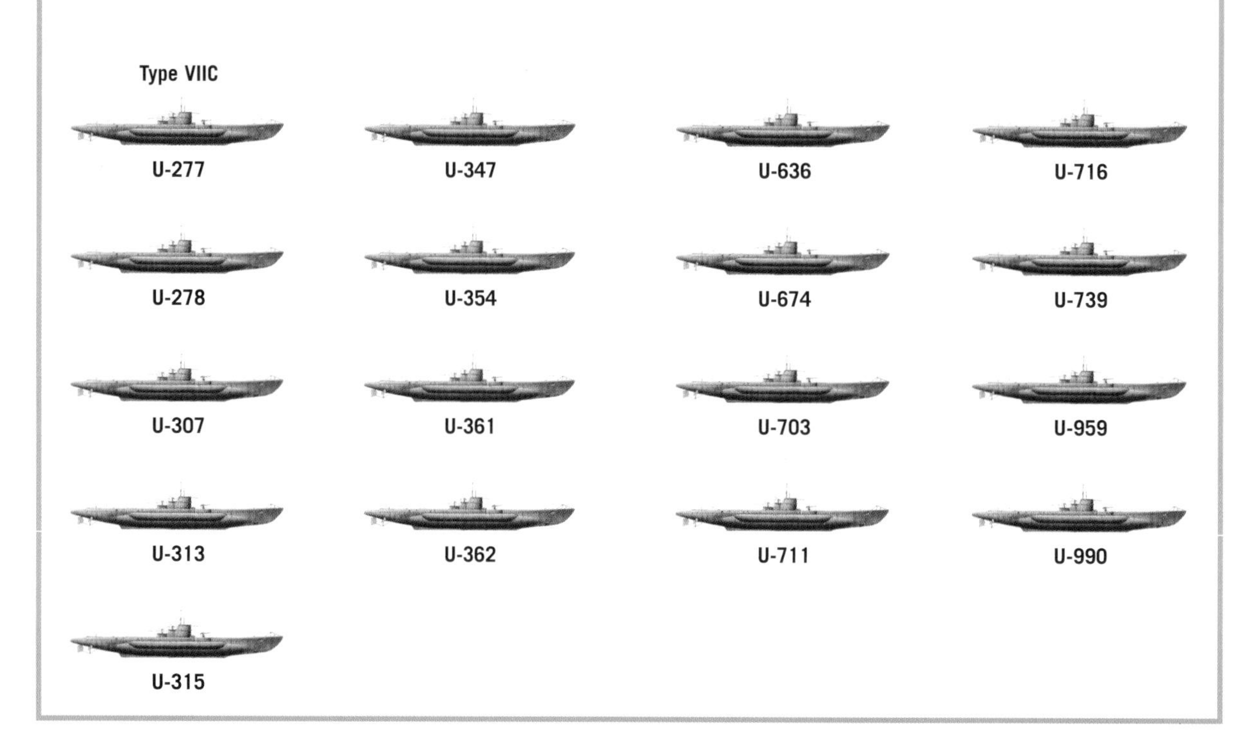

destination on the 20th, 10 ships had been sunk by air attack, but some 40 German aircraft had been shot down, heavy losses for a formation with limited resources to begin with.

For the U-boats, the action against PQ18 also brought worrying results. On the 13th, *U-408* sank two merchant vessels, and on the 14th, *U-408* and *U-457* between them sank the tanker *Atheltemplar* (*U-457* severely damaged the ship, and *U-408* essentially sank the abandoned wreck). These successes, however, were balanced out by the sinking of four U-boats during the onslaught, including *U-457*, which went down after an attack by the destroyer *Impulsive* on the 16th. It should be noted that *U-408* would also later end her days in Arctic waters. After a service life in three flotillas – 5th, 9th and 11th – during which time she claimed three sinkings, she was finally caught by a Catalina aircraft north of Iceland on 5 November 1942 and depth-charged to destruction. All 48 of her crew died in the sinking.

Breaking point

Despite the improved escort, the combined sinkings of PQ17 and PQ18 gave the Allies mounting concern, and further Arctic convoys were suspended for the rest of 1942. When they returned in December – coinciding with the Allies' renewed grip on Ultra intelligence, the better use of air cover and improved anti-submarine escort techniques – the Allies had changed the convoy

U-BOAT LOSSES 1944	
Month	**Boats lost**
January	U-972, U-426, U-757, U-81, U-231, U-305, U-544, U-377, U-641, U-263, U-271, U-571, U-364, U-314, U-592
February	U-854, U-177, U-762, U-238, U-734, U-545, U-666, U-283, U-424, U-738, UIT-23, U-7, U-406, U-264, U-386, U-257, U-713, U-761, U-601, U-91
March	U-358, U-603, U-709, U-472, U-366, U-744, U-973, U-343, U-450, U-625, U-845, U-380, U-410, UIT-22, U-575, U-653, U-392, U-28, U-801, U-1013, U-1059, U-976, U-851, U-961, U-223
April	U-360, U-288, U-355, U-302, U-455, U-856, U-2, U-962, U-515, U-68, U-108, U-448, U-550, U-342, U-986, U-974, U-311, U-193, U-488, U-803, U-421
May	U-277, U-674, U-959, U-852, U-371, U-846, U-66, U-473, U-765, U-1224, U-731, U-240, U-616, U-241, U-960, U-1015, U-453, U-675, U-476, U-990, U-292, U-549, U-289
June	U-477, U-505, U-740, U-629, U-955, U-970, U-373, U-441, U-821, U-980, U-490, U-1191, U-715, U-860, U-987, U-423, U-767, U-971, U-1225, U-269, U-317, U-719, U-998, U-988, U-478
July	U-543, U-154, U-233, U-390, U-586, U-642, U-678, U-243, U-1222, U-415, U-319, U-347, U-361, U-672, U-742, U-742, U-212, U-1164, U-214, U-2323, U-250, U-333
August	U-3, U-4, U-10, U-21, U-239, U-671, U-471, U-736, U-952, U-969, U-6, U-608, U-872, U-385, U-967, U-198, U-981, U-270, U-618, U-741, U-107, U-129, U-621, U-123, U-466, U-9, U-188, U-413, U-984, U-1229, U-230, U-766, U-344, U-180, U-354, U-445, U-18, U-24, U-178, U-667
September	U-247, U-394, U-362, U-484, U-865, U-20, U-23, U-19, U-855, U-703, U-1054, U-925, U-407, U-867, U-743, U-859, U-565, U-596, U-871, U-276, U-863, U-1000, U-1062
October	U-921, U-993, U-228, U-437, U-168, U-2331, U-92, U-777, U-1006, U-957, U-256, U-673, U-1060, U-1226
November	U-537, U-771, U-1200, U-479, U-985, U-1020, U-482, U-80
December	U-196, U-297, U-387, U-650, U-365, U-400, U-772, U-1209, U-737, U-2342, U-877, U-735, U-322, U-547, U-2530

U-255 TIMETABLE		
Patrol Dates	**Operational Area**	**Ships Sunk**
15 Jun 1942 – 15 Jul 1942	Northern waters	4
4 Aug 1942 – 9 Sep 1942	Spitzbergen/Soviet Arctic	0
13 Sep 1942 – 25 Sep 1942	Greenland Sea	1
29 Sep 1942 – 3 Oct 1942	Transit to Kiel for refit	0
7 Jan 1943 – 18 Jan 1943	Transit from Kiel to Hammerfest	0
23 Jan 1943 – 9 Feb 1943	Barents Sea	3
22 Feb 1943 – 15 Mar 1943	Norwegian Sea	2
29 Mar 1943 – 29 Apr 1943	Northern waters	0
19 Jul 1943 – 19 Sep 1943	Soviet waters/Novaya Zemlya	1
26 Feb 1944 – 11 Apr 1944	North Atlantic	1
6 Jun 1944 – 15 Jun 1944	Bay of Biscay	0
17 Apr 1945 – 21 Apr 1945	Minelaying off the French coast	0
22 Apr 1945 – 8 May 1945	Moved between La Pallice and St Nazaire several times	0
8 May 1945 – 15 May 1945	Transit to Loch Alsh and surrender	0

designation system. From now on, the PQ/QP suffixes became JW (eastbound) and RA (westbound).

What became apparent over 1943 and into 1944 was how few rewards the U-boats were gaining from attacking the Arctic convoys when compared with the risks taken. To take one U-boat as an example, *U-354*: between October 1942 and August 1944, it made nearly 20 operational patrols in northern waters. In that time, it sank only two enemy merchant ships. Its end came on 24 August 1944, when it was depth-charged in a ferocious attack by four Allied escort vessels, sinking off the North Cape with all 51 crew.

Similar stories were repeated throughout the remainder of the Arctic U-boat campaign. Each convoy usually brought some kills, but often with equal or greater losses. For example, in late March and early April, the assault on convoy JW58 by a total of 17 U-boats brought no merchant losses, but resulted in the destruction of four U-boats. Of the 492 ships that sailed in RA convoys, only 10 were sunk by U-boats, and in the process the U-boats lost 9 craft.

Redeployments

The same tactical and technological innovations that had given the Allies the edge in the Atlantic also won out in the Arctic. Although during the liberation of France most submarines fled to the north, swelling the ranks of formations such as the 11th and 13th Flotillas

13TH FLOTILLA (1 MAY 1945)

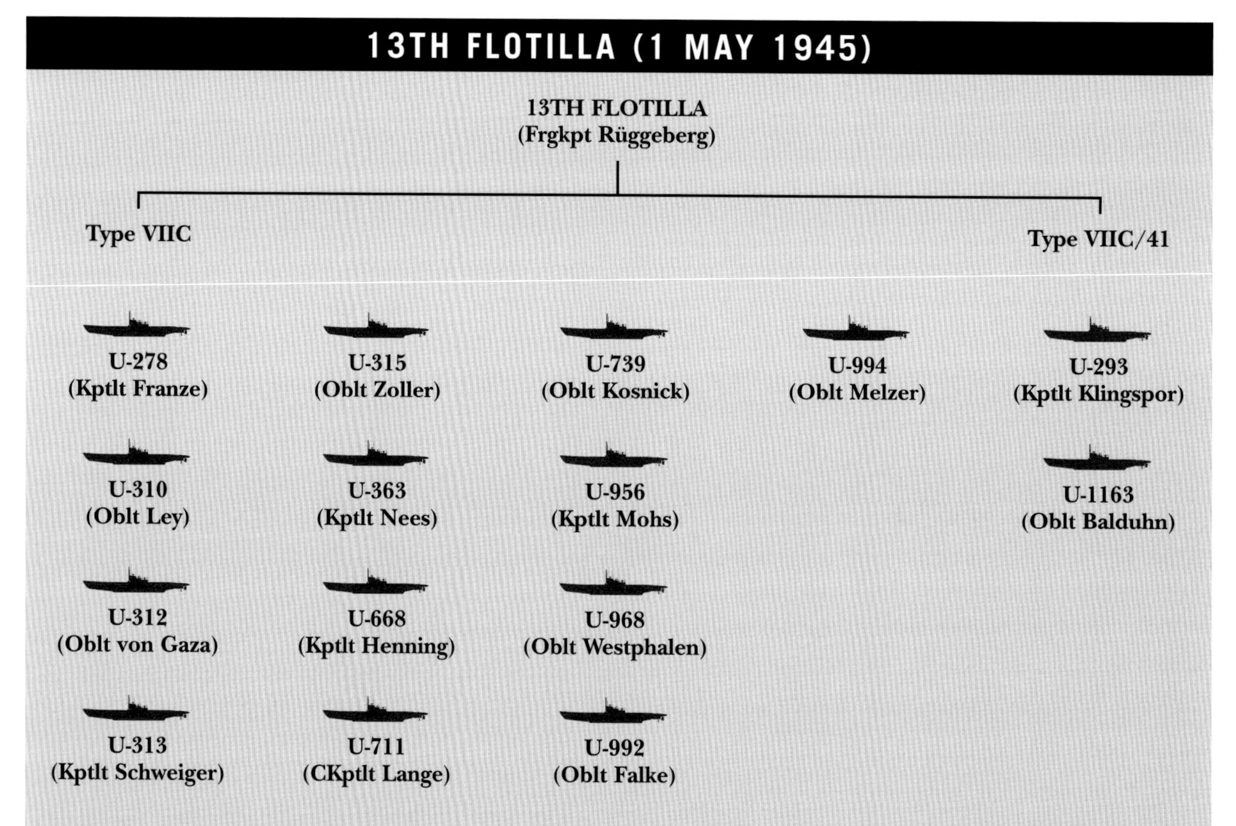

Based up in Trondheim, the 13th Flotilla was active until the very end of World War II, being disbanded only when Germany finally surrendered in May 1945. By the first of that month, the formation still had 15 U-boats on its establishment and was still under the command of Rolf Rüggeberg. Many of these U-boats were subsequently scuttled by the Allies during the Operation *Deadlight* action, in which they disposed of 121 submarines.

dramatically, there was still little the U-boat arm could do by the end of 1944, such was the strength of the Allied escorts. A telling figure is that in January and February 1945, outside the Atlantic, the German forces in total – both the *Kriegsmarine* and *Luftwaffe* – managed to sink only 14,521 tonnes (14,292 tons) of merchant shipping. In fact, the last submarine of World War II to be sunk was destroyed off the Norwegian coastline. This was *U-320*, launched on 6 November 1943 and destined to make only two, unsuccessful, patrols. It was depth-charged by a Catalina flying boat off Bergen on 7 May 1945, the end of the war being insufficient to save it.

Mediterranean operations: 1941–45

The Mediterranean became another major theatre of action for the U-boats from the summer of 1941. These were confined and difficult waters for the U-boats, which had to cope with several major Royal Navy fleets.

By mid-1941, Germany was locked in a dramatic to-and-fro battle with the British in North Africa. The theatre was a unique one, with both Allies and Axis fighting along a narrow coastal strip of North Africa, across terrain and distances that stretched logistics to their absolute maximum. For both sides, the maritime supply convoys were absolutely central in fuelling the war. For the Germans, the principal supply convoys came from Italy, mainly using Italian merchant ships and running into ports such as Tripoli, Benghazi and, when it was

U-BOAT MEDITERRANEAN BASES

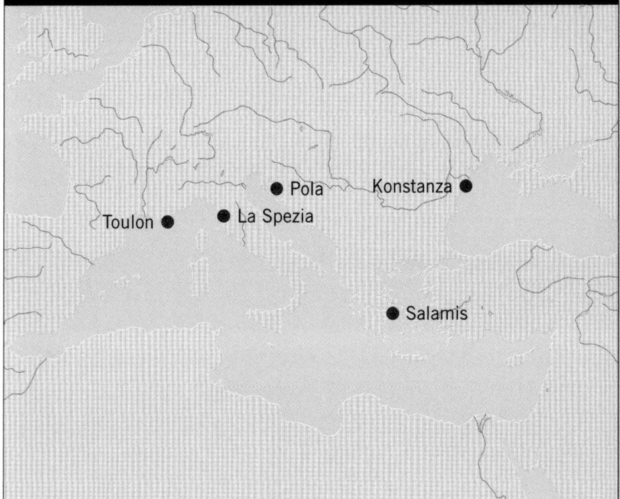

Pola
Konstanza
Toulon
La Spezia
Salamis

Spreading bases

The first Mediterranean U-boat base was established at Salamis on the southern tip of Greece following the formation of the 23rd Flotilla in September 1941. The 29th Flotilla was established a few months later, with its headquarters first at La Spezia in northwest Italy and then, from late summer 1943, at Toulon on the coast of southern France. Between them the two flotillas utilized a spread of bases and forward operating anchorages across the Mediterranean and on the Black Sea.

From west to east the main Mediterranean U-boat bases were Toulon/Marseilles, La Spezia, Pola on the Croatian coast and Salamis, with Konstanza on the Black Sea. Together these bases had the geographical distribution necessary for the U-boats to patrol the Mediterranean from its entrance into the Atlantic over to the coastal waters of the Middle East.

U-75 TIMETABLE		
Patrol Dates	**Operational Area**	**Ships Sunk**
10 Apr 1941 – 12 May 1941	South of Iceland	1
29 May 1941 – 3 Jul 1941	Central North Atlantic	1
29 Jul 1941 – 25 Aug 1941	Central North Atlantic	2
27 Sep 1941 – 2 Nov 1941	Transit from St Nazaire to Salamis	2
22 Dec 1941 – 28 Dec 1941	Off Egyptian coast	1

U-73 TIMETABLE		
Patrol Dates	**Operational Area**	**Ships Sunk**
8 Feb 1941 – 2 Mar 1941	West of British Isles	1
25 Mar 1941 – 24 Apr 1941	Southwest of Ireland	4
20 May 1941 – 24 Jun 1941	Bismarck escort North Atlantic/South Iceland	0
29 Jul 1941 – 2 Aug 1941	Mission aborted due to engine trouble	0
7 Aug 1941 – 7 Sep 1941	Southwest of Iceland	0
11 Oct 1941 – 11 Nov 1941	Southeast of Greenland	0
4 Jan 1942 – 20 Jan 1942	Through Strait of Gibraltar to Messina	0
31 Jan 1942 – 26 Feb 1942	Off Cyrenaica	0
16 Mar 1942 – 26 Mar 1942	Against convoy MW10 Alexandria/Malta	0
4 Aug 1942 – 5 Sep 1942	Against Malta resupply convoy Pedestal	1
20 Oct 1942 – 19 Nov 1942	Western Mediterranean against Operation Torch	0
22 Dec 1942 – 13 Jan 1943	Western Mediterranean off Algeria	1
12 Jun 1943 – 1 Jul 1943	Off Algerian coast	1
2 Aug 1943 – 29 Aug 1943	Off coast of Sicily	0
5 Oct 1943 – 30 Oct 1943	Special operations	0
4 Dec 1943 – 16 Dec 1943	Off Algerian coast	0

later in German hands, Tobruk. Major Royal Navy and RAF deployments worked hard to interdict these supply lines, particularly from Mediterranean naval centres such as Gibraltar (home of 'Force H') and Alexandria (home of the Mediterranean Fleet). The British-held island of Malta, under Axis siege from June 1940 to December 1942, was another thorn in the German side, as it sat across the Axis supply lines to North Africa.

By mid-1941, following a series of hefty Italian naval defeats, Hitler ordered Raeder to make immediate U-boat deployments into the Mediterranean. Six boats were pulled from the Atlantic straightaway and sent into the warmer waters, followed by over 30 more by the end of the year.

Operational structure

Two main U-boat formations dominated operations in the Mediterranean: the 23rd Flotilla and the 29th Flotilla. The 23rd was the first to be established in the region, on 11 September 1941. The German occupation of Greece made it possible for the flotilla to be based at Salamis on the southern edge of the country, a convenient location for striking at British convoys to Egypt. The 23rd would never be a large flotilla – during its existence it was equipped with only three Type VIIB and six Type VIIC vessels. This being said, the flotilla was not in existence long – it was disbanded in May 1942 and its boats were taken over into the newer and far larger 29th Flotilla. (Note that the 23rd Flotilla was later re-formed in 1943 as a training flotilla.)

The 29th Flotilla was originally created in December 1941, and had a much improved capability when compared with its predecessor – it operated three Type VIIB and 49 Type VIIC submarines between its foundation and the date on which it was disbanded, in September 1944. The 29th's bases stretched from Salamis in the east to Toulon and Marseilles in the west. (From its formation until August 1943, it was headquartered in La Spezia in Italy, but following a deterioration of the land campaign situation in Italy, it relocated to Toulon.)

Combat operations

U-boat combat operations against the Allies' Mediterranean convoys began before 1941 was out, and initially had limited success. A fundamental problem was that the Mediterranean sea lanes carried a much larger amount of coastal shipping, which had a shallower draft than the ocean-going ships that coursed the deep Atlantic. The result was that many torpedoes, set to run at a depth of around 4.5m (15ft), actually passed beneath the intended target. (The problem could be

29TH FLOTILLA (1 JANUARY 1942)

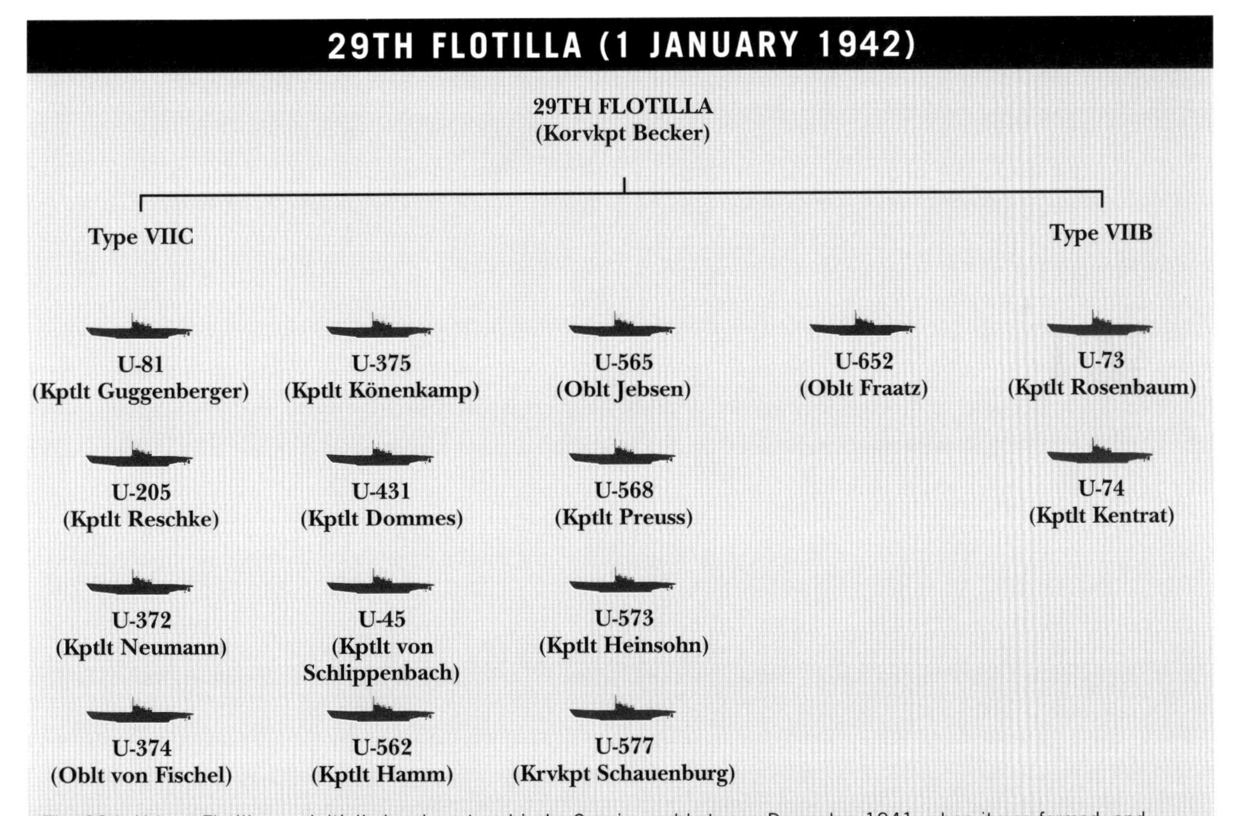

The 29th U-boat Flotilla was initially headquartered in La Spezia, and between December 1941, when it was formed, and September 1944, when it was disbanded, a total of 52 U-boats passed through its establishment. In the summer of 1943, the flotilla was forced to relocate its headquarters to Toulon as the Allies began their advance into Italian territory from the south, unsettling the naval power balance in the Mediterranean further in favour of the Allies.

partly overcome by using magnetic influence detonating pistols, but these were not always reliable.) Better luck was had against some of the larger British warships, as was proved in spectacular style in November 1941.

During that month, the U-boats scored two major victories. On the 13th off Gibraltar, while actually serving under the 1st U-boat Flotilla, *U-81* torpedoed the British aircraft carrier *Ark Royal*, which sank the following day. Then, on 25 November, the battleship HMS *Barham* received three torpedoes from *U-331* as she waded into a fight against Italian convoys. During her sinking, her 381mm (15in) main ammunition magazine exploded, blowing the ship to bits and killing two-thirds of the crew.

Increased momentum

The U-boat momentum now seemed to increase, as December brought more big victories. On 14/15 December, *U-557*, commanded by *Korvettenkapitän* Ottokar Paulshen, sank the *Arethusa* class cruiser HMS *Galatea* near Alexandria in a night action. The British also lost another cruiser and a destroyer to mines over the subsequent week, and with the beginning of war against Japan, major British warships were diverted from the Mediterranean to the Far East, where many of them became casualties.

For Hitler, these sinkings seemed to prove that his redeployment policy was a judicious move. German naval historian Horst Boog, however, has noted how the sinkings were treated with less jubilation by Dönitz:

'These spectacular successes appeared fully to justify the massive U-boat operations and soon led to the confident assessment that the U-boats – in comparison with the Luftwaffe and Italian navy – were "the only really efficient weapon" in the Mediterranean. However, Dönitz warned against overestimation of German prospects and against the illusion that naval supremacy could be achieved by the U-boats.'

Dönitz was right to express caution about the future of the U-boats in the Mediterranean. The theatre presented some uniquely dangerous conditions for the U-boat crews, especially once the Allies began to gain dominance in the land campaign from late 1942. First, entry into the Mediterranean was through the narrow, British-controlled Strait of Gibraltar, one of the most dangerous stretches of water for U-boat crews anywhere in the world. Significant numbers of German submarines were sunk just making this fraught passage, and in December 1941 Dönitz predicted to the German Naval Staff that up to one-third of his boats would be casualties in the strait. The assessment may have been

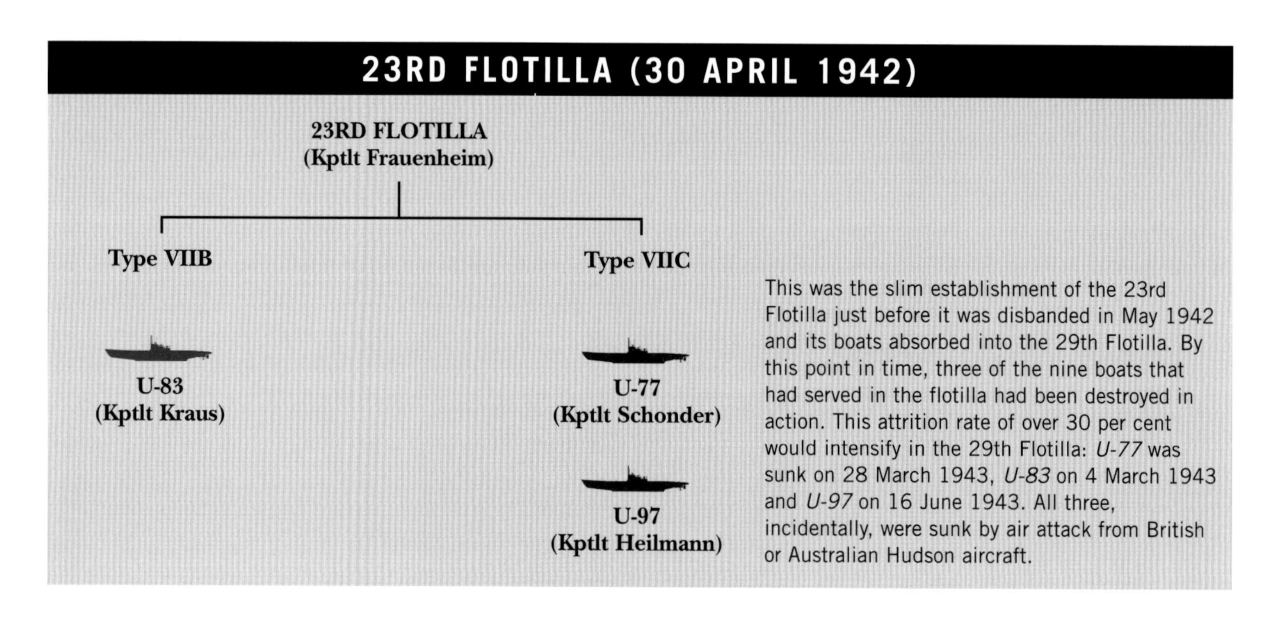

This was the slim establishment of the 23rd Flotilla just before it was disbanded in May 1942 and its boats absorbed into the 29th Flotilla. By this point in time, three of the nine boats that had served in the flotilla had been destroyed in action. This attrition rate of over 30 per cent would intensify in the 29th Flotilla: *U-77* was sunk on 28 March 1943, *U-83* on 4 March 1943 and *U-97* on 16 June 1943. All three, incidentally, were sunk by air attack from British or Australian Hudson aircraft.

U-371 TIMETABLE		
Patrol Dates	**Operational Area**	**Ships Sunk**
5 Jun 1941 – 1 Jul 1941	West of British Isles	1
23 Jul 1941 – 19 Aug 1941	Southwest of Ireland	2
16 Sep 1941 – 24 Oct 1941	Transit from Brest to Mediterranean	0
4 Dec 1941 – 10 Jan 1942	Eastern Mediterranean off Egyptian coast	0
4 Mar 1942 – 25 Mar 1942	Off Tobruk	0
21 Apr 1942 – 18 Sep 1942	Eastern Mediterranean	0
12 Oct 1942 – 16 Oct 1942	Transit from Salamis to Pola	0
1 Dec 1942 – 4 Dec 1942	Transit from Pola to Messina	0
7 Dec 1942 – 10 Jan 1943	Western Mediterranean	1
14 Feb 1943 – 3 Mar 1943	Off Algerian coast	1
7 Apr 1943 – 11 May 1943	Off Algerian coast	1
3 Jul 1943 – 12 Jul 1943	Western Mediterranean	0
22 Jul 1943 – 11 Aug 1943	Off Algerian coast	1
21 Aug 1943 – 3 Sep 1943	Western Mediterranean	0
7 Oct 1943 – 28 Oct 1943	Off Algerian coast	3
15 Nov 1943 – 23 Nov 1943	Western Mediterranean	0
22 Jan 1944 – 13 Feb 1944	Off the Anzio beachhead	0
4 Mar 1944 – 25 Mar 1944	Off Algerian coast	2
23 Apr 1944 – 4 May 1944	Off Algerian coast	0

30TH FLOTILLA (1 NOVEMBER 1942)

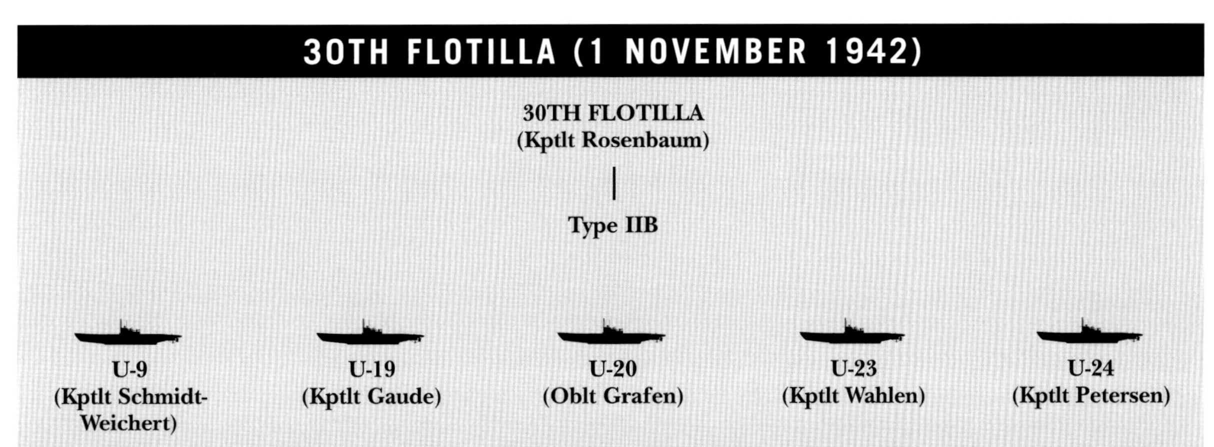

The 30th Flotilla was the *Kriegsmarine*'s Black Sea U-boat flotilla, and was established in October 1942. It was commanded at this point by *Kapitänleutnant* Helmut Rosenbaum, a successful U-boat commander who had led *U-73* when it torpedoed and sank the British aircraft carrier HMS *Eagle* in the Mediterranean on 11 August 1942. Note how the short ranges involved in the Black Sea deployment led to only Type IIB submarines being on the establishment. *U-18* joined the flotilla in May 1943.

excessively bleak – Dönitz was keen to keep his boats in the Atlantic, after all – but there was no doubt that passage into the Mediterranean was no easy matter.

Nor was life necessarily easier once the U-boats were inside the blue waters. The strong countercurrent flowing through the Strait of Gibraltar meant that the submarines inside the Mediterranean were essentially trapped there.

Furthermore, the Mediterranean is a geophysically complicated area of water, and Allied air patrols or escort vessels might often catch U-boats in shallow waters, where it was harder to hide from bombs and depth charges. As with the war in the Atlantic, 1942 was the year in which fortunes changed in favour of the Allies in the Mediterranean. We can see this in the pattern of merchant ship kills – admittedly to all causes, but to which the U-boat arm was integral.

Figures rise and fall

During the year, the strength of the U-boats in this theatre rose to 26 boats on station, with six further U-boats patrolling around the entrance to the Strait of Gibraltar. In January 1942, the Allies lost one merchant ship in the Mediterranean, and four the following month. In April and May, the numbers climbed to six each month, but in June the figure leapt to 16, primarily

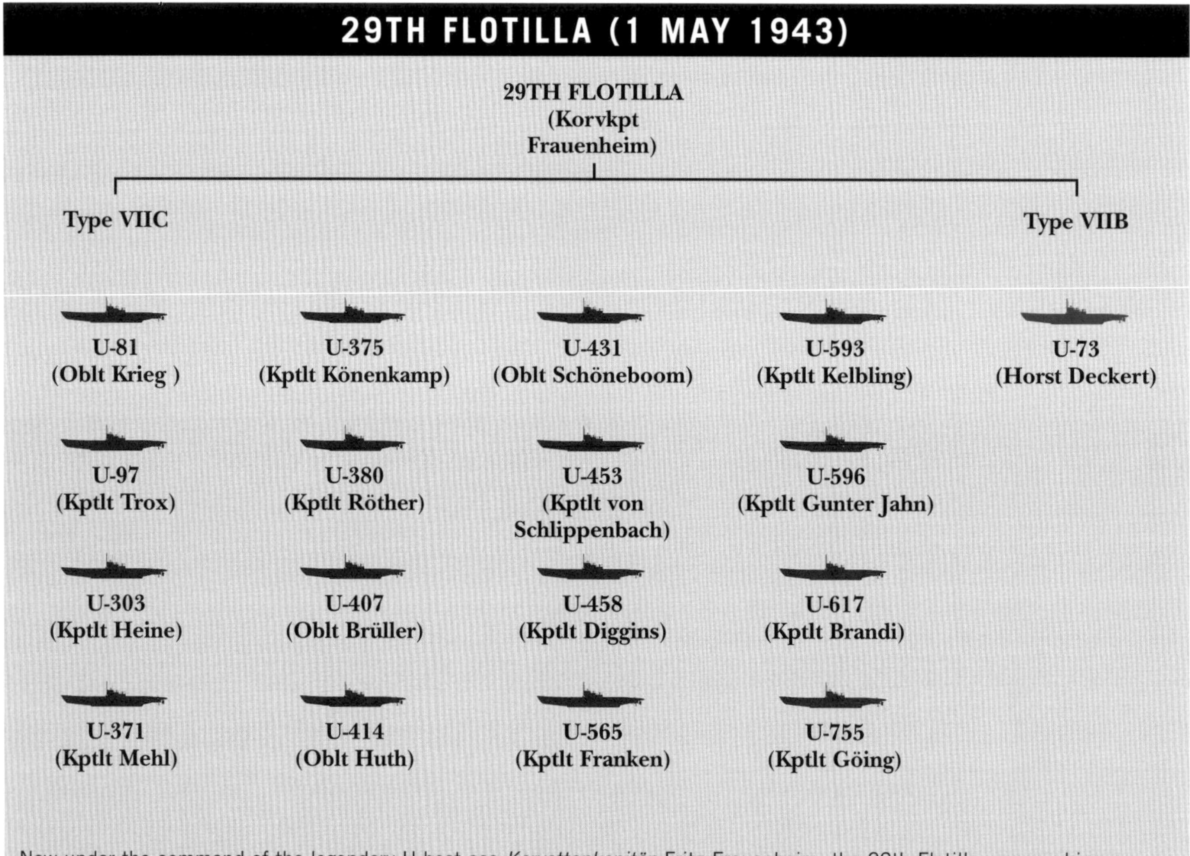

Now under the command of the legendary U-boat ace *Korvettenkapitän* Fritz Frauenheim, the 29th Flotilla was reaching a respectable strength by the beginning of May 1943, but its losses were continual and heavy. Later in this month, for example, *U-303* was sunk after it was torpedoed by a British submarine, and on 20 May, near Majorca, *U-755* was destroyed by an air attack from an RAF Hudson.

on account of actions against the Malta convoys. Thirteen ships went down in August, but for the rest of the year the figures plunged dramatically, and in October no merchant ships at all were sunk. The decrease has several explanations, not least the reversal of superiority in the Atlantic, which meant that fewer submarines were being sent down to the Mediterranean to replace losses, plus the fact that U-boats were being sunk in increasing numbers through all the tactics we have seen being applied in the Atlantic. By the mid-months of 1943, the Allies essentially had air superiority over the whole region, and plenty of operating bases, which meant that anti-submarine air patrols became the bane of the U-boat crews.

In 1943–44, the Allies implemented the 'Swamp' tactic, by which escort ships and aircraft would flood an

29TH FLOTILLA (1 AUGUST 1944)

29TH FLOTILLA
(Korvkpt Jahn)

Type VIIC

For a flotilla that had 52 boats pass through its establishment, the slump in numbers here is evident. Most of the U-boats pictured would also become victims of the growing Allied anti-submarine superiority. *U-471*, for example, was destroyed by US bombing on Toulon on 6 August 1944, as were *U-952* and *U-969*. *U-565* was damaged in Greece by another air raid and was scuttled on 24 September.

U-230 (Kptlt Siegmann) — **U-471** (Kptlt Kloevekorn) — **U-596** (Oblt Kolbus) — **U-967** (Oblt Eberbach)

U-466 (Kptlt Thäter) — **U-565** (Kptlt Henning) — **U-952** (Kptlt Curio) — **U-969** (Oblt Dobbert)

30TH FLOTILLA (1 SEPTEMBER 1944)

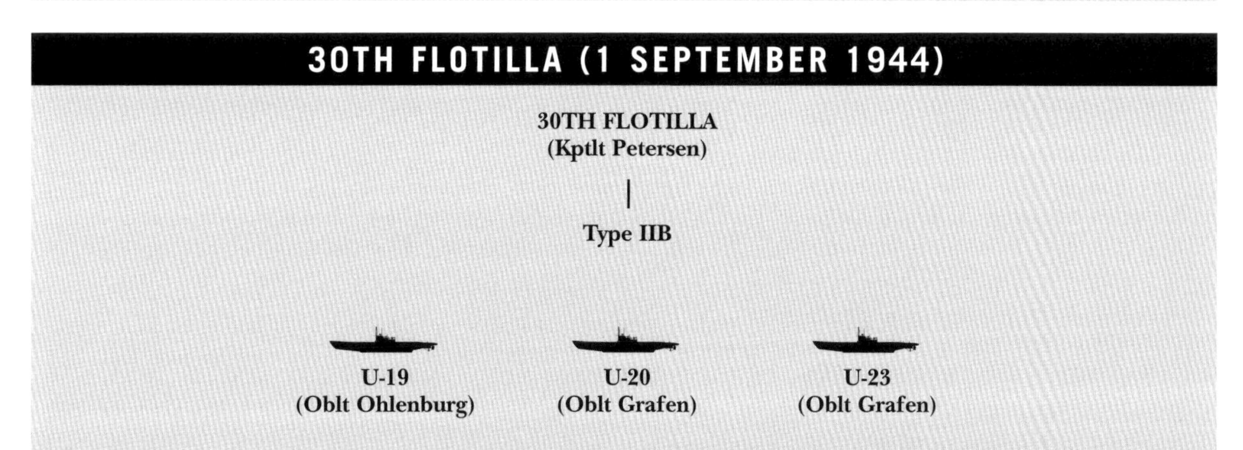

Here is the 30th Flotilla shortly after it had been forced to abandon its Konstanza base owing to the surrender of Romania and the advance of the Soviet ground forces towards the port. All three of these submarines were scuttled on 10 September off the coast of Turkey, the flotilla's location in the Black Sea meaning that there was no escape to safer waters. All six boats assigned to the flotilla were therefore destroyed by the time the unit was disbanded.

area of sea in which U-boats were believed to be (made easier by the Allied awareness of viable sea lanes back to U-boat bases), and hunt down the submarines without mercy. If one looks at the data relating to the 23rd and 29th U-boat Flotillas, almost every single submarine that passed through these formations was sunk – unlike many other flotillas, there was no escape to Norway.

Furthermore, during 1944, by which time the 29th Flotilla had lost many of its eastern bases, the USAAF pounded the French port of Toulon in bombing raids, destroying or damaging several U-boats as they sat at anchor. Ultimately, the Mediterranean became a graveyard for U-boats.

Black Sea operations

One of the most unusual theatres for the U-boats during World War II was the Black Sea. The chief problem of deploying submarines to the Black Sea was getting them there in the first place, as the Type IIs most suited to the waters did not have the range to reach them, nor was access through the Bosphorus viable anyway.

To overcome this problem, the U-boats deployed to the Black Sea as the 30th Flotilla were transported there using a mixture of canal and river boats and massive road transporters. The submarines were initially divided up into sections and packages of equipment, and were then reassembled at their final destination.

The purpose of the Black Sea operations was to intercept Soviet supply vessels reinforcing Stalin's land offensives in the Caucasus and Ukraine. It proved to be a poor use of resources. Not only were the submarines worryingly trapped once deployed, their base at Konstanza in Romania had to be abandoned as the Soviet advance approached in August 1944. Those vessels that had survived the attentions of Soviet naval forces and air attacks, were consequently scuttled at various locations around the Black Sea.

Operations in the Indian Ocean

The U-boat arm spread its influence far and wide, although with varying degrees of success. Not only were U-boats to be found operating in the Black Sea, but they also deployed in respectable numbers to the Indian Ocean and Pacific.

As the *Kriegsmarine* developed its Type IX submarines to ever greater operating radii, and also refined its systems of on-station refuelling through tankers and the *Milchkühe* submarines, ever more distant waters around the world became prospective areas for U-boat deployment. In the Atlantic itself, the distances covered, as we have seen, were truly vast. U-boats operated off the coasts of both South America and South Africa, or penetrated deep into Caribbean waters. U-boats sat on station for weeks off northern US cities, enormously isolated from their home bases. Yet during 1943, with the Battles of the Atlantic and Mediterranean slipping finally from Germany's grasp, Dönitz and the German high command began casting around for other locations in which they could exert some influence. In reality, the resulting deployments were often pointless exercises in diverting valuable boats to areas where they could have little overall strategic significance.

Operations around Cape Town

By 1942, Germany had another major ally, albeit a very distant one, in the war against the Allies. Japan was fighting half a world away, but as the year played out Hitler became increasingly interested in utilizing some of Japan's newly acquired bases in the Pacific and the Indian Ocean for his submarines. Specifically, U-boats in the Far East could deliver two important

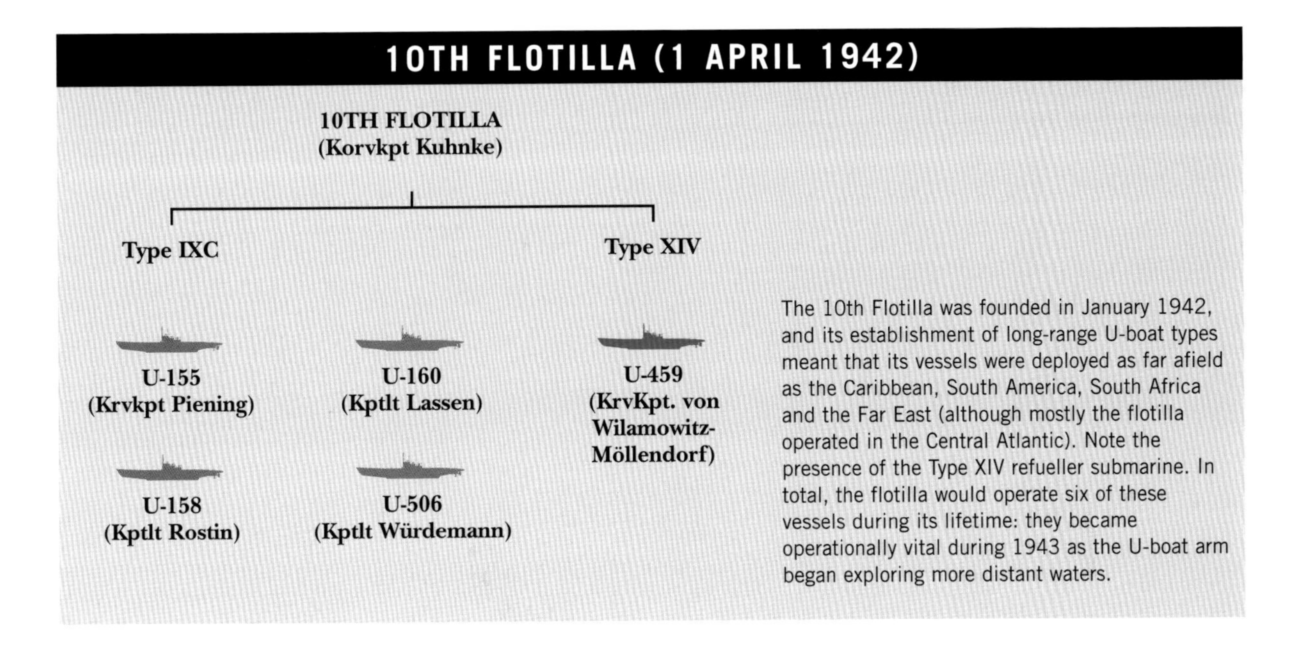

The 10th Flotilla was founded in January 1942, and its establishment of long-range U-boat types meant that its vessels were deployed as far afield as the Caribbean, South America, South Africa and the Far East (although mostly the flotilla operated in the Central Atlantic). Note the presence of the Type XIV refueller submarine. In total, the flotilla would operate six of these vessels during its lifetime: they became operationally vital during 1943 as the U-boat arm began exploring more distant waters.

benefits. First, they could help out in the Japanese attempt to win the naval war in the Pacific, and maybe even take some of the pressure off the Atlantic. Second, and more important, was that U-boats might be capable of acting as cargo transports for some of the vital raw materials that Germany lacked, but which the Far East had in abundance, such as rubber, tin, tungsten and molybdenum. In return, the Germans could provide the Japanese with any materials they needed via the outward journey. For the combat and the logistics operations, it was planned to use the *Kriegmarine*'s variety of long-range combat and transport submarines, the Types VIIF, IXC, IXD, XB and XIV. The first German deployments into the Indian Ocean (although not far into those waters) began in the spring of 1942, with four U-boats deployed to the Cape Town and Madagascar regions for operations against British African coastal traffic up to Freetown and other more northerly African destinations. In total, over 20 U-boats were sent into these waters, and by relocating to better hunting grounds around the southern African coast they had real successes – in October–December 1942, they sank over 50 Allied ships.

Inspired by these figures, the naval high command maintained operations in the western Indian Ocean during early 1943, but as the months went on, sinkings of U-boats increased, as the Allies spread their improved anti-submarine capabilities and adopted stronger convoy systems in African waters from December 1942. By August 1943, U-boat operations in this area were effectively wrapped up.

The *Monsun* boats

During the spring of 1943, Germany had negotiated with the Japanese to secure U-boat basing rights at Penang, Malaya. The U-boats based here were intended to form a logistical chain from the Far East to Europe, transporting the vital above-mentioned raw materials back to Germany. They were to be codenamed *Monsun* (Monsoon) boats, the name chosen on account of their expected arrival in Malaya in September, during the monsoon season. *U-178*, a Type IXD boat of the 12th Flotilla, headed over first to establish its commander, *Korvettenkapitän* Wilhelm Dommes, as the base commander at Penang.

The first batch of *Monsun* boats, a force of 11 vessels, departed from Europe in June 1943, facing journeys across thousands of kilometres of potentially and actually hostile waters. In fact, of the 11 boats that set out, only five actually reached their destination at

Penang; the rest were lost, mostly in the Atlantic transit phase, or diverted away because of fuel crises. (A critical *Milchkuh* vessel had been sunk by the US Navy.)

Eventually, over 40 U-boats would operate in the Far East, from bases that included Penang and Kobe (in Japan), plus repair facilities at Singapore, Jakarta and Surabaya. Their combat achievements, however, were limited. At least 20 of the U-boats were sunk by the

12TH FLOTILLA (1 AUGUST 1944)

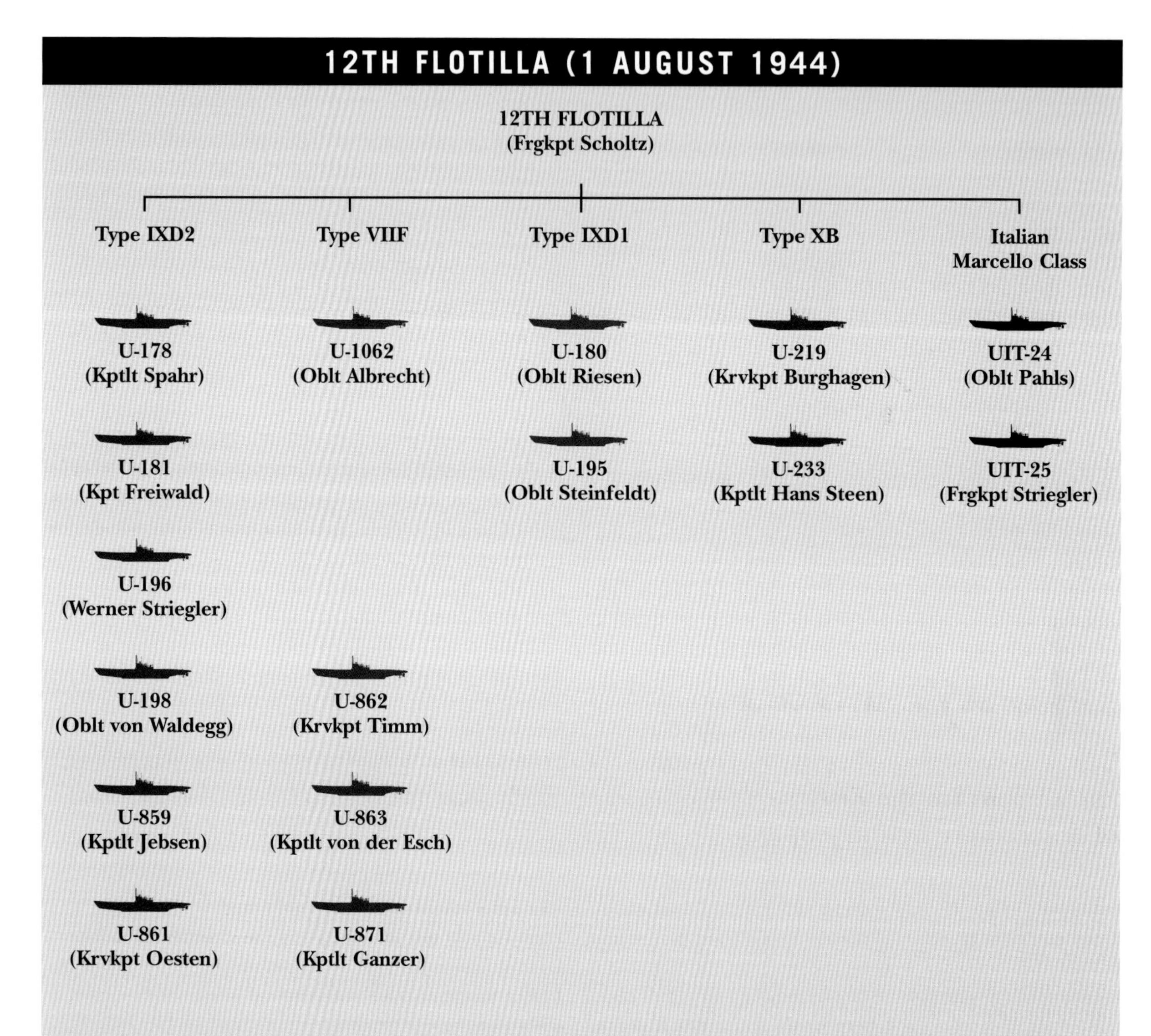

This is the final snapshot of the 12th Flotilla establishment, shortly before the unit was disbanded at the end of the month and its last surviving U-boats left Bordeaux to make the journey north. *U-178* made the first *Kriegsmarine* deployment to Penang, setting off in March 1943 and finally arriving in August, having made one of the longest patrols in U-boat history at that point. *U-178*'s commander, *Korvettenkapitän* Wilhelm Dommes, became base commander at Penang; he eventually became chief of all *Monsun* boats in January 1945 in the rank of *Fregattenkapitän*.

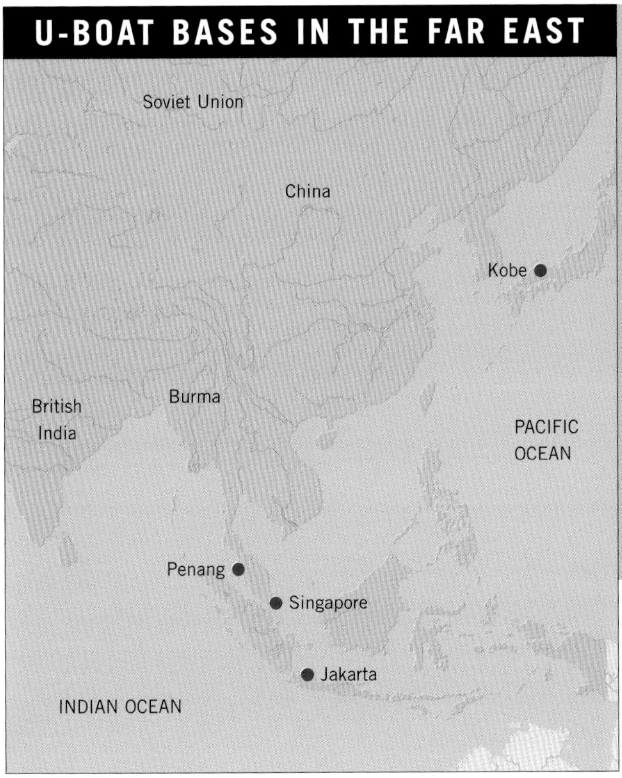

U-BOAT BASES IN THE FAR EAST

Eastern stations 1944

By the end of 1944, the U-boat arm had established a network of bases throughout the Far East, which assisted their patrols west into the Indian Ocean, while one U-boat, *U-862*, also ventured into the Pacific in late 1944 and operated around Australia.

The first of the bases was set up at Penang in Malaya, in 1943, and this remained the main Far East operations base for much of the war, until British land campaigns in Malaya forced its abandonment.

Just off the southern tip of Malaya, Singapore also acted as a repair base, as did Kobe in Japan much further to the north (although combat patrols also sailed from both these facilities). Jakarta and Surabaya, in modern Indonesia, were important locations for loading the U-boats with raw materials.

Allies, and the hunting was actually rather muted. Interestingly, however, the logistical function of the deployments was continued right up to the very end of the war, so these must have been paying dividends to Germany to some extent.

D-Day: 1944

D-Day was not just a highly significant day for the land war in Europe. It also had huge implications for the *Kriegsmarine*, as its once vitally important naval bases on the coast of France were now in jeopardy.

On 6 June 1944, the Allies invaded France in Operation *Overlord*, the beginnings of the liberation of Europe. An inadequate German response had enabled the Allies to establish a foothold on the Normandy beaches, and over the subsequent weeks this became the jumping-off point for penetration into the French interior.

D-Day

There was little that the U-boats could do to stem the massive tide of Allied shipping that deployed British, American and Canadian forces along the French coastline. By this time, many of the U-boats had adopted the *Schnorchel* (snorkel) device, described in more detail below, which enabled submarines to stay submerged without the need to surface for battery recharging. This innovation was undoubtedly tactically significant, but it came too late in the war to make any strategic impact. Nevertheless, *Schnorchel*-equipped submarines were in position off the British coast by the spring of 1944, waiting to counter an Allied invasion force, and on the

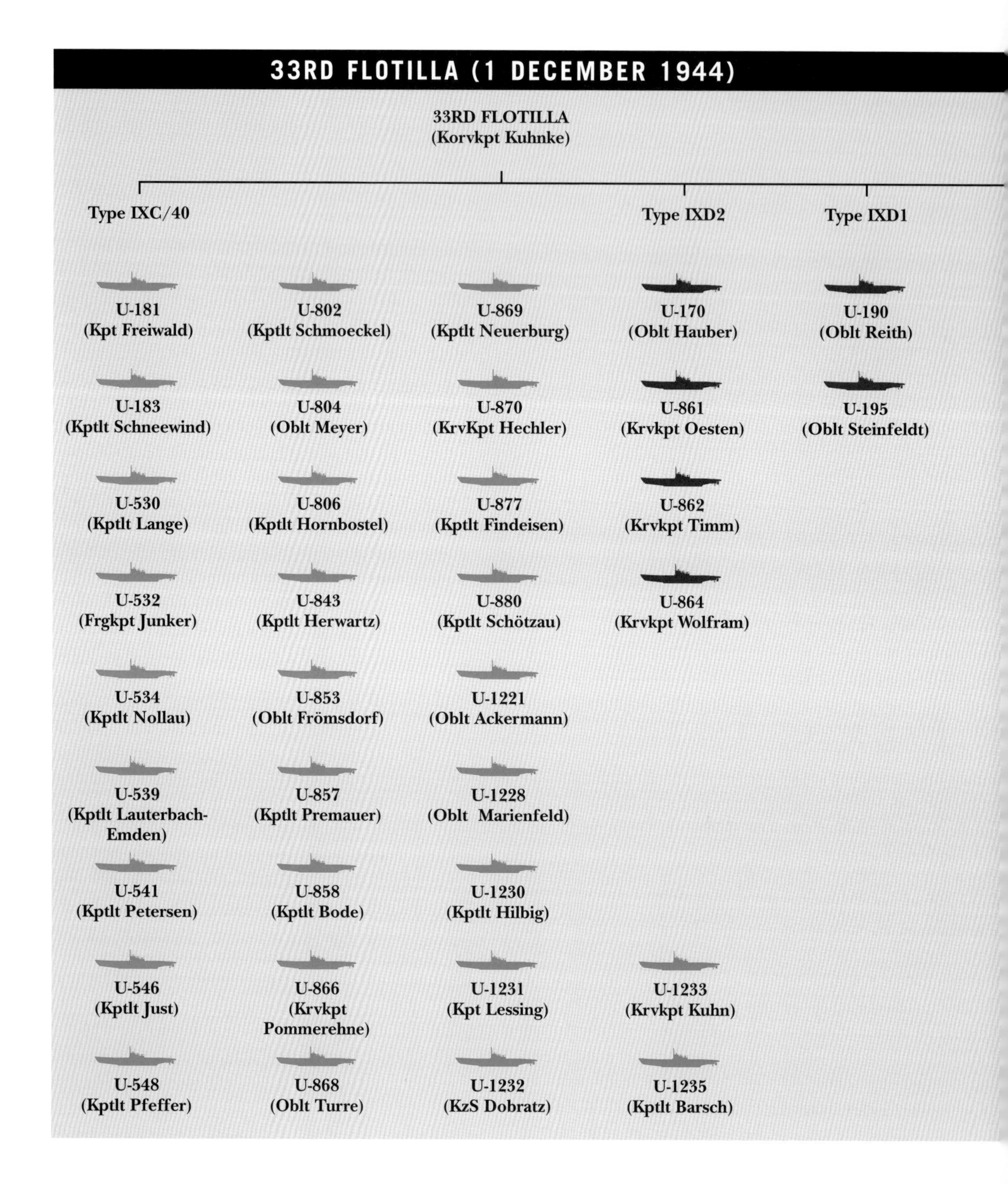
33RD FLOTILLA (1 DECEMBER 1944)
33RD FLOTILLA
(Korvkpt Kuhnke)
Type IXC/40
Type IXD2
Type IXD1
U-181
(Kpt Freiwald)
U-802
(Kptlt Schmoeckel)
U-869
(Kptlt Neuerburg)
U-170
(Oblt Hauber)
U-190
(Oblt Reith)
U-183
(Kptlt Schneewind)
U-804
(Oblt Meyer)
U-870
(KrvKpt Hechler)
U-861
(Krvkpt Oesten)
U-195
(Oblt Steinfeldt)
U-530
(Kptlt Lange)
U-806
(Kptlt Hornbostel)
U-877
(Kptlt Findeisen)
U-862
(Krvkpt Timm)
U-532
(Frgkpt Junker)
U-843
(Kptlt Herwartz)
U-880
(Kptlt Schötzau)
U-864
(Krvkpt Wolfram)
U-534
(Kptlt Nollau)
U-853
(Oblt Frömsdorf)
U-1221
(Oblt Ackermann)
U-539
(Kptlt Lauterbach-Emden)
U-857
(Kptlt Premauer)
U-1228
(Oblt Marienfeld)
U-541
(Kptlt Petersen)
U-858
(Kptlt Bode)
U-1230
(Kptlt Hilbig)
U-546
(Kptlt Just)
U-866
(Krvkpt Pommerehne)
U-1231
(Kpt Lessing)
U-1233
(Krvkpt Kuhn)
U-548
(Kptlt Pfeffer)
U-868
(Oblt Turre)
U-1232
(KzS Dobratz)
U-1235
(Kptlt Barsch)

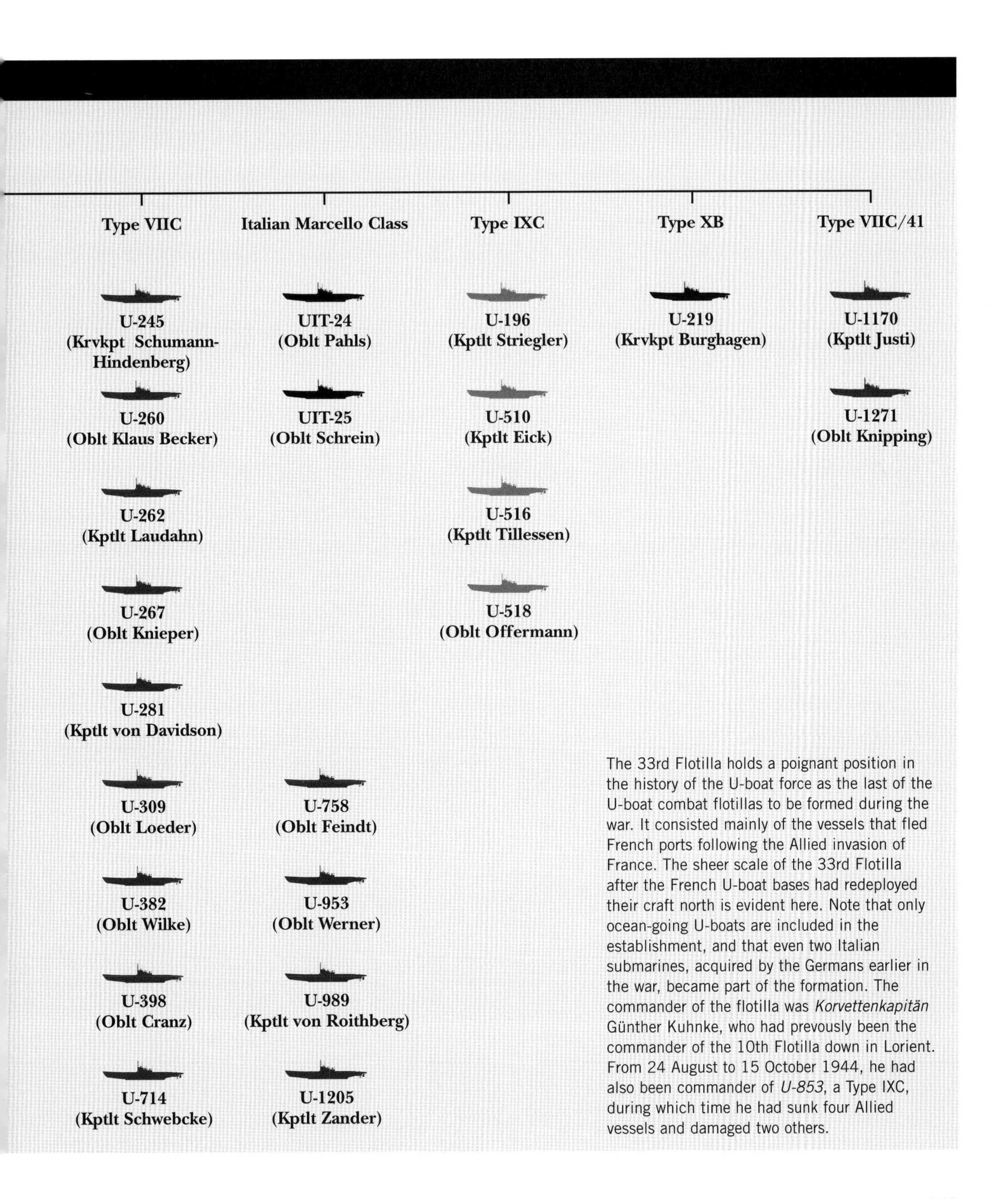

The 33rd Flotilla holds a poignant position in the history of the U-boat force as the last of the U-boat combat flotillas to be formed during the war. It consisted mainly of the vessels that fled French ports following the Allied invasion of France. The sheer scale of the 33rd Flotilla after the French U-boat bases had redeployed their craft north is evident here. Note that only ocean-going U-boats are included in the establishment, and that even two Italian submarines, acquired by the Germans earlier in the war, became part of the formation. The commander of the flotilla was *Korvettenkapitän* Günther Kuhnke, who had prevously been the commander of the 10th Flotilla down in Lorient. From 24 August to 15 October 1944, he had also been commander of *U-853*, a Type IXC, during which time he had sunk four Allied vessels and damaged two others.

day of the invasion itself 16 such submarines operating in the English Channel attacked the landing fleet, with 19 more submarines making combat patrols to the west in the Bay of Biscay.

Battles around Normandy

During the battles around Normandy over the next two months, the U-boats managed to sink 22 Allied vessels. Yet in return, 15 of their number were also destroyed. With the loss ratios approaching parity, the campaign against the Allied landings was simply unsustainable. For the commanders of the German U-boat bases further down in France, the invasion signalled that the end was approaching. Nevertheless, despite the proximity of the landings to some of the most northerly U-boat bases in France – particularly Lorient and Brest – the Allied invasion did not result in the immediate evacuation of all of the U-boats.

Flight to the north

The spread of the Allied forces out from Normandy began to put increasing pressure on the German U-boat bases on the French coast. The only option for those directly in the firing line was to pull out.

In August 1944, the decision was taken to extract the U-boats from those bases that were directly under threat of capture, and deploy them north to safer bases in Norwegian and German waters. Many of these boats subsequently came under the command of a new formation, the 33rd U-boat Flotilla, based around the German port of Flensburg.

The 33rd grew to become a sizeable command of dispossessed vessels. It was not only in control of the vessels that arrived in the north, but it also held authority over many vessels scattered in distant parts of the world, such as in the Far East, off South America or around the southern waters of Africa.

Fleeing the bases

Lorient and Brest were two obvious candidates for quick evacuation, being next door to the landing zones. As far as Lorient was concerned, fighting around the town's outskirts began on 7 August 1944. The withdrawals were already under way at this point, and the last U-boat to leave was *U-155* on 5 September. Those boats that could not be crewed or repaired were scuttled. As it turned out, the Allies actually bypassed Lorient, and the town's garrison did not surrender until May 1945, with the end of the war. Lorient had been home to the 2nd and 10th Flotillas; both flotillas were disbanded in October 1944.

Brest underwent one of the most violent dissolutions of all the U-boat bases. In August 1944, RAF Bomber Command hit it several times with 5454kg (12,000lb) Tallboy bombs. In total, 26 of these bombs were dropped in three air raids, and the aircraft scored nine direct hits on the U-boat pens. Five of the bombs actually penetrated the pens, but surprisingly they did limited damage to the boats within. Nevertheless, such earth-shaking attacks were a clear sign that staying put was not a good idea, so the 1st and 9th Flotillas began to leave, the last boat, *U-256*, leaving on 4 September. As a good indication of how long the journey to Norway took, *U-256* did not arrive at Bergen until 17 October, by which time Brest had been captured in a ferocious city battle that cost a total of 10,000 Allied lives.

Remaining bases

St Nazaire and La Rochelle/La Pallice, in common with Lorient, remained in German hands for the remainder of the war, although most of the U-boats left these bases in the August and September of 1944. They continued,

however, to serve sporadic U-boat traffic for many more months. Bordeaux fell to the Allies on 25 August 1944, by which time most of the U-boats had already left (the exceptions being those that could not sail). The last of the submarines to leave arrived at Flensburg at the end of October.

At Toulon, the 29th Flotilla went through a steady reduction in U-boat numbers over June–July, much of it on account of heavy US bombing raids, so that by 17 August it had only one boat, *U-230*, left in operation. This left the base and was scuttled a few days later.

Late kills

By August 1944, the writing was clearly on the wall for the U-boat force. Yet the fact remained that the U-boats,

U-2511 **(TYPE XXI)**	
Commissioned	29 September 1944
Crew	57–60
Displacement	1819 tonnes (1790 tons) submerged
Dimensions	Length: 76.7m (252ft); Beam: 6.6m (22ft)
Range	Surfaced: 24,944km (15,500 miles) at 18.5km/h (10kts); Submerged: 547km (340 miles) at 7.4km/h (4kts)
Armament	6 x 533mm (21in) torpedo tubes; 4 x 20mm (0.79in) AA guns
Powerplant	Surfaced: diesels 2985kW (4000hp); Submerged: electric 3730kW (5000hp)
Performance	Surfaced: 29km/h (15.5kts); Submerged: 30km/h (16kts)

U-BOAT BASES (SEPT 1944)

ATLANTIC OCEAN
Trondheim
Bergen
Flensburg
Kiel
Hamburg

Dwindling bases

This map of U-boat flotilla bases could hardly be more different from that of just over a year earlier (see page 101). All the French coastal bases have gone as official flotilla headquarters, although some remained open as stop-offs for isolated submarines looking to make repairs or trying to acquire some fuel. Toulon on the Mediterranean also closed as a flotilla base in September 1944, as did Konstanza on the Black Sea.

Those submarines that were not scattered in distant foreign waters generally made their way up to the north, settling in the old bases on the German coastline and also in Norwegian bases acquired back in 1940. From here, they still had opportunities to make strikes against Allied shipping crossing to the Soviet Union or operating in the North Sea, but the sheer strength of Allied air power and naval forces made such actions increasingly suicidal.

alongside isolated and bold units of small surface vessels, still managed to sink small numbers of Allied ships. On the grand scale of the entire war, the sinkings were admittedly more irritating than strategically significant, but they meant that the Allies still needed to channel resources into naval escorts. Looking at the numbers of Allied merchant ships lost in the Atlantic (through which a large part of the Normandy traffic moved) during the first six months of 1944, we see something of a boost provided by the D-Day landings:

January	13	February	5
March	8	April	8
May	3	June	22

The blip in June 1944, a sevenfold jump compared with the previous month, was scarcely an encouragement to the *Kriegsmarine.* Nearly 7000 vessels were used in the *Overlord* landings, so it was clear that the U-boats could do nothing against *die Materialschlacht* (the war of material) of the Allies, with their massive output of naval vessels.

Compounding this impotence was the fact that U-boats were being sunk at ever faster rates. Taking the first six months of 1944 once again, the figures for U-boats sunk across the Atlantic, Arctic and Baltic showed a general upward trend:

January	14	February	19
March	20	April	19
May	17	June	25

After June 1944, the figures for U-boat sinkings stayed in the low to mid-20s for July and August, then dropped quite dramatically from 14 in September through to 6 in November, rising again to 11 the following month.

These figures reveal several patterns. First, the loss of submarines in 1944 was roughly the same as that in 1943 – 237 compared with 242. The difference in 1944 was that the losses were incurred at a time when the U-boats had a critically diminished offensive capability – in short, there were same number of U-boats lost for much less return (the volume of merchant shipping sunk by U-boats dropped by 200 per cent in 1944). Second, the

3RD FLOTILLA (30 SEPTEMBER 1944)

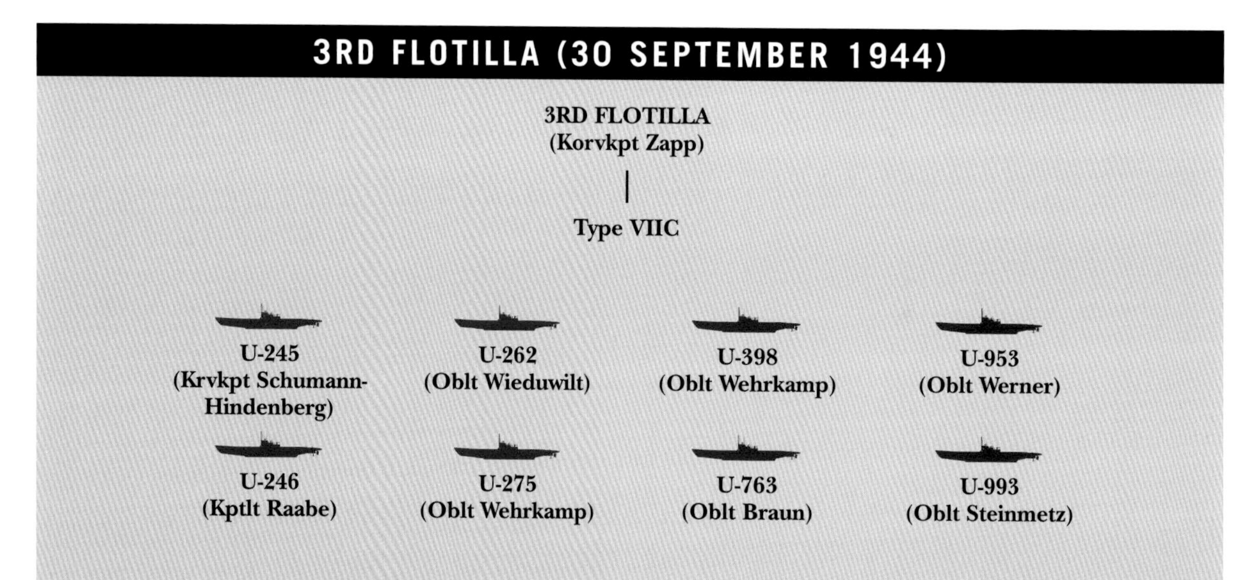

The final commander of the 3rd U-boat Flotilla was *Korvettenkapitän* Richard Zapp, a extremely highly decorated U-boat ace. The 3rd Flotilla had been based at La Rochelle/La Pallice, but at the time of the establishment pictured here all the surviving and operable boats had fled from there to the north, and the flotilla had only one month of existence left. One noteworthy point is that many 3rd Flotilla naval personnel remained in La Rochelle, and were formed into *Marine-Regiment Zapp*, a fighting unit that assisted in the ground defence of the town against the Allies up until the surrender of the German garrison in May 1945.

drop in U-boat losses from September is likely an indication that many U-boats had successfully escaped to the north, having made the dangerous passage from southern France through the Atlantic, Channel or North Sea. By the end of the year, it was clear that the U-boats' war was approaching its end.

9TH FLOTILLA (1 FEBRUARY 1944)

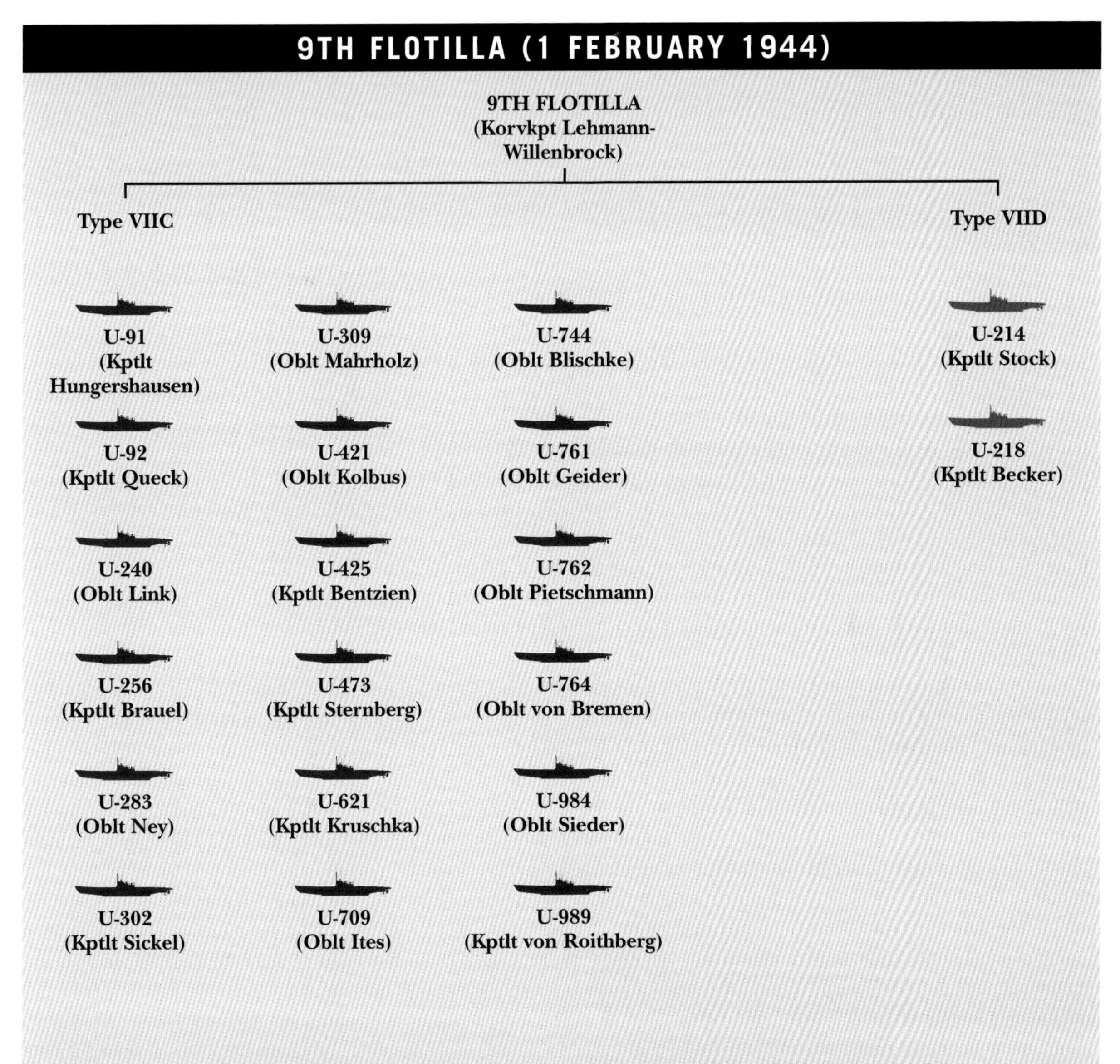

The 9th Flotilla, as this diagram shows, was still a powerful U-boat formation during the early months of 1944, with 20 operational submarines on its establishment. It was stationed in Brest, which was the third-busiest of all the U-boat bases in France (Lorient and St Nazaire fielded more U-boats). The Type VIIC was the flotilla's most prolific submarine, with 73 in total being assigned during the unit's three-year existence.

Technologies

As occurred elsewhere in the German armed forces during the last years of the war, the *Kriegsmarine* experienced a rush of technological innovations as it sought engineering solutions to Allied naval supremacy.

By 1945, U-boat technology had come a long way since the early war years, with the newer U-boats offering greater capabilities in everything from range and speed to dive depth and lethality. Many of the innovations occurred as specific responses to new Allied technologies.

Schnorchel

The *Schnorchel* (snorkel) was inspired by the fact that from 1942 the increased use of centimetric radar by the Allies meant that surfaced U-boats were now extremely vulnerable. Underwater, however, the U-boat could not use its diesels, and its electric motors provided limited endurance, speed and power. Building upon Dutch experiments from the 1930s, the *Kriegsmarine* engineers developed the *Schnorchel* as a solution. It was basically a long air intake tube that could be raised above the water when the submarine was submerged, allowing it to keep running the diesels. This meant massively improved submerged endurance, although that created problems in terms of sanitation. The *Schnorchel* underwent trials in 1943, and in 1944 installation began on the U-boat fleet. The installation programme was limited – by mid-1944 50 per cent of the French-based Atlantic boats had the system – but it undoubtedly improved the survivability of the U-boats. Yet the *Schnorchel* raised as many problems as it provided solutions. It compelled the submarine to operate at a slow speed of 11km/h (6 knots), depriving it of the fast attack speed useful for taking on the convoys. The tubes had a tendency to block up, resulting in the diesel engines switching to the crew compartments for their source of oxygen, causing illness.

Electro boats

Considering the performance limitations of the *Schnorchel*, better solutions were sought to the problem of underwater operations. One alternative was already in development, the Walter turbine, named after engineer Professor Helmuth Walter. This engine was a closed-cycle powerplant that ran on a combination of diesel and hydrogen peroxide, making it independent of atmopheric oxygen. This remarkable innovation was installed in four Type XVIIA submarines in 1943, and

U-BOAT LOSSES 1945

Month	Boats lost
January	U-679, U-248, U-2515, U-2523, U-1199, U-1051, U-1172, U-3520
February	U-1279, U-745, U-1014, U-864, U-923, U-869, U-989, U-1053, U-309, U-425, U-1273, U-1278, U-2344, U-676, U-683, U-1276, U-300, U-480, U-927, U-3007, U-327, U-1018, U-1208
March	U-3519, U-3508, U-1302, U-275, U–681, U-682, U-296, U-714, U-1021, U-367, U-758, U-866, U-399, U-722, U-905, U-1106, U-1169, U-96, U-348, U-350, U-870, U-965, U-1167, U-2340
April	U-747, U-1232, U-262, U-321, U-1221, U-2542, U-749, U-3003, U-242, U-246, U-677, U-1195, U-774, U-1001, U-2509, U-2514, U-3512, U-804, U-843, U-982, U-1065, U-2516, U-878, U-486, U-1024, U-235, U-1206, U-103, U-285, U-857, U-1063, U-1235, U-78, U-880, U-1274, U-398, U-251, U-548, U-325, U-636, U-518, U-183, U-396, U-1055, U-546, U-326, U-1197, U-56, U-286, U-307, U-1017, U-879, U-1107
May	U-315, U-2359, U-1210, U-2521, U-3032, U-3502, U-3505, U-711, U-2338, U-393, U-534, U-579, U-2367, U-2551, U-853, U-862, U-881, U-3523, U-181, U-320

gave these vessels an amazing submerged performance of 48km/h (26 knots).

A number of production U-boats were fitted with the Walter turbine, but the powerplant was massively expensive, and as the progression of the war imposed greater austerities and rationalizations on German industry, it was simply not the way forward. In 1942, however, a partial solution had been offered by two German naval engineers. The Walter U-boats required a vast fuel tank, which formed the lower part of the hull. The two designers suggested that they utilize this space for additional batteries instead of fuel, thereby increasing the power and endurance of the U-boat when submerged, but using conventional means.

The resulting U-boat was called the Type XXI, and offered a submerged speed of 22–26km/h (12–14 knots) for 10 hours or 9km/h (5 knots) for 60 hours. The Type XXI seemed a decent solution to the problems of submerged operations, and Hitler approved a production programme in August 1943.

The Type XXI was too large for shallow water operations, so a smaller Type XXIII was also developed for these roles. Trials of the new types gave exciting results, and both submarines could have made a significant impact on the German naval war effort. It was Germany's increasingly chaotic production process, however, that undid the *Electro* boats, as they were called. Dönitz made plans for 381 Type XXI and 91 Type XXIII boats to be delivered by May 1945. In the event, with numerous other forces competing for production facilities (particularly the *Luftwaffe*), only one Type XXI made it to the fully combat-ready state, and just six

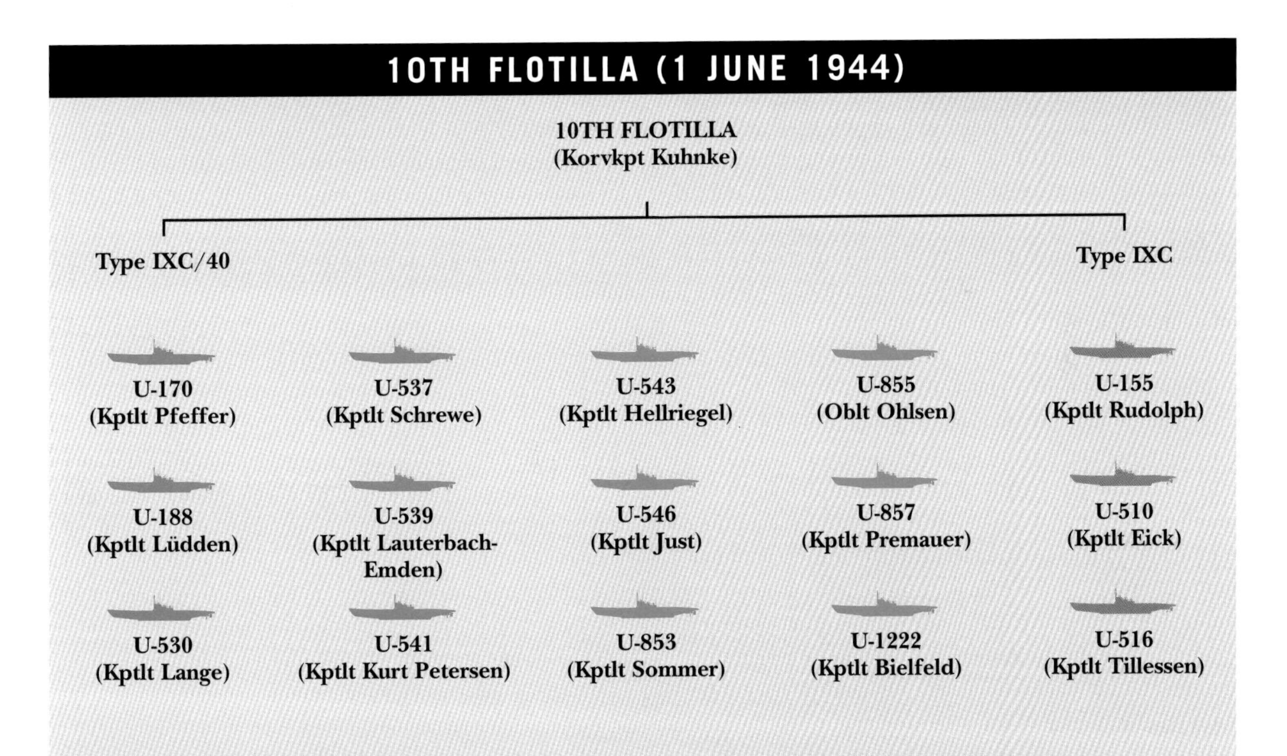

The 10th Flotilla had, by 1 June 1944, an establishment weighted towards the Type IXC/40, which had been in production since 1940. Overall, 41 of these U-boats passed through the 10th Flotilla, compared with 26 Type IXCs, 2 Type IXD1s, 4 Type IXD2s, 1 Type XB and 66 Type XIVs. The Type IXC/40 had an improved range and surface speed compared with the Type IXC.

Type XXIIIs. Much larger numbers reached training, trial or fitting-out stages, but essentially all the *Electro* boats achieved was to divert production away from the regular U-boat types that could have served the Germans well during the last years of the war.

Torpedoes

As well as in the U-boats themselves, Germany also made major leaps in torpedo technologies, research that went on to inform marine warfare development in the wider postwar world. The basic German G7a (gas-steam) and G7e (electric) torpedoes, when launched, ran straight and true. The FAT variant, however, introduced during 1942, was a pattern-running torpedo. It could be programmed to alter course at specific intervals, each time making an 180-degree turn. The FAT, and a later variant known as the LUT, which was capable of more subtle and wide-ranging programming variations, was particularly useful when fired into large convoys – if it missed its initial intended target, it would keep running within the convoy until it struck a target, ran out of power or self-detonated.

In March 1943, an even more sophisticated torpedo type was introduced, the G7es *Falke* (Falcon). This was the world's first homing torpedo, and tracked itself to the target using passive acoustic homing technology (it steered towards the sound of a ship's propellers and engines). Not fitted with a magnetic detonator, the *Falke* was of limited application, but an improved model known as the *Zaunkönig* (Wren) entered service later in the year.

Allied ships were certainly sent to the bottom by the homing torpedoes, but they could be an operational headache to use. The *Zaunkönig* was designed to lock on to the loudest aquatic noise after it had run 400m (437 yards). Unfortunately, this might actually be the launch submarine, and it is known that two U-boats were destroyed by their own torpedoes in this fashion (*U-972* and *U-377*). As a consequence, the U-boat commanders often had to follow a torpedo launch with an immediate dive to lower depths and also a strict silence policy aboard the boat. The torpedo technologies were undoubtedly impressive, but in their nascent state they had a limited impact on the outcome of the naval war.

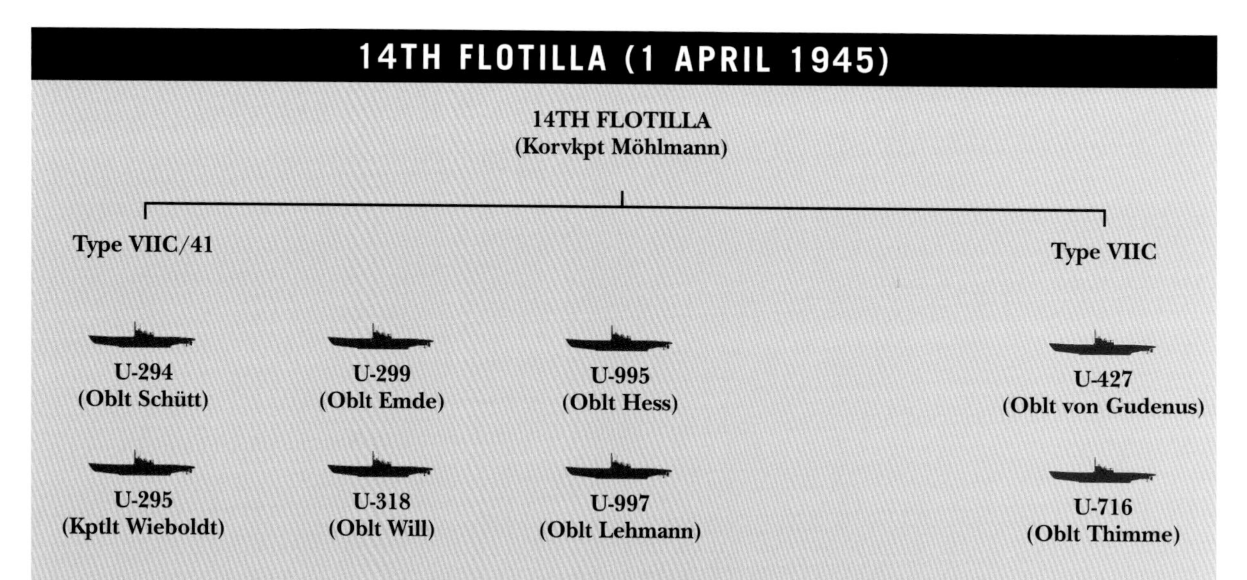

The 14th Flotilla was formed late in 1944, and only ever possessed the boats depicted here. These vessels had come from the French coastal bases evacuated following the D-Day landings. The flotilla's eight vessels were based up in Narvik, and although these U-boats made forays against the Allied Arctic convoys, incredibly all of them survived the war and their crews surrendered to the British in May 1945.

Strategic lessons

In 1945, the U-boat war finally collapsed altogether in favour of the Allies. By the later weeks of the war, it was virtually an act of suicide to take a U-boat into action against escorted ships.

The U-boat war was a tragedy of intense proportions, not only for the thousands of merchant and naval seamen who died following torpedo attacks, but also for the U-boat crews themselves. Over 60 per cent of the *Kriegsmarine*'s submariners would not survive the war, giving the U-boat crews one of the highest fatality rates of any arm of service in World War II.

Final defeat

In the five months from January 1945 until the end of the war the following May, Germany lost 151 submarines, compared with the loss of 242 for the whole of the previous year. In April alone, 55 U-boats were destroyed. The reasons behind the epic losses have partly been explained above, but added to these were the scuttling of U-boats to prevent their acquisition by the Allies and the destruction of submarines at their bases by the Allied advance on the ground. Note also that after the war, the Allies scuttled 121 U-boats, a sad end for admittedly deadly vessels once crewed with passion and intelligence.

Unlike the previous world war, World War II saw the submarine as the central foe for the Allies in Western waters, and it was a weapon that came close to theatre victories on at least two occasions. Its defeat, however, brought some major strategic and tactical lessons in naval warfare to both the victors and the vanquished.

The first lesson was that detection rather than weapons was the critical element of submarine warfare. Once the Allies had introduced their full panoply of detection technologies, the U-boats lost much of the invisibility that they had enjoyed previously. The U-boats introduced some new technologies in an attempt to counter those of the Allies, but ultimately the

30 MOST SUCCESSFUL U-BOAT COMMANDERS

Name	Success (in order of tonnage)
Otto Kretschmer	46 ships sunk; 5 ships damaged
Wolfgang Lüth	46 ships sunk; 2 ships damaged
Erich Topp	35 ships sunk; 4 ships damaged
Heinrich Liebe	34 ships sunk; 1 ship damaged
Viktor Schütze	35 ships sunk; 2 ships damaged
Heinrich Lehmann -Willenbrock	25 ships sunk; 2 ships damaged
Karl-Friedrich Merten	27 ships sunk
Herbert Schultze	26 ships sunk; 1 ship damaged
Günther Prien	30 ships sunk; 8 ships damaged
Georg Lassen	26 ships sunk; 5 ships damaged
Joachim Schepke	36 ships sunk; 4 ships damaged
Werner Henke	24 ships sunk; 2 ships damaged
Carl Emmermann	26 ships sunk
Heinrich Bleichrodt	24 ships sunk; 2 ships damaged
Robert Gysae	25 ships sunk; 1 ship damaged
Ernst Kals	20 ships sunk; 1 ship damaged
Johann Mohr	27 ships sunk; 3 ships damaged
Klaus Scholtz	25 ships sunk
Adolf Cornelius Piening	25 ships sunk; 1 ship damaged
Helmut Witte	23 ships sunk; 1 ship damaged
Günter Hessler	21 ships sunk
Ernst Bauer	25 ships sunk; 4 ships damaged
Engelbert Endrass	22 ships sunk; 4 ships damaged
Reinhard Hardegen	22 ships sunk; 5 ships damaged
Werner Hartmann	26 ships sunk
Hans Jenisch	17 ships sunk; 3 ships damaged
Richard Zapp	16 ships sunk; 1 ship damaged
Victor Oehrn	23 ships sunk; 1 ship damaged
Jürgen Oesten	19 ships sunk; 4 ships damaged
Wilhelm Rollmann	22 ships sunk

Kriegsmarine was never quite able to get ahead of the technology curve, at least in terms of ways that could be applied to all its production boats.

The exposure to detection technologies became especially critical when Allied systems were fully linked with anti-submarine air power, the number one killer of U-boats during the entire conflict. Just as U-boat endurance increased throughout the war, so did aircraft endurance, with the result that the U-boats had fewer and fewer places in which they could hide, and they

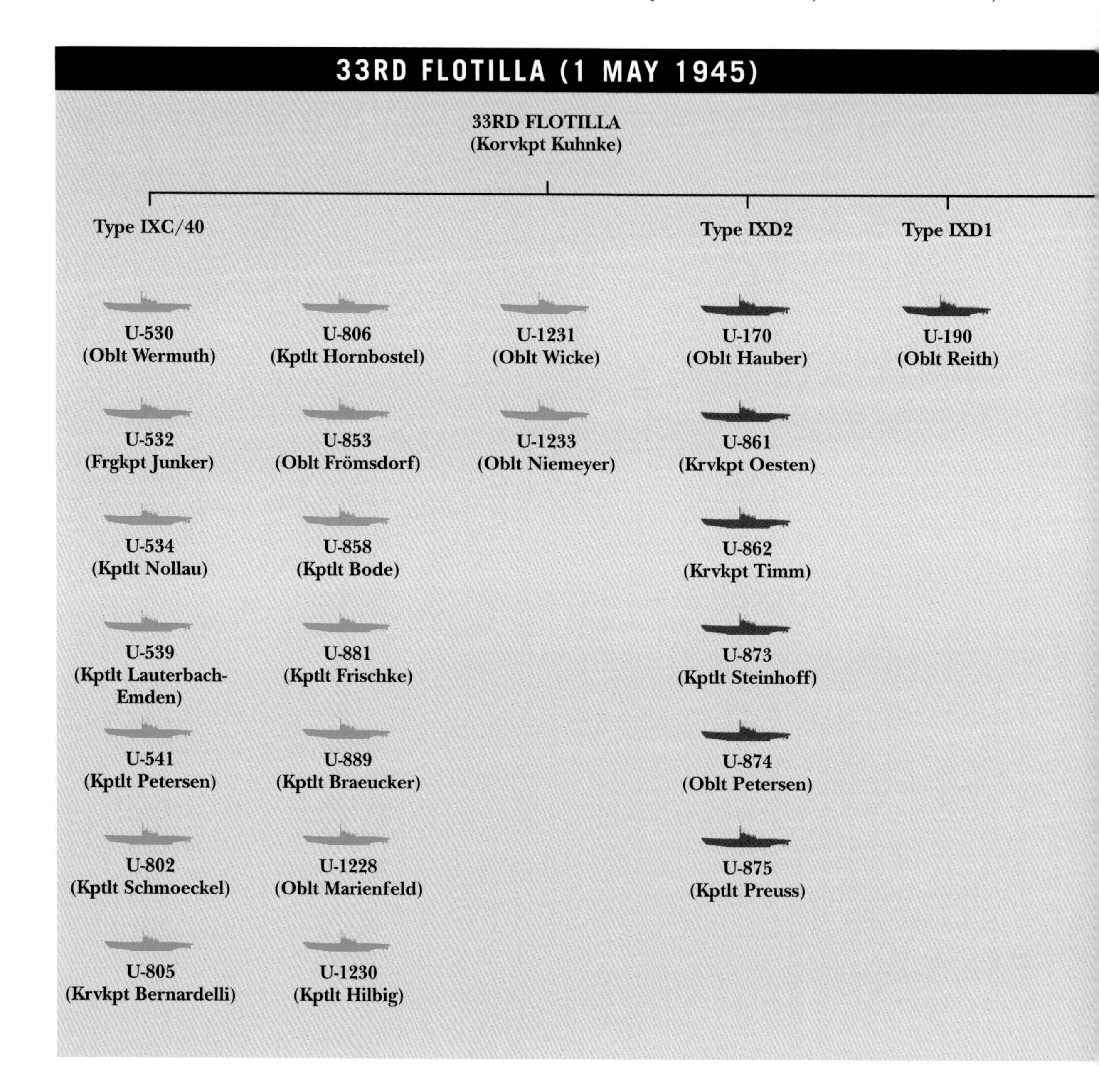

were forced to divert away from the best hunting grounds to more remote waters to avoid destruction by aircraft from Coastal Command.

One final factor that the U-boats could not defeat was simply the industrial might wielded by the Allies, particularly the United States. Germany sank in total 17,170,326 tonnes (16,899,146 tons) of merchant shipping in the Atlantic, but the United States alone produced twice this tonnage of vessels. In the final analysis, the U-boats fought an unequal war.

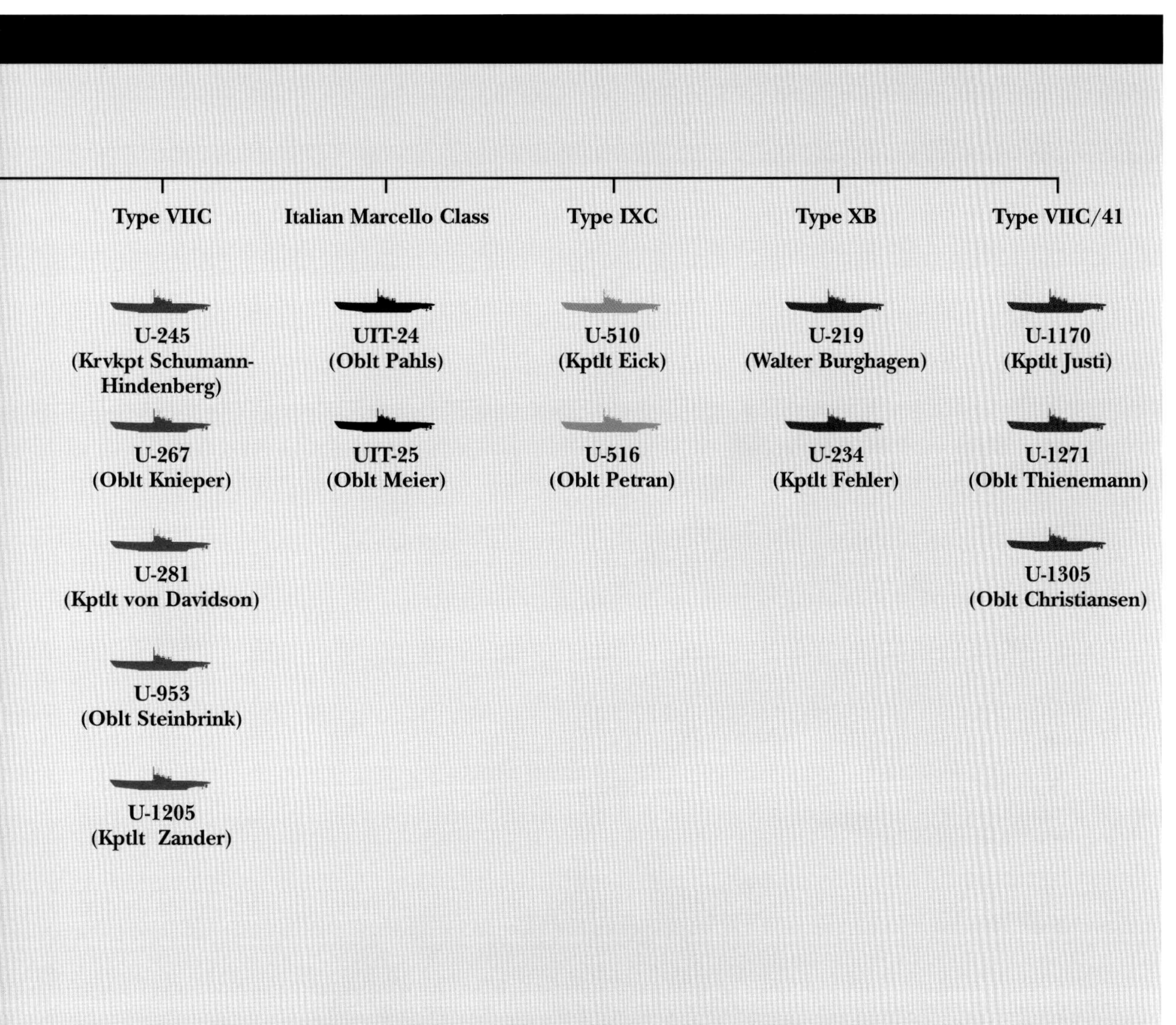

Korvettenkapitän Günter Kuhnke led the 33rd Flotilla until the very end of the war, when it was finally surrendered to the Allies. A quick glance at this establishment shows how theoretically powerful the flotilla had become, but lack of fundamentals such as fuel and munitions meant that many of the U-boats were effectively out of service. The crews of these craft were lucky in that most, although not all, would survive the war.

The Mediterranean: 1941–45

Germany's failure to take and control the Mediterranean waters was one of the great missed strategic opportunities of World War II, and it meant that the German Navy was on a path to another theatre defeat.

A formation of German S-boats open up to full speed while conducting a patrol in the Mediterranean.

By the end of 1940, two major events had occurred that changed the balance of naval power in the Mediterranean. First, the French fleet was effectively removed from the war, and the French bases around the Mediterranean now posed no substantial threat to any German ambitions in the region. Second, Italy joined the war on the part of the Axis, bringing with it a naval force that included six battleships and 19 cruisers, all stationed in the Mediterranean. The Royal Navy also had a menacing presence in the Mediterranean, but this was territorially split between Gibraltar in the west and Alexandria in the east, with Italy dividing the two territories. Add the fact that much of Britain's navy was wrapped up in the desperate struggle in the Atlantic, and Raeder decided the moment was right to act decisively in the Mediterranean.

Changed plans

During 1940, Raeder conceived of a plan to take sweeping control of the Mediterranean, seizing Gibraltar in a combined naval/land operation through southern France, Spain and French North Africa, while also taking the Suez Canal, a move that would give Germany effective control over the Middle East and Balkans, and over vital Allied maritime oil traffic.

The plan was submitted to Hitler, who then prevaricated over committing to it, most likely because his mind was far more occupied with the coming operation against the Soviet Union. This left the British with an opening, which they took forcefully. The French fleet at Mers-el-Kébir was wiped out by a British raid on 3 July 1940, lest it fall into German hands. The Royal Navy also increased the size of its Alexandria fleet to include four battleships and two destroyers.

To add to Raeder's problems, the war took different turns in late 1940 and early 1941. The Italian fleet suffered major damage under British air attack at Taranto harbour on 11 November. Italy invaded Greece in October 1940, and became embroiled in a conflict that it could not handle, which led to a German war in the Balkans from April 1941. Similar Italian troubles against the British in North Africa led to Germany beginning its North African war in February 1941. For Raeder, the involvement in these two theatres made a major Mediterranean operation even more imperative, but to Hitler the Mediterranean was a peripheral theatre, officially rendered so by his stated intention in December 1940 to make the Soviet Union his main operational focus. Raeder's dream of conquering the Mediterranean was over, and instead he was locked into a major battle with frequently limited resources.

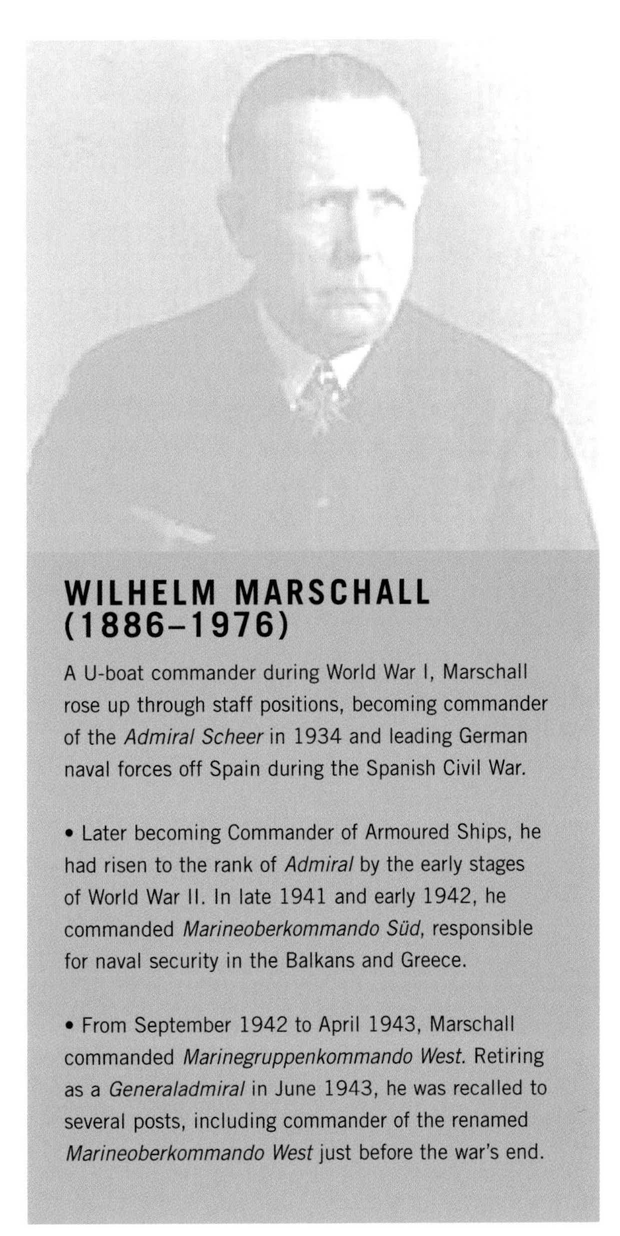

WILHELM MARSCHALL (1886–1976)

A U-boat commander during World War I, Marschall rose up through staff positions, becoming commander of the *Admiral Scheer* in 1934 and leading German naval forces off Spain during the Spanish Civil War.

• Later becoming Commander of Armoured Ships, he had risen to the rank of *Admiral* by the early stages of World War II. In late 1941 and early 1942, he commanded *Marineoberkommando Süd*, responsible for naval security in the Balkans and Greece.

• From September 1942 to April 1943, Marschall commanded *Marinegruppenkommando West.* Retiring as a *Generaladmiral* in June 1943, he was recalled to several posts, including commander of the renamed *Marineoberkommando West* just before the war's end.

Fast-boat war

For the *Kriegsmarine*, the surface naval war in the Mediterranean was to be a fast-boat conflict, conducted with torpedo boats, corvettes, destroyers, S-boats, minesweepers and motor launches.

The surface war in the Mediterranean was primarily about protecting or interdicting supplies. For the *Kriegsmarine*, its offensive perspective was twofold: destroy Allied supply shipping running to British-held ports on the North African coastline, and implement a naval siege of the island of Malta, which sat in the eastern Mediterranean astride the Axis North African supply routes. From a defensive point of view, the *Kriegsmarine* had to do its best to prevent the Allies severing the Italian convoy routes to Libya, without which the German and Italian land and air forces there would begin to wither.

The Mediterranean became a bitterly contested naval theatre, and naval historian Edward P. von der Porten notes the retaliatory nature of the conflict:

> 'The Mediterranean conflict degenerated into a series of vicious battles – employing every weapon from battleships to mine-carrying swimmers – which exacted heavy losses from each side. The Italians tried to reinforce North Africa; the British in Malta tried to cut the Afrika Korps' lifeline; and the British in Alexandria and Gibraltar tried to keep Malta reinforced – in what proved to be the most dangerous convoy run of all.' (Edward P. von der Porten, *The German Navy in World War Two.*)

In addition to the operations surrounding convoy protection or attack, the *Kriegsmarine* was also tasked with the broad range of coastal support and patrol duties, from ferrying supplies along coastlines to sweeping the approaches to harbours and anchorages free of mines.

MOTOR TORPEDO BOAT FLOTILLAS (1939–45)

Flotilla	Theatre
1st S-boat	Baltic, North Sea, Black Sea
2nd S-boat	North Sea, English Channel, Baltic
3rd S-boat	North Sea, English Channel, Baltic, Mediterranean
4th S-boat	English Channel
5th S-boat	Baltic, English Channel
6th S-boat	North Sea, English Channel, Baltic
7th S-boat	Baltic, Mediterranean
8th S-boat	Norway/Arctic
9th S-boat	English Channel
10th S-boat	English Channel
11th S-boat	Baltic, French coast
21st S-boat	Baltic, Mediterranean
22nd S-boat	Baltic
24th S-boat	Mediterranean

Organization

By the time that Hitler opened his campaign against Russia in June 1941, the *Kriegsmarine* command structure around the Mediterranean had settled into two main elements. As part of *Marinegruppenkommando West,* which was the main *Kriegsmarine* structure for operations in western seas, the *Admiral französischen Südküste* (Admiral Commanding, French South Coast) essentially took charge of all *Kriegsmarine* operations between Spain and Italy. In turn, this stretch of sea was divided into two sectors: *Seeko Languedoc* to the west covered a territory from Spain to Cany-le-Rouet, and *Seeko Riviera* to the east extended from Cany-le-Rouet to Italy.

Further east, Hitler's conquest of the Balkans had brought into his possession the Greek mainland and islands as operating bases, useful for applying pressure against the British shipping moving across the Mediterranean from Alexandria. These waters were the responsibility of *Marinegruppenkommando Süd,* a blanket

organization covering the Balkans, Black Sea and Greek waters. The main subordinated units within this formation were *Kommandierender Admiral Ägäis* (Admiral Commanding, Aegean), *Kommandierender Admiral Schwarzes Meer* (Admiral Commanding, Black Sea) and *Kommandierender Admiral Adria* (Admiral Commanding, Adriatic). Between them, all these *Kriegsmarine* formations and units, allied to the efforts of the Italian Navy, were able to extend Axis authority across the whole of the Mediterranean.

TYPE 23 TORPEDO BOAT	
Name	*Seeadler*
Commissioned	1 May 1927
Crew	120–29
Displacement	1290 tonnes (1270 tons)
Dimensions	Length: 87.7m (288ft); Beam: 8.43m (27.7ft)
Range	5753km (3575 miles) at 31km/h (17kts)
Armament	3 x 105mm (4.1in); 7 x 20mm (0.79in) AA; 6 x 533mm (21in) torpedo tubes; 30 mines
Powerplant	2 x steam turbines, 17,151kW (23,000hp)
Performance	61km/h (33kts)

Malta convoys

At least, that was the theory. One of the striking features of the Mediterranean campaign was the limited extent to which the German surface fleet could influence operations there. The most important reason was for this was the primacy of air power. The biggest threat to the Allied convoys was not from the S-boats or torpedo boats – such vessels could be handled by the Royal Navy's convoy escorts – but from U-boats and, to a much greater extent, air power. The *Luftwaffe* deployed massive resources into the Mediterranean during 1941, primarily for the suppression of convoys sailing to Malta, and British aircraft operating from there against German convoys. As soon as the Malta convoys sailed, the *Luftwaffe* He 111s, Ju 87s and Ju 88s swarmed over them, with catastrophic effects for many merchant and naval vessels. Sometimes the convoys would slip through without too much damage. Operation *Substance* in July 1941, for example, managed to sail from Gibraltar to Malta and successfully deliver 66,043 tonnes (65,000 tons) of supplies while under incessant Italian air attack, resulting in one cruiser damaged and one destroyer sunk, but with all the vital merchant ships getting through. By contrast, in February 1942 three transports attempting to get through to Malta from Alexandria were decisively stopped by repeated air attacks. This would not be surprising had not the ships' escort been genuinely strong – three cruisers and 16 destroyers. The disparity between the number of merchant ships and the strength of the escort is a clear indication of how big a problem air power was for the Allies.

Yet the fortunes of Axis air power would wax and wane in the Mediterranean, and each time they waned Malta was given some respite. Not only that, drops in *Luftwaffe* air resistance meant that the Allied air forces and Royal Navy ships were able to take revenge on Italian and German supply shipping.

Nowhere is this more strikingly demonstrated than in the first half of 1941, leading up to the German invasion of the Soviet Union in June. If we look at the tonnages of Axis supply ships sunk between January and April, we can see in graphic fashion the marked effect produced by the withdrawal of large numbers of *Luftwaffe* aircraft to the Eastern Front in April:

January	23,500 tonnes (23,129 tons)
February	39,406 tonnes (38,784 tons)
March	31,026 tonnes (30,536 tons)
April	154,570 tonnes (152,129 tons)

Although the *Luftwaffe* pulled back resources into the Mediterranean when the theatre started to prove truly problematic in 1942, the German air force steadily lost air supremacy by 1943, just as the strength of the Allied forces was growing at an accelerated pace. This was not only bad news for the *Luftwaffe*, it was equally bad news for the numerous *Kriegsmarine* craft plying the waters of the Mediterranean.

Mining operations

Although, as we shall see, there were significant engagements between the *Kriegsmarine*'s surface ships and the Royal Navy in the Mediterranean, the bulk of the big gunbattles were fought between the British and the Italians. A major task of the German Navy, however, was to use its S-boats and torpedo boats on minelaying operations, particularly using the smaller craft to target regular Allied convoy routes.

The S-boats were particularly useful in this regard. The 3rd S-boat Flotilla was was transferred from the Baltic to Derna, Libya, in December 1941, and between that date and June 1942 its primary job was laying mines around Malta. Then, however, it was employed in actual attack missions against the Allied convoys. Using speed as their main weapon, the S-boats were actually highly competent in this role. On 14 June 1942, in the flotilla's first action, S-boats torpedoed the destroyer HMS *Hasty*, which was so badly damaged she had to be sunk the next day, and severely damaged the cruiser HMS *Newcastle*. Combined with the losses inflicted on the Allies by the U-boats (see above), such actions showed that the *Kriegsmarine* was not entirely playing second fiddle to the *Luftwaffe*.

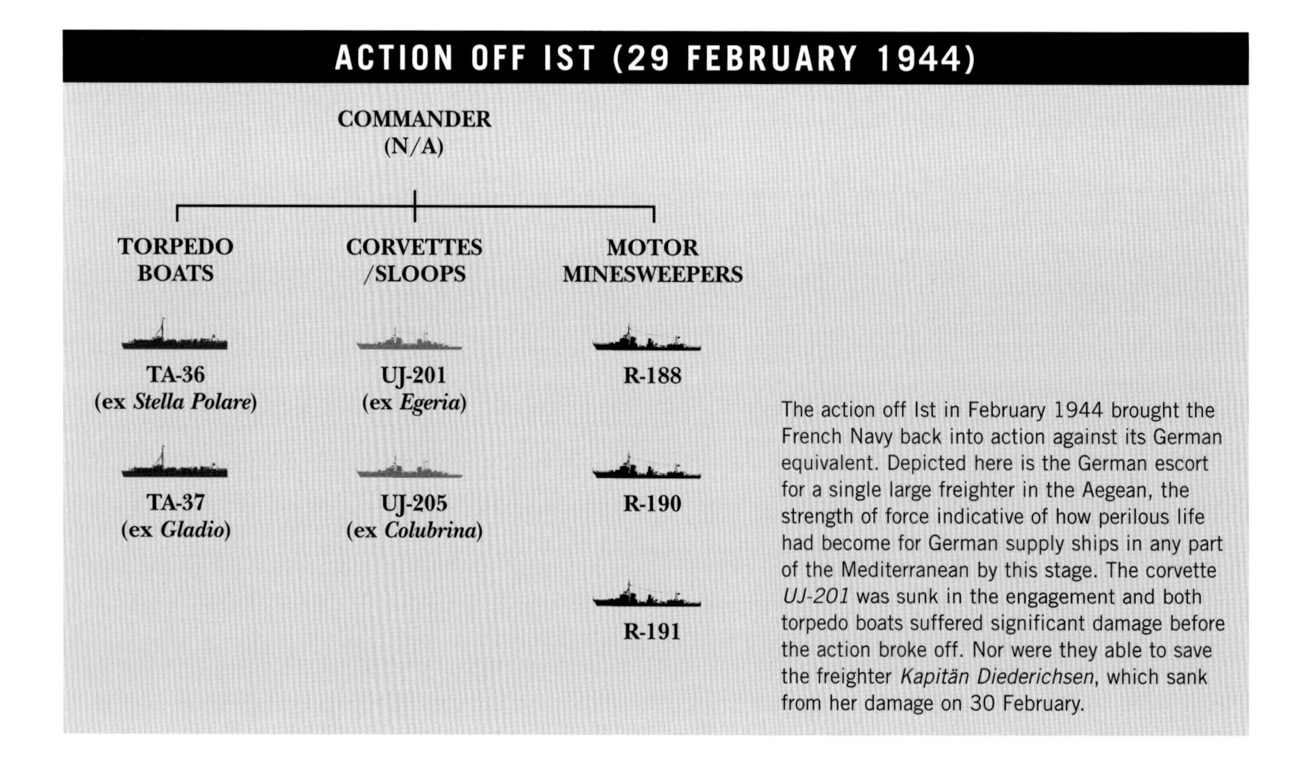

The action off Ist in February 1944 brought the French Navy back into action against its German equivalent. Depicted here is the German escort for a single large freighter in the Aegean, the strength of force indicative of how perilous life had become for German supply ships in any part of the Mediterranean by this stage. The corvette *UJ-201* was sunk in the engagement and both torpedo boats suffered significant damage before the action broke off. Nor were they able to save the freighter *Kapitän Diederichsen*, which sank from her damage on 30 February.

ACTION OFF IST (29 FEBRUARY 1944)					
Name	Displacement	Speed	Guns	Torpedoes	Damage
TORPEDO BOATS					
TA-36	1128 tonnes (1110 tons)	50km/h (28kn)	2x100mm (3.9in)	6x450mm (17.7in)	Moderate
TA-37	1128 tonnes (1110 tons)	50km/h (28kn)	2x100mm (3.9in)	5x450mm (17.7in)	Major
CORVETTES/SLOOPS					
UJ-201	740 tonnes (728 tons)	32km/h (18kn)	1x100mm (3.9in)	2x450mm (17.7in)	Sunk
UJ-205	740 tonnes (728 tons)	32km/h (18kn)	1x100mm (3.9in)	2x450mm (17.7in)	–
MOTOR MINESWEEPERS					
R-188	128 tonnes (126 tons)	41km/h (23kn)	1x37mm (1.5in)	–	–
R-190	128 tonnes (126 tons)	41km/h (23kn)	1x37mm (1.5in)	–	–
R-191	128 tonnes (126 tons)	41km/h (23kn)	1x37mm (1.5in)	–	–

Allied dominance: 1943–45

With the Italian armistice in September 1943, the situation for *Kriegsmarine* vessels in the Mediterranean changed dramatically. Not only did the German Navy face new enemies, but its own resources were dwindling.

The Italian armistice presented the *Kriegsmarine* with its most worrying development in the Mediterranean. The German Navy had no big gun warships – nothing bigger than a destroyer, in fact – in the Mediterranean, and this gap had previously been filled by the capabilities of the Italian Navy. As Vincent O'Hara notes:

> 'The Italian armistice signed in September 1943 transformed the balance of naval power in the western Mediterranean. With a simple signature the threat presented by Italy's six battleships, nine cruisers, eighty destroyers and escorts, and many smaller vessels, disappeared from the naval balance sheet.' (O'Hara)

In contrast to the Royal Navy, which had built up a massive unified force in the Mediterranean by 1943, the *Kriegsmarine* was operating a disparate collection of small vessels, ranging from torpedo boats down to requisitioned yachts and trawlers.

To add to the *Kriegsmarine*'s woes at this time, the land campaign surrounding the Mediterranean waters was going badly for Germany. German forces had already been ejected from North Africa, the navy having been unable to keep the Axis resupplied in the Western Desert, and equally having been unable to prevent the epic Allied amphibious landings in Morocco and Algeria in November 1942.

It was also impotent when the Allies went ashore in Sicily in July 1943. The 7th S-boat Flotilla, for example, had only just reached the Mediterranean after having been redeployed from France. On 16/17 July, in a night action, five of its boats were severely damaged in an engagement with numerous British motor torpedo boats (MTBs). After this, it was largely out of service as a combat unit, although later in the year seven of its boats undertook minelaying operations off the coast of Italy.

In September 1943, the Allies kept their momentum going and invaded mainland Italy itself. As the German occupied zones contracted, the *Kriegsmarine* was faced with an unenviable spread of operations, from combat runs against major Allied landing forces, through to fraught troop evacuations under the muzzles of Allied naval guns. By this time, too, the siege of Malta had been broken and the convoy routes reopened.

Eastern Mediterranean

In the eastern Mediterranean, the situation for the *Kriegsmarine* in the Aegean and Adriatic was particularly grave. The British were looking to reclaim control of both seas by force, and the *Kriegsmarine* resources were eclectic, to say the least. In the Aegean, they included 17 submarine chasers, two requisitioned minesweepers, five submarines, as well as landing barges, patrol boats, plus some requisitioned Italian warships.

Nevertheless, the British were unable to prevent the German occupation of the island of Rhodes, pre-empting an intended British operation there. One saving grace for the *Kriegsmarine* in the Aegean was that the *Luftwaffe* still retained some presence over the Balkans, making life dangerous for British ships during the hours of daylight.

During the fight over the Aegean, the Royal Navy tended to achieve results through its superior firepower, sinking a good number of the German torpedo boats

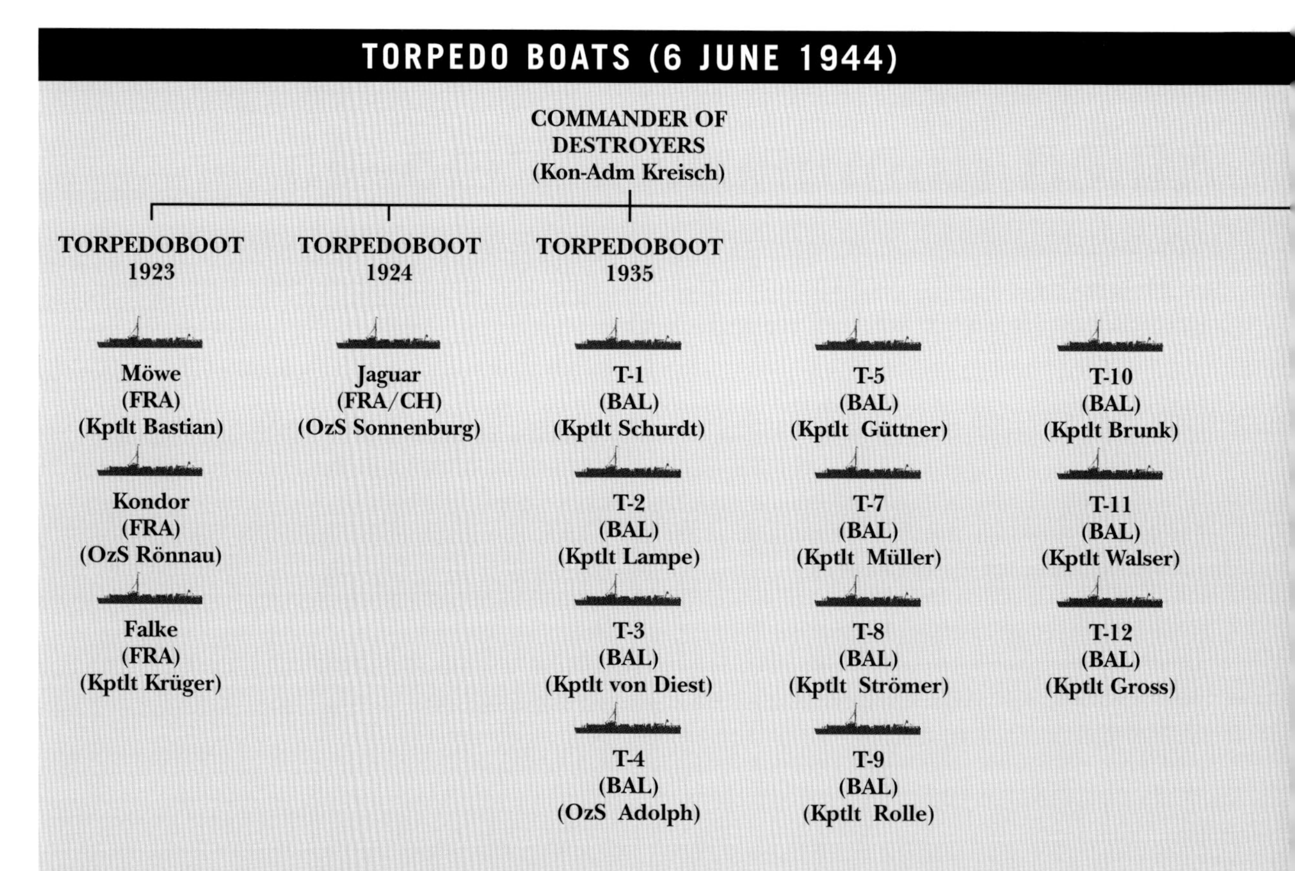

Here we see the full establishment of *Kriegsmarine* torpedo boats at the time of the D-Day landings on 6 June 1944. In addition to these vessels, however, Germany also took into service 41 vessels from other nations and utilized these in the torpedo boat role. In the Mediterranean, in particular, 26 torpedo boats were seized from the Italian Navy at the time of the Italian armistice in September 1943. In total, 37 French or Italian ships of all types were used, of which 26 were sunk.

and other craft. Yet incredibly, the *Kriegsmarine* and *Luftwaffe* together prevented the British from attaining their goal: the reoccupation of the Dodecanese islands before the Germans could claim them from the Italian garrisons. The campaign cost the Allies a shocking total of 18 ships, including six destroyers. Although direct surface actions between German and British warships often hit the Germans equally heavily, the *Kriegsmarine* had proved itself capable of influencing the war zone through amphibious deployments of troops and through mining operations.

In the Adriatic, there were also multiple naval engagments as the Allies attempted to interdict German

CAPTURED TORPEDO BOATS		
TA-9 (MED)	TA-10 (AEG)	TA-11 (MED)
TA-14 (AEG)	TA-16 (AEG)	TA-17 (AEG)
TA-19 (AEG)	TA-20 (ADR)	TA-21 (ADR)
TA-22 (MED)	TA-24 (MED)	TA-25 (MED)
TA-26 (MED)	TA-27 (MED)	TA-28 (MED)
TA-29 (MED)	TA-30 (MED)	TA-31 (MED)
TA-32 (MED)	TA-34 (ADR)	TA-35 (MED)
TA-37 (ADR)	TA-38 (AEG)	TA-39 (MED)
TA-40 (MED)	TA-45 (MED)	TA-49 (MED)

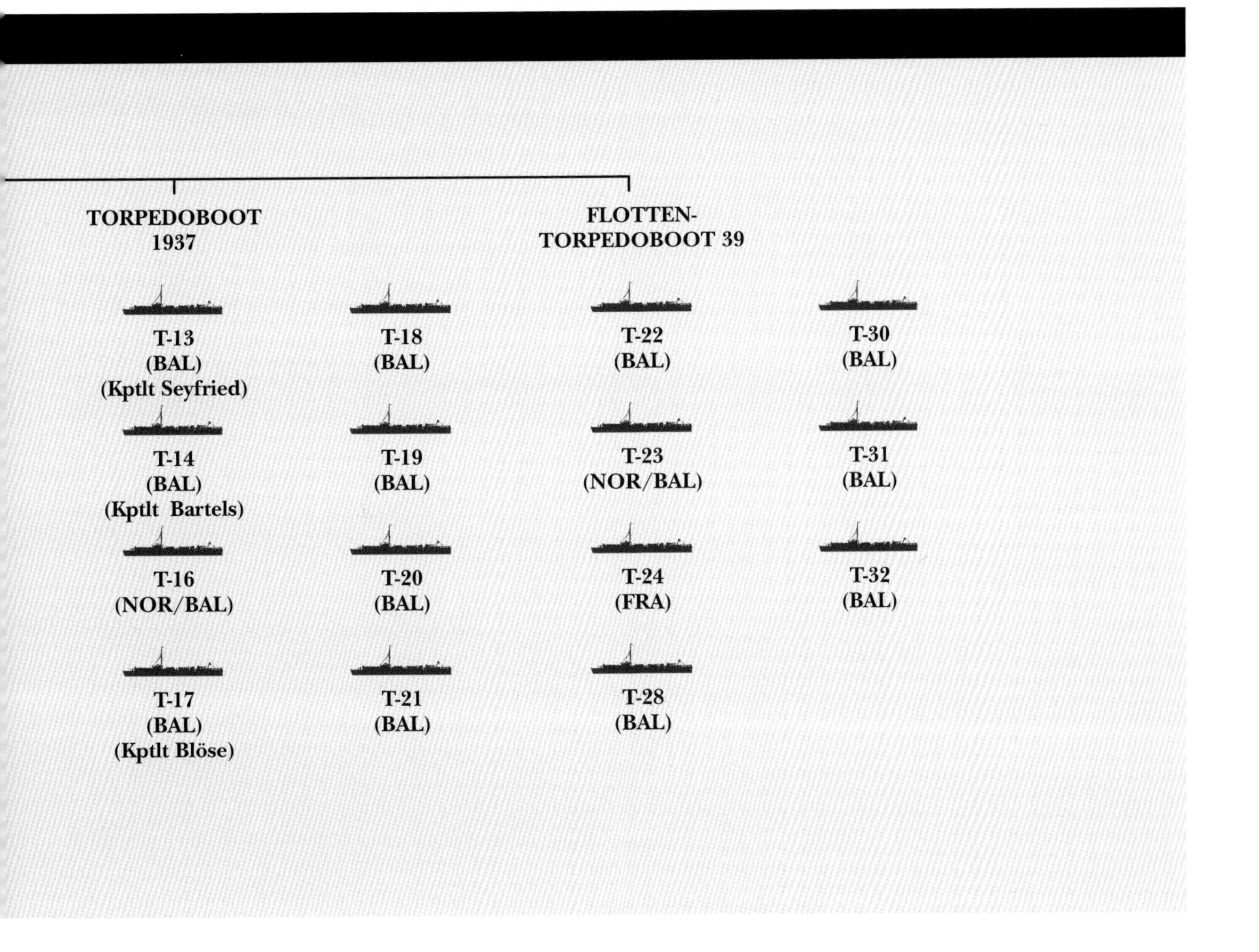

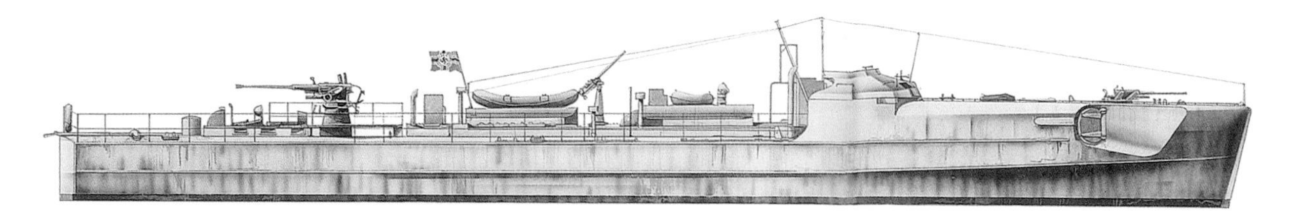

SPECIFICATIONS	
Name	S-Boot (*Schnellboot*)
Crew	24–30
Weight	80.17 tonnes (78.9 tons)
Dimensions	32.76m x 5.06m x 1.47m (107ft 6in x 16ft 6in x 4ft 9in)
Range	800 nm at 30 knots
Armament	2x 533mm (21in) torpedo tubes (4 torpedoes), 1 x 40mm (1.57in)cannon, 1x 20mm (1.8in) C/30 cannon, 1 x 7.92mm (0.3in) MG, or 6 mines
Powerplant	3x Daimler Benz twenty-cylinder diesel engines MT 502; 3960 hp
Performance	43.8 knots

coastal traffic around the Balkans. One engagement of particular note was the action off Ist on 29 February 1944. It brought German forces into battle with three large French destroyers (*Le Terrible*, *Le Malin* and *Le Fantasque*), these having joined the British 24th Destroyer Flotilla stationed at Bari. Off Ist, the three ships encountered a German freighter, the *Kapitän Diederichsen*, escorted by two German torpedo boats and two corvettes (although all of these were of Italian origin) and three minesweepers.

The French ships closed on the German convoy. Engaging at a range of around 8000m (8750 yards), they hit the freighter and set it ablaze (it sank the next day). The corvette *UJ-201* was hit by torpedoes from *Le Malin* and was destroyed in a catastrophic magazine explosion,

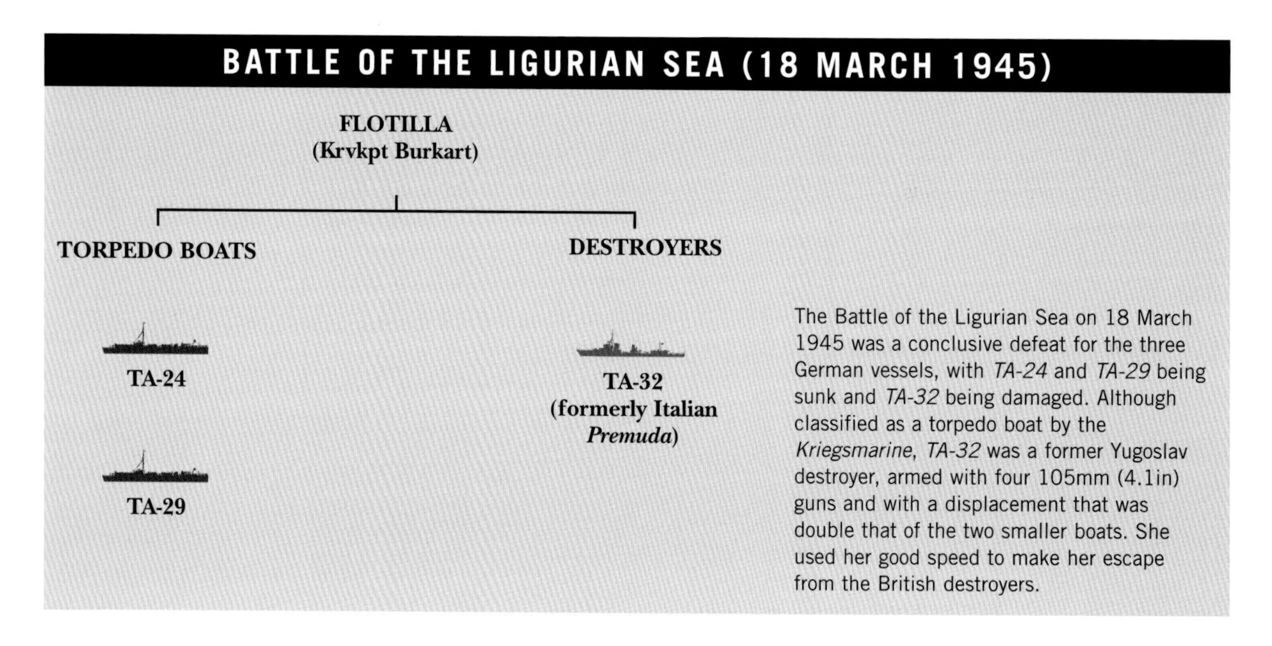

The Battle of the Ligurian Sea on 18 March 1945 was a conclusive defeat for the three German vessels, with *TA-24* and *TA-29* being sunk and *TA-32* being damaged. Although classified as a torpedo boat by the *Kriegsmarine*, *TA-32* was a former Yugoslav destroyer, armed with four 105mm (4.1in) guns and with a displacement that was double that of the two smaller boats. She used her good speed to make her escape from the British destroyers.

BATTLE OF THE LIGURIAN SEA (18 MARCH 1945)					
Name	Displacement	Speed	Guns	Torpedoes	Damage
TORPEDO/ESCORT BOATS					
TA-24	1128 tonnes (1110 tons)	54km/h (31kn)	2x100mm (3.9in)	6x450mm (17.7in)	Sunk
TA-29	1128 tonnes (1110 tons)	54km/h (31kn)	2x100mm (3.9in)	6x450mm (17.7in)	Sunk
DESTROYER					
TA-32	2032 tonnes (2000 tons)	67km/h (37kn)	4x105mm (4.1in)	3x533mm (21in)	Light

and the two torpedo boats were damaged by shell strikes before the French ships broke off the action, the commander of the squadron believing he had spotted approaching German MTBs.

The naval war in the eastern Mediterranean began drawing to a close in the summer of 1944, when the British poured a mighty naval force into the Aegean to complete the takeover they had attempted previously. By this time, the German defence was collapsing owing to developments on land, as the Soviet advance swarmed towards the Balkans.

The *Kriegsmarine* units in the theatre were principally employed in evacuating German troops from the islands, and they paid a heavy price in doing so. The September and October evacuations cost the German Navy 10 warships, including 5 torpedo boats, and 29 merchant ships, most of which were sunk by Allied air attack.

Western Mediterranean

The western Mediterranean was the last enclave of the *Kriegsmarine* in the region. The Allied Italian campaign pushed the German naval presence further into the north, but from September 1944 until the end of the war the *Kriegsmarine* managed to retain a presence on the Ligurian coastline between La Spezia and the French border.

The actions in the western Mediterranean during this period were chaotic and opportunistic, with the Allies attempting to crush the remnants of German naval power in the region, but actually failing to do so completely. The major *Kriegsmarine* unit in the area was the 10th Torpedo Boat Flotilla, which was primarily established by using captured Italian vessels. Initially nine ships strong, the 10th Flotilla was gradually whittled down through Allied air and naval attacks, plus mine strikes. Four ships were left by 15 August 1944, and subsequent months saw further craft damaged.

The end for the 10th Flotilla came on 18 March 1945, by which time only three of the torpedo boats were fully operational. The three boats sailed out to conduct a mining operation around Corsica, which they completed, laying 132 mines between them. As they were returning to Genoa, they were intercepted by two British destroyers, *Meteor* and *Lookout*. The latter ship massacred *TA-29* in a close-range gunbattle, and *Meteor* also sent *TA-24* to the bottom of the Ligurian Sea. *TA-32* was badly damaged, but managed to make her escape.

End in the Mediterranean

Over the last five months of World War II, those *Kriegsmarine* units still operating in the Mediterranean suffered a traumatic time, as the might of the victorious British and American navies, plus contributions from the French and Italians, worked to crush all remaining resistance. The German Mediterranean units recognized the end was nigh, and in the last few weeks of conflict began scuttling vessels at an ever increasing rate. In five months, over 110 Axis warships of varying sizes, plus nearly 120 auxiliary ships, were sunk in the Mediterranean, by either Allied or German hands.

In a sense, the Mediterranean was a naval battle that would be decided on land. In the territories surrounding the confined waters, the advances of land armies changed basing opportunities along the coast, and over the course of the war forced the *Kriegsmarine* into ever-shrinking defensive pockets, from which there was ultimately no option for escape.

Defeat in the North: 1942–45

The far north would become the graveyard of Germany's major surface vessels. Deployed to threaten the Allied Arctic convoys, they were in fact largely helpless in the face of Allied air power.

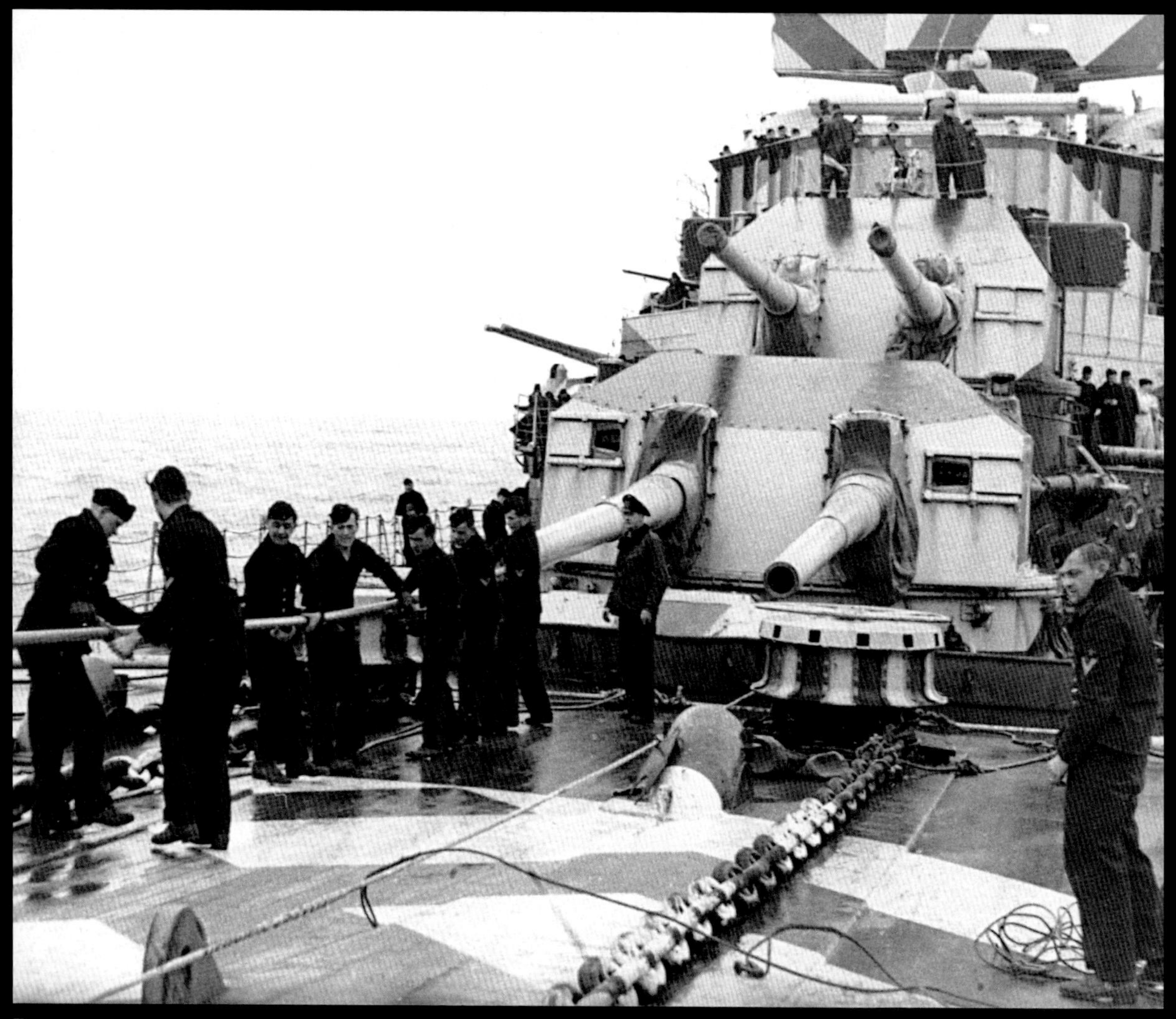

The crew of the *Admiral Hipper*, one of Germany's premier heavy cruisers, clean the main 203mm (8in) guns.

By early 1942, the *Kriegsmarine* had something of a crisis of identity. For decades the world's navies had been defined by their capital ships, the battleships and heavy cruisers that could carry big guns to any point on the globe. Since the sinking of the *Bismarck* in May 1941, however, Hitler's confidence in large warships largely evaporated. In consequence, the *Kriegsmarine*'s major surface fleet was consigned to operations in the far north around Norway, the Baltic and in Arctic waters. The *Scharnhorst* and *Gneisenau* made their Channel Dash in early 1942; the heavy cruisers moved back to the German ports to become part of the Baltic fleet; and the *Tirpitz*, the monolithic new battleship that so unnerved the Allies, was coming to the end of its trial phase in the Baltic. With such a powerful fleet up north, and a defined target in the Allied Arctic convoys, there was the chance for the surface warships to prove themselves.

Strategic reinforcements

As we have already acknowledged, the deployment of the great German warships to the north was the product of much disagreement between an inflexible *Führer* and a frustrated Raeder. Raeder wanted his warships concentrated in the Atlantic and Mediterranean, not stuck up in the frozen north, while Hitler felt, probably correctly, that keeping the warships in those theatres would ultimately end in their destruction by Allied air power, with concomitant propaganda blows akin to the sinking of the *Bismarck*.

Hitler won out, but by early 1942 the increase in Allied Arctic convoys, plus the way the war was evolving on the Eastern Front, gave Raeder's surface force a new purpose. In the first few months of 1942, therefore, the *Kriegsmarine* began to concentrate its fleet around Norway, ready to begin the incursions against the Allied convoys. *Tirpitz* herself moved into the region, slipping into Trondheimsfjord with the destroyers *Richard Beitzen, Bruno Heinemann, Paul Jakobi* and *Z-29*, while on 20 March the *Admiral Hipper* sailed into Trondheim with the destroyers *Z-24, Z-26* and *Z-30* plus the torpedo boats *T-15, T-16* and *T-17.*

Although the build-up of forces in the north was physically and militarily impressive, the picture in reality was more complex than it might initially appear. Taking a snapshot of the German Navy on 1 March 1942, all its major capital vessels were in the north, but not all were ready for action. *Tirpitz* was now operational, but both the *Scharnhorst* and *Gneisenau* were under repair at Kiel. (The former would return to operations in January 1943, while *Gneisenau* would never serve again.) Of the heavy cruisers, *Admiral Scheer* and *Admiral Hipper* were both operational, but the *Lützow* and *Prinz Eugen* were under repair, the former returning to service by May but the latter taking until January 1943 to ready itself for war. Three light cruisers (*Emden, Leipzig* and *Nürnberg*) were in the Baltic conducting training, while the *Köln* was undergoing a refit in Wilhelmshaven. A total of 17 destroyers were in the north, distributed between Denmark, Germany and Norway, but only five were actually fully operational at this time, a further nine returning to service by August 1942.

This quick breakdown of the northern surface fleet shows that its operational status was patchy to say the least, particularly amongst the heavy warships. In fairness to Hitler's decision-making capabilities, the fact that so many battleships or cruisers were confined to port or dry dock on account of damage was hardly likely to inspire confidence in their use.

Initial clashes

March 1942 brought the first clashes between Allied and German surface naval forces in the Arctic. On 6 March, the mighty *Tirpitz* ventured out against convoy PQ12, accompanied by three destroyers. It was a disappointing outing, as the German ships simply missed the convoy in appalling weather. A more substantial clash, however, came on 29 March in the Barents Sea off Bear Island. Three destroyers from the 8th Flotilla – *Z-24, Z-25* and *Z-26* – sailed out to intercept convoy PQ13, which had been scattered by earlier bad weather. *Z-26* found and sank the freighter *Bateau,* but then the German destroyers ran into the convoy's powerful escort group, which included the cruiser *Trinidad* and five destroyers. *Trinidad* and *Eclipse* sank *Z-26* with gunfire and *Z-25* was damaged, although in return both British ships were seriously hit (the *Trinidad* by one of its own torpedoes, which circled back and hit the cruiser). This action was to be one of the first major engagements in what became a vicious Arctic war.

Balance of power: 1942

The war against the Arctic convoys turned into a naval slugging match, with both sides taking losses. At the Battle of the Barents Sea, the *Kriegsmarine*'s surface fleet met one of its biggest challenges to date.

The attack on convoy PQ17 in July 1942, as we have already noted, was an important event not just for the Allied response, but also for the status of the German surface fleet. To counter PQ17 and its potent escort, Raeder put together virtually the entire *Marinegruppenkommando Nord*. The *Tirpitz* plus three heavy cruisers and 10 destroyers were channelled into the battle, but ultimately the lion's share of the convoy's destruction was accomplished by submarines and aircraft. Subsequent convoys resulted in equally abortive missions for the surface fleet, and most of 1942 was spent simply shifting the vessels around from place to place, waiting for the moment to strike.

Barents Sea

At the very end of December 1942, convoy JW51B was cruising into the danger zone off Bear Island. It consisted of 14 merchant vessels plus a major escort of two cruisers, five destroyers, two corvettes and one minesweeper. A German submarine had spotted the convoy, and in response the area naval command began making plans for a major surface combat deployment. The *Admiral Hipper* and six destroyers from the 5th Destroyer Flotilla were assembled for the action, a force which was then expanded dramatically with the addition of the *Lützow*, Hitler having given his personal permission for the ship to be deployed.

The plan of action, as devised by *Vizeadmiral* Oskar Kummetz (*Befehlshaber der Kreuzer*) involved splitting his forces in two, each side having one heavy cruiser and three destroyers. By attacking with one half of his force, he hoped to draw away the escort, then crush the convoy with waiting half, led by the *Lützow*. Yet even as the warships sailed, Kummetz received an order from Raeder that ran to the effect: 'Despite previous operational orders regarding contact against the enemy, exercise caution even against an enemy of equal strength because it is undesirable for the cruisers to take

BATTLE OF THE BARENTS SEA (31 DECEMBER 1942)					
Name	**Displacement**	**Speed**	**Guns**	**Torpedoes**	**Damage**
HEAVY CRUISERS					
Admiral Hipper	18491 tonnes (18,200 tons)	58km/h (32kn)	8x203mm (8in) 12x105mm (4.1in)	12x533mm (21in)	Significant
Lützow	16459 tonnes (16,200 tons)	50km/h (28kn)	6x280mm (11in) 8x150mm (5.9in)	8x533mm (21in)	–
DESTROYERS					
Friedrich Eckoldt	3216 tonnes (3165 tons)	68km/h (38kn)	5x127mm (5in)	8x533mm (21in)	Sunk
Richard Beitzen	3206 tonnes (3165 tons)	68km/h (38kn)	5x127mm (5in)	8x533mm (21in)	–
Theodor Riedel	3160 tonnes (3110 tons)	68km/h (38kn)	5x127mm (5in)	8x533mm (21in)	–
Z-29	3655 tonnes (3597 tons)	68km/h (38kn)	4x150mm (5.9in)	8x533mm (21in)	–
Z-30	3655 tonnes (3597 tons)	68km/h (38kn)	4x150mm (5.9in)	8x533mm (21in)	–
Z-31	3655 tonnes (3597 tons)	68km/h (38kn)	4x150mm (5.9in)	8x533mm (21in)	–

great risks.' Once again, it appeared that the naval high command wanted the surface fleet to fight with one hand behind its back.

Move to contact

To find the convoy, Kummetz spread his ships out in a line over 129km (80 miles) long, and just before dawn on the 31st *Hipper* caught its first sighting of the enemy vessels. At 0929, the gunbattle began, the German destroyer *Friedrich Eckoldt* opening the firefight. *Hipper* joined the engagement at 0941, making splinter and concussion strikes on the destroyer *Achates*.

Poor visibility was producing a sporadic engagement, but at 1016 *Hipper* obtained serious hits on the destroyer *Onslow*, and put her out of action, and another British destroyer was also damaged. The fight seemed to be going Kummetz's way. Yet when *Lützow* arrived on the scene around 1045, it simply glided past in the bad weather, missing the Allied ships, and leaving *Hipper* to continue the fight, which it did with aplomb. *Hipper* destroyed and sank the minesweeper *Bramble*, and finished off the *Achates*, which also later sank. Several other ships were also seriously damaged. Yet at around 1130, the two British cruisers, *Sheffield* and *Jamaica*, swung into action against the *Hipper* in a surprise attack. The German cruiser was hit by three huge shell strikes and was forced to break off the action, saved primarily by the low visibility that was part and parcel of the terrible weather.

With *Lützow* still out of the battle, the engagement was continued by the German destroyers. However, the *Friedrich Eckoldt* was caught with a full broadside from

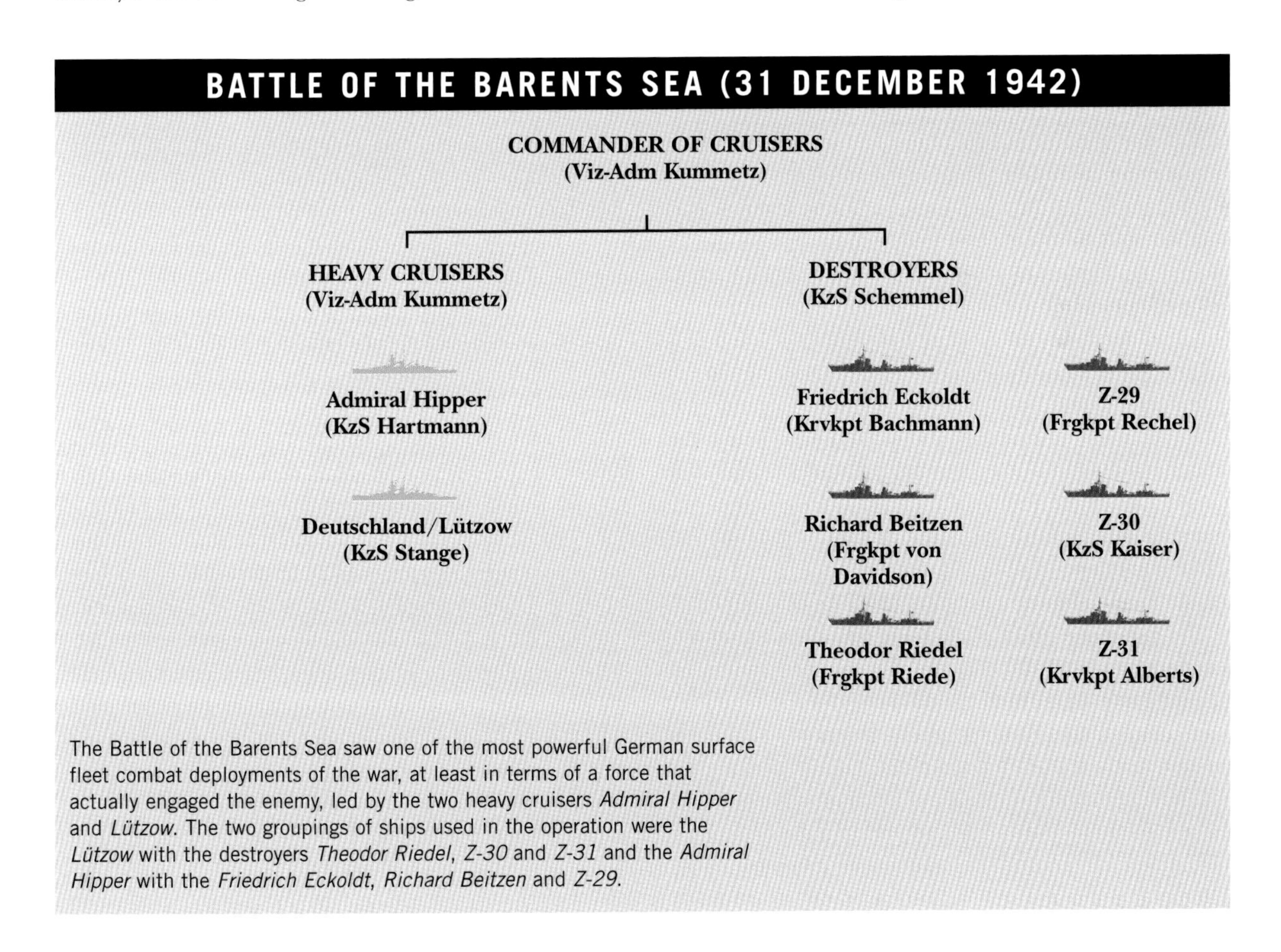

The Battle of the Barents Sea saw one of the most powerful German surface fleet combat deployments of the war, at least in terms of a force that actually engaged the enemy, led by the two heavy cruisers *Admiral Hipper* and *Lützow*. The two groupings of ships used in the operation were the *Lützow* with the destroyers *Theodor Riedel*, *Z-30* and *Z-31* and the *Admiral Hipper* with the *Friedrich Eckoldt*, *Richard Beitzen* and *Z-29*.

the *Sheffield*, and the destroyer went down, taking all 340 crew members with it.

Eventually, at 1138, the *Lützow* finally swung into action, but apart from inflicting some splinter damage on a couple of British ships, it achieved no decisive hits. Furthermore, night was now approaching, and the German battlegroup received orders to withdraw.

The Battle of the Barents Sea was over, but we have already noted the huge repercussions of this event. The German capital ships would wade into action again, but as we shall see, they no longer impressed Hitler, who now viewed them as costly liabilities, rather than mighty warships capable of controlling the waters.

BATTLE OF THE BARENTS SEA

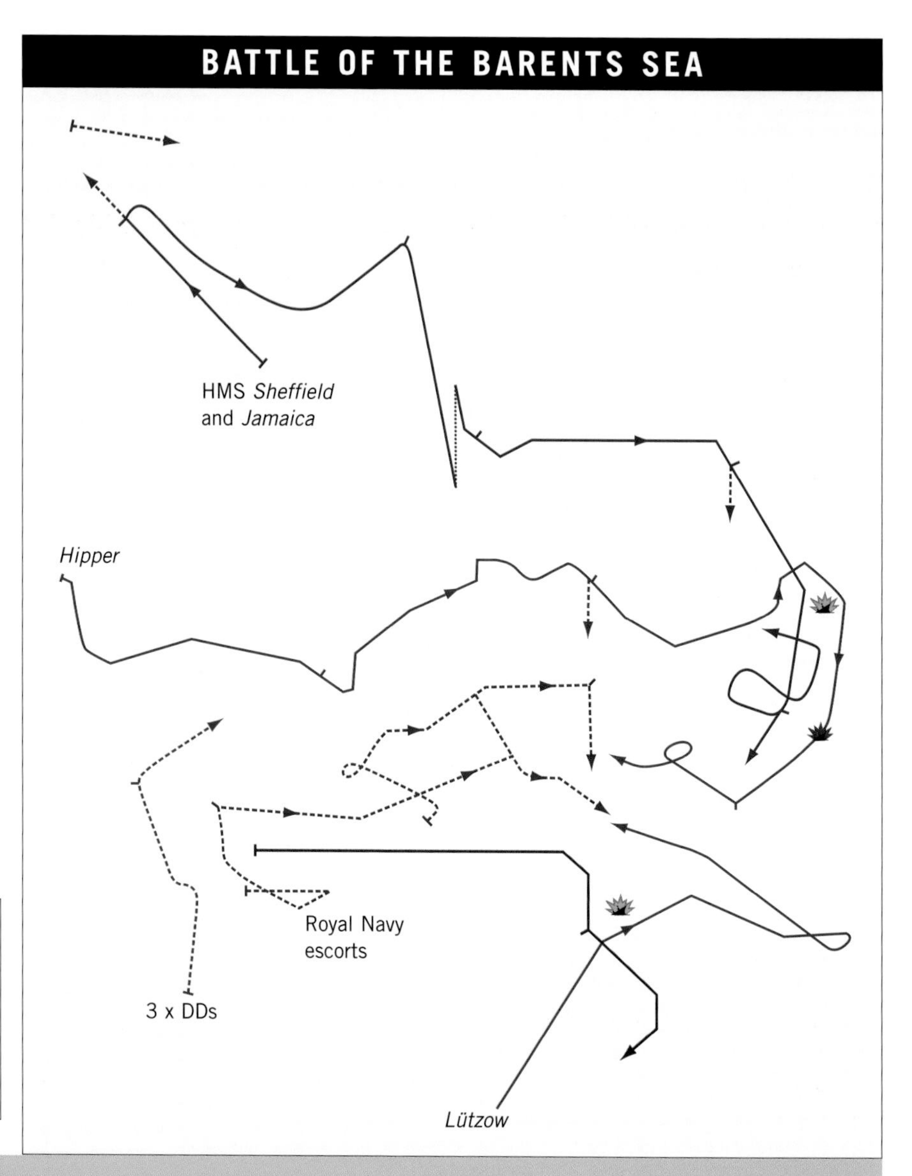

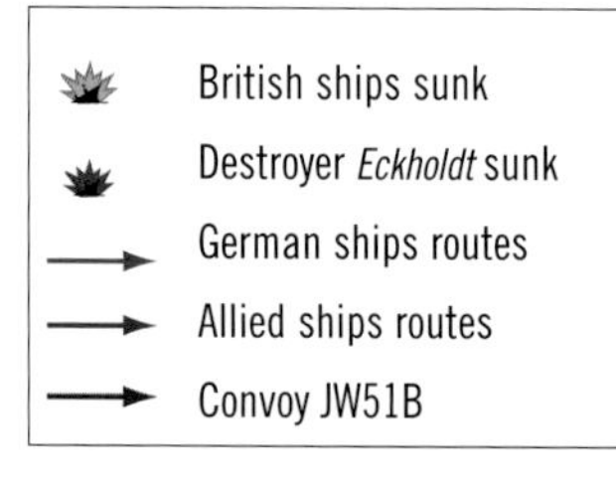

31 December 1942

The Battle of the Barents Sea illustrates how much environmental conditions could affect convoy actions in the far north. In the poor visibility, the battle squadron led by *Lützow* actually missed the British ships in the first instance, and only the clearing weather plus the flashes of gunfire later enabled her to orient back into the action.

As the British were initially outgunned, a favoured tactic was to make mock torpedo runs against the *Hipper*, thereby causing the great cruiser to execute evasive manoeuvres and restrict the volume of fire that she could put out. Once the British cruisers *Sheffield* and *Jamaica* arrived, such was the element of surprise that at first the German destroyers thought that the *Hipper* was mistakenly firing on them.

Loss of the capital ships: 1943–45

After the Battle of the Barents Sea, the *Kriegsmarine* was enslaved to a policy of caution when it came to utilization of its major surface vessels. This did not prevent many of these great warships subsequently being destroyed by shell and bomb.

From 1943 to 1945, the *Kriegsmarine*'s surface fleet was steadily destroyed. It was an acutely painful process, not least because it illustrated how appallingly vulnerable the big battleships and cruisers really were in a new era of warfare. Here we will look at the fates of the big-name warships that have so often graced the earlier chapters of this book, illustrating the scale of the disaster that overtook the *Kriegsmarine* in the north as the war went through its final cataclysmic stages.

Scharnhorst

Of all the German capital ships, with the exception of the *Bismarck*, the *Scharnhorst* arguably underwent the most dramatic end. By December 1943, the *Scharnhorst* was essentially the only major German warship still operationally viable in the north. (For more about the fate of the *Tirpitz*, see below.) Allied Arctic convoys were now slipping through the German net with great regularity, and those that were intercepted were usually confronted with only a small collection of destroyers and torpedo boats at worst.

On 25 December, however, the *Scharnhorst* was deployed along with five destroyers (*Z-29, Z-30, Z-33, Z-34* and *Z-38*) to intercept the ships of two Arctic convoys: the outward-bound JW55B and the returning RA55A, both protected by the nearby presence of two massive Royal Navy escort forces, which between them fielded one battleship (*Duke of York*), four cruisers and eight destroyers (one of them Norwegian).

The commander of the German force, *Konteradmiral* Erich Bey, had received orders to attack JW55B direct from Dönitz, the Nazi high command having for once relinquished its operational caution with regard to its surface fleet. German intelligence had not revealed that the convoy's immediate support included a battleship.

On the morning of 26 December, the German force was approaching the hunting grounds. Bey took *Scharnhorst* north, while his destroyers scouted to the southwest, a fateful decision that left the German battleship on its own.

At around 0930, star shells bursting above the *Scharnhorst* told the captain that his ship had been spotted. The initial Allied salvos from the cruisers *Norfolk* and *Belfast* made quick hits on the German battleship destroying its forward radar. *Scharnhorst* turned for home, ordering the destroyers to keep hunting for the convoy. Shortly after noon, *Scharnhorst* was again engaged by the British cruisers, but hit the *Norfolk* and managed to outpace the pursuers.

This was not the end, however. Just after 1600 *Scharnhorst* was surprised by the combined fire of the *Duke of York* and the cruiser *Jamaica*. In the ensuing running gun battle, *Scharnhorst* was crippled by four shell strikes, then was torpedoed in an opportunistic attack by two destroyers. The once great battleship was now dead in the water, but for 36 minutes the British force swarmed around it, pumping in shells and torpedoes until the vessel finally capsized and sank, taking with it over 1900 men.

Tirpitz

The destruction of the *Tirpitz* was a protracted affair that took place over two years, and which ensured that the ship never made any serious attack on Allied shipping, an ironic situation given the sheer muscular power of the vessel.

On 22 September 1943, in one of history's most audacious raids, two British four-man midget submarines (out of six deployed) managed to slip into Altenfjord, Norway, where the *Tirpitz* was anchored. They placed massive explosive charges beneath *Tirpitz*'s hull, and

OSKAR KUMMETZ (1891–1980)

Oskar Kummetz joined the navy in 1910, rising to become *Führer der Torpedoboote* (Chief of Torpedo Boats) in 1934 in the rank of *Fregattenkapitän*.

• In June 1942, as a *Vizeadmiral*, Kummetz was appointed *Befehlshaber der Kreuzer* (Commander of Cruisers), in which capacity he oversaw the Barents Sea operation. The following February, he became *Befehlshaber der Kampfgruppe* (Commander of the Battlegroup), the new organization responsible for Germany's battle fleet.

• Kummetz remained in this post until February 1944, when he was appointed commander-in-chief of *Marineoberkommando Ostsee* in the Baltic, a position that he held for the rest of the war.

these, when detonated, did enough damage to put the battleship out of action until March 1944.

Not that the *Tirpitz* would be allowed to rest during this time. While it was being repaired, it was anchored in the Kaajfjord, which led off from the Altenfjord. The Kaajfjord was selected because its preciptous mountain surroundings partly protected the *Tirpitz* from air attack, although the Allies still made repeated raids in an attempt at putting the great ship out of action before it could be repaired. On 10–11 February, for example, Russian bombers from the Soviet Naval Arm made an attack, causing minor damage through a near miss.

Operation *Tungsten*

The second major attack, this time by the British, had far more serious consequences. On 2 April 1944, two British carriers (*Victorious* and *Furious*) positioned off Norway, heavily protected by Home Fleet warships, launched an attack, codenamed Operation *Tungsten*, with dozens of maritime aircraft. In spite of the massive anti-aircraft protection from on board and around the *Tirpitz*, the battleship was hit in two waves by 14 armour-piercing bombs that killed 122 of its crew and wounded 316 others. Although the damage was limited to the superstructure, the vessel was still put out of action for an additional three months.

Repeated raids were made on the *Tirpitz* over the coming months, some of them battered off by the increasingly powerful anti-aircraft gun systems that now ringed the beleaguered battleship, although some minor bomb hits were achieved. (Another of the battleship's main defences was its ability to lay a massive smokescreen within minutes of the air raid warning.)

Yet by the end of the summer of 1944, RAF Bomber Command was also looking at how it could take out the *Tirpitz*. It decided to examine whether the new 5454kg (12,000lb) Tallboy deep-penetration bomb had applications against the battleship. By using the Tallboy, the Allies hoped that they could punch right through the battleship's armoured decks and detonate deep inside the ship, with decisive consequences.

Flying out of northern Russia, the first Tallboy attack went in on 11 September, but dreadful weather prevented it even reaching its target. Then, on 15 September, 27 Lancaster bombers made a further attempt, and this time there was a definite result. One of the Tallboy bombs smashed straight through *Tirpitz*'s bow and detonated in the water beneath, smashing much of the front end of the ship and pushing back repair estimates by nine months.

At this point, *Tirpitz* was relocated to Tromsø for extra safety. Furthermore, in blunt recognition that it was unlikely to play much of a part in open-ocean warfare again, the ship was assigned a coastal defence role in case the Allies attempted an invasion of Norway. The British, however, had no reliable intelligence on the extent of the *Tirpitz*'s damage, so still considered it a genuine threat to the British fleet.

For this reason, the air attacks continued. A Tallboy attack on 20 October made no headway through low cloud and the enemy smokescreen, achieving only one near miss. Then, on 12 November 1944, another two squadrons of Lancasters made an attack run, and this time caught the *Tirpitz* in clear, unobscured daylight.

Despite the blazing anti-aircraft fire from the ship,

BATTLE OF THE NORTH CAPE (26 DECEMBER 1943)

Name	Displacement	Speed	Guns	Torpedoes	Damage
BATTLESHIP					
Scharnhorst	39,522 tonnes (38,900 tons)	58km/h (32kn)	9x280mm (11in) 12x150mm (5.9in)	6x533mm (21in)	Sunk
DESTROYERS					
Z-29	3655 tonnes (3597 tons)	68km/h (38kn)	4x150mm (5.9in)	8x533mm (21in)	–
Z-30	3655 tonnes (3597 tons)	68km/h (38kn)	4x150mm (5.9in)	8x533mm (21in)	–
Z-33	3750 tonnes (3691 tons)	68km/h (38kn)	5x150mm (5.9in)	8x533mm (21in)	–
Z-34	3750 tonnes (3691 tons)	68km/h (38kn)	5x150mm (5.9in)	8x533mm (21in)	–
Z-38	3750 tonnes (3691 tons)	68km/h (38kn)	5x150mm (5.9in)	8x533mm (21in)	–

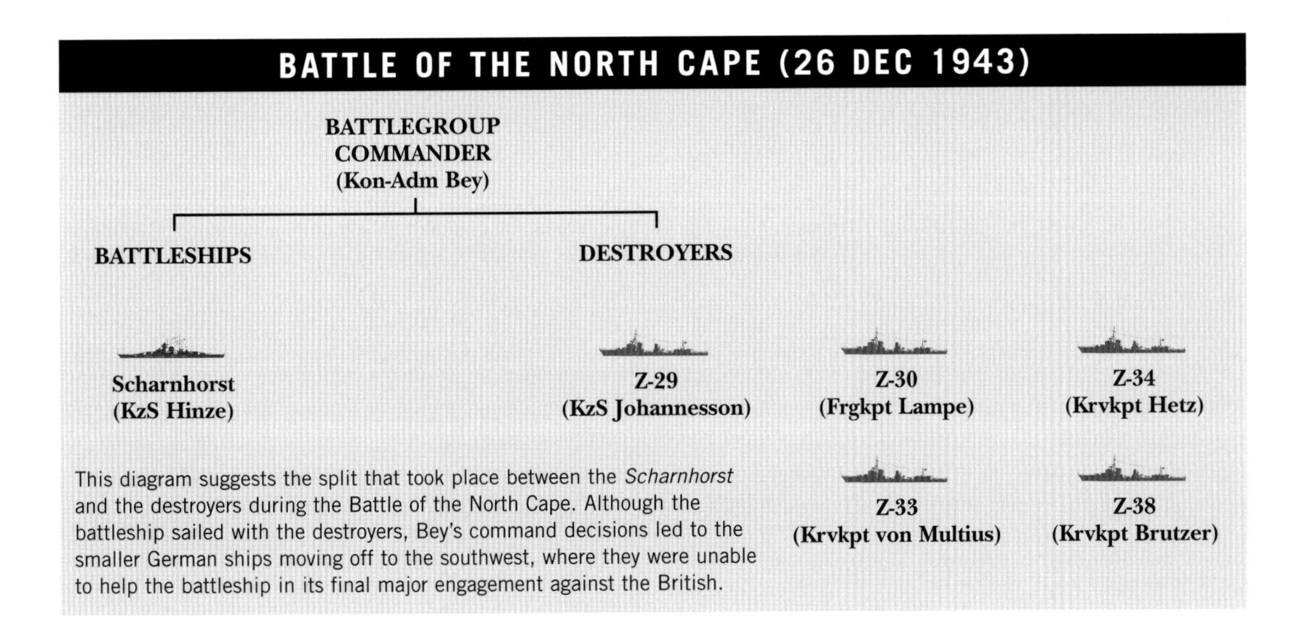

This diagram suggests the split that took place between the *Scharnhorst* and the destroyers during the Battle of the North Cape. Although the battleship sailed with the destroyers, Bey's command decisions led to the smaller German ships moving off to the southwest, where they were unable to help the battleship in its final major engagement against the British.

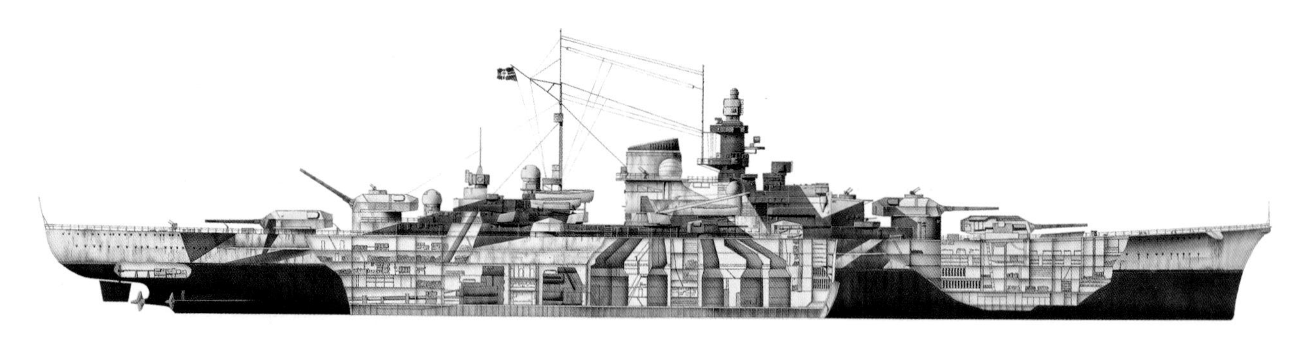

TIRPITZ	
Name	*Tirpitz*
Commissioned	25 February 1941
Crew	2608
Displacement	52,600 tonnes (51,769 tons)
Dimensions	Length: 250m (822ft); Beam36m (118ft)
Range	14,274km (8870 miles) at 35km/h (19kts)
Armour	Belt: 320mm (12.6in); Decks: 50–120mm (2–4.7in); Turrets: 230–355mm (9–14in)
Armament	8 x 381mm (15in); 114 x AA guns; 8 x 533mm (21in) torpedo tubes
Powerplant	3 x steam turbines, 102,907kW (138,000hp)
Performance	54km/h (29kts)

the end of the *Tirpitz* was only minutes away. The ship was hit square-on by three of the Tallboy bombs, which blew apart huge sections of the vessel. *Tirpitz* had finally had enough, and capsized, with the superstructure actually resting on the bottom of the fjord, thus exposing the hull above the water. In total, 874 of its crewmen died in the attack. As a final indignity, the *Tirpitz* lay in its capsized state for over 10 years, still with the bodies of some of the crew inside, while the ship was slowly cut up for scrap, a process that was not completed until 1957.

The heavy cruisers

Few of the *Kriegsmarine*'s warships were to be spared the horrors unleashed against Germany in the last months

KRIEGSMARINE BASES (JAN 1945)

Narvik
Trondheim
ATLANTIC OCEAN
Bergen
Flensburg
Kiel
Gotenhafen
Wilhelmshaven
Hamburg
Lorient
La Pallice
La Spezia

Reduced bases

By January 1945, the number of *Kriegsmarine* bases around Europe had declined considerably. In France, Lorient, St Nazaire and La Pallice remained in German hands, with occasional U-boat and fast boat traffic, until the end of the war.

In the Mediterranean, La Spezia and Genoa were still operational bases. Yet it was in the far north that the bulk of the *Kriegsmarine* bases were located at this point in time. In Norway, these included Trondheim, Bergen and Narvik, although the navy also made use of the dozens of natural anchorages available among the fjords.

Meanwhile, in Germany and on the Baltic Sea, the principal naval bases were Kiel, Wilhelmshaven, Hamburg, Flensburg, Bremen and Gotenhafen. By this stage of the war, however, many of these bases were under heavy Allied air attack and were scarcely operational.

of the war, as defeat became inevitable. The warships in the north were rarely assigned roles against the enemy's fleets. Instead they were employed in shore bombardment roles against the approaching Soviet forces, or in the panicked evacuation of hundreds of thousands of refugees fleeing the Russian offensive into East Prussia. The scenes played out in these last months of the war were nightmarish in the extreme, and cost the lives of hundreds of naval personnel.

The *Admiral Scheer*, that venerable *Panzerschiff/ Schwerer Kreuzer*, entered service again in October 1944 after repairs, and mainly served in a ground-support role for the German Army around the northern coastlines. It also performed refugee evacuation missions. In March 1945, *Admiral Scheer* was engaged in its last gun action, bombarding Soviet forces attacking the Wollin bridgehead in East Pomerania. Such were the firepower demands of the action, that the ship was then sent to Kiel, having worn out its main gun barrels. While at Kiel, the cruiser was found by RAF Bomber Command on 9–10 April, and hit with several bombs. *Admiral Scheer* capsized, and was later buried under rubble after the war when the Allies filled in the anchorage basin. (*Admiral Scheer* was finally broken up in 1946.)

Admiral Hipper

As for the *Admiral Hipper*, its last mission was as a refugee ship sailing from Gotenhafen on 30 January 1945, carrying on board over 1500 refugees from the approaching apocalypse further east. As it departed, the cruiser was accompanied by the passenger liner *Wilhelm Gustloff*, which was packed with over 10,000 refugees.

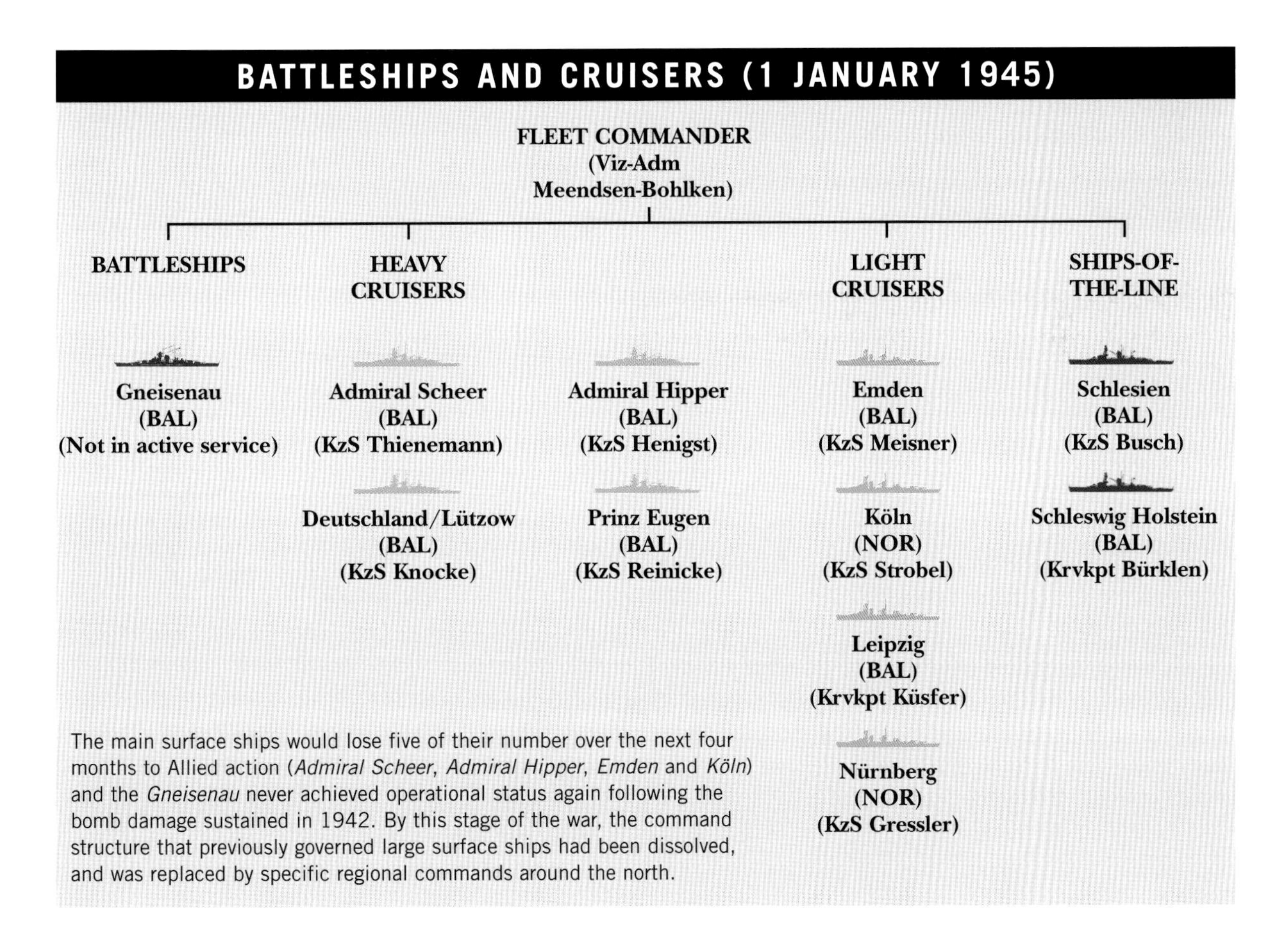

The main surface ships would lose five of their number over the next four months to Allied action (*Admiral Scheer*, *Admiral Hipper*, *Emden* and *Köln*) and the *Gneisenau* never achieved operational status again following the bomb damage sustained in 1942. By this stage of the war, the command structure that previously governed large surface ships had been dissolved, and was replaced by specific regional commands around the north.

Shortly after leaving harbour into sub-zero Baltic weather, the *Wilhelm Gustloff* was torpedoed by a Russian submarine, and sank. Over 9000 people, most of them women and children, died in the sinking, making the tragedy of the *Wilhelm Gustloff* the worst maritime disaster of all time.

Admiral Hipper managed to reach its destination safely, arriving at Kiel in early February. There, however, it became another victim of Allied air attacks, which were becoming particularly intense and confident. On 9–10 April *Hipper* was heavily damaged by British bombs. The cruiser sat in a wrecked state for several weeks until, on 3 May, it was scuttled.

Prinz Eugen

Like *Admiral Scheer*, *Prinz Eugen* also found itself on shore bombardment duties during the last months of the war, and yet was unusual in actually surviving the final collapse of the Third *Reich*. On 8 April 1945, *Prinz Eugen* sailed to Copenhagen, and at war's end was placed under British command. Transferred to US service in 1946, the cruiser was used in several atom bomb tests that resulted in its final destruction.

DEUTSCHLAND/LÜTZOW	
Name	*Deutschland/Lützow*
Commissioned	1 April 1943
Crew	619–951
Displacement	14,519 tonnes (14,289 tons)
Dimensions	Length:186m (610ft); Beam: 21.3m (70ft)
Range	30,013km(18,650 miles) at 28km/h (15kts)
Armour	Belt: 80mm (3.1in); Deck: 45mm (1.8in); Turrets: 85–140mm (3.3–5.5in)
Armament	6 x 280mm (11in); 8 x 150mm (6in); 24 x AA guns; 8 x 533mm (21in) torp. tubes
Powerplant	8 x diesels, 41,760kW (56,000hp)
Performance	53km/h (28.5kts)

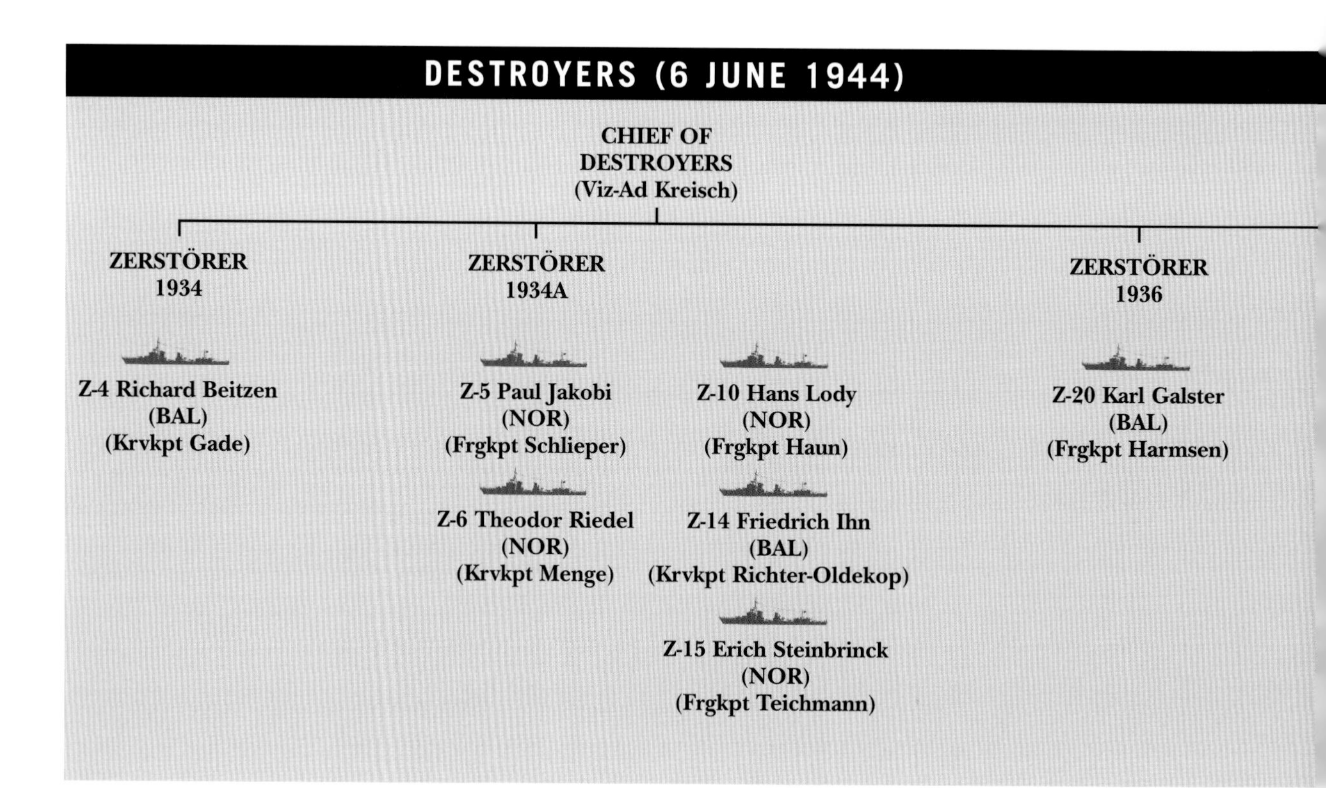

Among the other great ships of the German Navy, some managed to see their crews safely through until the surrender. The light cruisers *Leipzig* and *Nürnberg*, for example, both ended their service in relative safety at anchor in Denmark.

Emden* and *Köln

Others were less lucky. As Allied aircraft hunted for final targets, *Emden* was pounded into submission by British air attacks as it sat out of action at Kiel, and *Köln* was destroyed after being hit by five aircraft bombs during a raid over Wilhelmshaven on 31 March 1945. The cruiser sank, but its superstructure remained above the shallow water, with its main gun turrets still operable.

In April 1945, in a remarkable show of defiance, these guns fired at (very suprised) Allied troops around the port. Although the German surface fleet had largely failed on a strategic level against a much larger Allied navy, the continued fight of ships like the *Köln* illustrated in bold measure that this failure was not due to a lack of courage.

Here is the German Navy's complement of destroyers at the time of the Allied invasion of France in June 1944. It amounted to 22 ships in total, but from this point until the end of the war it would lose a further eight of its number, most of them to Allied air power operating over northern waters.

ZERSTÖRER 1936A		**ZERSTÖRER 1936A (MOB)**		**ZERSTÖRER 1936B**
Z-23 (FRA) (Krvkpt von Mantey)	**Z-28 (BAL) (Frgkpt Gerlach)**	**Z-31 (NOR/BAL) (KK Paul)**	**Z-37 (FRA) (Kptlt Ullrich)**	**Z-35 (BAL) (Krvkpt Bätge)**
Z-24 (FRA) (Krvkpt Birnbacher)	**Z-29 (NOR) (Krvkpt von Mutius)**	**Z-32 (FRA) (Frgkpt von Berger)**	**Z-38 (NOR) (Krvkpt Brutzer)**	**Z-36 (BAL) (Krvkpt von Hausen)**
Z-25 (FRA) (Frgkpt Gohrbrandt)	**Z-30 (NOR) (Frgkpt Lampe)**	**Z-34 (NOR) (Krvkpt Hetz)**	**Z-39 (BAL) (Krvkpt Loerke)**	**Z-43 (BAL) (Krvkpt Loerke)**

Final reckoning

A month before the end of the war, the *Kriegsmarine* still had in service 14 destroyers and 14 torpedo boats, plus several cruisers (although many were inactive) and a large collection of smaller craft.

It is inevitable that in any history of the German Navy the capital ships and the U-boats, those craft that exercised the most strategic influence over the naval war, should attract the lion's share of interest. In doing so, dozens of histories go untold, those of the hundreds of smaller craft that performed important service to the *Reich*, from minesweepers clearing channels through dangerous waters, to S-boats making torpedo runs at Allied vessels far more powerful than themselves, and often paying a terrible price.

Z-40 (TYPE 1941 – PROPOSED)	
Name	*Z-40*
Commissioned	-
Crew	-
Displacement	4540 tonnes (4468 tons)
Dimensions	Length: 152m (498ft); Beam: 14.6m (48ft)
Range	22.250km (13,826 miles) at 35km/h (19kts)
Armament	3 x twin 150mm (6in); 1 x twin 88mm (3.5in); 20 x AA guns in multiple mounts; 10x 533mm (21in) torp. tubes; 140 mines
Powerplant	2 x steam turbine and 1 x diesel, 68,605kW (92,000hp)

Some of these stories are full of intense drama and sadness. On 12 November 1944, for example, a British strike force of two cruisers and four destroyers ventured into Norwegian waters, seeking out an Axis convoy revealed by Ultra intelligence. They found it around the Listerfjord – four freighters escorted by three minesweepers and three corvettes.

For the German sailors, the sight of the powerfully armed British force bearing down upon them must have been a moment of sharp terror, as the enemy vessels began lighting up their targets with star shells. It was to be a completely unequal struggle. One minesweeper and all three corvettes were sunk in a thunderous roll of gunfire. Acts of desperate heroism were commonplace. *UJ-1713*, for example, managed to avoid the initial barrages, but returned to the scene to try to pick up survivors, an act for which she was blasted out of existence. And despite being so totally outclassed, the German force still managed to damage two British destroyers. When the waters settled, only one German freighter had escaped the massacre without damage.

Long view

The Listerfjord action was just one of hundreds of naval engagements fought by the *Kriegsmarine* in the last stages of the war, most of which went largely unrecognized in the wider world. They illustrate the point that in many

ways the *Kriegsmarine* fought a small-boat war rather than a conflict of capital ships, although the larger vessels naturally attracted the attention of the Allied navies.

Yet in the final months of the war the *Kriegsmarine* could make no effective strategic contribution to the German war effort, apart from providing the weight of their guns in shore bombardment roles, or in evacuating refugees. One telling statistic is that from October 1943 to the end of the war, the Allies sank a total of 39 German warships, but in return the Germans took only seven of the Allies' combat vessels. For most of 1944 and 1945, the *Kriegsmarine*'s focus was on survival rather than victory, and hence it wisely avoided head-on combat where it could.

ATTACK OFF LISTERFJORD (12/13 NOVEMBER 1944)

Name	Displacement	Speed	Guns	Torpedoes	Damage
MINESWEEPER					
M-416	787 tonnes (775 tons)	31km/h (17kn)	1x105mm (4.1in)	–	Sunk
M-427	787 tonnes (775 tons)	31km/h (17kn)	1x105mm (4.1in)	–	Major
M-446	787 tonnes (775 tons)	31km/h (17kn)	1x105mm (4.1in)	–	Significant
CORVETTE/SLOOP					
UJ-1713	986 tonnes (970 tons)	22km/h (12kn)	1x88mm (3.5in)	–	Sunk
UJ-1221	986 tonnes (970 tons)	22km/h (12kn)	1x88mm (3.5in)	–	Sunk
UJ-1223	986 tonnes (970 tons)	22km/h (12kn)	1x88mm (3.5in)	–	Sunk

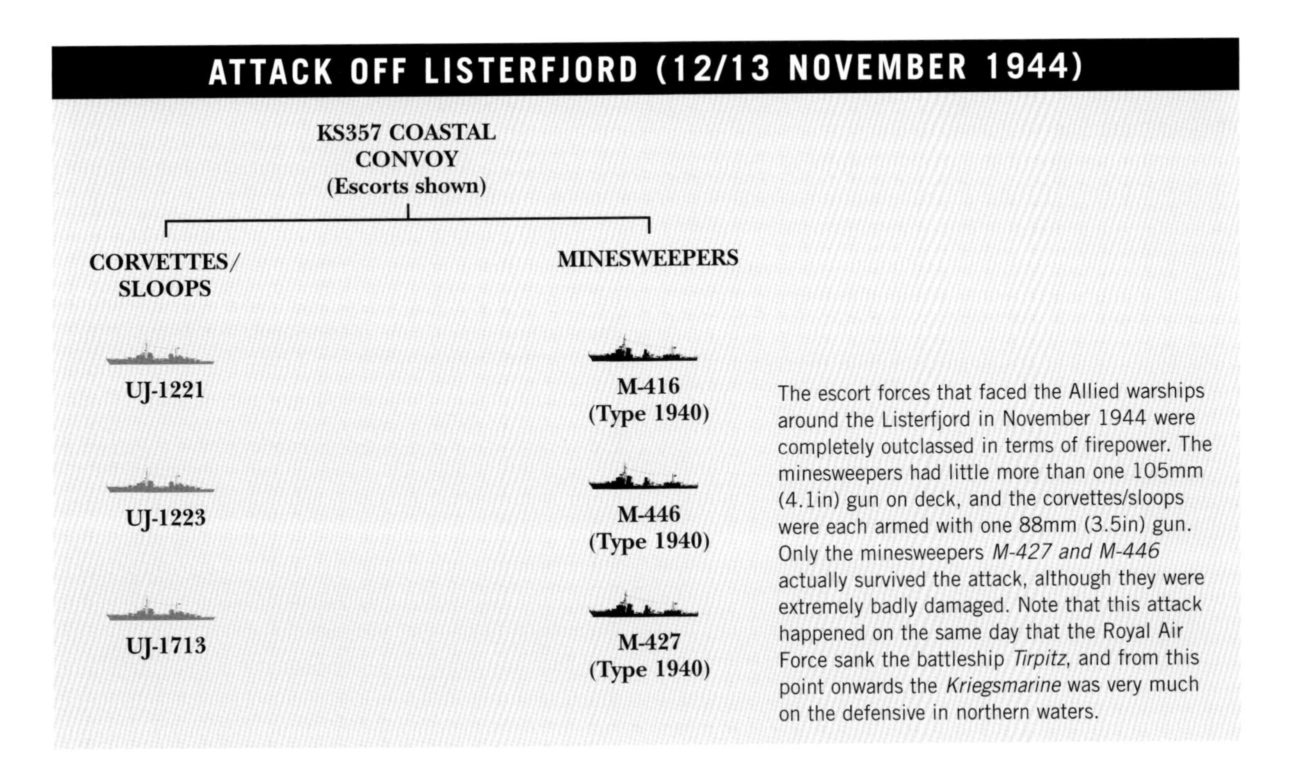

The escort forces that faced the Allied warships around the Listerfjord in November 1944 were completely outclassed in terms of firepower. The minesweepers had little more than one 105mm (4.1in) gun on deck, and the corvettes/sloops were each armed with one 88mm (3.5in) gun. Only the minesweepers *M-427 and M-446* actually survived the attack, although they were extremely badly damaged. Note that this attack happened on the same day that the Royal Air Force sank the battleship *Tirpitz*, and from this point onwards the *Kriegsmarine* was very much on the defensive in northern waters.

Strategic Lessons

The *Kriegsmarine* suffered tremendous losses throughout the war, and had few serviceable major warships left by May 1945. Yet in the context of the entire war, it had still taken a heavy toll upon the Allied fleets.

For the *Kriegsmarine*, the war proved several points about the future of naval warfare. First, the days of the large battleships were truly over, the scale of these vessels turning them into little more than delicious targets for submarines and air raids. Prior to World War II, the German Navy had envisaged great warships such as the *Bismarck* and *Tirpitz* roaming the blue-water theatres, preying on commerce and posing a threat to entire Allied convoys. This vision did not materialize for two main reasons: airpower and escort power. Airpower emerged as the true deciding factor in naval combat, becoming the biggest killer of U-boats and small warships by the end of the war. For the battleships, airpower meant that a single torpedo bomber could disable a major capital vessel (as was the case with the *Bismarck*). Furthermore, Allied aircraft could prey on warships when they were in harbour, where they were nothing more than static objectives. Torpedo-armed fast escorts were another grave concern for the large warships, which meant that in action they were often preoccupied with evasive rather than aggressive manoeuvres.

The second major lesson was that, as with the German Army and *Luftwaffe*, the *Kriegsmarine* had been unable to win the war of production. Quite simply, the combined navies of the United Kingdom, United States and Soviet Union had overwhelmed the *Kriegsmarine* through sheer numbers of ships, guns and aircraft, while also improving their tactics and technologies to an extent the German Navy could not match. The *Kriegsmarine* had paid the price for Hitler's overreaching ambitions as much as any other fighting force in the Third Reich.

Costly victory

Despite these lessons, however, we must never deny that the *Kriegsmarine* still wielded influence on the high seas. Apart from the massive volume of merchant ships downed by the Germans, the tables on this and the adjacent page show just what a severe cost the Allies suffered in terms of warships while fighting the *Kriegsmarine*, including three battleships, seven carriers and nine cruisers. The *Kriegsmarine* was ultimately destined for a bloody defeat, but it went down fighting.

***KRIEGSMARINE* KILLS – ALLIED CAPITAL SHIPS**

Name	Sunk	Nationality
BATTLESHIPS/BATTLECRUISERS		
Royal Oak	14 Oct 1939	GB
Hood	24 May 1941	GB
Barham	25 Nov 1941	GB
CARRIERS		
Courageous	17 Sep 1939	GB
Glorious	08 Jun 1940	GB
Ark Royal	13 Nov 1941	GB
Audacity	22 Dec 1941	GB
Eagle	11 Aug 1941	GB
Avenger	15 Nov 1942	GB
Block Island	29 May 1944	US
CRUISERS		
Sydney	19 Nov 1941	AU
Dunedin	24 Nov 1941	GB
Galatea	14 Dec 1941	GB
Naiad	11 Mar 1942	GB
Edinburgh	02 May 1942	GB
Hermione	16 Jun 1942	GB
Charybdis	23 Oct 1943	GB
Penelope	18 Feb 1944	GB
Dragon	08 Jul 1944	GB/PL

KRIEGSMARINE KILLS – ALLIED DESTROYERS

Name	Sunk	Nationality
DESTROYERS		
Exmouth	21 Jan 1940	GB
Daring	18 Apr 1940	GB
Glowworm	08 Apr 1940	GB
Hardy	10 Apr 1940	GB
Hunter	10 Apr 1940	GB
Jaguar	23 May 1940	GB
Grafton	29 May 1940	GB
Wakeful	29 May 1940	GB
Sirocco	31 May 1940	FR
Acasta	08 Jun 1940	GB
Ardent	08 Jun 1940	GB
Whirlwind	05 Jul 1940	GB
Exmoor	25 Feb 1941	GB
Bath	19 Aug 1941	NZ
Broadwater	18 Oct 1941	GB
Cossack	23 Oct 1941	GB
* Reuben James	31 Oct 1941	US
Stanley	19 Dec 1941	GB
Gurkha	17 Jan 1942	GB
Matabele	17 Jan 1942	GB
Belmont	31 Jan 1942	GB
Vortigern	15 Mar 1942	GB
Jaguar	26 Mar 1942	GB
Hasty	15 Jun 1942	GB
Ottawa	14 Sep 1942	CA
Somali	20 Sep 1942	GB
Veteran	26 Sep 1942	GB
Martin	10 Nov 1942	GB
Isaac Sweers	13 Nov 1942	NL
Penylan	03 Dec 1942	GB
Porcupine	09 Dec 1942	GB
Blean	11 Dec 1942	GB
Firedrake	16 Dec 1942	GB
Partridge	18 Dec 1942	GB
Achates	31 Dec 1942	GB
Harvester	11 Mar 1943	GB
Lightning	12 Mar 1943	GB
Beverley	11 Apr 1943	GB
Eskdale	14 Apr 1943	NO
Puckeridge	06 Sep 1943	GB
Rowan	10 Sep 1943	US
St. Croix	20 Sep 1943	CA
Orkan	08 Oct 1943	PL
Buck	09 Oct 1943	US
Bristol	13 Oct 1943	US
Limbourne	23 Oct 1943	GB
Borie	2 Nov 1943	US
Hurricane	24 Dec 1943	GB
Leary	24 Dec 1943	US
Hardy (II)	30 Jan 1944	GB
Warwick	20 Feb 1944	GB
Mahratta	25 Feb 1944	GB
Leopold	09 Mar 1944	US
Laforey	30 Mar 1944	GB
Athabascan	29 Apr 1944	CA
Fechteler	05 May 1944	US
Svenner	06 Jun 1944	NO
Isis	20 Jul 1944	GB
Fiske	02 Aug 1944	US
Quorn	03 Aug 1944	GB
Deyatelnyy	16 Jan 1945	USSR
La Combattante	23 Feb 1945	FR
Frederick C. Davis	24 Apr 1945	US

KEY
GB – Great Britain
US – United States
AU – Australia
PL – Poland
FR – France
NZ – New Zealand
CA – Canada
NO – Norway
USSR – Soviet Union

* Sunk while the US was still officially neutral.

Glossary of key abbreviations

Rank:

Adm	Admiral
Frgkpt	Fregattenkapitän
Gen-Ad	Generaladmiral
Gr-Adm	Grossadmiral
Kom	Kommodore
Kon-Ad	Konteradmiral
Kptlt	Kapitänleutnant
Krvkpt	Korvettenkapitän
KzS	Kapitän zur See
OzS	Oberleutnant zur See
Viz-Ad	Vizeadmiral

Operational area abbreviations:

Note: The following abbreviations, given in the orders of battle for surface vessels, denote the waters to which the vessels were ascribed for operations and/or stationed at the date given. Note that when several operational areas are shown, this suggests the operation movement that the ship was undergoing at that time.

ADR	Adriatic
AEG	Aegean
ARC	Arctic
BAL	Baltic
BR	British (coastal)
CH	English Channel
FRA	France (coastal)
IND	Indian Ocean
N.AT	North Atlantic
NOR	Norwegian/North Sea
PAC	Pacific
S.AT	South Atlantic

Acknowledgements

Books

Becker, Cajus. **Hitler's Naval War**
(New York, Bantam, 1974)

Bishop, Chris. **Kriegsmarine U-boats 1939–45**
(London, Amber, 2006)

Gardiner, Robert (ed.). **Conway's All the World's Fighting Ships, 1922–1946**
(New York, Mayflower, 1980)

Jackson, Robert. **The German Navy in World War II**
(London, Brown, 1999)

Miller, David. **U-Boats: The Illustrated History of the Raiders of the Deep**
(London, Brassey's, 2002)

O'Hara, Vincent P. **The German Fleet at War 1939–1945**
(Annapolis, MD, Naval Institute Press, 2004)

Porten, Edward von der. **The German Navy in World War Two**
(London, Pan, 1972)

Showell, Jak P. Mallmann. **German Navy Handbook 1939–1945**
(London, Sutton, 1999)

Williamson, Gordon. **German Battleships 1939–45**
(Oxford, Osprey, 2003)

Williamson, Gordon. **German Destroyers 1939–45**
(Oxford, Osprey, 2003)

Williamson, Gordon. **German Pocket Battleships 1939–45**
(Oxford, Osprey, 2003)

Recommended websites

German Naval History – http://www.german-navy.de/index.html

Feldgrau (Kriegsmarine section)
– *http://www.feldgrau.com/kriegs.html*

ubootwaffe.net – *http://www.ubootwaffe.net/*

uboat.net – *http://www.uboat.net/index.html*

Axis History Factbook – http://www.axishistory.com/

Kriegsmarine of the Reich
– http://www.kriegsmarine-reich.co.uk/index.htm

Scharnhorst & Gneisenau
– http://www.scharnhorst-class.dk/index.html

Vessel Index

Page numbers in *italics* refer to illustrations and tables.

Index

General Index

Page numbers in *italics* refer to illustrations and tables.

Index

Index